THE BEST OF
KARPOV

TO LYNDA

THE BEST OF KARPOV

P. R. MARKLAND

OXFORD UNIVERSITY PRESS
1975

Oxford University Press, Ely House, London W. 1

GLASGOW NEW YORK TORONTO MELBOURNE WELLINGTON
CAPE TOWN IBADAN NAIROBI DAR ES SALAAM LUSAKA ADDIS ABABA
DELHI BOMBAY CALCUTTA MADRAS KARACHI LAHORE DACCA
KUALA LUMPUR SINGAPORE HONG KONG TOKYO

ISBN 0 19 217534 3

© *Oxford University Press 1975*

*Printed in Great Britain
by J. W. Arrowsmith Ltd., Bristol*

Preface

Anatoly Karpov needs no introduction to those of us who have followed his meteoric career over the past five years, but to the more casual player the emergence of a new Soviet star to challenge Bobby Fischer for the world championship crown may come as something of a surprise. One of my aims in writing this book, therefore, was to explain how he has achieved so much in so short a time.

The main purpose of this book, however, is to enable players of all standards to enjoy the best of Karpov's play and thus to become better acquainted with the intricacies of his style. I have devoted a whole chapter to some common middle-game themes in order to try and give the reader a greater understanding of the way Karpov thinks and plans, and to explain the reasons for some of his choices in the games.

Karpov himself was kind enough to select the games, and has given us triumph and disaster, positional squeezes and tactical strikes. I hope you enjoy playing them over as much as I have.

January 1975   Peter Markland

Acknowledgements

I should like to thank

Anatoly Karpov for giving up some of his free time at the Nice Olympiad to select his best games for this book.

Penguin Books Ltd (Harmondsworth) and Random House Inc (New York) for permission to reproduce a passage from C.H.O'D. Alexander's book *Fischer v. Spassky Reykjavik 1972.*

Notation

The great majority of the countries of the world use algebraic notation for their chess publications, and this has been an important factor in international chess communication. English- and Spanish-speaking countries have hitherto clung to the descriptive system, but even in these countries there is an increasing tendency for the leading players to prefer algebraic notation, because it is more concise, and because it assists clear, logical thought about the game.

For readers who are not familiar with the algebraic system we give below a game (Charousek–Wollner) in full algebraic, in condensed algebraic, and in descriptive notation. The main differences are that in algebraic all the squares on the board are identified by a single map-reference system; that pawns are not named, but understood when no piece is named; and that in a capture the captured man is not identified.

1 e2-e4 e7-e5	1 e4 e5 2 d4 exd4 3 c3 dxc3	1 P-K4 P-K4
2 d2-d4 e5xd4	4 Bc4 Nf6 5 Nf3 Bc5 6 Nxc3 d6	2 P-Q4 PxP
3 c2-c3 d4xc3	7 0-0 0-0 8 Ng5 h6 9 Nxf7 Rxf7	3 P-QB3 PxP
4 Bf1-c4 Ng8-f6	10 e5 Ng4 11 e6 Qh4 12 exf7+ Kf8	4 B-QB4 N-KB3
5 Ng1-f3 Bf8-c5	13 Bf4 Nxf2 14 Qe2 Ng4+ 15 Kh1	5 N-B3 B-B4
6 Nb1xc3 d7-d6	Bd7 16 Rae1 Nc6	6 NxP P-Q3
7 0-0 0-0		7 0-0 0-0
8 Nf3-g5 h7-h6		8 N-KN5 P-KR3
9 Ng5xf7 Rf8xf7		9 NxP RxN
10 e4-e5 Nf6-g4		10 P-K5 N-N5
11 e5-e6 Qd8-h4		11 P-K6 Q-R5
12 e6xf7+ Kg8-f8		12 PxRch K-B1
13 Bc1-f4 Ng4xf2		13 B-B4 NxBP
14 Qd1-e2 Nf2-g4+		14 Q-K2 N-N5ch
15 Kg1-h1 Bc8-d7		15 K-R1 B-Q2
16 Ra1-e1 Nb8-c6		16 QR-K1 N-QB3
(see diagram)		*(see diagram)*

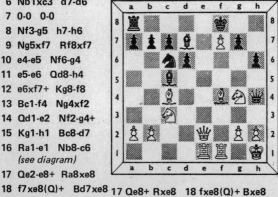

17 Qe2-e8+ Ra8xe8	17 Qe8+ Rxe8 18 fxe8(Q)+ Bxe8	17 Q-K8ch RxQ
18 f7xe8(Q)+ Bd7xe8		18 PxR(=Q)ch BxQ
19 Bf4xd6 mate	19 Bxd6 mate	19 BxQP mate

! good move   ? bad move   + check

!? double-edged but probably good move   ?! double-edged but probably bad move

± with advantage to White   ∓ with advantage to Black

 K   Q   R   B   N   ♙ P

Contents

1 Anatoly Karpov — a personal view

The first time I saw Anatoly Karpov was when I was a spectator of the last round of the World Junior Championship in Stockholm in 1969. By this time Karpov had already secured the title, and so to some extent his play in that game, against Diaz of Cuba, was not so concentrated and intense as in the previous rounds. I was nevertheless impressed by the way he played. Although he remained seated for virtually the whole of the time, he appeared to be far away, dreaming of other things. As soon as it was his turn to move he stared hard at the board and moved surprisingly quickly. The game was over in a couple of hours. Karpov allowed a dangerous-looking queen-for-two-rooks 'sacrifice' and then proceeded to demonstrate the superiority of the queen in this particular situation. Howard Williams, the British Chess Federation representative in Stockholm, assured me that Karpov was in a class of his own, and told me how impressed he had been with the Champion's play. It was not until the Nice Olympiad preliminaries in 1974 that Howard was to experience personally the Karpov 'treatment'.

More than two years later Karpov was invited to the Hastings International Congress. By this time he had already gained the Grandmaster title and won the strongest chess tournament since the war—the Alekhine Memorial Tournament in Moscow. Both his fame and his strength had increased since I had last seen him, but he was still the same small, thin figure that I had seen in Stockholm. He must certainly be the lightest grandmaster in the World, and I was left to wonder how such a small frame would cope with the fifteen rounds at Hastings, coming only ten days after the seventeen games he had played in Moscow. I was not left in doubt for long, as he won seven of his first ten games!

But it was not only his immense stamina and energy that took my notice. He was, and is, a friendly and cheerful young man away from the board. Many of his spare hours were spent around the bridge table in the hotel where he gladly took on all comers with Viktor Korchnoi as his partner. This appeared to be a good arrangement until, every so often, a mass of quickly-spoken Russian would be exchanged on the merits (or otherwise) of the partner's bidding or play. His natural modesty and almost fluent English make Karpov excellent company, and in early 1972, shortly after the end of the Hastings tournament, I was able to treat him to dinner when he visited Oxford to give a simultaneous display at the University Chess Club.

His most impressive and noticeable feature, however, is his style of play. To beat the World's leading grandmasters is no small task, and the ease with which Karpov achieves this is quite staggering. Leaving aside Bobby

Fischer for the moment, it can safely be said that in recent times no player has been able to match his winning power and his solidity at the same time. Of course, Petrosian at his best has surpassed Karpov in solidity, as has Tal in the number of wins scored, but never before has such a remarkable double record as Karpov's been held for such a long period of time. In all the U.S.S.R. Championships, Olympiads (including Students' Olympiads) and other International team and individual events between 1969 and 1974, Karpov scored over one hundred wins in less than two hundred and fifty games, and only fifteen losses!

To begin to understand this phenomenon we must try to categorize chess players into two types, tacticians and strategists. Of course no player slots exactly into either category, but every player has a dominating style. The tactician will play the sharpest opening variations, and may even accept slightly dubious positions, provided that they contain tactical possibilities. This kind of player can usually be identified by his middle-game situations. Always, the trend will be towards open positions, or closed positions in which the counterattacking chances are good (for example the King's Indian Defence). Given a choice between exchanging pieces and retaining tension, the tactician will choose the latter course, unless the former is clearly much better. He may even, as at the opening stage, accept a slight deterioration of his position to keep the tactical chances alive. Tacticians' games are therefore complicated, inventive, and full of sacrifices of one kind or another. In recent times this school has produced three world champions—Mikhail Tal, Boris Spassky, and of course Bobby Fischer.

The second category is the strategist. His opening repertoire will be aimed at the quieter and simpler variations. He will try to outmanœuvre his opponent with spatial advantage, or a Q-side majority, and will try to suppress the tactical aspects of the position and thus enforce his own strategical plan. His middle-game aims will be to further his plan by the best means available, and all sacrifices will be 'positional' or completely calculated, and rarely, if ever, speculative. This school has also produced three recent world champions—Mikhail Botvinnik, Vassily Smyslov, and Tigran Petrosian.

There are differences between the two schools of thought on many aspects of middle-game play. Perhaps one of the more obvious is the relative attitudes towards an isolated-queen's-pawn position.

The type of position in Diagram 1 can be reached from the Caro-Kann defence, the Queen's Gambit Declined, or the Nimzo-Indian Defence, although in the latter case White will usually have his a-pawn on a3 already. There are many different deployments of pieces for both sides. For example, Black could have fianchettoed either or both of his bishops; or White could have played his queen to e2, intending to play the king's rook to d1; or chosen to play with his king's bishop on the a2-g8 diagonal, by a2-a3 and Bf1-c4 instead of Bf1-d3. But the basic elements in the position are the

same. White must play for the
attack and hope either to win by
a direct K-side onslaught, or to
play a timely advance d4-d5 when
the greater freedom of his pieces
will give him the better chances.

BLACK TO MOVE

WHITE

Black, on the other hand, will
seek to take advantage of the
weak white pawn on d4 (a weakness because it must be supported
by pieces) and keep a blockade
on the d5 square (thus preventing
the weak pawn from advancing).
To this end, he may well fianchetto
his queen's bishop and prepare to
attack the pawn by central exchanges. In general, White's chances are
superior in this type of position, but the important point to note is that a
tactician will always be happy to play the White side of this position, but
will try to avoid the Black side if he possibly can. On the other hand the
strategist will tend to prefer the Black side of the position, because it is
'positionally superior', but even he may be tempted to try the 'tactically
superior' White position.

Karpov falls quite definitely into the strategist category, and it is rare to
find him playing with an isolated pawn (unless he has been in difficulties
and is trying to avoid something worse). Some of his finest wins, and there
are many of them in this book, have been while playing against the isolated
queen's pawn in the French Defence, Tarrasch variation, although here
Black has the isolated pawn and White has a c-pawn instead of the usual
e-pawn, thus giving more scope to his pieces. On the other hand three of his
rare losses (Ivkov, Caracas 1970; Smyslov, 39th USSR Championship,
Leningrad 1971; and Portisch, San Antonio 1972) have been caused by his
failure to keep control of the Black side of an isolated-queen's-pawn
position.

This is just one of the many points to look out for in the game collection.
Another is Karpov's attitude to the closed Ruy López. With the White side
he will nearly always play the advance d4-d5 rather than the exchange
d4xc5. The reason for this is his liking for spatial advantage in blocked
positions. Thus he deviates from the López theory of pawn exchange and
occupation of the d5 square. In this respect he differs quite distinctly from
Fischer, who is, in the main, an 'exchanger'. Here again is an example of the
underlying trend of play—the strategist prefers a closed game with spatial
advantage, whilst the tactician chooses a more open game with attacking
chances.

Against the Sicilian defence Karpov plays 2 Nf3 and 3 d4, but thereafter he aims for positional lines of play. The best examples of this are 1 e4 c5 2 Nf3 Nc6   3 d4 cxd4   4 Nxd4 Nf6   5 Nc3 d6 when Karpov plays the 'positional' Richter-Rauzer attack 6 Bg5, rather than the Fischer-inspired Sozin attack 6 Bc4; and against the Najdorf variation (1 e4 c5   2 Nf3 d6 3 d4 cxd4   4 Nxd4 Nf6   5 Nc3 a6) when he chooses the solid 6 Be2 rather than the attacking 6 Bc4 or 6 Bg5. (Although he played 6 Bg5 against Quinteros at the Leningrad Interzonal in 1973, this was very much an exception.)

With the black pieces his Breyer variation against the Ruy López is solid and reliable rather than aggressive; his Sicilian—with a variety of e6, a6, Nc6, and Qc7—although more risky, is generally employed against weaker opponents. He rarely varies from these two openings against 1 e4, but in his match with Spassky he played the equally solid Caro-Kann Defence. Against a 1 d4 player his choices are the Nimzo-Indian Defence and the Queen's Gambit Declined—probably the two most solid defences to 1 d4.

It is therefore something of a surprise that Karpov is a 'win with white, draw with black' player. His opening repertoire with the white pieces gives him a fabulous rate of success. His loss to Spassky in the first game of their 1974 match was his first loss with white for over two years, and only his third loss with white since the World Junior Championship of 1969. This extraordinary record is due mainly to the narrow field of opening theory on which he concentrates. Because he seldom varies his openings he is rarely caught by an improvement or a new move. His repertoire with black is based on solidity and reliability rather than the 'playing for a win with either colour' attitude adopted by some of the leading players, notably Fischer and Tal. Here again, his openings are well-learnt and rarely changed. His winning rate with black is far below that with white and this is reflected in the game collection by the fact that the great majority of the games show Karpov as White. His rapid rise to fame in the early 1970s has been a result mainly of the improvement in his play with the black pieces. Over the last three years he has managed wins against Korchnoi (three times), Stein, Taimanov, Smejkal, Uhlmann, Planinc, and Spassky—a formidable list of opponents.

In the field of calculation and analysis at the board, we again see the difference between strategists and tacticians, whose thoughts may be directed on entirely separate areas of play. Whilst a tactician may be busy analysing the tactical possibilities of the position, or, more likely, how tactical possibilities can best be introduced into the game, the strategist's thoughts will be 'How can I further my positional aims without allowing a tactical backlash?' The first part of a strategist's thinking would have to be 'Has my opponent any threats?', and then 'What is my plan?'. It is in the area of the first question that Karpov's true power and strength lies. The reason that his wins look so easy and convincing is his vast under-the-surface analysis. His whole thinking is based on the question 'How can I further my positional aims without allowing a tactical backlash?' So although his opponent may appear to have been mercilessly crushed by a strategical idea without ever getting into the game, he has, in fact, been out-calculated. Karpov has seen and outflanked any tactical tricks whilst pursuing his own ideas. The power of a strategical idea carried out in this way is enormous, and many of Karpov's wins in the game selection are due entirely to this method of thinking. The great majority of his losses occur when the 'master plan' is broken by tactical considerations (i.e. when Karpov has analysed the tactics incorrectly or when the strategical idea inherent in the position is not strong enough to cope with the tactical possibilities for the opponent).

Karpov is also a quick thinker. It is very rare to find him in any sort of time-trouble and he is frequently half an hour to an hour 'up' on his opponent. As Korchnoi is a slowish mover Karpov was almost invariably ahead in their 1974 match by up to an hour on the clock. This is again a surprise in view of the amount of analysis necessary to play the way he does. In the Hastings tournament, I remember watching the post-mortem of the Karpov—Hartston game. Hartston had done well in the game, but it became obvious that Karpov had seen and analysed a great many more possible variations. Even in lines not considered by Hartston, Karpov was producing deep analysis and his comment 'The only move' was backed up by subvariations of analysis at every stage.

To play Karpov is a somewhat disconcerting experience. It is rather like facing a boxer whose reach is far greater than yours, and who spends the whole fight keeping you at arm's length and wins on points by scoring punch after punch without possible retaliation. You feel that you can never get a punch in and that the tactical opportunities are strangely lacking. Never is it possible to get close enough to even worry him and, of course, never is it possible to see a continuation that has not already been analysed, checked, and catered for. This was the sentiment expressed by Howard Williams after his game with Karpov in the Nice Olympiad, and was exactly the way I felt in my first game with him. It seems appropriate to end this chapter on my own view of Karpov with that game taken from the 1971—2 Hastings Tournament, round 15.

White **Karpov**   Black **Markland**   French Defence, Winawer Variation

1 e2-e4 e7-e6   2 d2-d4 d7-d5   3 Nb1-c3

    A surprise. I was expecting 3 Nd2, but perhaps Karpov was influenced
    by my score of 0/3 in this variation.

3 ... Bf8-b4   4 e4-e5 c7-c5   5 a2-a3 Bb4xc3+   6 b2xc3 Qd8-c7   7 Ng1-f3 Ng8-e7   8 a3-a4 b7-b6   9 Bf1-b5+ Bc8-d7   10 Bb5-d3

That manœuvre was to prevent 9 . . . Ba6

10 . . . Nb8-c6   11 0-0 h7-h6   12 Rf1-e1 Nc6-a5   13 Qd1-d2?!

Perhaps the best move here is the 13 Be3 played by Robert Byrne against me in an earlier round.

13 . . . Ra8-c8!

I played 13 . . . 0-0 against Mecking but 14 Qf4 f5   15 exf6 Qxf4 16 Bxf4 Rxf6   gave him the advantage.

14 h2-h4

14 Qf4 f5! gives Black at least equality.

14 . . . 0-0   15 Qd2-f4 f7-f5   16 e5xf6 Rf8xf6   17 Qf4xc7 Rc8xc7 18 d4xc5! b6xc5   19 Nf3-e5

If played last move this could have been answered by 18 . . . cxd4 19 cxd4 Nec6 with good counterchances for Black.

19 . . . Bd7-c8   20 c3-c4

Karpov criticized this move and gave 20 g3 followed by Bf4 as better.

20 . . . Na5-c6   21 Bc1-b2 Nc6-b4

Sokolov suggested 21 . . . Na5.

22 a4-a5!! *(see Diagram 2)*

It was only at this point that I began to feel uncomfortable. White has no obvious way in which to improve his position and chooses the obscure, but strong, advance of the a-pawn. However, I felt I could see a good line . . .

MARKLAND TO MOVE   2

KARPOV

22 . . . Rf6-f8   23 Bb2-a3 d5xc4 24 Ne5xc4 Rf8-f4

My analysis extended to seeing that my threats of 25 . . . Rxh4   25 . . . Rxc4 and   25 . . . Nxc2 could not be satisfactorily met by 25 Re4 as   25 . . . Nxd3   26 cxd3 Rxe4 27 dxe4 Nc6! would be excellent for Black. Karpov's actual move therefore came as no surprise.

25 Nc4-d6! Nb4xd3   26 c2xd3 Rf4xh4   27 Nd6-e4

27 Rac1 is met by 27 . . . Ra4! and now   28 Bxc5 by   28 . . . Bd7! and not 28 . . . Rxa5? when 29 Bb4 is strong.

27 . . . Rh4-h5   28 Re1-c1

It was only now that I saw the effect of Karpov's 22nd move. My escape by 28 . . . c4 is met by 29 Bd6, Rd7   30 a6! preventing both 30 . . . cxd3 and 30 . . . Bb7, and thus giving White a great advantage. I suspect that the whole of this variation was seen by Karpov *before his 22nd move*— or at least before his 23rd move, but in any case about five moves before it entered my head!

Not only did Karpov now have a strong, if not already winning, position but also he had destroyed some of my confidence. The rest was relatively easy for him.

28 ... Bc8-b7   29 Ne4xc5 Bb7-d5   30 f2-f3 Rh5-f5   31 a5-a6!
The noose is rapidly closing, but what could I do?

31 ... Rf5-f7   32 Nc5-e4 Ne7-f5   33 Ba3-c5 Rc7-c8   34 Bc5-f2 Rf7-c7
35 Rc1xc7 Rc8xc7   36 Ra1-b1
Although the bishops are of opposite colours, this does not help Black to draw. The black bishop cannot come to attack the weak a6 pawn and can only watch as White surrounds and picks up the a7 pawn.

36 ... Nf5-e7   37 Rb1-b8+ Kg8-h7   38 Kg1-h2 Ne7-g6   39 Ne4-c5
Threatening 40 Rb7.

39 ... Rc7-c6
To meet 40 Rb7 by 40 ... Rxa6! The try 39 ... Ne5 loses to 40 Rb7 Bxb7 41 axb7 and now 41 ... Nd7 42 d4! or 41 ... Nc6 42 Bg3 wins for White.

40 Rb8-d8! Rc6-c7   41 Rd8-d7 Rc7xd7   42 Nc5xd7 Bd5-c6   43 Nd7-b8
Bc6-b5   44 Bf2xa7 Ng6-e7   45 Ba7-b6!
45 Bc5 could be answered by 45 ... Nd5 intending 46 ... Nc7.

45 ... Ne7-c8   46 Bb6-c5 Kh7-g6?
Better resistance could have been offered by 46 ... Bxd3   47 a7, Nxa7 48 Bxa7 Bb5 but in any case Black is lost.

47 a6-a7 Nc8xa7   48 Bc5xa7 e6-e5   49 d3-d4 e5xd4   50 Ba7xd4 Kg6-f7
51 f3-f4 g7-g5   52 f4xg5 h6xg5   53 Kh2-g3 Kf7-g6   54 Kg3-f3 Kg6-f5
55 g2-g3 Black resigns

POSTSCRIPT

'Judgement is the power to assess the soundness of one's ideas; many imaginative players lack judgement—so they win one brilliancy prize and lose three unsound attacks. Analytic power is essential to carry out the detailed calculations that are constantly necessary to carry any plan into effect; it is a lower-order quality than imagination or judgement (as is shown by the fact that it is the one that is the least difficult to simulate in a computer programme), but you can't do without it. Determination is the quality to make the others effective. Recently I watched the new Soviet star, twenty-year-old Anatoly Karpov, play his Oxford contemporary, Peter Markland, at Hastings. A late middle game was reached which was very nearly equal—many players in Karpov's position would have given it

up as a draw. Karpov manœuvred, probed, made difficulties, kept the
position unbalanced; Markland fought hard, but the position was just too
hard for him—from looking about equal, it began to look awkward, then
desperate, and in fifty-five moves he resigned. This was a victory for
technique, talent and will-power in equal proportions.' These words, written
by C.H.O'D. Alexander in his book *Fischer v. Spassky, Reykjavik 1972*
(Penguin), sum up many of my thoughts about this game.

It would not be fitting to pass over this reference without especial
mention of the author. Hugh Alexander's death on 15 February 1974 was
a tragic blow to the many people who counted him as a true friend, and his
departure left British chess without one of its greatest players and most
hard-working supporters.

2 Some middle-game themes

There are a number of middle-game (and endgame) themes which crop up frequently in the text. In order to give the reader a fuller understanding of terms such as 'the two bishops' or 'a spatial advantage' I have sifted through many of Karpov's games and have selected a few positions that seem to me to illustrate some of these principles. Whilst it is impossible to place a numerical pawn value on the advantage of two bishops over two knights, or to estimate the winning chances of a passed pawn, it should be understood that any one of the aspects discussed will guarantee a substantial advantage, and may be sufficient to win.

In compiling this section I have collected only those ideas which are recurrent in Karpov's style of play, and hence there are no sections on such combinational possibilities as 'Sacrifice for mate'. There are, nevertheless, some mating attacks in the selected games—the most brilliant of these in my opinion being Karpov's wins against Taimanov (Game 38) and Korchnoi (Game 71).

THE TWO BISHOPS

In a simple ending (i.e. one in which two bishops and pawns are opposed by bishop, knight, and pawns, or two knights and pawns) the advantage of the two bishops, especially in an open position, can be decisive. The two following examples show how the proper use of the two bishops in an open position can even be sufficient to outweigh a material deficit.

KARPOV TO MOVE   3

GARCIA

The position shown in Diagram 3 was reached after Silvano Garcia's 39th move of his game with Karpov at Madrid in 1973.

The material situation here is rook and two pawns against Karpov's two bishops. This in itself constitutes a small advantage for Black, but because of the mating possibilities against the white king, and the weak, exposed white e-pawn, Black is already well on the way to a win. The continuation was:

39 ... Bh6-g7

Threatening 40 ... Bxe5+! 41 Rxe5 Rg2+ 42 Kh1 Re2+, winning a piece.

40 Rf1-f7 Kh7-h6
Renewing the threat.

41 h3-h4
After 41 Rc7 Bf3! 42 Re3 Bxe5+! decides the game instantly.

41 . . . Kh6-h5!
Black now has another weak pawn to attack.

**42 Kh2-h3 Bc6-e8 43 Rf7-a7 Be8-g6 44 Ra7xa6 Bg6-d3 45 Re2-f2
Bd3xc4 46 Ra6-a3 Bg7-h6?**
   Quicker was 46 . . . Bxe5! 47 Ra5, Rg3+ 48 Kh2 Re3+ followed by
49 . . . Bd5.

47 Ra3-g3 Rg8-a8 48 Rf2-f7 Ra8-a1 49 Rf7-h7
Threatening 50 Rg5 mate, but the h-pawn is lost, and so therefore is
the game.

**49 . . . Ra1-h1+ 50 Kh3-g2 Rh1xh4 51 Kg2-g1 Bc4-e2 52 Kg1-f2 Be2-g4
53 b4-b5 Bg4-f5 54 Rh7-h8 Rh4-b4 55 Rg3-g1 Rb4-b2+ 56 Kf2-f3
Rb2-b3+ 57 Kf3-f2 Bf5-e4 58 Rg1-g3 Rb3-b2+ 59 Kf2-g1 Be4-f5
60 Rg3-g2 Rb2xg2+ 61 Kg1xg2 Bf5-e4+ 62 Kg2-g3 Kh5-g6 63 b5-b6
Be4-d5 64 Rh8-b8**
   If 64 Rd8 then 64 . . . Kf5 65 Rd7 (65 Rxd5? exd5 66 b7 Bf4+ 67 Kf3
Bxe5 wins) 65 . . . Bf4+ 66 Kf2 Bxe5 67 b7 Ke4! followed by 68 . . . Bc6
69 Re7 Kd5 etc. wins comfortably.

**64 . . . Kg6-f5 65 b6-b7 Kf5xe5 66 Kg3-g4 Bh6-e3 67 Kg4-g3 Be3-g5!
68 Kg3-f2 Bg5-e7! White resigns**
The pawn is lost.

Let us look now at the power of the two bishops in the middle-game. In
the first two cases the bishops become winning factors when the position
is opened up and, in the third, we see

them manœuvred to create a decisive
breakthrough.

   In Sloth—Karpov (Skopje Olympiad 1972) the position of Diagram
4 was reached after Karpov's 33rd
move.

   The fall of the white f-pawn is
imminent and an attempt to save it
by 34 Qg3 would allow 34 . . . g5!
when 35 f5 Be5 36 Bc3 Nd4 wins
for Black. Thus White is obliged to
capture the b-pawn in exchange,
but the opening-up of the position,

SLOTH TO MOVE

and the forced loss of a bishop, lead to a speedy defeat.

34 Nd5xb6 Ne6xf4 35 Bd2xf4

> After 35 Rxf4 Be5 36 Bc3 Qg7! 37 Kh1 Rxf4 38 Nd7! Bxc3 39 Nxb8 Be5 40 Nc6 Bxc6 Black has a small advantage.

35 ... Rf7xf4 36 Nb6-d7 Rf4xf1!

> So as to meet 37 Nxf8? by 37 ... Be5+ 38 Qg3 Rfxf8 winning.

37 Qd3xf1 Qf8xf1 38 Bg2xf1 Rb8-d8 39 Nd7-b6 Bb7xe4

> Winning a pawn and hence the game. The finish was

40 Nc2-e3? Bg7-e5+ 41 Kh2-g1 Be5-d4 White resigns

Against Saren, also at the Skopje Olympiad, Karpov was in some trouble. A speculative pawn break some five moves before had left him with weak centre pawns and an exposed rook.

Play continued;

20 ... Qd8-f8

> A tricky move. After 21 Bg4 Rf6 22 Ne4 Rg6 23 Bh5 Rh6 24 Bf3 White would have a clear advantage. However, Saren sees a pawn en prise and decides to capture it. The result is to release the bishops, which quickly mate the white king.

KARPOV TO MOVE 5

SAREN

21 b4-b5? a6xb5 22 c4xb5 Nc6-a5 23 Be3xb6? Nd7xb6 24 Qf2xb6 Be7-d8! 25 Qb6-a7

> After 25 Qxd6 Qxd6 26 Rxd6 Rc5 Black wins a piece.

25 ... Rb8-c8 26 Qa7-e3 e6-e5 27 Be2-g4 Na5-c4 28 Qe3-d3?

> Better was 28 Qe2 when 28 ... Bb6+ 29 Kf1 Rxf4+ 30 gxf4 Qxf4+ 31 Ke1 Rf8 threatening 32 ... Bf2+ would eventually win for Black.

28 ... Bd8-b6+ 29 Kg1-f1 Rf5xf4+ 30 g3xf4 Qf8xf4+ White resigns

The final position in this section comes from the Leningrad Interzonal of 1973.

Uhlmann, having made the injudicious advance h3-h4 some time ago, is now in some difficulty. He decides to sacrifice this pawn, but in doing so opens up the g6 square for Karpov's other bishop to come round and demolish the rest of his position—a fine example of domination by a pair of bishops.

**34 Qe3-h3 Rd7-d6   35 Ba2-b1
Rd6-d2   36 h4-h5 g6xh5!**

There is no point in allowing
White any counterplay.

37 Nc3-d1 Bb7-c6!

When this bishop reaches g6 the
end is in sight.

38 Qh3-f3 Bc6-e8   39 b2-b4 Be8-g6

The threats along the b1-h7
diagonal have been neutralized,
and Black can now concentrate
on picking off the e4 pawn.

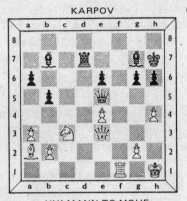

KARPOV   6

UHLMANN TO MOVE

40 Nd1-f2 Qe5-d4   41 Nf2-h3 e6-e5

Preventing 42 Nf4. Either the a-pawn or the e-pawn must now fall.

**42 Nh3-f2 Rd2-b2   43 Kh1-h2 Qd4-c4   44 Rf1-d1 Rb2-b3   45 Nf2-d3
Qc4xe4   White resigns**

THE PASSED PAWN

A passed pawn, or even just a Q-side majority, is a dangerous weapon in the
hands of any grandmaster, and in Karpov's possession it often proves fatal
for his opponent. The game collection contains so many examples of this
theme that I shall give here only a few positions to whet the reader's
appetite.

A passed pawn almost always constitutes an advantage, except in the
rare cases when the pawn can be successfully blockaded (as in Karpov's win
against Spassky in the sixth game of their match—Game 65). The pawn may
be advanced either in the middle-game (as in the first two examples below)
or in the ending (as in the third). In each case the cramping effect is similar,
and the promotion of the pawn or the win of material is always the end
result.

The first example is taken from the game Barcza—Karpov Caracas 1970.

White is about to play his 23rd move. Already he has made a couple of
mistakes, as the cramped nature of his position will testify. The imminent
creation of a passed pawn will push the white forces back even further, and
the black bishops, beautifully positioned on the a2-g8 and a1-h8 diagonals,
will force the pawn home.

23 Bd2-e3 Rf8-c8   24 Qc1-d2 b5-b4!   25 a3xb4 c5xb4

So the passed pawn is born and is already guaranteed to reach b3.

26 Be3-a7 Rb8-b5 27 Re1-c1 Rc8xc1+ 28 Qd2xc1 b4-b3

Black is well on the way to a win. The immediate threat is 29 ...b2! 30 Rxb2 Rxb2 31 Qxb2 e4 winning a piece. With his next move White seeks some freedom, but in fact brings about a quick finish.

29 Qc1-c6? Qd6xc6 30 Bf3xc6 Rb5-a5 31 Ba7-e3 Ra5-a2

The threat is not so much 32 ... Rxe2 as 32 ...b2! followed by 33 ... Ra1 etc. to which there is no reply.

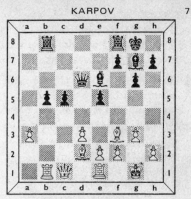

KARPOV 7

BARCZA TO MOVE

32 Bc6-b5 b3-b2! 33 Kg1-g2 e5-e4! 34 d3-d4

34 dxe4 loses to 34 ... Ra1 35 Bd3 Ba2. After the text move however White loses control of the c4 square.

34 ... Be6-b3 White resigns

White no longer has the resource Bb5-c4, and hence must lose at least a piece.

The second example shows the boot on the other foot. This time it is Karpov on the receiving end of a mighty passed pawn driven into his position by former world champion Vassily Smyslov. The game was played in the 39th USSR Championship at Leningrad in 1971.

Were it Black's move here, the isolated queen's pawn would come under fire by either ... Nc6-e7!, blockading the d5 square and incidentally threatening Ne7-f5 winning a piece, or ... Re8-d8 with a direct threat to the d4 pawn on account of the 'hanging' h6 bishop. As it is, White is to make his 21st move and Black is allowed no chance to save himself.

KARPOV 8

SMYSLOV TO MOVE

21 d4-d5!

To capture this pawn would allow mate in two. The threat to the e6 pawn forces Black's reply.

21 ... Nc6-d8 22 d5-d6 Rc8-c5

The only move to save the b6 pawn and prevent the fork by d7.

23 d6-d7 Re8-e7

By 23 ... Rf8 Black would lose the exchange but could probably prolong the game slightly. After the text move Smyslov exploits the weakness of Black's back rank.

24 Qe3-f4! Bf6-g7   25 Qf4-b8 Qh5xh6   26 Qb8xd8+ Bg7-f8   27 Re1-e3

White could win a piece here, but can afford to spend an extra move on
improving his position, since Black is powerless to prevent the threat.

27 ... Bb7-c6   28 Qd8xf8+! Qh6xf8   29 d7-d8=Q Black resigns

Karpov usually prefers to play against an isolated queen's pawn rather than
with it (see Game 41) but this game must have made him regret such a
preference.

In his game with Kaplan from Madrid 1973, Karpov established a dangerous
pawn centre and in the diagrammed position (see Diagram 9) this is about
to become a winning passed pawn.

The continuation was:

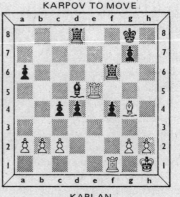

KARPOV TO MOVE   9

KAPLAN

**30 ... d4-d3!   31 c2xd3 c4xd3
32 b2-b3 Rf6-g6   33 h2-h3 d3-d2**

Threatening 34 ... Bxg2+!
35 Kxg2 d1=Q winning the
exchange.

34 Rf1-d1 Bd5-f7   35 Kh1-g1

After 35 Bh5 Rc6! is strong.

**35 ... Rg6-c6   36 Kg1-f2 Rc6-c2
37 Re5-a5 Rd8-d6   38 Bg4-e2
Rc2-c1   39 Be2-f3 Kg8-h8
40 Ra5-e5 Rc1-c2   41 Re5-a5
Bf7-g6!**

With the idea of meeting 42 Be2 by 42 ... Rc1 and 43 ... Bc2 winning.

42 Ra5-d5 Rd6xd5   43 Bf3xd5 Bg6-d3!

Black must preserve his passed pawn and thus avoid 43 ... Rxa2 44 Ke2
Bh5+ 45 Bf3 Bxf3+ 46 gxf3 Rb2 47 Rxd2 Rxb3 48 Ra2 with a drawn
rook and pawn ending.

44 a2-a3 g7-g5   45 Bd5-c4?

Falling into a trap. The last chance was 45 g3 fxg3+ 46 Ke3! Bf5 47 Rxd2
and now either 47 ... Rc3+ followed by 48 ... Bxh3 or 47 ... Rxd2
followed by 48 ... Bxh3 gives Black good winning chances.

45 ... Rc2-c1!

Now 46 Rxd2 allows 46 ... Rf1 mate; so White loses the exchange.

46 Bc4xd3 Rc1xd1 47 Kf2-e2 Rd1-g1 48 Ke2xd2 Rg1xg2+ 49 Kd2-c3
Rg2-g3 50 Kc3-c2 Rg3xh3 51 Bd3xa6 g5-g4 52 a3-a4 g4-g3 **White resigns**

SPATIAL ADVANTAGE

A 'spatial advantage' is a further example of 'natural advantage'. Although,
if it is well-defended, a cramped position may be tenable, and may in some
cases even offer the better prospects, it is in general difficult to construct a
satisfactory defence against breakthrough possibilities when restricted in
space.

The winning procedure is to use the spatial advantage to improve the
positioning of the pieces; then to play for a pawn breakthrough, and finally
to infiltrate into the opponent's position. In this section we shall consider
only one example, but there are two further examples of spatial advantage
in the next section. An excellent illustration in the collection is Karpov's
win against Gligorić from San Antonio 1972 (see Game 44)

The diagrammed position (10) was
reached after 25 moves of Karpov-
Wirthensohn at the Skopje
Olympiad in 1972.

According to Karpov's notes
in *Informator 14* the position is
level. It is true that White has a
small spatial advantage, but
Black's counterplay against the
weak c4 pawn should balance
this. If White is to win at all, then
it must be by a K-side pawn storm.
The continuation was:

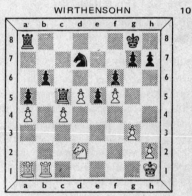

WIRTHENSOHN 10

KARPOV TO MOVE

26 Kh1-g2 Kg8-f8
The active plans 26 ... h5 and 26 ... e4 27 Kf2 Ne5 were both superior.

27 Kg2-f3 Kf8-e7 28 g3-g4 Ra8-h8 29 h2-h4
Now White has a genuine advantage. The white king is within reach of
the weak c4 pawn and the threat of g5 is beginning to take shape.

**29 ... Rh8-f8 30 Kf3-e3 h7-h6 31 Rb1-g1 Rc5-c8 32 Ra1-b1 Rc8-b8
33 Nd2-e4!**
White has achieved the first part of his objective, namely the improvement of the positioning of his pieces in preparation for a breakthrough.

33 ... Rb8-c8 34 Rg1-c1
This would also be the best reply to 33 ... Rfc8, since the speculative

advance 34 g5?! would turn out to be bad after 34 ... hxg5 35 h xg5
Rxc4 36 d6+ (if 36 gxf6+ Nxf6! 37 Rxg7+ Kf8 38 Rf7+! Kxf7
39 Nd6+ Ke7 40 Nxc4 Nxd5+ is to Black's advantage) 36 ... Kf7
37 g6+ Kg8 when White has no more attack.

34 ... Rf8-e8   35 Rb1-b5 Re8-d8   36 Ke3-d3 Ke7-f8?
The back rank should be kept open for the rooks. Now the long-planned
breakthrough is possible.

37 g4-g5! h6xg5   38 h4xg5 Kf8-e7   39 Rc1-g1 Rd8-h8
If 39 ... Rg8 then 40 d6+ Kf8 41 gxf6 gxf6 42 Rxg8+ Kxg8 43 c5!

**40 g5xf6+ g7xf6   41 Rg1-g7+ Ke7-d8   42 Ne4-d6! Rh8-h3+   43 Kd3-e2
Rh3-h2+   44 Ke2-e3 Black resigns**
After 44 ... Rc7 45 Rg8+ Ke7 46 Re8+ Kxd6 47 Re6 is mate, whilst
after 44 ... Rb8 White wins quickly by 45 Rb1 followed by 46 R1g1.

THE BETTER MINOR PIECE

In this section we shall look at the four possible single-minor-piece end-
games—i.e. those with one bishop or knight on each side.

BISHOP v. BISHOP

The two examples here are strikingly similar, and both rely to some extent
on the possession of a spatial advantage in addition to the 'better bishop'.
In general, a bishop is strong when the opponent's pawns are fixed on the
same coloured squares as the bishop, and weak when its fellow-pawns are
fixed on the same coloured squares. (This refers only to bishops of the same
colour—a section on opposite-colour bishops appears later.) So, for example,
with white-squared bishops, both sides will strive to place their blockaded
pawns on black squares.

SMITH TO MOVE   11

KARPOV

The position in Diagram 11 was
reached after White's 41st move in
the Karpov-Smith game at San
Antonio in 1972.

   White has a small spatial advantage
but his winning chances lie in the
superiority of his black-squared
bishop. So Karpov starts on the
preliminary work of removing the
knights and white-squared bishops.

**41 ... Be7-d8   42 Bf3-e2! Nc8-e7
43 Be2-c4! Bf7xc4   44 b3xc4**

Rg8-h8   45 Rg1-h1

45 Rxg7 would have been quicker, but Karpov is in no rush. The bishop will triumph in the end.

45 ... Kb7-c6   46 Kb2-b3 Rh8-h7
47 Bf2-e3 Rh7-h8

Black can only wait. There is no way for him to improve the placing of his pieces.

48 Kb3-b4 Rh8-h7?

Better was 48 ... Kb7 so as to meet 49 Nd5 by 49 ... Nc6+.

49 Nc3-d5 Ne7xd5

Better was 49 ... Nc8.

50 c4xd5+ Kc6-b7   51 Kb4-b5

White has achieved the ending he was aiming for and quickly demolishes Black's remaining defences. As soon as the position is broken up White's bishop wreaks havoc amongst the black pawns.

51 ... Bd8-c7   52 a2-a4 Rh7-h8   53 Be3-d2 Rh8-h7   54 Bd2-b4 Rh7-h8
55 Rh1-g1 Rh8-h7   56 Rg1-g6! Bc7-b8   57 h5-h6! g7xh6

Clearly 57 ... Rxh6? would be disastrous for Black after 58 Rxg7+ followed by 59 Kc6 (58 ... Bc7 loses a piece to 59 Bxd6).

58 Rg6xf6 h6-h5   59 Bb4xd6 Bb8xd6   60 Rf6xd6 h5-h4   61 Rd6xb6+
Kb7-a7   62 Rb6-g6 h4-h3   63 Rg6-g1 Rh8-h4   64 Rg1-g7+! Ka7-a8
65 f5-f6! Rh4-f4   66 f6-f7 h3-h2   67 Rg7-h7 Rf4xf7   68 Rh7xh2 Rf7-f4
69 d5-d6 Rf4xe4   70 Rh2-h8+ Black resigns

The second example is from the Karpov-Ribli game at the European Team Championship finals at Bath in 1973.

The superiority of White's bishop over Black's was established at an early stage in the game, and after much manœuvring and several exchanges Karpov has reached his optimum position. The win is by no means guaranteed here, but White's initiative is so strong that Ribli's position seems to fall apart.

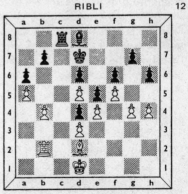

RIBLI   12

KARPOV TO MOVE

52 b4-b5! a6xb5   53 Rb2xb5
Kd7-c7   54 Kd1-e2 Kc7-b8

After 54 ... Ra8 55 Rb4 Be7
56 Rb6 Ra7 57 Kf3! the
threat of 58 g5! is difficult to

meet. The text move is aimed at the bishop-and-pawn ending reached in the game, but this, unfortunately for Black, turns out to be lost.

55 Bd2-b4 Bd8-c7　56 a5-a6 Kb8-a7!　57 a6xb7 Rc8-b8　58 Bb4-d2! Rb8xb7　59 Rb5xb7+ Ka7xb7　60 g4-g5! h6xg5　61 h4xg5 Bc7-d8
After 61 ... fxg5 62 Bxg5 Kc8 63 Be7 Bd8 64 Bxd6 or 63 ... Kd7 64 Bf8 White wins a pawn.

62 Ke2-f3! Kb7-c8　63 Kf3-g4 Kc8-d7　64 Kg4-h5 Kd7-e8　65 Bd2-b4!
Black's position is hopeless. The possibilities are:
(a) 65 ... Be7 66 gxf6 gxf6 67 Kg6 followed by Bb4-e1-h4xf6;
(b) 65 ... Bc7 66 gxf6 gxf6 67 Kg6 as in (a);
(c) 65 ... Ke7 66 gxf6+ gxf6 67 Kg6 similarly;
(d) 65 ... Kd7 66 gxf6 (the simplest) Bxf6 67 Kg6 Ke7 68 Ba3! Kd7 69 Kf7 Kc7 70 Ke6 winning the d-pawn.

65 ... f6xg5　66 Bb4xd6
The g5 pawn falls; so Black could safely resign here. The finish was:

66 ... Bd8-f6　67 Bd6-b4 Ke8-f7　68 Bb4-d2 Bf6-e7　69 Bd2xg5 Be7-a3 70 Bg5-d8 Ba3-d6　71 Kh5-g5 Black resigns

The two examples above involved closed positions. Game 45 is an excellent example of a bishop-ending in a more open setting.

BISHOP v. KNIGHT

A bishop is basically a long-range piece and it is therefore not surprising that it exerts its greatest pressure in an open position. Whereas the bishop can attack both sides of the board simultaneously, the knight can exert pressure over only a comparatively small area, and so, in a position offering play on both sides of the board, the bishop is generally superior. The bishop is still bad if its own pawns are fixed on the same-coloured squares, but in a fluid-pawn situation the bishop comes out best.

The three examples in this section show how even a well-placed knight is unable to deal with a bishop. Each ending illustrates a different aspect: the first shows the bishop dealing with a passed-pawn race; the second, the creation of a passed pawn; and the third, a direct rook-and-bishop mating attack.

The bishop triumphs in the first position (Karpov-Dueball, Skopje Olympiad 1972) because it can both support the advance of its own pawn and also prevent the advance of the Black one.

Play continued:

36 ... Rb8-a8　37 c3-c4! a5xb4　38 a3xb4 b5xc4+　39 Kb3xc4 Ke7-d8 40 Kc4-b5 Kd8-c7　41 Rd2-c2+ Kc7-b7　42 Bf5-d7!

After 42 Rc6? Ne2! is strong.

42 ... Ra8-a3   43 Rc2-c6!

Now 43 ... Ne2 is met by 44 Bc8+
Kb8 45 Kb6 with a mating attack,
and 43 ... Rxf3 by 44 Ra6 again
mating. A possible alternative to
the text plan was 43 ... Nxd5
44 Rxd6 Nxb4! when 45 Kxb4
Rxf3 gives Black good drawing
chances. However 45 Rxf6! is
stronger.

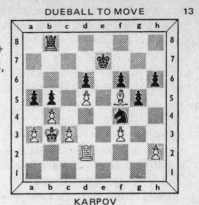

DUEBALL TO MOVE   13

KARPOV

43 ... Ra3-d3   44 Rc6-b6+ Kb7-c7

**45 Bd7-c6 Nf4xd5   46 Rb6-b7+
Kc7-c8   47 Rb7-f7**

Quicker was 47 Rh7!

**47 ... Kc8-d8   48 Rf7-d7+ Kd8-c8   49 Rd7-f7 Kc8-d8   50 Kb5-c4 Nd5-f4
51 Rf7xf6 d6-d5+**

A neat point here is that 51 ... Kc7 is met by 52 Kb5 and not 52 Rxf4
when 52 ... Ra3! regains the piece.

**52 Kc4-c5 Kd8-e7   53 Rf6xh6 Rd3-c3+   54 Kc5-b6 Rc3xf3   55 b4-b5
g5-g4?**

The last chance was 55 ... Rb3.

56 Rh6-h4! Rf3-h3   57 Rh4xg4 Nf4-e2

Both 57 ... Nd3 58 Rg3 and 57 ... Ne6 58 Bxd5 Rxh2 59 Re4 win
for White.

58 Kb6-c7 Rh3-h7   59 b5-b6 Ke7-e6+   60 Kc7-d8!! Ne2-d4

If 60 ... Kd6 then 61 Rg6+ Kc5 62 b7 wins immediately.

61 Rg4xd4 Ke6-d6   62 Bc6xd5! Kd6-c5

After 62 ... Rh8+ 63 Bg8+ Kc6 64 Rg4 or 62 ... Rxh2 63 b7 Rh8+
64 Bg8+ Kc6 65 b8=N+! Kb7 66 Rb4+ Ka7 67 Kc7! White wins.

63 Rd4-d2 Kc5xb6   64 Rd2-c2 Black resigns

The second example is similar in many ways. The conversion of a Q-side
majority into a passed pawn is sufficient to bring the Black position down.
This time, the knight is excellently placed and the bishop is to some extent
'bad' owing to the fixed pawns on e4, g2, and h3, but this is no compensation for a passed pawn. The diagrammed position (14) was reached after
White's 38th move in the fourth game of the 1974 Karpov-Polugaevsky
match.

38 ... Ke7-d8   39 c3-c4 Kd8-c7?

Better was 39 ... b6. The Q-side pawns now overwhelm the black pieces.

40 b2-b4 Ne5-g6   41 b4-b5 a6xb5

After 41 ... Rc5 42 b6+ Kc6 43 Bd1! White has a winning position.

42 c4xb5 Rc6-c2   43 b5-b6+ Kc7-d7

After 43 ... Kc6 44 Ke3 the threat of 45 Bb5 mate is unanswerable (44 ... Rxe2+ 45 Kxe2 Nf4+ 46 Kf3 Nxd5 47 exd5+ Kc5 48 dxe6 wins).

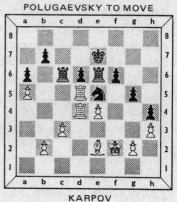

POLUGAEVSKY TO MOVE   14

KARPOV

44 Rd4-d2!

To prevent 44 ... Rxe2+, or 44 ... Nf4.

44 ... Rc2xd2   45 Rd5xd2 Re6-e5

If 45 ... Rxe4 then 46 Bb5+ Kc8 47 Rc2+ Kb8 48 a6 bxa6 49 Bxa6 Re8 50 b7 Ne7 51 Re2 wins.

46 a5-a6! Kd7-c6

46 ... bxa6 47 Bxa6 Ne7 48 Rb2 Nc6 49 Bb5! also wins for White.

47 ... Rd2-b2 Ng6-f4   48 a6-a7 Re5-a5   49 Be2-c4 Black resigns

The final example in this section gives an idea of the true power of a bishop in an open situation. The white rook and bishop prove an effective mating force against the exposed black king. The black knight is unable to join in the defence, as it is dominated by the white bishop.

The game is Karpov-Pomar, Nice Olympiad 1974. Pomar, having just regained a sacrificed pawn, is somewhat exposed on the first and second ranks.

POMAR   15

KARPOV TO MOVE

34 Rf1-f8+ Kc8-c7   35 Bb4-a5+ b7-b6   36 Ba5-d2 Ng5-e4 37 Bd2-f4+ Kc7-b7   38 Rf8-f7+ Kb7-a8

38 ... Ka6? is met by 39 Bb8.

39 Rf7-f8+ Ka8-b7   40 b2-b4

Rg6xg4   41 Rf8-f7+ Kb7-a8?

Better was 41 . . . Kc8! 42 Be5 c5!

**42 Kc1-c2 h6-h5   43 a3-a4 h5-h4   44 Kc2-d3 Ne4-g5   45 Rf7-f8+ Ka8-b7
46 Rf8-b8+ Kb7-a6   47 Bf4-d2! Rg4-g3+   48 Kd3-c2 Black resigns**

Mate by 49 b5+ is unstoppable.

KNIGHT v. BISHOP

Karpov is essentially a 'bishop man' and so examples of his play with good
knight against bad bishop are rare. A knight can be superior to a bishop only
when the position is blocked, or closed, or when the field of action is
limited to one side of the board. Even with a closed position the bishop
may be the better piece—this depends solely on the relative pawn structures.

In the two examples below the underlying reason for the defeat is the
good-knight-v.-bad-bishop theme, although in one case Karpov is a pawn to
the good, and in the other he engineers a winning attack.

In the Rukavina-Karpov game at the Leningrad Interzonal in 1973, Black
has already won the white c4 pawn. White's bishop is not an especially bad
piece but the black knight decides the game quickly when it reaches the
outpost at c4.

Play continued:
**21 e3-e4 d7-d6   22 Qb5-g5 Nf6-d7
23 Qg5-e7 Nd7-e5! 24 Qe7xc7
Rc6xc7   25 Rb2-b5**

25 Rxb6? loses a piece to
25 . . . Nc4.

Ne5-c4   26 Bd2-c1 Ra8-c8

If the pawn situation were level
here Black would still stand much
better.

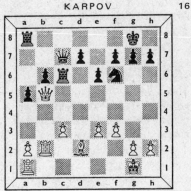

KARPOV   16

RUKAVINA TO MOVE

**27 Ra1-b1 Rc7-c5   28 Kg1-f1 Kg8-f8
29 Kf1-e2 Kf8-e7   30 Rb5-b3 Ke7-d7
31 a2-a4 Kd7-c7   32 Bc1-f4 Kc7-b7
33 Bf4-e3 Rc5-c6   34 Be3-d4 f7-f6
35 Rb1-d1 Rc8-d8   36 f3-f4 d6-d5!
37 Bd4-f2 Rc6-d6   38 Bf2-c5 Rd6-c6
39 Bc5-f2 Rd8-d6   40 e4xd5 Rd6xd5   41 Rd1xd5 e6xd5   42 Rb3-b5
Rc6-e6+   43 Ke2-d3 Kb7-c6   44 g2-g3 Re6-e7   45 Rb5-b1 Re7-b7
46 Rb1-b5 Nc4-d6   47 Rb5-b2 b6-b5   48 a4xb5+ Rb7xb5   49 Rb2-e2
White resigns.**

The second example is Karpov-Grigorian from the 39th USSR Championship, Leningrad 1971. At first sight it appears that Black's problems centre round the open e-file. It is true that he is unable to relieve the pressure on this file, but the main reason for this is that the bishop on g7 is useless. Were this a white-squared bishop on, say, d7 Black would easily achieve equality, but the black-squared bishop, hemmed in so badly behind its own pawns, can neither help to relieve the e-file pressure nor cover the weak d5, f5, g6, and h5 squares. As a direct

GRIGORIAN   17

KARPOV

result of this, White is able to work his way in on the white squares, and makes short work of the game.

**25 ... Nc6-e7   26 f4-f5! Bg7-f8   27 Re2-e6 Ne7-g8   28 Nf3-h2 Re8-c8
29 Re1-e3 Rc8-c6   30 Qc2-e2 Ra8-c8   31 Qe2-f3 Qf7-c7   32 Ng3-e2
Qc7-a5   33 a2-a4   Rc6-c7**

> The black queen would have been more useful on f7. Now the weak
> white squares are infiltrated.

**34 Re6-e8 Bf8-g7   35 Qf3-h5 Qa5-b6   36 Nh2-g4 Rc8xe8   37 Re3xe8
Rc7-e7   38 Ng4xh6! Re7xe8   39 Nh6-f7 mate**

> Examples in the game collection are Game 21 (v. Klovan) and Game 25
> (v. Taimanov).

KNIGHT v. KNIGHT

This is a very rare, and often ignored, aspect of minor-piece play. In itself, an aggressively-posted knight against a passively-posted knight rarely constitutes a winning advantage, but, in conjunction with a secondary element, such as spatial advantage (see the example Karpov-Wirthensohn above), or a Q-side pawn majority (see Game 43 against Browne), it can be a decisive factor.

The following examples show how a win can be squeezed out from the smallest advantage.

The position of Diagram 18 arose after Black's 34th move in the Karpov-Tukmakov game in the 39th USSR Championship at Leningrad in 1971. White's only advantage lies in the fact that he can establish a more aggressive position for his knight. This alone should not be sufficient to win, but it

requires only a small error from
Black before his position collapses.

**35 Nc2-b4 a6-a5 36 Nb4-c6 a5-a4
37 Kg1-f2 Kf8-e8 38 Kf2-e3 Ke8-d7
39 Nc6-e5+?!**

Even better was 39 Nd4 Nd6
40 Kd3 Kc7 41 Kc3 Kb6 42 Kb4.

39 ... Kd7-e6 40 Ke3-d4 f7-f6?
The simple 40 ... Ne7 was better.

41 Ne5-d3 Ke6-d6 42 Nd3-f4 g7-g6
The threat was 43 Nh5, winning
a pawn.

TUKMAKOV 18

KARPOV TO MOVE

43 Nf4-d5 f6-f5 44 g2-g4 Nc8-a7
Threatening 45 ... Nc6+, winning the knight.

**45 Nd5-b4 f5xg4 46 f3xg4 Na7-c8 47 Nb4-d3 Nc8-e7 48 Nd3-e5 Kd6-e6
49 a2-a3 Ne7-d5 50 Ne5-d7!**

Gaining further ground, since the king and pawn ending after 50 ... Kxd7
51 Kxd5 would be totally lost for Black.

50 ... Ke6-d6 51 g4-g5! Nd5-e7 52 Nd7-f8 Ne7-c6+ 53 Kd4-c3 Nc6-e5?
A losing blunder. The best chance was given by 53 ... Ke5 54 Nxh7 Kf5
55 Kd3 when White has only a small advantage.

54 Nf8xh7 Ne5-f3 55 Kc3-b4 Black resigns

After 55 ... Kc6 56 Nf8 Nxh2 57 Nxg6 Nf3 58 Ne7+ followed by
59 g6 after 58 ... Kb6, or 59 Nf5+ after 58 ... Kd6, White's extra pawn
will soon win.

BETTER-QUALITY PIECES

This general heading can cover a whole range of ideas in middle-game play,
including the exploitation of weak pawns, the use of better-placed pieces,
and combinations of all the themes discussed above. I have chosen just two
examples.

The first is from the Ghizdavu-Karpov game in the European Team
Championship finals at Bath in 1973.

This is basically a good-knight-v.-bad-bishop situation. Black is able to
control the open c-file and eventually infiltrates with his pieces. The
other aspects working in Black's favour are more space on the Q-side
and an absence of weaknesses. It is most instructive to see how Black
makes use of all his advantages.

27 ... d6xe5   28 d4xe5
The exchange of bishop for knight
after 28 Nxe5+ Bxe5 would be
very much in Black's favour.

28 ... Rf8-c8   29 Nf3-d4 Bg7-f8
30 Ra1-a6 Rb7-b6   31 Ra6-a7+
Rc8-c7   32 Ra7-a8 b4-b3   33 Ra8-
a4 Bf8-c5   34 Nd4-e2 Bc5-b4
35 Re1-d1 Rb6-c6   36 Ra4-a1
Rc6-b6   37 Rd1-d3 Bb4-e7   38 g2-g3
After 38 Nd4 Ra6! 39 Rb1 Ra4
40 Nxb3 Nxf4 41 Bxf4 Rxf4
the white e-pawn would soon fall.

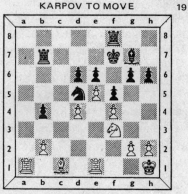

GHIZDAVU

38 ... Rc7-c4   39 Kh1-g2
If 39 Nd4 then 39 ... Nb4! is strong.

39 ... Rc4-c2   40 Kg2-f3 Rb6-b4   41 h2-h4
Better was 41 Nd4 Rxh2 42 Ra7!

41 ... Be7-c5   42 Bc1-d2 Rb4-e4   43 Ra1-c1 Bc5-b4!   44 Rc1xc2 b3xc2
45 Bd2-c1
After 45 Bxb4 Rxe2 Black wins immediately.

45 ... Re4-c4   46 Rd3-d4 Rc4-c7   47 b2-b3 Bb4-e1   48 Rd4-c4 Rc7xc4
49 b3xc4 Nd5-c3   50 Ne2xc3?
Better was 50 Nd4! Ne4 51 Nxc2 Bxg3 52 c5! Bxh4 53 c6 Bd8
54 Nd4 Nc3! when Black's advantage is only small. The text move gives
White a lost bishop-and-pawn ending.

50 ... Be1xc3   51 g3-g4
51 c5 is met by 51 ... h5!

51 ... f5xg4+   52 Kf3xg4 h6-h5+   53 Kg4-f3
After 53 Kg5 Bb4! White is still lost.

53 ... Bc3-e1   54 Kf3-e2 Be1xh4   55 Ke2-d3 Bh4-f2   56 Kd3xc2 h5-h4
57 Kc2-d3 h4-h3   White resigns

The second example combines the elements of exploitation of weak pawns,
superior piece-placing, and a superbly-conducted endgame. It shows how a
minute advantage in co-operation between the pieces can be gently and
surely converted into a win.

The position of Diagram 20 occurred after Black's 38th move of the
Karpov-Rashkovsky game in the RSFSR Championship in 1970.

The game appears to be level, as the placing of the white pieces is not

especially constructive, but with a
few quick blows Karpov changes the
nature of the struggle completely.

RASHKOVSKY 20

KARPOV TO MOVE

**39 e4-e5! d6xe5 40 Rd2-d7+ Rf8-f7
41 Rd7x f7+ Kg7xf7 42 Rd1-d7+
Kf7-e6 43 Rd7xa7 Ne8-f6
44 Ra7-c7 Ba6-d3 45 Rc7xc5
Rb6-a6 46 Rc5-c6+ Ra6xc6
47 Bg2xc6**

The resulting ending is difficult
to win, since the black king can
work his way into the heart of the
white position. The win is achieved
only after a most delicate series of
moves.

**47 ... Ke6-d6 48 Bc6-g2 Kd6-c5 49 a2-a3 Kc5-d4 50 Kg1-f2 e5-e4
51 a3-a4 Kd4-c3 52 a4-a5 Nf6-d7 53 h3-h4 Kc3xb3 54 Ne3-d5! Nd7-c5
55 Kf2-e3 Kb3-a4 56 Nd5-f4! Ka4xa5 57 Nf4xg6 Nc5-d7 58 Bg2xe4
Bd3-c4**

Now if Black can give up either bishop or knight for the h-pawn the
game is drawn.

**59 Ke3-d4 Bc4-e2 60 Be4-f5 Nd7-f6 61 Kd4-e5 Nf6-e8 62 Ng6-f4
Be2-d1 63 Bf5-g6 Ne8-c7 64 Bg6-h5 Bd1xh5 65 Nf4xh5 Nc7-e8
66 Nh5-f4 Ka5-b6 67 h4-h5 Kb6-c7 68 h5-h6 Ne8-d6 69 h6-h7 Kc7-d7
70 Ke5-f6 Black resigns**

ENDINGS WITH ROOKS, AND BISHOPS OF OPPOSITE COLOUR

A discussion of this particular type of ending seems appropriate in view of
the remarkably similar situations that arose in Games 33 (against Robert
Byrne) and 35 (against Mecking).

The major problem in all endings with bishops of opposite colour is to
win the opposing pawns. If these are placed on squares of the same colour
as the opposing bishop then there is little to be done and an alternative
winning plan must be found. In the two games mentioned above, the strategy
was to attack the opposing king directly, and thus force mate or win material.
Bishops of opposite colours are often involved in effective attacks on the king.

The example below shows the other side of the coin. The white pawns
fall like ripe apples, and Black's extra pawns decide the issue. The position
of Diagram 21 was reached after Black's 39th move in the Beliavsky-Karpov
game from the USSR Championship of 1973.

White is already in some trouble, and must at least lose the g2 pawn.

**40 Bg3-h4+ g6-g5! 41 f4xg5+ h6xg5
42 Bh4-g3 Ra3-a2+ 43 Kf2-e3
Ra2xg2 44 Bg3-c7 Rg2-a2**

White has a further problem: his
h-pawn is not easy to defend.

45 Rd7-h7 Ra2-a8!

A necessary preparation for
46 ... Kg6. Black does not want
to allow the white rook to go to h8.

**46 Ke3-f2 Kf6-g6 47 Rh7-d7 Ra8-a3
48 Rd7-d8 Ra3-f3+ 49 Kf2-g1
Rf3xh3**

The rest is relatively simple.

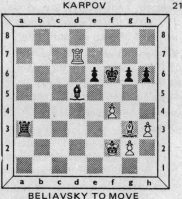

KARPOV   21

BELIAVSKY TO MOVE

**50 Rd8-b8 Rh3-c3 51 Bc7-d6 Rc3-c2 52 Rb8-f8 Rc2-c6 53 Bd6-e5
g5-g4 54 Rf8-f6+ Kg6-g5 55 Rf6-f8 Bd5-f3 56 Be5-f4+ Kg5-g6 57 Kg1-f2
Rc6-c2+ 58 Kf2-g3 Rc2-g2+ 59 Kg3-h4 Rg2-e2 60 Bf4-g3 e6-e5
61 Rf8-b8 e5-e4 62 Rb8-b5 Re2-e3 63 Rb5-b6+ Kg6-f7 64 Kh4-g5
Re3-d3 65 Kg5-f5 e4-e3 66 Rb6-d6 Rd3-b3 67 Rd6-d7+ Kf7-e8
68 Kf5-e6 e3-e2 69 Rd7-e7+ Ke8-f8 70 Ke6-f6 Bf3-d5 71 Bg3-h4,
Rb3-f3+ 72 Kf6-g6 Bd5-f7+ White resigns**

Tournament and match record

YEAR	EVENT	PLACE	SCORE W	D	L
1967	Třinec, Czechoslovakia	1	7	8	0
	European Junior Championship	1	4	3	0
1968	USSR v. Yugoslavia match, Junior board		3	1	0
	USSR v. Scandinavia match, Junior board		0	1	1
	Moscow University Championship	1	7	6	0
	Soviet Team Championship, Junior board		9	2	0
1969	World Junior Championship, selection tournament	1	5	5	2
	USSR v. Yugoslavia, Junior match		2	2	0
	World Junior Championship, preliminaries	1	3	3	0
	World Junior Championship, final	1	9	2	0
	RSFSR v. Hungary match, Junior board		0	2	2
1970	RSFSR Championship	1	8	9	0
	Caracas	4-6	8	7	2
	38th USSR Championship	5-7	5	14	2
1971	39th USSR Championship, semi-final	1	9	8	0
	18th Student Olympiad, board 3		7	1	0
	Soviet Team Championship, Junior board		6	1	0
	Army Team Championship, board 1		2	4	1
	39th USSR Championship	4	7	12	2
	Alekhine Memorial Tournament	1-2	5	12	0
	Hastings	1-2	8	6	1
1972	Soviet Team Championship, board 2		4	3	2
	19th Student Olympiad, board 1		5	4	0
	20th Olympiad, board 5		12	2	1
	San Antonio	1-3	7	7	1
1973	Budapest	2	4	11	0
	USSR Match Tournament, board 1		2	2	0
	Interzonal Tournament	1-2	10	7	0
	European Team Championship, board 4		4	2	0
	40th USSR Championship	2-6	5	11	1
	Madrid	1	7	8	0
1974	Match v. Polugaevsky		3	5	0
	Match v. Spassky		4	6	1
	21st Olympiad, board 1		10	4	0
	Match v. Korchnoi		3	19	2

List of games

32   *List of games*

3 World Junior Champion

Anatoly Evgenyevich Karpov was born in Zlatoust, some 850 miles east of Moscow, on 23 May 1951. He learned to play chess at the age of four and achieved the third-category rating (equivalent to a British Grading of 130-140) at the age of seven, the second-category rating (British Grade 150-160) at the age of eight, and the first-category rating (British Grade 175-180) at the age of nine. Two years later he achieved the title of Candidate Master (British Grade 195 and above) and at the age of fifteen he became the youngest Master in the Soviet Union by winning a Candidates/Masters tournament in Leningrad.

In comparison with other leading grandmasters of today this progress may be described as 'average'. Boris Spassky was a Candidate Master at twelve, and took part in the world championship series at the age of eighteen. Mikhail Tal was sixteen before he won the Candidate Master title; he won the USSR Championship (a feat that has so far eluded Karpov) at twenty and was world champion at twenty-three. Tigran Petrosian, on the other hand, did not achieve his first-category rating until he was thirteen and his Master title until he was eighteen. The 'unfair' example would be Bobby Fischer who, by winning the USA Championship, qualified for the Interzonal at fourteen, played in the Interzonal at fifteen and represented his country in the Olympiad at Leipzig at seventeen.

It was not until 1967 that Karpov opened his international career, and, when he did, it was with the outstanding success with which we have become familiar. He was selected to play in a tournament at Třinec in Czechoslovakia by mistake. The tournament was not for juniors (as had been thought by the Soviet Chess Federation) but for adults. Nevertheless, Karpov was included, and came first without a loss! The leading scores were: Karpov 11, Kupka and Kupreychik 9½, Smejkal 8½.

In 1967 Karpov had perhaps the greatest failure in his entire chess career: he lost three games in the same tournament. This, of course, was no great tragedy, but it serves to illustrate the consistency of Karpov's career. The occasion was a junior selection tournament held to decide who should represent the USSR in the 1967 world junior championship. All the leading junior players took part, and so it was no disgrace for the young Anatoly to lose to the older and more experienced players Balashov, Timoshenko, and Kupreychik. His turn was soon to come.

At the end of 1967 and the beginning of 1968, Karpov took part in, and won, the International Youth Tournament in Groningen, Holland. This was his first trip to the West. The Groningen tournament was at the time the *de facto* European Junior Championship and has subsequently been re-named as such. The top final scores were Karpov 5½ (out of 7), Jocha 5, Levi 4½, Zara and Timman 3½, Moles, Hostalet, and Ligterink 2. Games 1 and 2 are taken from this event, and show two entirely different aspects of Karpov's play in those early days. One is a Ruy López, the other an English Opening, but both have that stamp of authority and control which was to become one of Karpov's trade-marks.

Back in the USSR for the whole of 1968, Karpov played in matches representing his country on the junior board against Scandinavia (in which he was beaten 1½-½ by Jacobsen) and against Yugoslavia. In the latter, he beat Vujakovic by 3½-½, and thus helped his side to a convincing victory. Game 3 is taken from this match, and a second of the games is included in the notes.

The other major events of 1968 were the Moscow University Champion-ship and the Soviet Team Championship at Riga. Karpov came first in the Moscow University Championship with seven wins and six draws (no losses), and scored nine wins and two draws on the junior board for the Armed Forces team in the Soviet Team Championship. Games 4 and 5 are taken from the former event and Games 6 and 7 from the latter.

In March/April 1969 Karpov played in a three-player tournament with six games between each pair to decide who would represent the USSR in the world junior championship in Stockholm later in the year. After six of the twelve rounds the scores were: Karpov 5, Vaganian 2½, Steinberg 1½. Karpov's poor finish of 2½/6 was still sufficient to give him a clear 1½-point victory. Immediately after this he scored two wins and two draws against Evrosimovsky in a USSR v. Yugoslavia junior match in Moscow.

Karpov had by now formed a strong partnership with his trainer, Grandmaster Semyon Furman. The next few months were spent in training for the world junior championship—improving every aspect of Karpov's game down to physical training and exercise! The preliminary rounds must have been a nightmare for Furman. Both Hug and Torre achieved winning positions against Karpov, but by some good luck and some excellent defensive play he managed to save both positions and thus enter the A-final.

Once he had qualified, Karpov mowed down the opposition relentlessly, and started with eight wins in a row! Then came a draw, and Karpov was sure of the title, but in the last two rounds (although he needed no more points) he scored a further draw and a win. This last-round demolition of Diaz was the first game I saw Karpov play. By winning the world junior championship Karpov automatically became an International Master.

Game 8 is a Ruy López against the young Ulf Andersson (now a grandmaster). The latter half of this game is excellently conducted by

Karpov and is only the prelude of many similar victories to come. Game 9 is Karpov's variation of the Alekhine Defence. Careful study of the opening will show this to be a valuable contribution to the realms of theory. Game 10 was a difficult one to annotate—White's mistake is not obvious and yet he is lost in only twenty-odd moves. Castro in Game 11 lasts a little longer after Karpov's daring pawn sacrifice in the opening.

This had been a highly successful start to his career and Karpov could only wait for an opportunity to qualify for his grandmaster title. It was not long in coming.

Game 1

BLACK Timman   English Opening
European Junior Championship, Groningen 1967-8

Although Karpov's style of play is, in general, based on strategy, he also has an impressive facility for analysis of tactical situations. In this game, he wins a pawn early on, defends against his opponent's sacrificial attack, and finally breaks through by returning some of the sacrificed material. Throughout he has the game under control and we shall see in later games that this is a feature of his play.

1 c2-c4   e7-e6

2 Nb1-c3   Ng8-f6

3 Ng1-f3

More aggressive is 3 e4.

3 ... Bf8-b4

4 Qd1-b3

With 4 d4 White could choose to play a Nimzo-Indian Defence. Also possible was:

(a) 4 a3 Bxc3 5 bxc3 0-0 6 g3 c5 7 Bg2 Nc6 8 d3 d5 9 cxd5 exd5 10 0-0 Re8 11 Bg5 h6 12 Bxf6 Qxf6 with an equal game (Matulović-Korchnoi, Bucharest 1966).

or probably best

(b) 4 Qc2 c5 5 a3 Ba5 (also possible is 5 ... Bxc3 followed by 6 ... b6); 6 e3 when 6 ... d5 allows 7 Na4! b6 8 Rb1 Na6 9 cxd5 Nxd5 10 Bb5+

with a clear advantage to White (Smyslov-Matanović, Monte Carlo 1967).

4 ... c7-c5

5 a2-a3   Bb4-a5

Naturally 5 ... Bxc3 6 Qxc3 is just what White would like.

6 e2-e3

6 g3 is more common here. The game Polugaevsky-Korchnoi, Sochi 1966 continued 6 ... Nc6 7 Bg2 d5 8 0-0 Bxc3! 9 Qxc3 d4 10 Qc2 a5 11 d3 0-0 12 Bf4 with advantage to White, but 11 ... e5 would have been an equalizing move.

6 ... 0-0

7 Bf1-e2   d7-d5

8 0-0   Nb8-c6

With this move Black prepares the

manœuvres 9 ... Bc7 or 9 ... d4. At
present 8 ... Bc7 could be met by
9 d4! when the possibility of Nc3-
b5xc7 (giving White the two bishops)
is always in the air, and 8 ... d4 by
9 Na4 when Black is embarrassed for
an adequate way to protect both the
c5 and d4 squares:

(a) 9 ... b6 10 exd4 cxd4 11 Qd3!
threatens both the d4 pawn and
12 b4 winning the bishop on a5.

(b) 9 ... Bb6 10 Nxb6 and Black has lost
his two bishops and has had his pawn-
structure permanently ruined.

(c) 9 ... Qd6 10 Qb5 Bb6 11 Nxb6 as in
(b) above.

9 Nc3-a4!

But Karpov doesn't give him time.
Now 9 ... b6 would leave the bishop
out on a limb and a simple retreat
10 Qc2 would leave White with a clear
advantage.

9 ... Qd8-e7

10 Qb3-c2 Nf6-d7

An awkward move, but the alternative
10 ... b6 is no better. 10 ... d4 on the
other hand could be strongly met by
11 exd4 Nxd4 12 Nxd4 cxd4 13 b4
or by 11 b4!?

11 d2-d4

The natural continuation. This move
increases the pressure on Black's c5
pawn.

TIMMAN TO MOVE   **1.1**

KARPOV

11 ... d5xc4

The alternative was 11 ... cxd4 but
this would also prove to be poor after
12 cxd5 exd5 13 b4 when Black must
choose between:

(a) 13 ... Bc7? 14 b5 winning a piece.

(b) 13 ... Bb6 14 Nxb6 Nxb6 15 b5
followed by 16 Nxd4 with a well-
developed position for White.

(c) 13 ... Bd8 with a cramped game.

12 d4xc5 e6-e5

12 ... Nxc5 13 Nxc5 Qxc5 14 b4!
costs Black a piece. This is the tactical
justification of 11 d4

13 e3-e4

Karpov prefers to increase the scope
of his queen's bishop before taking
the crippled c-pawn

13 ... Nc6-d4

14 Nf3xd4 e5xd4

15 Be2xc4

White now has a sound extra pawn
although Black has some K-side
chances. The c5 pawn is still untouchable.

15 ... Nd7-e5

16 b2-b4 Ba5-c7

17 Bc4-d5

A difficult decision but undoubtedly
correct. 17 Be2 would allow Black to
establish his second bishop on c6 with
a menacing attack. On the other hand
the bishop on e2 could be used to
defend the K-side. Karpov, however,
chooses 17 Bd5 because from this
dominating position the bishop
hinders the development of Black's
Q-side and blocks any pressure from a
black rook on the d-file.

17 ... d4-d3

18 Qc2-d1 Bc8-g4

19 f2-f3 Bg4-h5

20 Ra1-a2!

Preparing to wrap the game up by
21 g4. 20 Ra2 defends the vulnerable
h2 and g2 squares and prepares to
transfer the rook to active service on
the K-side. Black cannot prevent the
following piece-winning plan and his

TIMMAN TO MOVE   1.2

KARPOV

TIMMAN   1.3

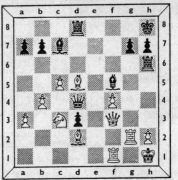

KARPOV TO MOVE

next move is the only try for complications.

20 ... Kg8-h8

21 g2-g4   Bh5-g6
and not 21 ... Bxg4 22 fxg4 Qh4
23 Rg2! and if then 23 ,.. Nxg4
24 Qxg4 Bxh2+ 25 Kh1 wins.

22 f3-f4
Winning at least a piece.

22 ... Ne5xg4

23 Qd1xg4   f7-f5

24 e4xf5   Bg6xf5

25 Qg4-f3   Ra8-d8

26 Na4-c3
White's only remaining problem is
how to mobilize his extra piece.
Karpov achieves this with an amazing
economy of effort.

26 ... Qe7-f6

27 Ra2-g2!
Preparing to develop the queen's bishop
on d2. Note that 27 ... Qxc3 is refuted
by 28 Bb2 and mate on g7.

27 ... Qf6-d4+

28 Kg1-h1   Rf8-f6

29 Bc1-d2   Rf6-h6
Black has conjured up a certain
number of threats: 30 ... Bh3 wins
the exchange, and 30 ... Rh3 followed
by 31 Qf2 Rxd5 wins two pieces for
a rook.

The following fine sacrifice decides
the game quickly since it removes all
Black's attacking pieces at minimal
cost. But it is difficult to see why
Karpov rejected (or overlooked)
30 Nb5! Qxd5 31 Qxd5 Rxd5
32 Nxc7 Rd7 33 Re1! which would
have won more rapidly.

30 Qf3-f2   Rd8xd5

31 Rf1-e1
The point of the previous move. Now
Black must allow White to exchange a
pair of rooks, since 31 ... Be6 would
allow 32 Qxd4 Rxd4 33 f5 followed
by 34 Re7 winning a piece.

31 ... Rh6-e6

32 Nc3xd5   Qd4xd5

33 Re1xe6   Bf5xe6

34 Kh1-g1
It is now only a matter of time before
the extra white material proves decisive.
Karpov forces the win by occupying
the weakened a1-h8 diagonal.

34 ... Qd5-b3
In order to prevent Bc3.

35 Qf2-e1!   Kh8-g8

36 f4-f5   Be6-f7

37 Bd2-h6   g7-g6

38 Qe1-a1!
The final point of White's 35th move.

38 ... Bc7-e5

39 Qa1xe5 Qb3-d1+
40 Kg1-f2 Qd1-c2+
41 Kf2-g3 **Black resigns**

Game 2

BLACK Moles   Ruy López, Wormald Variation
European Junior Championship, Groningen, 1967-8

This game shows how relentless pursuit of a straightforward and simple plan
can produce a win. The white strategy of bombarding the weakened a-pawn
cannot satisfactorily be met and although Black appears to have some
counterplay this is merely an illusion.

1 e2-e4   e7-e5

2 Ng1-f3   Nb8-c6

3 Bf1-b5   a7-a6

4 Bb5-a4   Ng8-f6

5 Qd1-e2
   The Wormald variation.

5 ... Bf8-e7
   More usual here is 5 ... b5 6 Bb3 Be7
   7 a4 when 7 ... Rb8 8 axb5 axb5
   9 d4 d5! 10 c3 Nxe4 11 Nxe5 Nxe5
   12 dxe5 0-0 13 0-0 Bf5 14 Be3 gives
   an equal game (Spassky-Kholmov,
   Leningrad 1954).

6 c2-c3
   Note that if 6 Bxc6 dxc6 7 Nxe5 Qd4,
   and Black regains the pawn.

6 ... b7-b5

7 Ba4-b3   d7-d6

8 a2-a4   Bc8-b7
   The best move. 8 ... b4 would be met
   by 9 Qc4 which wins a pawn owing
   to the double threat of 10 Qxf7 mate
   and 10 Qxc6+, but 8 ... Rb8, although
   a little passive, is playable.

9 0-0
   The tactical justification of 8 ... Bb7
   is that after 9 axb5 axb5 10 Rxa8
   Qxa8 11 Qxb5 Nxe4 both
   (a) 12 Bxf7+ Kxf7 13 Qd5+ Ke8
   14 Qxe4 Nd4!

and (b) 12 Qd5 Nd8!
   give Black the better game.

9 ... 0-0

10 d2-d3   h7-h6
    To prevent a possible Bg5 by White
    and with the following manœuvre in
    mind, but Black would have been
    wiser to play 10 ... b4 or 10 ... Re8
    and d5.

11 Rf1-e1   Nf6-h7?

MOLES   2.1

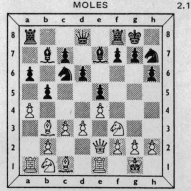

KARPOV TO MOVE

A mistake. Black is trying to exchange
some pieces on g5 but should instead
be contesting the central squares with
11 ... Re8 and 12 ... Bf8.

12 d3-d4

White has pressure against the black e5 pawn. The removal of Black's knight from f6 reduces the counterplay against White's e4 pawn, and thus White is suddenly menacing the b5 pawn. After the further advance 13 d5 Black is obliged to retreat 13 ... Na7 when the focus of the game will switch to the b5 pawn and the partly open a-file.

12 ... Nh7-g5

13 Bc1xg5   h6xg5

If 13 ... Bxg5 then 14 axb5 axb5 15 Rxa8 Qxa8 16 Qxb5 and now
(a) 16 ... Na7 17 Qd3, or
(b) 16 ... Na5 17 Bc2,
and White retains his extra pawn. After the text move, however, 14 axb5 axb5 15 Rxa8 Qxa8 16 Qxb5 is met by 16 ... g4 followed by the capture of the d4 pawn, and 16 dxe5 by 16 ... g4 17 Nd4 Nxd4 18 cxd4 dxe5 when although Black loses a pawn he has adequate compensation in the two bishops.

14 d4-d5   Nc6-a7

If 14 ... Na5 15 Bc2 the immediate threat to the b-pawn in conjunction with the plan of 16 Nbd2 and 17 b4 would leave Black with an uncomfortable position.

15 Re1-d1

To provide a square for the king's knight after g4 and also to dissuade Black from a c6 push.

15 ... g5-g4?

This move Black cannot afford. Already his position is critical and after this it is lost. He simply sets up a further target for White's attack. It is worth noting that since move eight Black has always been able to play bxa4 but has rejected it because of the resulting weakness to the a-pawn. Now he forces the same pawn structure on himself!

16 Nf3-e1

Preparing to attack a6 via c2 and b4.

16 ... Bb7-c8

17 a4xb5

The moment White has been waiting for. Now 17 ... axb5 is impossible on account of 18 Nd2 followed by 19 Ra2 and 20 R1a1.

17 ... Na7xb5

18 Bb3-c4   Bc8-d7

19 Ne1-c2

White bombards the a6 pawn.

19 ... Qd8-c8

20 Nb1-d2   g7-g6

21 Nc2-b4   Be7-g5

After 21 ... a5 22 Nc6! Bxc6 (White threatened both 23 Bxb5 and 23 Nxe7+) 23 dxc6 Na7 (the only move to save the knight on b5) 24 Bd5 White captures the a5 pawn next move with a crushing game.

22 Ra1-a5   Qc8-b7

23 Nd2-b3   Kg8-g7

24 Rd1-a1

MOLES TO MOVE   2.2

KARPOV

The culmination of White's opening strategy—the a-pawn is won by an extraordinary concentration of the white pieces. As in the previous game Black tries some tactical tricks but Karpov is now completely in control.

24 ... f7-f5

25 Nb4xa6   Qb7-b6

The knight is lost since after 25 ... Na7 26 Nbc5 dxc5 27 Nxc5 followed by 28 Nxd7 and 29 Rxa7 White has two extra pawns and an easily won game.

26 Bc4xb5   f5xe4

Black's threats against f2 seem quite promising, but Karpov's next move removes all his hopes.

MOLES TO MOVE   2.3

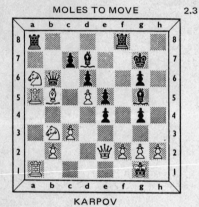

KARPOV

27 c3-c4!   Rf8xf2

28 c4-c5

Black's attack is over and best here would be to resign.

28 ... Rf2xe2

29 c5xb6   Bg5-e3+

30 Kg1-h1   Bd7xb5

31 b6-b7   Ra8-h8

32 b7-b8=Q   Rh8xb8

33 Na6xb8   Bb5-c4

34 Ra5-a3   Re2xb2

35 Nb3-a5   Rb2xb8

36 Na5xc4   Be3-d4

37 Ra1-d1   Rb8-b4

38 Nc4-e3   Rb4-b5

39 g2-g3   Rb5-c5

40 Kh1-g2   Rc5-b5

41 Rd1-c1   **Black resigns**

Game 3

BLACK Vujaković   Pirc Defence
USSR v. Yugoslavia match, Suchumi 1968

All great players have the ability to win from every kind of position. Just as Tal wins positional games, or Petrosian plays a mating attack, so Karpov shows here that he is just as much at home delivering the death blow with a sharp K-side assault.

1 e2-e4   d7-d6

2 d2-d4   g7-g6

3 Nb1-c3   Ng8-f6

4 h2-h3

This game was played on the junior board of this match. Each player plays his opponent four times, twice with white and twice with black, and Karpov scored 3½. In the first encounter with Karpov white the continuation had been 4 f3 c6 5 Be3 b5

6 Qd2 Nbd7 7 Nge2 Bg7 8 g3 0-0 9 Bg2 Nb6 10 b3 a5 11 0-0 Qc7 12 h3 Bb7 13 Nf4 Rfd8 14 Qf2 Rac8 15 Nd3 Nfd7 16 Rad1 b4 17 Ne2 c5. A curious opening. White now begins a winning K-side advance. 18 f4 Ba6 19 f5 Rf8 20 Rd2 cxd4 21 Bxd4 Bxd3 22 cxd3 Bxd4 23 Nxd4 Qb8 24 h4 Nf6 25 Bh3 Rc5 26 Qe3 Nbd7 27 Ne2 Qc7 28 g4 Rc2 29 Rxc2 Qxc2 30 g5 Nh5 31 fxg6 Ne5 32 gxh7+ Kxh7 33 d4 Nc6

34 Rc1 Black resigns.
This second encounter was shorter
and more decisive.

4 . . . Bf8-g7

5 Bc1-e3   0-0

6 Qd1-d2   c7-c6

7 g2-g4

An interesting idea. The game should
now develop into a race between the
white g- and h-pawns and the black
a- and b-pawns. However, Black
chooses to contest the centre with his
next move—not in itself a mistake but
in my opinion distinctly inferior to
7 . . . b5.

7 . . . e7-e5?!

8 0-0-0   Qd8-e7

9 d4-d5

Black's position has already become
difficult. The immediate threat of
10 dxc6 and 11 Qxd6 can only be
satisfactorily met by the text move as
9 . . . Rd8 would leave the black game
passive and cramped, and 9 . . . cxd5
would be met by 10 Nxd5 (but *not*
10 g5 Nxe4) with control of d5 and a
superior position for White.

9 . . . c6-c5

10 Ng1-e2   Nb8-a6

10 . . . b5 would be met by 11 g5 b4
12 gxf6 bxc3 13 Nxc3 Bxf6 (or 13 . . .
Qxf6 14 Bg5 Qf3 15 Rh2 threatening
both 16 Be2 and 16 Be7) 14 Bh6
when White's attack is the quicker.

11 Ne2-g3   Na6-c7

12 Kc1-b1   Nf6-e8?

An extraordinary move. Black would
do better to begin Q-side operations
at once with 12 . . . Rb8, 12 . . . a6 or
even 12 . . . Bd7. The idea of 12 . . .
Nfe8? is to bring the king's knight to
the Q-side and also to enable Black to
defend the K-side along the second
rank after f6.

13 Bf1-e2   Ra8-b8

14 Rd1-g1   b7-b5

Karpov has completed his preparations

KARPOV TO MOVE

and now begins his assault.

15 h3-h4

It is worth noting that with a knight
still on f6 this would be a pawn sacrifice and hence would be much more
hazardous. Furthermore Black would
also be a tempo ahead with his own
attack.

15 . . . b5-b4

16 Nc3-d1   Nc7-b5

17 h4-h5   c5-c4?!

An incorrect sacrifice, but Black's
attack was too slow in any event.

18 Qd2xb4

18 Bxc4 would be met by 18 . . . Bxg4.

18 . . . Ne8-c7

19 Qb4-d2   Bc8-d7

Black has gained two or three tempi
for his pawn, but this is insufficient
compensation: White's attack is still
the stronger.

20 c2-c3   a7-a5

21 Kb1-a1

Safety-first—although White has no
need to play this move he does so to
remove the king from the half-open
file and hence reduce his opponent's
tactical chances.

21 . . . a5-a4

22 Ng3-f5!

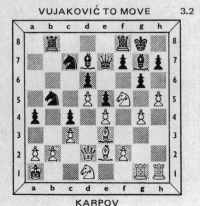

VUJAKOVIĆ TO MOVE   3.2

KARPOV

An elegant sacrifice that breaks open Black's position. Black must take this knight, since the threat of Nxg7 followed by attack on the h-file is too dangerous.

22 ... Bd7xf5

After 22 ... gxf5 23 gxf5 (threatening both 24 h6 and 24 Bh6) 23 ... Kh8 comes the real point—24 Rxg7! Kxg7 25 f6+! Qxf6 (or 25 ... Kxf6 26 Bg5+ winning the queen) 26 Bg5 winning the queen.

23 g4xf5   a4-a3

24 h5xg6   a3xb2+

25 Nd1xb2   f7xg6

26 f5xg6   Rb8-a8

27 Be2xc4

Typical Karpov. With this move he wins a further pawn and safeguards his king at the same time, although no doubt both 27 Rxh7 and 27 Bh6 would also win. Black could resign here.

27 ... Ra8-a3

28 Be3-h6   h7xg6

29 Rg1xg6   Rf8-f7

30 Rh1-g1   Black resigns

Game 4

BLACK Gik   Sicilian Defence, Dragon Variation, Rauzer Attack
Moscow University Championship 1968

Karpov has often criticized himself for his lack of opening knowledge in his early days. In this game, however, we see him refuting Black's 16th move, and indeed Karpov's 17th move has led to this variation being abandoned in master chess. It is interesting to note the effect that current (i.e. 1968) opening theory had on the game.

1 e2-e4   c7-c5

2 Ng1-f3   d7-d6

3 d2-d4   c5xd4

4 Nf3xd4   Ng8-f6

5 Nb1-c3   g7-g6

6 Bc1-e3   Bf8-g7

7 f2-f3

The move 7 Be2 would lead to the Classical Variation. Nowadays the

Rauzer attack is much more popular.

7 ... Nb8-c6

8 Bf1-c4   0-0

9 Qd1-d2   Qd8-a5

10 0-0-0   Bc8-d7

Also possible is 10 ... Nxd4 11 Bxd4 Be6 12 Bb3!

11 h2-h4   Nc6-e5

12 Bc4-b3   Rf8-c8

13 h4-h5

This thematic pawn sacrifice leads to a sharp struggle.

13 ... Nf6xh5

The best reply.

(a) 13 ... gxh5 14 Kb1! Nc4 15 Bxc4 Rxc4 16 Nb3 Qc7 17 Bg5 with a small advantage to White according to Gufeld and Lazarev.

(b) 13 ... Nc4 14 Bxc4 Rxc4 15 hxg6 fxg6 and now either 16 Kb1 or 16 Nb3 leads to a white advantage.

14 Be3-h6

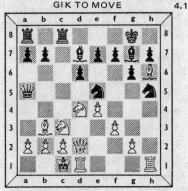

GIK TO MOVE   4.1

KARPOV

Karpov must have prepared this variation before the game. In the diagrammed position, Black has the surprising move 14 ... Nd3+! This was discovered by Westerinen and played by him against Gheorghiu in the world student championship at Örebro in 1966, and against Hartston in the Havana Olympiad later in the same year. It was considered to be good for Black (e.g. 15 cxd3 Bxd4 or 15 Qxd3 Bxh6+) but in 1968 (before this game was played) Dueball played 15 Kb1! against Mista in the world student championship at Ybbs. The analysis of this move was:

(a) 15 ... Bxd4 16 Nd5! (as in the original Dueball-Mista game) 16 ... Qxd2 17 Nxe7+ Kh8 18 Rxd2 Re8 19 Rxd3 Bg7 20 Bxg7+ Kxg7

21 Nd5 and White won the d-pawn and hence the game.

(b) 15 ... Nf2? 16 Qxf2 Bxh6 17 g4 and White wins.

(c) 15 ... Bxh6 16 Qxh6 Rxc3 (or 16 ... Nxb2 17 Nd5!) 17 bxc3 Nf2 18 Rxh5 gxh5 19 Rf1 traps the knight (Berkovich-Svensson, USSR v. Scandanavia match, 1968).
Since then the move 15 ... Nxb2! has been shown to give Black more chances

BLACK   4.2

WHITE TO MOVE

Despotović suggested the move, and gave analysis to justify his claim that Black had good chances. More recently, however, grave doubt has been cast on one of the main lines. Mecking-Joksić from Vrsac 1971 continued 16 Kxb2 Bxh6 17 Qxh6 Rxc3! 18 g4 Nf6 19 e5! Rxb3+ 20 axb3 dxe5 21 Ne2 Be6 22 Nc3! with clear advantage to White.

14 ... Bg7xh6

15 Qd2xh6 Rc8xc3

A typical Dragon exchange sacrifice.

16 b2xc3 Qa5xc3?

A blunder. Estrin suggested 16 ... Nf6 17 g4 Qxc3! in his notes to this game, but 17 Kb1! is a better try and leads to advantage for White. Black's best course of action is 16 ... Rc8! with great complications and chances for both sides.

17 Nd4-e2!

Black is, in all probability, already lost. Karpov allows his opponent no further chance.

17 ... Qc3-c5

The variations (a) 17 ... Qa1+ 18 Kd2 Qb2 19 Rxh5 gxh5 20 Rh1 and (b) 17 ... Nd3+ 18 Rxd3 Qa1+ 19 Kd2 Qxh1 20 g4 Ng3 21 Qxh1 Nxh1 22 Ke3 followed by Rd3-d1xh1, both give White a winning position.

18 g2-g4   Nh5-f6

19 g4-g5   Nf6-h5

20 Rh1xh5! g6xh5

21 Rd1-h1 Qc5-e3+

22 Kc1-b1! Qe3xf3

After 22 ... Qxe2 23 Qxh5 Black is mated. e.g.

(a) 23 ... Ng6 24 Qxh7+ Kf8 25 Qxf7
(b) 23 ... e6 24 Qxh7+ Kf8 25 Qh8+ Ke7 26 Qf6+ Ke8 27 Rh8.

23 Rh1xh5 e7-e6

24 g5-g6! Ne5xg6

Both 24 ... hxg6 25 Qh8 mate, and 24 ... fxg6 25 Qxh7+ Kf8 26 Qh8+ Ke7 27 Rh7+ Nf7 28 Qxa8 Qxe2 29 Qxb7 are disastrous for Black.

25 Qh6xh7+ Kg8-f8

26 Rh5-f5!

The point of Karpov's fine sacrifice at move 24—the Black queen is lost.

26 ... Qf3xb3+

27 a2xb3 e6xf5

28 Ne2-f4 Ra8-d8

If 28 ... Nxf4 then 29 Qh8+ followed by 30 Qxa8 wins easily for White.

29 Qh7-h6+ Kf8-e8

30 Nf4xg6 f7xg6

31 Qh6xg6+ Ke8-e7

32 Qg6-g5+ Ke7-e8

33 e4xf5 Rd8-c8

34 Qg5-g8+ Ke8-e7

35 Qg8-g7+ Ke7-e8

36 f5-f6   Black resigns

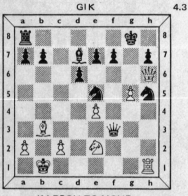

GIK   4.3

KARPOV TO MOVE

Game 5

BLACK Pronin   Benoni Defence
Moscow University Championship 1968

Although Karpov is essentially a strategist and prefers a positional game, he is always ready to strike with a decisive attack. Unlike Tal or Spassky, Karpov launches tactical ventures that are based on deep analysis and contain little speculation.

1 e2-e4   e7-e6

2 d2-d4   c7-c5

Played mainly by Larsen. The idea of the move is to reach a Benoni-type

position with an open e-file—i.e. one in which White has been forced to recapture on d5 with the e-pawn—whereas in the modern Benoni (1 d4

Nf6 2 c4 c5 3 d5 e6 4 Nc3 exd5
5 cxd5) White captures with the
c-pawn on d5 and the e-file remains
only half-open,

3 d4-d5

Also possible is 3 Nf3 or 3 c3 leading
to an open-Sicilian or an Alapin
Variation, respectively.

3 ... e6xd5

4 e4xd5   d7-d6

5 Ng1-f3

The most flexible move. 5 c4 or 5 Nc3
are also possible but the text move
allows for a later c4, without excluding
the possibilities of Bb5+ and Nb1-d2-c4.

5 ... a7-a6

This move cannot really be criticized
since it prevents a possible Bb5+ by
White and prepares the thematic
Q-side advance b5. The game Gligorić-
Larsen, Busum 1969 continued here
5 ... Nf6 6 Bb5+ Nbd7 7 0-0 Be7
8 a4 0-0 9 Re1 Re8 10 Nc3 a6
11 Bf1 b6 with equality.

6 a2-a4   Bc8-g4?!

7 Bf1-e2   Bg4xf3

8 Be2xf3   b7-b6

The plan of playing Bc8-g4xf3 is not
uncommon in this opening. The game
Gligorić-Barcza, Ljubljana 1969 went
5 ... Bg4 6 Be2 Bxf3 7 Bxf3 Be7
8 0-0 Nf6 9 Na3 and White already
held the advantage. However, in this
game the extra moves 5 ... a6 6 a4
have done nothing but weaken Black's
position. He now feels obliged to play
8 ... b6 to prevent 9 a5 and a subsequent Nb1-d2-c4 with a Q-side bind.
White's natural moves 9 0-0 10 Nd2
11 Re1 12 Nc4 13 Bf4 etc. will ensure him the advantage owing to his
greater command of space, the two
bishops and the better co-ordination
of his pieces. Black would have been
wiser to continue his development
with 6 ... Be7 followed by Nf6 and
0-0.

9 0-0   Bf8-e7

10 Nb1-d2   Nb8-d7

Black would like to play 10 ... Nf6
but then 11 Nc4 0-0 12 Bf4 would
leave him unable to develop his Q-side
owing to the threat to the d6 pawn.

11 Rf1-e1!

By far the most difficult move of the
game(!) The natural 11 Nc4 would be
met by 11 ... b5 12 axb5 axb5
13 Rxa8 Qxa8 and the knight must
retreat. The point of the move is twofold. Firstly, after 11 ... Ngf6 12 Nc4
(threatening Nxd6+) 12 ... 0-0 13 Bf4,
Black's position is lost. The threats of
14 Bxd6 (or 14 Nxd6) and 14 Rxe7
followed by Bxd6 force Black to play
13 ... Ne8, when 14 Qe2 Bf6 15 Nxd6
completes the demolition of Black's
game. The second point of 11 Re1 is
the game continuation.

11 ... Nd7-e5

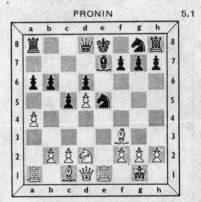

PRONIN   5.1

KARPOV TO MOVE

12 Re1xe5!

This pawn sacrifice leads to a complete rout of Black's position. Already
Black is lost but the method of execution is instructive.

12 ... d6xe5

13 d5-d6   Be7xd6

Forced. 13 ... Ra7 14 dxe7 would
leave White with two pieces for rook
and pawn, and an enormous advantage.

14 Bf3-c6+   Ke8-f8

The alternative 14 ... Ke7 would fare

no better. After 15 Bxa8 Qxa8
16 Nc4 Bc7 17 a5 b5 18 Ne3! and
now

(a) 18 ... Qd8 19 Nf5+ Kf8 20 Be3!

(b) 18 ... Nf6 19 Nf5+ Kf8 20 Bg5

(c) 18 ... Bd8 19 Nf5+ Kf8 20 Qd6+
Ne7 21 Bg5 f6 22 Bxf6

(d) 18 ... Bd8 19 Nf5+ Kf8 20 Qd6+
Be7 21 Nxe7 Nxe7 22 Bg5.

In each case Black's position is hopeless.

15 Bc6xa8 Qd8xa8

16 Nd2-c4 Bd6-c7

17 Bc1-e3

PRONIN TO MOVE   5.2

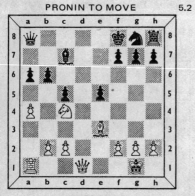

KARPOV

The unanswerable 'quiet' move. White's
threats are 18 a5 and 18 Qd7. For
example:

(a) 17 ... a5 18 Qd7 and now:

  (a1) 18 ... Qd8 19 Rd1 wins a piece!

  (a2) 18 ... Qb7 (or Qa7) 19 Nd6 wins.

  (a3) 18 ... Bd8 19 Rd1 Be7 20 Nxb6

  (a4) 18 ... Bb8? 19 Qd8 mate.

  (a5) 18 ... Qb8 (best) 19 Rd1 Nf6
  20 Qc6 and Black is completely movebound (20 ... Ke7 21 Nxa5, 20 ...
  Ng4 21 Rd7, 20 ... Bd8 21 Nxe5
  etc.).

(b) 17 ... Nf6 18 a5 Nd5 (18 ... Qa7
(or Qb7) allows 19 axb6 Bxb6 20

Qd6+ winning a piece and after
18 ... Qb8 (or Qc6) 19 axb6 Bxb6
20 Rxa6 wins) 19 axb6 and now:

  (b1) 19 ... Nxb6 20 Nxb6 Bxb6
  21 Qd6+ winning a piece

  (b2) 19 ... Bxb6 20 Nxb6 Nxb6
  21 Bxc5+ winning a piece

  (b3) 19 ... Nxe3 20 fxe3 Bd8
  21 Rxa6 winning.

So Black would be obliged to try
18 ... bxa5 19 Bxc5+ Kg8, but
White has a choice of easy wins, for
example, by 20 Bd6 Qb8 21 Bxc7
Qxc7 22 Rxa5 g6 23 b3, etc.

The game continuation is equally
decisive. The whole attack is beautifully played by Karpov—Black is
never given a chance to recover.

17 ... Ng8-e7

18 a4-a5 b6xa5
The refutation of 18 ... Nd5 is given
in the previous note. 18 ... b5 could
be met by 19 Nb6 Bxb6 20 axb6, etc.
and if the queen defends b6 then
19 Qd7 (in the case of 18 ... Qa7 or
18 ... Qb7) or 19 axb6 and 20 Rxa6
(after 18 ... Qb8 or 18 ... Qc6).

19 Be3xc5 Qa8-c6

20 Nc4xe5
A neat combination: 20 ... Qxc5
21 Nd7+ costs Black his queen, while
20 ... Bxe5 21 Qd8+ Qe8 22 Bxe7+
Kg8 23 Qxe8 mate.

20 ... Qc6-e8

21 Qd1-d4 h7-h5

22 Ra1-e1
If 22 ... Bd8 then 23 Nc6.

Black resigns

Game 6

WHITE Nisman   Nimzo-Indian Defence, Saemisch Variation
Soviet Team Championships, Riga 1968

This game is a classical demonstration of the method of undermining and destroying an over-extended centre. The Saemisch variation is noted for its sharpness, and when the white attack fails it is only a matter of time before the weak doubled c-pawn falls.

1 c2-c4   Ng8-f6

2 Nb1-c3   e7-e6

3 d2-d4   Bf8-b4

4 a2-a3

> The Saemisch Variation. This move is seldom played in International tournament chess. The Rubinstein Variation (4 e3) is the most common here, although the Classical Variation (4 Qc2) and Spassky's variation (4 Bg5) still have many advocates.

4 ... Bb4xc3+

5 b2xc3   c7-c5

> Black can try many other moves here 5...d5 5...d6 5...0-0 5...b6 and 5...Ne4 are all possible. In fact the most unlikely looking of these, 5...Ne4, was played in the 14th, 16th, 18th, and 20th games of the 1960 world championship match between Botvinnik (White) and Tal. All these four games were drawn, but by winning the 17th and 19th games, Tal took the world title.

6 e2-e3

> The other possibility here is 6 f3 which leads to a much more open game after the normal 6...d5 7 cxd5 Nxd5 8 dxc5 etc.

6 ... Nb8-c6

7 Ng1-e2

> More usual here is 7 Bd3. The text is inaccurate because of the commitment of the white knight to go to g3. White intends to play 8 Ng3 and 9 Bd3 but by playing 7 Bd3 and 8 Ne2 he could keep the knight at e2 and retain the possibility of Ne2-c1-b3 and thus relieve the pressure on the c4 pawn from a black knight at a5. For example, the game Geller-Lisitsyn, 22nd USSR Championship, 1955 went: 7 Bd3 b6 8 e4 d6 9 Ne2 Qd7 10 0-0 Ba6 11 Bg5 0-0-0 12 Nc1! Na5 13 Nb3! Qa4 14 Nxa5 Qxa5 15 Qc2 h6 16 Bd2 with advantage to White.

7 ... b7-b6

8 Ne2-g3   Bc8-a6

9 Bf1-d3?

> A mistake. Correct is 9 e4 after which Black must play with care. For example, if Black replies 9...Na5, then 10 e5 Ng8 11 Ne4 is very strong, or, if 9...d6, then 10 Qa4. So Black must try 9...0-0 10 Bg5 h6 11 h4! when White has the initiative. After this lapse, Karpov is able to develop his pieces on their natural squares.

9 ... Nc6-a5

> Note that 9...d6 is still a mistake owing to 10 Qa4.

10 Qd1-e2   d7-d6

11 Bc1-b2   Qd8-d7

12 e3-e4   0-0-0

13 a3-a4

KARPOV TO MOVE   6.1

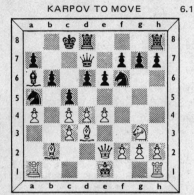

NISMAN

The opening has not been successful
for White. He has already been driven
on to the defensive by Karpov's
development. His last move was forced
to prevent the manœuvre Qd7-a4 when
the weak c4 pawn would fall. Black's
position is very solid and well defended;
so he begins a flank attack and thus
illustrates the lack of cohesion between
the white pieces.

13 ... h7-h5
This move does not merit an ex-
clamation mark as it is the logical
course of action. It highlights the
error made by White at move 9 and
the inaccuracies at moves 7 and 11
(White's black-squared bishop should
be on the c1-h6 diagonal)

14 0-0
Not a pleasant move to have to make,
but the alternative 14 h4 e5!
(threatening the strong 15 ... Qg4!
16 Qf1 [What else?] Rhe8 or 16 ...
g5!?) 15 f3 leaves White weak on f4,
h4, c4, and a4! Also he will never
then be able to castle.

14 ... h5-h4

15 Ng3-h1   e6-e5
The threat of Nf6-h5-f4 is very unpleasant for White.

16 f2-f4   Nf6-h5
Winning material by force.

17 f4xe5

17 Bc1 would lose the d-pawn, while
after 17 g3 hxg3 18 hxg3 Qh3
threatens 19 ... Qxh1+ as well as
19 ... Nxg3.

17 ... d6xe5

18 d4-d5
The only way to save the d-pawn.
White still loses the exchange but,
what is more important, Black's attack
continues unabated.

18 ... Nh5-f4

19 Rf1xf4
After a queen move 19 ... Nxd3
20 Qxd3 Bxc4 would win the exchange
and a pawn.

19 ... e5xf4

20 e4-e5   h4-h3

21 g2-g4
White cannot allow the opening of the
h-file, since hxg2, Rh4, R8h8 must win
for Black.

21 ... Kc8-b8
It is possible that 21 ... Bxc4! is
already playable; e.g. 21 ... Bxc4
22 Bxc4 Nxc4 23 Qxc4 Qxg4+
24 Ng3 Rh4 25 Qa6+ Kb8 26 a5 fxg3
27 axb6 gxh2+ 28 Kf2 Qg2+ 29 Ke3
Re4+ 30 Kd3 Rxd5 mate.
Karpov prefers the sure way. White
cannot prevent both the Bxc4 sacrifice
and the threat to attack and win the
e5 pawn. The move 22 ... f3! is also
in the air.

22 Bb2-c1   *(see Diagram 6.2)*

22 ... Ba6xc4!
This combination brings the game
into an easily won ending for Black.
Now 23 Bxf4 is met by 23 ... Bxd3
or 23 ... Qxd5.

23 Bd3xc4   Na5xc4

24 Qe2xc4
After 24 Bxf4 Qxd5 25 e6+ Ka8
26 e7 Rde8 Black will soon pick off
the advanced pawn.

24 ... Qd7xg4+

25 Nh1-g3
25 Kf2 would allow Qg4-g2xh1, all
with check.

KARPOV TO MOVE   6.2

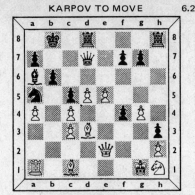

NISMAN

25 ... Rh8-h4
The point of the combination. Black wins back the sacrificed piece with an easy ending in view. White's Q-side attack is always one tempo too slow.

26 Qc4xf4 Qg4xf4

27 Bc1xf4 Rh4xf4
White could safely resign here; his remaining pawns are very weak and Karpov picks them off at will.

28 Ra1-d1 g7-g6

To prevent a possible Nf5 or Nh5—the a-pawn cannot run away.

29 Rd1-d2 Rf4xa4

30 Kg1-f2 Ra4-c4

31 Rd2-d3 a7-a5

32 Kf2-e3 Rd8-e8
Winning a third pawn.

33 e5-e6 f7xe6

34 d5-d6 Re8-d8

35 Ng3-e4 Kb8-c8

36 Ne4-f6 Rd8-d7!
The simplest way. White should take the hint and resign.

37 Nf6xd7 Kc8xd7

38 Ke3-d2 Rc4-h4

39 Kd2-c2 b6-b5

40 Rd3-g3 Kd7xd6

41 Rg3xg6 Rh4-f4

42 Kc2-b3 c5-c4+

43 Kb3-a3 Rf4-f3

44 Ka3-b2 b5-b4

45 c3xb4 a5xb4

46 Rg6-g4 Kd6-d5

White resigns

Game 7

BLACK Miklyaev   Ruy López, Modern Steinitz Defence
Soviet Team Championships, Riga 1968

A slightly passive choice in the opening gives Karpov no advantage. He has an uphill struggle to make anything out of the position and the fruits of his labour become apparent only in the second session, when he gains a pawn and wins the ending in exemplary fashion.

1 e2-e4 e7-e5

2 Ng1-f3 Nb8-c6

3 Bf1-b5 a7-a6

4 Bb5-a4 d7-d6
The Modern Steinitz Defence.

5 c2-c3

The most aggressive continuation. Also possible here are 5 Bxc6+, 5 d4, 5 0-0 and the Duras variation 5 c4.

5 ... Bc8-d7
Black avoids the tremendous complications of the variation 5 ... f5 6 exf5 (6 d4?! fxe4 7 Nxe5 dxe5

8 Qh5+ Ke7! 9 Bxc6 bxc6
10 Bg5+ Nf6 11 dxe5 Qd5! promises
White no more than a draw)
6 . . . Bxf5   7 0-0 (7 d4 is the alternative) 7 . . . Bd3   8 Re1 (8 Qb3!? b5!
9 Qd5 Nd4! 10 cxd4 Ne7 11 Qe6
Bxf1 12 Bb3 Bc4 13 Bxc4 bxc4
is unclear) 8 . . . Be7 and now White
can choose to play for attack by
9 Qb3 or 9 Re3 or can simply play
9 Bc2! Bxc2 10 Qxc2 Nf6 11 d4
0-0 12 dxe5 Nxe5 13 Nxe5 dxe5
14 Nd2 Bc5 15 Nb3 Bb6 16 Be3
with a small but clear edge.

6 0-0

It is more usual to play 6 d4 and 7 0-0.

6 . . . g7-g6

An enterprising if somewhat dubious
system of development. Safer was
6 . . . Nge7.

7 d2-d4   Bf8-g7

8 h2-h3

There was no need for such a passive
move. Better was 8 dxe5 dxe5 9 Be3
Nf6 10 Nbd2 when 10 . . . 0-0 11 Bc5
Re8 12 Bc2 b6 13 Ba3 Qc8 14 Nc4
Nh5 15 Ne3 Rd8 16 Bb3 Be6 is to
White's advantage (Parma-Darga, Bled
1961). The moves 8 Bb3, 8 a3, 8 Bg5
and 8 Be3 have also been tried here.

8 . . . Ng8-f6

9 Nb1-d2   0-0

10 Rf1-e1   Rf8-e8

11 Ba4-c2

So as to be able to manœuvre the d2
knight via f1 to g3. *(see Diagram 7.1)*
Karpov's somewhat passive play in the
opening has given him little advantage.
He has only a minimal pressure against
the black e5 pawn and no especially
cohesive plan of development. His
long-term plan will be to entice a Q-
side pawn advance by Black and then
blockade the centre and subsequently
work up a K-side attack, whilst Black
attacks on the Q-side.

11 . . . h7-h6

12 a2-a3   Kg8-h7

13 Nd2-f1   b7-b5?!

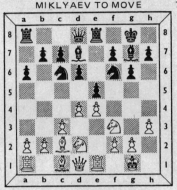

MIKLYAEV TO MOVE   7.1

KARPOV

It would have been better to play
quietly in the centre by 13 . . . Qe7
14 Ne3 exd4 15 cxd4 Qf8.

14 Nf1-g3   Nc6-a5

15 b2-b3   c7-c5

16 d4-d5   c5-c4

17 b3-b4   Na5-b7

Both sides are happy at having completed the first part of their plans.
Black can quickly force the opening
of the a-file down which he hopes to
infiltrate. White, on the other hand,
has control of the c5 square and
hence can prevent the knight on b7
from entering into the game. He hopes
to build up a K-side attack to counter-
balance Black's control of the a-file.

18 Bc1-e3   Qd8-c7

19 Nf3-h2   a6-a5

20 Qd1-d2   Ra8-a6

21 Re1-f1   Re8-a8

22 Ra1-c1!   a5xb4

23 a3xb4   Nf6-g8

24 f2-f4

With his 22nd move White removed
all Black's Q-side chances along the
a-file. Now he achieves his aim of an
f4 advance and thus a K-side attack.
Already White stands a little better.

24 . . . f7-f6

25 h3-h4!   Bd7-e8
The advance 26 h5 cannot be allowed.

26 Nh2-g4
Tempting a further weakening of
Black's K-side pawn-position. After
this the advance g2-g4 by White will
put Black under serious pressure

26 ... h6-h5

27 Ng4-h2   e5xf4
The threat of 28 f5! was unpleasant
for Black.

28 Be3xf4   Nb7-d8!
A fine defensive move. The knight
comes to f7 and hence to e5.

29 Qd2-d1
Threatening 30 e5! dxe5   31 Qxh5+
etc. and hence Black's reply.

29 ... Kh7-h8

30 Ng3-e2   Nd8-f7

31 g2-g4!

MIKLYAEV TO MOVE   7.2

KARPOV

Black's position is now under heavy
pressure. By allowing the exchange on
h5 Black not only saddles himself
with weak pawns at f6 and h5, but also
loses control of the f5 square. The
best here for Black would have been
31 ... hxg4! 32 Nxg4 Ne5 33 Ng3
Qd7! when his defensive chances,
although not good, are better than in
the game continuation.

31 ... Nf7-e5

32 g4xh5   g6xh5

33 Ne2-g3   Qc7-f7
The only way to defend h5.

34 Nh2-f3
The threat now is 35 Bxe5 dxe5
36 Nxe5 winning a pawn.

34 ... Ne5-g4

35 Nf3-d4
The f5 point is completely under
White's control.

35 ... Bg7-h6
This bishop exchange is desirable for
Black, or else a knight at f5, with a
bishop at f4, would seriously threaten
the d6 pawn. This move must be
played now, since 36 N4f5 would
surely be White's next.

36 Qd1-d2   Bh6xf4

37 Qd2xf4   Ng8-h6
Hoping to contest the f5 square.

38 Ng3-f5   Nh6xf5

39 Nd4xf5   Qf7-f8

40 Bc2-d1!
At last the bishop joins in the action.
Black soon loses a pawn.

40 ... Ng4-e5
Threatening a fork at d3.

41 Rc1-c2!   Ra6-a2

42 Rc2xa2   Ra8xa2

43 Nf5-g3!

MIKLYAEV TO MOVE   7.3

KARPOV

The threats to the f6 and h5 pawns can be met in a number of ways. Suetin analysing this position gives:

(a) 43 ... Ra1 44 Bxh5 Rxf1+ 45 Kxf1 wins for White

(b) 43 ... Ra3! 44 Qxf6+ (44 Qd2 Qg7! is difficult to meet) 44 ... Qxf6 45 Rxf6 Bd7! (45 ... Rxc3 is met by 46 Kf2!) 46 Rh6+ Kg8 47 Rxd6 Rxc3 48 Nxh5 Rc1 49 Nf6+ and now

(b1) 49 ... Kg7 50 Nxd7 Rxd1+ 51 Kf2 c3 52 Nxe5 c2 53 Rc6! (53 Nd3? Rd2+! 54 Ke1 Rxd3 wins for Black) 53 ... c1=Q 54 Rxc1 Rxc1 55 Ke3 wins for White.

(b2) 49 ... Kf7! 50 Nxd7 Rxd1+ 51 Kf2 Ke7! (recommended by Geller and Furman) 52 Re6+ Kxd7 53 Ke2! (After 53 Rxe5 c3 Black again wins) 53 ... Rd4 54 Rxe5 c3 55 d6! with equality.

In the game Black chooses a third possibility, but it seems that 43 ... Ra3! was the only chance of holding the position.

43 ... Qf8-g7

44 Qf4xf6 Qg7xf6

45 Rf1xf6 Ra2-a1

46 Rf6-f1 Ra1-c1

47 Ng3-e2!
The exchange of Black's h-pawn for White's c-pawn is something that White must avoid.

47 ... Rc1-a1

48 Ne2-d4 Kh8-g8

49 Nd4-f5! Ra1-a6
The loss of the d6 pawn would be fatal for Black, and the alternative defence of 49 ... Nf7 allows 50 Bxh5 etc.

50 Kg1-f2 Be8-g6

51 Kf2-e3 Bg6xf5

52 e4xf5
Although White is a pawn ahead with bishop against knight, this ending is far from an easy win, owing to the

strong unchallengeable position of the black knight. However, a little of Karpov's deadly accuracy decides the issue.

52 ... Ra6-a2

53 Ke3-d4 Ra2-a1

54 Bd1-e2! Ra1-a2
After 54 ... Rxf1 55 Bxf1 Nf3+ 56 Ke4 Nxh4 57 Be2 White retains his extra pawn and wins comfortably.

55 Be2xh5 Ra2-h2

56 Rf1-f4 Rh2-d2+

57 Kd4-e4 Rd2-d3

58 f5-f6 Rd3xc3

59 Ke4-f5!
The entry of the white king is decisive.

59 ... Rc3-e3

60 Rf4-f1 Ne5-d7

61 Rf1-g1+! Kg8-f8

62 Rg1-a1 Re3-e5+

63 Kf5-g6
We now see the point of 61 Rg1+!— the square f8 is no longer available to the black knight.

63 ... Re5-e8

64 Ra1-a7 Re8-d8

65 Ra7-c7!
Preventing for ever the advance of the c-pawn. Black could resign here, but in any event the end is not far away.

65 ... Kf8-g8

66 Kg6-g5 Kg8-h8

67 Bh5-g6 Kh8-g8

68 h4-h5 Kg8-h8

69 h5-h6 c4-c3

70 Rc7xc3 Rd8-f8

71 f6-f7 Black resigns

Game 8

BLACK Andersson   Ruy López, Closed Variation
World Junior Championship Finals, Stockholm 1969

Although this game was played early in his career Karpov has since demonstrated great ability with the Closed Ruy López. He seems to be most at home in the blocked, or almost blocked, positions arising from this opening. In Game 2 he defeated Moles on the Q-side and now he deals with Andersson in the centre. For a beautiful example of a K-side attack, see his game with Spassky (49).

1 e2-e4   e7-e5

2 Ng1-f3   Nb8-c6

3 Bf1-b5   a7-a6

4 Bb5-a4   Ng8-f6

5 0-0   Bf8-e7

6 Rf1-e1   b7-b5

7 Ba4-b3   0-0

8 c2-c3   d7-d6

9 h2-h3   Nc6-a5

The move 9 . . . Nb8 (Breyer variation) has become popular again recently in master chess. For examples of this see Games 44, 49, and 52.

10 Bb3-c2   c7-c5

11 d2-d4   Qd8-c7

12 Nb1-d2

So far this is the main line of the Chigorin defence. Black's next move is unusual.

12 . . . Bc8-b7

This move is generally preceded by the exchange of pawns 12 . . . cxd4 13 cxd4. White can now safely close the position with no fear of an attack along the c-file. Unzicker tried 12 . . . Nc6 against Karpov in the 1974 Nice Olympaid but was drastically beaten in one of Karpov's most impressive performances (Game 69).

13 d4-d5

Because Karpov prefers a closed game he does not allow his opponent a further chance to open the c-file. The alternative 13 Nf1 cxd4   14 cxd4 Rac8 would lead back into standard variations.

13 . . . Bb7-c8

Black wishes to move his knight via b7 to c5 (after playing c5-c4).

14 Nd2-f1   Bc8-d7

15 b2-b3

To meet the advance c4 by b4 and so keep the Q-side closed.

15 . . . Na5-b7

Aiming for 16 . . . c4   17 b4 a5 when Black has the initiative. However, Karpov's 15th move also allows him to solidify the Q-side position and prevent any possibility of a c4 break-through. Preferable therefore was the immediate 15 . . . c4 and if 16 b4 Nb7 to be followed by 17 . . . a5.

16 c3-c4!   Rf8-b8

This rook is preferred since, by moving it, Black gives his King's bishop a retreat square in anticipation of a white knight's reaching f5.

17 Nf1-e3   Be7-f8

18 Ne3-f5   *(see Diagram 8.1)*

Thus White prevents the regrouping manœuvre 18 . . . g6 and 19 . . . Bg7.

ANDERSSON TO MOVE   8.1

KARPOV

The opening has turned out well for
him. By letting White play 16 c4!
Black has reduced his chances of a
Q-side attack; the open b-file is not a
great asset, since the white bishops
can control the squares b1, b2, b3 and
b4, so that no entry square for the
black rooks is available; the c4 pawn
is secure; and so White can conduct
his own K-side attack without harass-
ment on the other side of the board.

18 ... Nb7-d8
Preparing a break by a6-a5-a4, and
also to move this knight to f7 and g5.

19 Nf3-h2   Nf6-e8
All part of Black's defensive plan, as
we shall see.

20 h3-h4   f7-f6

21 h4-h5
White continues to occupy more space
and to prepare for an eventual K-side
breakthrough.

21 ... Nd8-f7

22 Re1-e3   Nf7-g5

23 Nf5-h4
White removes the knight from g5,
or, as in the game, forces Black to
weaken his K-side pawns.

23 ... Qc7-d8

24 Re3-g3   Ne8-c7

25 Nh2-f3

The culmination of the manœuvre
begun on move 22. Black must choose
between a weakening pawn move
25 ... h6, the retreat 25 ... Nf7, or
the defending 25 ... Be7.

25 ... h7-h6
The other possibilities were also unpleasant:

(a) 25 ... Nf7 would be met by 26 Nf5
(threatening 27 Nxg7!) and now Black
is obliged to play 26 ... Bxf5 since
26 ... Kh8 is strongly met by 27 N3h4
(and 28 Ng6+).

(b) 25 ... Be7 26 Nxg5 fxg5 27 Nf5 h6
and White's attack will surely win.
25 ... h6 has the advantage of maintaining the blockade of the g5 square.

26 Nh4-g6   a6-a5
The long awaited Q-side advance.
Karpov is ready for this and stops an
a5-a4 break instantly.

27 a2-a4   b5xc4

28 b3xc4   Nc7-a6

29 Qd1-e2!   Ra8-a7
Preparing to double rooks, and if
necessary to help defend the weakened
K-side.

30 Bc1-d2
Going to c3 and thus keeping the
enemy rooks out.

30 ... Ra7-b7

31 Bd2-c3   Na6-b4

32 Bc2-d1
The point of 29 Qe2! With the queen
still on d1 Black's move would have
posed grave problems. White cannot
allow the exchange of his white-
squared bishop, since Black's rooks
would then rule the b-file.

32 ... Nb4-a6
Black would be content to draw.

33 Nf3-d2
But White still strives to win.

33 ... Na6-b4
Black can achieve nothing on the
Q-side. He therefore removes the
threat to his a-pawn so his queen
can come to the defence of his K-side.

ANDERSSON   8.2

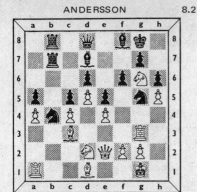

KARPOV TO MOVE

34 Rg3-e3

White's next step is to exchange the
white-squared bishops and leave Black
seriously weakened on the white
squares.

34 ... Bd7-e8

35 Nd2-f1

This knight keeps an eye on f5 and
also makes way for the manœuvre
Qd2, Be2, Qd1, Bg4.

35 ... Qd8-c8

35 ... Na6 would be met by 36 Qd2!
and if Rb1? 37 Rxb1 Rxb1 38 Bc2!
followed by 39 Bxa5 winning.

36 Nf1-g3   Be8-d7

Preventing the threatened 37 Nf5.

37 Qe2-d2   Ng5-h7

38 Bd1-e2   Kg8-f7

39 Qd2-d1   Bf8-e7

40 Ng3-f1

Going to h2 and thus achieving the
Bg4 idea.

40 ... Be7-d8

41 Nf1-h2   Kf7-g8

42 Be2-g4

At last the objective is reached. Note
how Black has had to resort to 'shuffling' moves. The bishop manœuvre to
d8 was with the idea of removing this
piece from the attack of the g6 knight
and also to enable Black to play Na6

(threatening rook infiltration) without
the a-pawn being en prise.

42 ... Nh7-g5

43 Bg4xd7   Qc8xd7

44 Nh2-f1

The knight heads back to g3 and f5.

44 ... f6-f5?

After this move White achieves his
breakthrough very quickly; but passive
defence would also have proved inadequate, for White can continue
Ng3, Nf5, g3, f4, Qg4, etc., after
which Black's game would collapse.

45 e4xf5   Qd7xf5

46 Nf1-g3   Qf5-f7

If 46 ... Qc2 then 47 f4! wins at least
a pawn.

47 Qd1-e2   Bd8-f6

To prevent the threatened 48 f4!

48 Ra1-f1   Qf7-d7

ANDERSSON   8.3

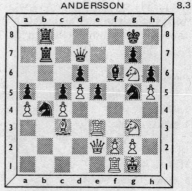

KARPOV TO MOVE

There is no defence to the coming
breakthrough.

49 f2-f4!

Black's position collapses like a pack
of cards, under the pressure of the
major pieces on the e- and f-files, the
mating possibilities, and the maraud-
ing white knights.

49 ... e5xf4

50 Rf1xf4   Bf6xc3

51 Re3xc3   Rb8-e8
Note that 52 ... Rxe2 is not a threat!

52 Rc3-e3   Rb7-b8

53 Qe2-f2!
Threatening to win the queen by
54 Rxe8+ and also preventing
53 ... Rxe3.

53 ... Ng5-h7

54 Ng3-f5
Gaining the e7 square by force.

54 ... Re8xe3

55 Qf2xe3   Nh7-f6

56 Ng6-e7+   Kg8-h8

57 Nf5xh6   Rb8-e8

58 Nh6-f7+   Kh8-h7

59 Rf4-e4!
Not 59 Rxf6? Rxe7 60 Qg5 Rxf7
and Black survives; but now the threats
of 60 Ng5+, or 60 Re6, are too much.

59 ... Re8xe7

60 Re4xe7   Black resigns
An impressive demonstration of
Karpov's strategical technique.

Game 9

BLACK Neckar   Alekhine's Defence, Modern Variation
World Junior Championship Finals, Stockholm 1969

Karpov played this—his own variation—twice against Vaganian in the pre-
world junior selection tournament. Although he had some trouble in those
games, he beat both Neckar and McKay with this variation in the world
junior finals.

1 e2-e4   Ng8-f6

2 e4-e5   Nf6-d5

3 d2-d4   d7-d6

4 Ng1-f3   g7-g6
The alternative to 4 ... Bg4 as chosen
by Bagirov in Game 19.

5 c2-c4   Nd5-b6

6 e5xd6   c7xd6

7 h2-h3
White can, if he wishes, omit this move
and play 7 Be2 Bg7 8 Be3 0-0 9 0-0
Nc6 and now either 10 Nbd2 or
10 Nc3! Bg4 11 b3 d5 12 c5 Nd7
13 b4! with sharp play.

7 ... Bf8-g7

8 Nb1-c3
White could also delay Bf1-e2 and
continue 8 Be3 Nc6 9 Nc3 0-0
10 Rc1 or 10 Qd2 with the threat of
11 d5 Na5 12 b3

8 ... 0-0

9 Bf1-e2   Nb8-c6

10 0-0
Now 10 Be3 would be inaccurate on
account of 10 ... d5! 11 c5 Nc4
12 Bxc4 dxc4 13 b3? (better is
13 0-0) 13 ... Qa5! 14 Rc1 Rd8
15 0-0 (Petkevic-Zukhovitski, USSR
1969) when 15 ... Be6 gives Black
the edge (Polugaevsky).

10 ... Bc8-f5
The advance 10 ... d5 would be
premature. With the white bishop still
on c1 the continuation 11 c5 Nc4
12 b3 N4a5 13 Be3 (Averbach-
Korchnoi, Moscow 1960) leaves White
well on top.

11 Bc1-f4
Karpov's idea *(see Diagram 9.1)*

He intends to meet the obvious 11 ...
e5 by 12 Bg5! and then if 12 ... f6
13 Be3 or 12 ... Qd7 13 d5! Nd4
(or 13 ... Na5 14 b3!) 14 Nxd4

KARPOV

exd4 15 Nb5 d3! 16 Bxd3 Bxb2
17 Rb1 Bxd3 18 Qxd3 Bg7 when
19 Be3 or 19 Bf4 gives White a substantial advantage.

In the McKay game Black played
11 . . . d5? but after 12 c5 Nc4 13 b3
N4a5 14 Rc1 b6 15 cxb6 axb6
16 Qd2 Nb7 17 Nb5 Rc8 18 Rc3
Qd7 19 R1c1 f6 20 Bc7! Black was
lost.

11 . . . h7-h6!

This renews the threat of 12 . . . e5
since 13 Bg5 is no longer available.

12 Bf4-e3

So as to meet 12 . . . e5 with 13 d5.
Two other moves have been played
here.

(a) 12 Rc1,e5 13 Be3 e4 14 Nd2 Re8
15 Nb3 d5 16 cxd5 Nb4! 17 Qd2
N4xd5 18 Nc5 Nxe3 19 fxe3 Qg5
20 Nh1 Rad8 with a tremendous
game for Black who went on to win
(Karpov-Vaganian, Leningrad match-
tournament 1969).

(b) 12 Qd2!? g5! (13 . . . Kh7 14 d5 Na5
15 b3!) 13 Be3 d5 14 c5 Nc4
15 Bxc4 dxc4 16 d5 Nb4 17 h4 Bd3
18 hxg5! hxg5 19 Bxg5 Nxd5! (The
d3 bishop must stay to protect the
b1-h7 diagonal) 20 Rfe1 f6 21 Bh6
Nxc3 22 Bxg7 Kxg7 23 Qxc3 Rh8
24 Nd4 and the game was agreed

drawn (Adorjan-Eales, Groningen
1970). Black can play 24 . . . Kf7 and
thus meet 25 Ne6 by 25 . . . Qd5 (-h5).

12 . . . d6-d5

13 b2-b3

The point of Karpov's idea. In the
position arising after 11 Be3 d5
(i.e. with the black h-pawn on h7)
the move 12 c5 is invariably played,
and after 12 . . . Nc4 13 Bxc4 dxc4
14 Qa4 Bd3 15 Rfd1 a complicated
position arises with chances for both
sides. Naturally 13 c5 is still possible
here, and was played in Stean-Timman,
Islington 1970, when after 13 . . . Nc4
14 Bxc4 dxc4 15 Qa4 Bd3 16 Rfd1
Qa5 17 Qxa5 Nxa5 18 Ne1 Bf5
White continued with the dubious
19 Rd2?! and eventually lost, whereas
19 Nd5 Nc6 20 g4 Bd3 21 Nxd3
cxd3 22 Rxd3 Rad8 is approximately
equal.

13 . . . d5xc4

14 b3xc4 Nc6-a5

Better is 14 . . . Rc8 15 Rc1 Na5
16 c5 N6c4 17 Bf4 and now 17 . . . e5!
equalizes (Boleslavsky). Karpov-Vaganian, also from the Leningrad match-
tournament 1969, went 17 . . . g5
18 Bg3 Qd7 19 Bxc4? (It would have
been better to play 19 Re1 for an
eventual Ne5 as in the game) 19 . . .
Nxc4 20 Qe2 Qe6 21 Rfe1 Qxe2
22 Rxe2 e6 23 Ne4 Bxe4 24 Rxe4
Na5 25 Be5 Rfd8 and Black stands
better, although the game was eventually drawn.

15 c4-c5   Nb6-c4

16 Be3-f4   g6-g5

17 Bf4-g3   Qd8-d7

18 Rf1-e1!

By playing for 19 Ne5! White secures
a small advantage.

18 . . . b7-b6

19 c5xb6   a7xb6

20 Nf3-e5!   Nc4xe5

21 d4xe5   *(see Diagram 9.2)*

NECKAR TO MOVE   9.2

KARPOV

After 21 ... Rfd8 White has a small
advantage, but after the text move
this is increased.

21 ... Qd7-e6?!

22 Be2-f3   Ra8-d8

23 Bf3-d5   Qe6-c8

24 Qd1-f3   e7-e6

25 Bd5-e4   Na5-c4

Black cannot contemplate 25 ... Bxe4
26 Nxe4, since his K-side defences
are weak enough as they are. The
white-squared bishop is needed to
defend the king. It is interesting to
note that White is not threatening
26 Bxf5 exf5, for Black's K-side
position would then be considerably
strengthened.

26 Ra1-c1!   Nc4-d2

27 Qf3-h5   Qc8-a6

After 27 ... Nxe4 28 Nxe4 White is
threatening Black's queen, and also
to land his knight on either f6 or d6.

28 Be4xf5!   e6xf5

29 h3-h4

Without this tactical idea the exchange
on f5 would have favoured Black as
at move 25.

29 ... f5-f4

30 Bg3-h2?

The logical move was 30 hxg5, since
30 ... fxg3 31 gxh6 and now 31 ...

gxf2+ 32 Kxf2 Bh8 33 h7+ Kg7
34 Qg5+ Kxh7 35 Rh1 mate or
31 ... Bh8 32 h7+ Kg7 33 Re3 gxf2+
34 Kxf2 and Black is lost. So Black
must try 30 ... hxg5 and after 31 Bh2
the g5 pawn is lost. Karpov had
probably overlooked Black's ingenious
resource to save his pawn.

30 ... Qa6-d3!

31 h4xg5   Qd3-f5

32 Nc3-e2   f4-f3?

Better was 32 ... Bxe5 33 Qxh6 Qg4!
when Black has a highly dangerous
attack.

33 Ne2-g3   Qf5xg5

34 Qh5xg5   h6xg5

Although Black appears to have
equalized, the weakness of the f5 and
h5 squares, together with the superior
white development, gives Karpov the
advantage.

35 Ng3-f5   f3xg2

36 Kg1xg2

NECKAR TO MOVE   9.3

KARPOV

White has a neat trick that Black
completely fails to notice. In any
event, the establishment of a white
knight at d6 will give White a substantial middle-game advantage.

36 ... Rd8-d3?

Losing rapidly. Better was 36 ... Rfe8.

37 Nf5-e7+   Kg8-h7

38 Re1-h1
Suddenly White has a winning attack.
Black must lose a piece.

38 ... Bg7-h6

39 Bh2-g3
Threatening both 40 Nf5 and 40 Rc6.

39 ... Nd2-e4

40 Rc1-c6
The simplest way to win.

40 ... f7-f6

41 Ne7-f5   Kh7-g6

42 Nf5xh6   Ne4xg3

43 f2xg3   Rd3-d2+

44 Kg2-f3   Rd2xa2
Even with the loss of a pawn this
ending presents no difficulties for
White.

45 Nh6-g4   Ra2-a3+

46 Ng4-e3   g5-g4+

47 Kf3-e4   Ra3-a4+

48 Rc6-c4   f6-f5+

49 Ke4-f4   Ra4xc4+

50 Ne3xc4   b6-b5

51 Nc4-d6   Rf8-a8

52 e5-e6   Black resigns

Game 10

WHITE Juhnke   Ruy López
World Junior Championship Finals, Stockholm 1969

Karpov has always had a ruthless streak that he reserves mainly for out-of-
form or weaker players. In this game he springs out from a theoretically
equal position and demolishes his opponent's defences in a mere ten moves.

1 e2-e4   e7-e5

2 Ng1-f3   Nb8-c6

3 Bf1-b5   a7-a6

4 Bb5-a4   Ng8-f6

5 d2-d4
An interesting move. It avoids the
main theoretical lines of either the
Open or the Closed Ruy López and
leads to an open game in which White's
chances are at least equal.

5 ... e5xd4
Also possible, but inferior, are:
5 ... Nxe4 6 Qe2 f5 7 d5 Nb8
8 Nxe5 etc., or 5 ... Nxd4 6 Nxd4
exd4 7 e5 Ne4 8 Qxd4 Nc5 9 Nc3
Be7 10 Qg4 as in Szabo-Pachman,
Spindleruv Mlyn 1948.

6 0-0   Bf8-e7

7 e4-e5
The move 7 Re1 offers White greater
chances of achieving an advantage.
For example:

(a) 7 ... 0-0 8 e5 Ne8 (or 8 ... Nd5
9 Bb3 Nb6 10 Nxd4 Nxd4 11 Qxd4
d5 12 exd6 Qxd6 13 Qe4 with
advantage to White: Suetin-Petrosian,
18th USSR Championship 1950)
9 Bf4 d5 10 Bxc6 bxc6 11 Nxd4 Bd7
12 Nb3! (Maric-Lokvenc, Sarajevo
1958)

(b) 7 ... b5! 8 e5 Nxe5 9 Rxe5 bxa4
10 Nxd4, or, if here, 9 ... d6, then
10 Re1 bxa4 11 Nxd4 (Szabo-
Balanel, Bucarest 1954).
In each line White's game is preferable.

7 ... Nf6-e4

8 Nf3xd4   0-0

The alternative plan for Black is
8 ... Nxd4 9 Qxd4 Nc5 10 Nc3 0-0
11 Bg5 Bxg5 12 Qxc5 Be7 13 Qe3
d5 with approximately equal chances.

9 Nd4-f5

Allowing Black to equalize completely,
but White's other moves also give no
advantage. Thus:

(a) 9 Re1 Nc5 10 Bxc6 dxc6 11 Nc3 f5
12 Nce2 Ne6 13 Nxe6 Qxd1 14 Rxd1
Bxe6 15 Nd4 Bc8 and Black stands
no worse.

(b) 9 c3 Nxe5 10 Re1 d5 11 f3 Bd6!
12 fxe4 Bg4 13 Qd2 Qh4 with a
powerful attack.

(c) 9 c4 Nc5 10 Bc2 Nxe5 11 Qh5 Ng6
12 b4 Ne6 13 Nxe6 dxe6 14 Rd1
Qe8 15 Rd3 f5! 16 Rh3 h6 17 Bxh6
Nh4! and White's attack is repulsed.

9 ... d7-d5

10 Ba4xc6 b7xc6

11 Nf5xe7+ Qd8xe7

12 Rf1-e1

KARPOV TO MOVE   10.1

JUHNKE

According to theory this position
offers equal chances. After 12 ... f6
13 f3 Ng5 (if 13 ... Nc5 then 14 b3!
is strong: e.g. 14 ... fxe5 15 Ba3 Rf6
16 Nc3 Rg6 17 g3 Qh4 18 Bxc5 and
White can beat the attack and win)

14 Nc3 Bf5 (if 14 ... fxe5 then
15 Nxd5!) 15 exf6 Qxf6 the game is
equal.
Karpov prefers to await events.

12 ... Rf8-e8!

13 f2-f3

White cannot try 13 Nd2 because of
13 ... Qxe5! and if then 14 f3? Qd4+
wins.

13 ... Ne4-d6

Heading for f5.

14 b2-b3

A difficult decision. To commit the
queen's bishop to the a3-f8 or b2-h8
diagonal allows the black queen free
use of the g5 square and with the
knight heading for f5 and bishop on
c8 this forms a winning combination.
White's problem is that he wishes to
develop his queen's bishop and at the
same time prevent the weakness on the
a7-g1 diagonal. 14 Be3 leaves the
e-pawn en prise and 14 Bd2 (or 14 Bf4)
Nf5 leaves Black with the nasty threat
of 15 ... Qc5+.
It appears that White must play to
establish some control of d4 and c5
by 14 Nd2 but then 14 ... f6! is a
strong reply.

14 ... Nd6-f5

15 Bc1-a3

15 Bb2 , 15 Nd2, or 15 Nc3 are all
met by 15 ... Qc5+.

15 ... Qe7-g5

16 Ba3-b2

And now 16 Bc1 Qg6 is no better.

16 ... Nf5-h4

Suddenly White is completely lost.
One can only say that White's 13 f3
must have been a mistake, but it is
difficult to suggest a better way to
tackle the position.

17 Qd1-e2 f7-f6

18 Qe2-f2 Bc8-h3

19 g2-g4 f6xe5 *(see Diagram 10.2)*

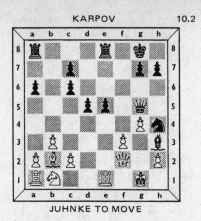

KARPOV   10.2

JUHNKE TO MOVE

Black's threats are overwhelming. White's next move merely shortens the game by a few moves.

20 Nb1-d2   Qg5xd2!

and if 21 Qxd2 then Nxf3+ 22 Kf2 Nxd2 23 Kg3 Bxg4 (or even 23 ... Bf1) 24 Kxg4 leaves Black three pawns up.

White resigns

Game 11

WHITE Castro   King's Gambit
World Junior Championship Finals, Stockholm 1969

The opening in this game is most interesting. Karpov plays a little-known move and his opponent, by accepting the forcing continuation thus offered, is soon in trouble. The latter part of the game is noteworthy for the technique shown by Karpov in converting a small material advantage and a position full of possibilities for White into a convincing win in only ten moves.

1 e2-e4   e7-e5

2 f2-f4

The King's Gambit is very rare in tournament chess these days. Bronstein and Spassky are two of its advocates.

2 ... e5xf4

3 Bf1-c4

The King's Bishop's Gambit.

3 ... Ng8-f6

Karpov, as always, plays a safe line. He avoids the tactical complications of the two other major alternatives, namely 3 ... Qh4+ and 3 ... d5. For example, after 3 ... Qh4+ 4 Kf1 g5 5 Nc3 Ne7 6 d4 Bg7 7 g3 fxg3 8 Kg2 Qh6 9 hxg3 Qg6 10 Nf3 h6

11 Nd5 White has a fierce attack. Alternatively, 3 ... d5 4 Bxd5 Qh4+ 5 Kf1 g5 6 Nc3 Bg7 7 d4 Ne7 8 Nf3 Qh5 9 h4 h6 10 Qd3 Nc6 and White has the better chances.

4 Nb1-c3

After 4 e5 d5! 5 Bb3 Ne4 6 Nf3 Bg4 7 0-0 Nc6 Black stands better.

4 ... Bf8-b4

Opening theory here suggests that 4 ... c6! is the best move for Black. After 5 Qf3 d5! 6 exd5 Bd6 7 d3 Bg4 8 Qf2 0-0 9 Bxf4 Re8+, or 5 Bb3 d5 6 exd5 cxd5 7 d4 Bd6 8 Nge2 0-0 9 0-0 g5! 10 Nxd5 Nc6 11 c3 Nxd5 12 Bxd5 Ne7 13 Be4 f5 (Spielmann-Bogolyubov, Mährisch-Ostrau 1923), Black has the advantage.

5 e4-e5

Putting the idea to the test. Safer would have been 5 Nf3 or 5 Nge2.

5 ... d7-d5

6 Bc4-b5+   c7-c6

7 e5xf6   c6xb5

8 f6xg7   Rh8-g8

9 Qd1-e2+   Bc8-e6

10 Qe2xb5+   Nb8-c6

11 Qb5xb7   Ra8-c8

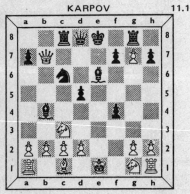

KARPOV   11.1

CASTRO TO MOVE

Every Black move since move 4 has been forced—that is to say the merit of 4 ... Bb4 is based upon an evaluation of this position. If, as is in fact the case, this position is good for Black then White should have played a different fifth move. Karpov must have judged that this variation was better for Black when choosing his fourth move!

12 Ng1-f3

Preventing a possible 12 ... Nd4.

12 ... Rg8xg7

13 0-0

13 Kf1 would leave the white queen precariously placed after 13 ... d4 (threatening 14 ... Bc4+ and 15 ... Rc7).

13 ... Be6-h3

14 Rf1-e1+

Unfortunately forced. If 14 Rf2 then 14 ... Bc5 and if 14 Ne1 Bc5+ 15 Kh1 (or 15 d4 Bxd4+ 16 Kh1) then 15 ... Qg5! is decisive.

14 ... Ke8-f8

15 Re1-e2   Bh3-g4!

KARPOV   11.2

CASTRO TO MOVE

White is now forced to give up the exchange by 16 Rf2. The other king moves 16 Kf1, 16 Kh1 and 16 Kf2 are all quickly refuted:

(a) 16 Kf1 Bxf3 17 gxf3 Rc7! 18 Qa6 (or 18 Qb5) Qg5 19 Rf2 (what else?) Qg1+ 20 Ke2 Nd4+ 21 Kd3 Qxf2.

(b) 16 Kh1 Bxf3 17 gxf3 Rc7 18 Qa6 (or 18 Qb5) Qg5.

(c) 16 Kf2 Bc5+ 17 d4 (17 Kf1 or 17 Ke1 allow Bxf3, and if 18 gxf3 Rg1 mate) 17 ... Nxd4.

16 Re2-f2   Bb4-c5

17 d2-d4

White must develop quickly to prevent an immediate catastrophe. If 17 Kf1 then ... Bxf2 18 Kxf2 Bxf3 followed by 19 ... Rc7 and 20 ... Qg5 will be decisive.

17 ... Nc6xd4

18 Nf3xd4   Bc5xd4

19 Bc1xf4

Also possible here is 19 Qb4+ Bc5 20 Qxf4.

19 ... Bd4xf2+

20 Kg1xf2

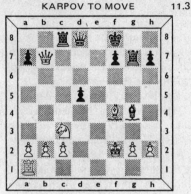

KARPOV TO MOVE   11.3

CASTRO

Now is the time to take stock of the situation. Black has a rook for knight and pawn. Both kings are relatively exposed and even a pure ending would not be easy for Black to win, owing to the poor position of his pawns—all four are isolated, whereas White's form two islands only.

20 ... Rg7-g6!

This move is aimed at removing all White's counterchances. (Note that White was not threatening 21 Bh6 on account of the reply 21 ... Qf6+ winning a piece.) After the obvious 20 ... d4 21 Nd5 Rxc2+ 22 Kf1 White has numerous threats, such as:

(a) 22 ... Be2+ 23 Ke1 (23 Kg1? Rxg2+) and now

(a1) 23 ... Bf3 24 Bd6+! Kg8 (24 ... Ke8 25 Qb5+ Qd7 26 Nf6+) 25 Ne7+ Kh8 26 Qxf3 and now if 26 ... Qxd6 27 Qa8+ mates.

(a2) 23 ... Rxg2 24 Bh6+ Ke8 (24 ... Kg8 25 Ne7+ and 26 Qxg2) 25 Nc7+! Qxc7 26 Qxg2 and the win is still a long way off. White may even try 24 Qb4+ Kg8 25 Ne7+ Kg7 and now 26 Nf5+ or 26 Be5+ with an unclear position.

(b) 22 ... f5?! 23 Qb4+ Kg8 24 Qxd4 and White may even stand better.

The text move avoids the possibilities of both Bd6+ and Bh6+ and allows the king a flight square in case of Qb4+. The rook on g6 can swing into play on e6 or f6 and possibly even try to trap the white queen on b6

21 Kf2-g1

After 21 Nxd5 Rxc2+ 22 Kf1 Be2+ 23 Ke1 Re6! is decisive since White has no swindles.

21 ... d5-d4

22 Ra1-f1

22 Nd5 would be met by 22 ... Bf3

22 ... Qd8-d7

22 ... dxc3?? 23 Bd6+ Kg7 (23 ... Kg8 24 Qxf7+ Kh8 25 Be5+) 24 Qxf7+ Kh6 25 Bf4+, etc. would be totally disastrous for Black.

23 Qb7-b4+   Kf8-g8

24 Nc3-e4

Hoping for some tricks on f6 or d6 but Karpov has his third rank well covered.

24 ... Qd7-d5

25 Qb4-e7   Qd5-e6

26 Qe7-b7

The exchange of queens would lead to the loss of a further white pawn.

26 ... Bg4-e2

27 Rf1-e1   Rc8xc2

28 Ne4-g5   Qe6-f5

29 Bf4-e5

Hoping for 29 ... Qxe5 30 Qxf7+ Kh8 31 Qxh7 mate or 29 ... Qxg5 30 Qb8+ and mate in two.

29 ... Rg6xg5

30 h2-h4

Threatening hxg5 and Rxe2.

30 ... Qf5xe5

Now 31 hxg5 can be met by 31 ... d3, 31 ... Qg3 or 31 ... Bf3 according to taste.

White resigns

4 Grandmaster

The rest of 1969 must have been an anti-climax after the success at Stockholm. In the RSFSR-Hungary match in Budapest Karpov was beaten by both the young Hungarian stars Ribli and Adorjan. His poor score, ½/2 against each, resulted in a crushing defeat for the Russian team.

However, 1970 was to be another successful year. In May and June, Karpov won a place in the 38th USSR Championship (to be held later in the year in Riga) by winning the RSFSR Championship in Kuibyshev. The final scores were Karpov 12½ (8 wins, 9 draws, no losses) Krogius 11, Antoshin and Dementiev 10½, Doroshkevich 10, Averkin, A. Zaitsev, and Kopelov 9½, etc. Game 12 against Krogius is the first of many Tarrasch French wins in the collection. I can safely guarantee that the reader will never see a more unusual win for Karpov than that of Game 13. The white king escapes from a barrage of black pieces and lives to see the rout of the black position. Game 14 is something of an oddity—a difficult game to understand—but with a pretty finish that justifies its inclusion.

In June and July, Karpov had his first chance to reach the granumaster title in the international tournament at Caracas. After seven rounds of long unrelenting struggles, Karpov was in the lead with 6 points, followed by Kaválek 5½, Panno 5, Bisguier, Stein, and Ivkov 4½, etc. He had already had an 84-move marathon draw with Bisguier, an excellent win over Parma (Game 15), and a somewhat fortunate win against O'Kelly (Game 16). But in his seven games he had played only one short game, and he seemed to tire in the second half of the tournament. The key game was Game 17 (against Ivkov) when, having achieved a winning position at an early stage, he rejected Ivkov's offer of a draw, and went on to lose. This was one of the few examples of tournament nerves ever exhibited by Karpov. In the next round he came close to losing to Panno with white and the tenth round saw him losing again—this time to Kaválek. By this time Karpov had given up all chance of first prize and concentrated on the grandmaster 'norm'. He coasted home, beating three tail-enders and drawing his last three games quickly to reach equal fourth place behind Kaválek, Panno, and Stein, but, more importantly, he reached the grandmaster norm at his first attempt.

The young grandmaster on returning to Russia took up his place in the 38th USSR Championship in Riga. This was not to be as successful a tournament as Caracas had been. There was a certain lack of finishing power evident in Karpov's play in the early stages of the tournament. He began with eight draws, some short but mostly hard-fought games where he just failed to secure the win, and then lost to Korchnoi. After two more draws, one against Averbakh, in which he displayed brilliant defensive ability, he broke through and won his first game against Bagirov (Game 19). Another draw was followed by a second win against Igor Zaitsev (Game 20), but an unfortunate reversal at the hands of Dementiev in the next round prevented him from reaching a high place. Nonetheless a finishing spurt of 4½/6 left him in a respectable fifth place with Gipslis and Savon, behind Korchnoi, Tukmakov, Stein, and Balashov. The game with Bagirov will repay careful study as it is, without doubt, one of the best examples of the use of a passed pawn to be found in any textbook. The other game selected from the Championship is a tense cut-and-thrust encounter with Stein from round 1 (Game 18). Both sides played excellently in this game and so the draw was a fair result.

Karpov had already made himself known in Soviet chess circles and by now his fame was spreading. The following year was to see him thrust to the forefront of the chess scene by winning the strongest tournament since the war.

Game 12

BLACK Krogius   French Defence, Tarrasch Variation
RSFSR Championship, Kuibyshev 1970

Grandmaster Krogius makes a serious error of judgement in the opening of this game, in the shape of a dubious pawn sacrifice. Karpov succeeds in maintaining the pawn, and the tide has already turned when Krogius makes a losing blunder.

1 e2-e4   e7-e6

2 d2-d4   d7-d5

3 Nb1-d2

The Tarrasch variation. Karpov almost invariably plays this against the French, but for an example of 3 Nc3 see the game at the end of Chapter 1!

3 ... c7-c5

The alternatives are 3 ... Nf6 and 3 ... Nc6.

4 e4xd5

White is playing to isolate Black's d-pawn and exploit it in the classical manner—blockade and then capture. Note that all White's pieces are developed on squares where they help control d4.

4 ... e6xd5

The recapture 4 ... Qxd5 leads to advantage for White after 5 Ngf3! cxd4 6 Bc4 followed by 7 0-0 8 Nb3 and 9 Nbxd4, etc.

5 Ng1-f3   Nb8-c6

Also possible is 5 ... Nf6 6 Bb5+ Bd7 7 Bxd7+ Nbxd7 8 0-0 Be7 9 dxc5 Nxc5 when White has only a small advantage.

6 Bf1-b5   Bf8-d6

7 0-0   Ng8-e7

8 d4xc5   Bd6xc5

9 Nd2-b3   Bc5-b6

More popular is 9 ... Bd6 when 10 Bg5 0-0 11 Bh4! (intending the exchange of black-squared bishops) leads to an interesting game with better chances for White (see Game 51).

10 Rf1-e1

The old way to play this position was with 10 Be3 Bxe3 11 Bxc6+! bxc6 12 fxe3 but after 12 ... Bg4! 13 Qd4 Bxf3 14 Rxf3 0-0 the chances are equal. The positional grip of the d4 and c5 squares by White is counter-balanced by Black's chances on the b- and e-files. The idea of 10 Re1 is to recapture on e3 with a rook.

10 ... 0-0

11 Bc1-e3

In Game 47 Karpov tries 11 Bg5 against his old rival Vaganian.

11 ... Bc8-g4?

A definite error. Either 11 ... Bf5 12 c3 Be4 13 Nbd4 Qd6 14 Bf1 Qf6 15 Qa4 h6 16 Rad1, or 11 ... Bxe3 12 Rxe3 Bg4 13 c3 Qd6 14 h3 leaves White with only a small advantage.

The text move is based on an incorrect pawn sacrifice.

12 Be3xb6   Qd8xb6

13 Bb5xc6   Ne7xc6

13 ... bxc6 or 13 ... Qxc6 would leave the knight e7 en prise.

14 Qd1xd5   Nc6-b4

15 Qd5-e4   Bg4xf3

16 g2xf3   a7-a5   *(see Diagram 12.1)*

The opening has been unsuccessful for Black, who has insufficient compensation for the sacrificed pawn, with only slight possible counterplay on the central files and against White's weak pawns. White's difficulty will be to advance his Q-side majority with so many pieces on the board and with his king so exposed. Karpov's solution to this problem is simple—he attacks on the K-side, using his extra Q-side pawn as a latent problem for Black in case of a possible piece exchange.

The exchange of any one piece would not hinder Black's chances very much, but if White could exchange say the

KROGIUS   12.1

KARPOV TO MOVE

knights and a pair of rooks he could then safely advance his Q-side majority to decide the game.

17 a2-a3   Nb4-c6

18 Qe4-e3   Qb6-b5

Black's chances of survival lie in his counterplay; so a queen exchange would be fatal for him.

19 a3-a4   Qb5-h5

20 Qe3-e4   Qh5-g5+

21 Kg1-h1   Qg5-f6

22 Nb3-c5

Threatening 22 Nd7.

22 ... Ra8-d8

After 22 ... Qxb2 23 Rab1 Qd4 24 Nxb7 Qxe4 25 Rxe4! White has a winning end-game owing to the weakness of Black's a5 pawn.

23 c2-c3

Having sewn up the Q-side against attack, White now switches to the K-side. The white queen dominates the board.

23 ... b7-b6

24 Nc5-d3   h7-h6

25 f3-f4

White is slowly creeping forward and now begins to increase his spatial advantage.

25 ... Rd8-d7

26 Re1-e3   Rf8-d8

27 Ra1-g1   Nc6-e7

28 Nd3-e5   Rd7-d1

29 Re3-e1!
Allowing no counterplay at all.
Karpov instinctively, and quite
correctly, avoids the dubious 29 Ng4.

29 ... Rd1xe1
The rook cannot be withdrawn to d6
because of 30 Ng4.

30 Rg1xe1   Ne7-f5

KROGIUS   12.2

KARPOV TO MOVE

Black's position looks impregnable.
Karpov continues to probe and push
until a crack appears.

31 Ne5-g4   Qf6-g6

32 Ng4-e5
Although 32 Rg1 would threaten
33 Qxf5!, Black would get in first
with 32 ... Ng3+.

32 ... Qg6-h5

33 Qe4-f3   Qh5-h4
33 ... Qxf3 34 Nxf3 Rd3 35 Kg2
followed by 36 Re5 etc. wins easily
for White.

34 Ne5-c4   Qh4-f6

35 h2-h3   Nf5-h4
This manœuvre leaves Black in great
difficulties. Preferable would be a
passive move such as 35 ... Kh7.

36 Qf3-e4   Nh4-g6

37 f4-f5   Ng6-h4

38 Nc4-e3!
After 38 Nxb6 Qxb6 (or 38 ... Nxf5
39 Nd5 Qc6 40 Qxf5 Rxd5 41 Re8+
Qxe8 42 Qxd5 Qxa4 with winning
chances for Black) 39 Qxh4 Rd2
Black has excellent play for the two
pawns. Again Karpov chooses the
most accurate move, avoiding counterplay.

38 ... Kg8-h8

39 Re1-e2   Qf6-g5

40 Kh1-h2   h6-h5

41 f2-f4   Qg5-h6?

KROGIUS   12.3

KARPOV TO MOVE

After this move White wins prettily.
The alternative 41 ... Qf6 is better.
After 42 Kg3, the threat of 43 Qe5!
can be met by 42 ... g5!, and if then
43 fxg6 Nxg6 gives Black good chances.
Note that 43 Qe5 here would fail to
43 ... gxf4+ and if 44 Kxf4 Ng6+.

42 Kh2-g3!   g7-g5
Forced.

43 f5xg6   Nh4xg6

44 Ne3-f5!   Qh6-f8
The alternative 44 ... Qh7 would be
met by 45 Qe8+ transposing to a
winning endgame.

45 Qe4-f3
Thus winning a second pawn.

45 ... Kh8-g8

46 Qf3xh5   Rd8-d3+

47 Kg3-g4!
   The white king is perfectly safe.

47 ... Qf8-a8

48 Nf5-d4   Rd3-d1

49 Nd4-f3   Rd1-d5
   Better was 49 ... Rd3 when Black
   could continue the struggle for a little
   longer.

50 Nf3-g5   Qa8-c8+

51 Kg4-g3   Rd5-f5

52 Qh5-h7+   Kg8-f8

53 Qh7-h6+   Kf8-g8   *(see Diagram 12.4)*

54 Ng5-e6!
   Forcing the win of a third pawn and
   exposing the black king to a mating
   attack. After 54 ... fxe6 55 Qxg6+
   Kh8 (or 55 ... Kf8) 56 Rxe6 Black
   is completely lost.

KROGIUS   12.4

KARPOV TO MOVE

... **Black resigns**

An excellent example of Karpov's
superb technique.

Game 13

BLACK Alexander Zaitsev   Caro-Kann Defence
RSFSR Championship, Kuibyshev 1970

This is the kind of game that one dreams (or has nightmares) about! Karpov
is caught out in the opening and is subjected to an extremely dangerous,
and by rights a winning attack. He needs a little help from his opponent
plus a very ingenious and resourceful defence to escape at all, but, having
done so, he makes no mistake about clinching the game.

1 e2-e4   c7-c6

2 d2-d4   d7-d5

3 Nb1-c3   d5xe4

4 Nc3xe4   Nb8-d7
   The safest variation. The alternatives
   4 ... Nf6 and 4 ... Bf5 are less solid—
   the latter was 'discredited' after the
   13th match game in the 1966 world
   championship final between Spassky
   (White) and Petrosian, but is still
   almost invariably played by the
   Spanish grandmaster Pomar.

5 Ng1-f3   Ng8-f6

6 Ne4xf6+ Nd7xf6

7 Nf3-e5
   7 c3 is without bite, but 7 Bc4 merits
   consideration here.

7 ... Bc8-f5
   In the 40th USSR Championship in
   Baku, 1972, Razuvaev showed that
   7 ... Be6! was the best move for Black

here. His game with Gufeld from round 12 of that event continued 8 c4 g6 9 Be2 Bg7 10 0-0 0-0 11 Be3 Qc7 12 h3 Rfd8 13 Nf3 b5 14 b3? (Better was 14 cxb5) bxc4 15 bxc4 c5! 16 d5 Bf5? (Better was 16 ... Ne4! so that 17 Qc2 Bf5 18 g4 Nxf2 19 gxf5 Qg3 mate) 17 Nh4! Bd7 18 Qc2 Rab8 19 Rab1 Rb6 20 Bd2 Ra6 21 Bd3 e6 22 dxe6?? Ba4 23 Rb3 Bxb3 24 axb3 Rxe6 25 Be3 Qe7 and White resigns. Although White lost by a blunder, the opening clearly favoured Black.

8 c2-c3

Aiming to exploit the position of the bishop on f5 by g4. The game could also develop on quieter lines by 8 Bc4 e6 9 0-0 Be7 10 Re1.

8 ... e7-e6

White was threatening 9 Qb3, winning a pawn, and would meet 8 ... Nd7 by 9 Nxf7! Kxf7 10 Qf3 e6 11 g4 Qf6 12 gxf5 Qxf5 with some advantage (Spassky-Donner, San Juan 1969, and Kaválek-Barcza, Caracas 1970).

9 g2-g4   Bf5-g6

10 h2-h4   Bf8-d6

11 Qd1-e2!

11 h5 Be4 12 f3 would be strongly met by 12 ... Bxe5.

11 ... c6-c5

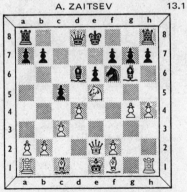

A. ZAITSEV   13.1

KARPOV TO MOVE

The game Jansa-Flesch from Sombor 1970 continued with 11 ... Bxe5 but 12 dxe5 Qd5 13 Rh3 Nxg4 14 Qxg4 Bf5 15 Qf3 Bxh3 16 Qxd5 cxd5 17 Bxh3 gave White a material advantage

12 h4-h5?

This is the move that leads to all the trouble for White. Kotov in his notes to the game in *Informator 9* gives 12 Bg2! and Boleslavsky in his *Skandinavisch bis Sizilianisch* suggests the exchange sacrifice 12 dxc5 Be4 13 Qb5+ Kf8 14 cxd6 Bxh1 15 Bf4. Both these are superior to the move played.

12 ... Bg6-e4

13 f2-f3   c5xd4!

and now 14 cxd4 is met by 14 ... Bb4+! 15 Bd2 Qxd4 16 Qb5+ Bc6! 17 Qxb4 Qxe5+, or 14 fxe4? by 14 ... Bxe5 15 Qb5+ Nd7, both leading to winning positions for Black.

14 Qe2-b5+   Nf6-d7!

The real point. After 15 Nxd7? Bc6 or 15 Qxd7+ Qxd7 16 Nxd7 Bxf3 Black is winning.

15 Ne5xf7!

The only chance for survival. This leads however, to White's king being exposed in a most amusing manner. I doubt whether White's next three moves have ever been seen in such a position.

15 ... Bd6-g3+

16 Ke1-e2(!)   d4-d3+

17 Ke2-e3(!!)   Qd8-f6

18 Ke3xe4(!!!)   *(see Diagram 13.2)*

A position that certainly merits a diagram. It is surprising that mate cannot be delivered instantly, but in fact White's king is remarkably safe. Black should, of course win but the mating idea that he misses is difficult to see.

A. ZAITSEV TO MOVE   13.2

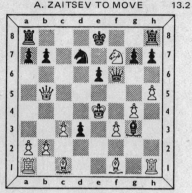

KARPOV

18 ... Qf6xf7

19 Rh1-h3   a7-a6

20 Qb5-g5   h7-h6?
According to Kotov, the correct way is 20 ...e5! 21 Rxg3 Nc5+ 22 Ke3 0-0 (threatening 23 ...Qf4+) and now

(a) 23 b4 Qf4+ 24 Qxf4 (24 Kf2?? Ne4+) 24 ...exf4+ 25 Kf2 fxg3+ 26 Kxg3 Rad8! 27 bxc5 d2 28 Bxd2 Rxd2 29 Rb1 when White has some drawing chances.

(b) 23 Rh3 Rad8 when

(b1) 24 Kf2? or 24 Kd2? allows 24 ...Ne4+.

(b2) 24 Qf5? Qe7 traps the queen.

(b3) 24 b4 h6! (if 24 ...Ne4!? 25 Kxe4? Qd5+ 26 Ke3 d2 then 27 Bc4 loses to 27 ...d1=N+ 28 Ke2 Qxc4+ etc.) 25 Qg6 (Qf5 Qd5!) Qf4+ 26 Kf2 d2 wins for Black.

(b4) 24 Bd2 is best answered by the lethal 24 ...h6! 25 Qf5 Qd5 26 Qg6 Rf6 winning the queen. Kotov's 24 ...Ne4!? (so that 25 Kxe4 Qd5+ 26 Ke3 Qc5+ 27 Ke4 Rd4+ or 25 fxe4 Qf2 mate) is dubious on account of 25 Qf5! Qe7 26 fxe4 when White will at least reach an ending by 26 ...g6 27 hxg6 Qc5+ 28 Kf3 hxg6 29 Be3!

21 Qg5-e3!
After 21 Qg6 Nc5+ 22 Kd4 is met by 0-0-0+! and the black queen comes across to mate.

21 ...e6-e5
Black cannot reconcile himself to take a draw. After 21 ...Nf6+ 22 Kxd3 Nxg4 the only sensible course for White is 23 fxg4 Qxf1+ 24 Kc2 Qxh3 25 Qxe6+ with perpetual check.

22 Ke4xd3!
Karpov removes his king to safety, capturing a pawn en route, and thus wins the game. 22 Rxg3? Qc4+ would be a disaster.

22 ...Bg3-f4

23 Qe3-g1   0-0-0

24 Kd3-c2   Bf4xc1

25 Ra1xc1   Qf7xa2

26 Rh3-h2   Rh8-f8

27 Rh2-d2!   Qa2-a4+

28 Kc2-b1

A. ZAITSEV TO MOVE   13.3

KARPOV

The remainder of the game is a perfect example of technique of the highest order. White's advantage is based on the superior quality of his pawns, the bishop's ability to dominate the knight, and the greater safety of his king.

28 ...Qa4-c6
After 28 ...Rxf3 29 Bg2 R3f8 (29 ...Rg3? 30 Bxb7+) 30 Qa7 Qb3

(best) White continues 31 R1d1!
(with the threat of 32 Qa8+ Kc7
33 Rxd7+) Qb6 32 Qa8+ Kc7
33 Rxd7+ Rxd7 34 Rxd7+ Kxd7
35 Qxf8 Qg1+ 36 Qf1 wins. In this
line 31 ... Rfe8 (to prevent the above-
mentioned threat) would be met by
32 Bxb7+ Qxb7 33 Qxb7+ Kxb7
34 Rxd7+ Rxd7 (34 ... Kc8 would
lose the king-and-pawn ending).
35 Rxd7+ Kc6 36 Rxg7 with a
winning rook-and-pawn ending.

29 Bf1-d3! Kc8-c7
The f-pawn is still untouchable.
If 29 ... Rxf3 30 Bf5 is a murderous
pin, and 29 ... Qxf3 30 Bf5 Qc6
31 R1d1 Rf7 32 Rd6 Qa4 33 Qc5+
Kb8 34 Qd5 and Black is helpless.
(If 30 ... Kc7? 31 Rxd7 Rxd7
32 Qc5+ wins.)

30 Bd3-e4 Qc6-b6

31 Qg1-h2
Karpov surrounds the isolated e-pawn
and forces a hopeless exchange sacrifice.

31 ... Rd8-e8

32 Rc1-d1 Nd7-f6

33 Be4-g6 Re8-e7

34 Rd1-e1 Qb6-b5

35 Rd2-e2 Nf6-d7

36 Bg6-f5!
The pawn falls, so Black sacrifices ...

36 ... Rf8xf5

37 g4xf5 Qb5-d3+

38 Kb1-a1 Qd3xf5 *(see Diagram 13.4)*

Karpov makes the rest look simple.

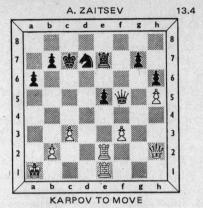

A. ZAITSEV   13.4

KARPOV TO MOVE

39 Qh2-h4 Nd7-f6

40 Qh4-c4+ Kc7-d8

41 Qc4-c5 Nf6-d7

42 Qc5-d5 Kd8-c8

43 Re2-e4 b7-b5
The end is already in sight.

44 Qd5-c6+ Kc8-d8

45 Qc6xa6 Qf5xh5

46 f3-f4 Qh5-f5

47 Qa6-a8+ Kd8-c7

48 Qa8-a5+ Kc7-c6

49 c3-c4 b5-b4

50 Qa5xb4 Re7-e6

51 f4xe5
This pawn is also lost since 51 ... Rxe5
52 Rxe5 Nxe5 53 Qb5+ Kd6 54 Qd5+
wins a piece.

... Black resigns

It is the mark of a great player that, after
making an error, he makes it as difficult
as possible for his opponent to take
advantage of it.

Game 14

BLACK Sergievsky   Irregular Defence
RSFSR Championship, Kuibyshev 1970

After a peculiar opening, Karpov is left with a passive position but a superior
pawn structure. He keeps his two bishops, and when the game is opened
up he uses them to deliver a swift and surprising mating attack.

1 e2-e4   d7-d6

2 d2-d4   Ng8-f6

3 Nb1-c3   Nb8-d7

Black could be trying for almost any
pawn structure here. He could have
been intending 4 ... g6 with a Pirc
Defence, 4 ... e5 with a kind of
Philidor's Defence, or 4 ... c6 or
4 ... c5 taking the game out of known
theory.

4 Ng1-e2

4 f4 or 4 Nf3 (both to enable 5 e5)
would be more logical.

4 ... b7-b5?!

Forcing White into a queen exchange.
5 a3 or 5 f3 would be too passive.

5 e4-e5   d6xe5

6 d4xe5   Nd7xe5

7 Qd1xd8+   Ke8xd8

8 Nc3xb5   a7-a6

9 Nb5-d4   Bc8-b7

10 Bc1-f4   Ne5-g6

11 0-0-0   Kd8-c8

After 11 ... Nxf4?? Black would be
mated by 12 Ne6+ (12 ... Kc8
13 Rd8 or 12 ... Ke8 13 Nxc7).

The opening has turned out quite well
for Black. The white queen's bishop is
threatened and White is very weak on his
f2 square. His Q-side majority, and slightly
superior pawn structure, can be effective
only in a much simpler position than this,
i.e. one in which more pieces have been
exchanged. So, for the time being at any
rate, White must fall back on the defensive.
As we have come to expect, Karpov
defends accurately.

12 Bf4-d2

The only square. 12 Be3 or 12 Bg5
would be met by 12 ... Ng4, and
12 Bg3 by Ne4, and in each case Black
would obtain the two bishops.

12 ... e7-e6

13 Nd4-b3!

Preventing the black king's bishop
developing on c5 and preparing to
obtain the two bishops himself.

13 ... Nf6-g4

14 Bd2-e1   Bf8-d6

15 h2-h3   Ng4-f6

After 15 ... Nh2 16 Rxd6! (not
16 Rxh2 Bxh2 17 g3 Rd8! when the
black bishop will ultimately escape)
16 ... Nxf1 17 Rd3 Bxg2 18 Rg1
Nh4 19 Nf4 Nf3 20 Rxf3 Bxf3
21 Rxf1 gives White excellent winning
chances.

16 Nb3-a5

The point of White's 13th move.

SERGIEVSKY TO MOVE   14.1

KARPOV

Black must now concede the bishop pair and this reduces his K-side play to virtually nil.

16 ... Rh8-d8

17 c2-c4
The bishop cannot escape.

17 ... Ng6-f4

18 Na5xb7   Kc8xb7

The removal of this bishop gives White the advantage. Although he is temporarily cramped, his two bishops will soon come into their own.

19 Kc1-c2
It is strange that Karpov did not try to reduce the pressure on his position with 19 g3. The move has no obvious drawbacks.

19 ... Bd6-e5

20 Ne2-c3   Rd8xd1

21 Nc3xd1   Ra8-d8
This marks the end of Black's threats. Now the white bishops take over.

22 g2-g3   Nf4-g6

23 Bf1-g2+   Kb7-b6
23 ... c6 would be safer.

24 Nd1-c3   Be5-d4

25 Nc3-e2   Bd4-e5

26 f2-f4   Be5-d6

27 Ne2-c3   c7-c6?

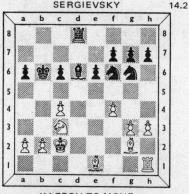

SERGIEVSKY   14.2

KARPOV TO MOVE

A mistake. Better was 27 ... c5. The white bishops dominate the two black knights. Black's king is exposed, and his Q-side minority and weak pawns on a6 and c6 are beginning to become real handicaps. All in all, White has a substantial advantage.

28 c4-c5+!
If 28 ... Kxc5 then 29 Bf2+ Kb4 30 Bb6! or 29 ... Kc4 30 Bf1+ Kb4 31 Bb6! and the threat of a3 mate cannot be parried.

28 ... Bd6xc5

29 Nc3-a4+   Kb6-b5

30 Kc2-b3!

SERGIEVSKY TO MOVE   14.3

KARPOV

30 ... Rd8-d3+

31 Be1-c3   Rd3xc3+

32 Na4xc3+   Kb5-a5

33 Nc3-a4!
Unfortunately for Black, the mating net still exists.

33 ... Bc5-f2

34 Rh1-c1   Ng6-e7
If 34 ... Bxg3 then 35 Rc5 is mate.

35 Rc1-c2   Bf2-e3

36 Bg2xc6   Nf6-h5
It would be better to resign here.

37 Bc6-e8   Nh5xg3

38 Kb3-c4

Now 39 b4 mate is the threat.

38 ... Ne7-d5

39 a2-a3   Nd5-b6+

40 Kc4-d3!   Nb6xa4

41 Kd3xe3   Ng3-f5+

42 Ke3-d3

The threat of 43 b4+ Kb6 44 Bxa4 can be stopped only by 42 ... Nb6, when 43 b4 or 43 Rc5 are both mate. A piece must be lost.

... Black resigns

Game 15

BLACK Parma   Nimzo-Indian Defence, Classical Variation
Caracas, 1970

Grandmaster Bruno Parma of Yugoslavia has a reputation as an expert on opening theory and is one of the most difficult players to beat. At Caracas he lost only one of his seventeen games—this one against Karpov. From an even opening Parma is slowly outplayed. The classical simplicity of the winning plan is Karpov's trade-mark. He creates a passed pawn in a major-piece ending, and the rest is remorseless technique.

1 c2-c4   Ng8-f6

2 Nb1-c3   e7-e6

3 d2-d4   Bf8-b4

4 Qd1-c2

The Classical Variation.

4 ... 0-0

The most flexible continuation for Black.

5 Ng1-f3

The alternative 5 e4 is today considered to be too loosening.

5 ... c7-c5

6 d4xc5   Nb8-a6

7 Bc1-d2

Other possibilities here are:

(a) 7 a3 Bxc3+ 8 Qxc3 Nxc5 9 e3 a5 10 b3! with equal chances.

(b) 7 e3 Nxc5 8 Bd2 transposing back to the game continuation.

7 ... Na6xc5

8 e2-e3

Alternatively 8 a3 Bxc3 9 Bxc3 N5e4 10 e3 b6 11 Be2 Bb7 12 0-0 Rc8

13 Bb4 Re8 14 Rfc1 Qc7 15 Be1 Qb8 16 b4 d5 gives chances for both sides (Kottnauer-Keres, Budapest 1952).

8 ... b7-b6

9 Bf1-e2   Bc8-b7

9 ... Ba6 is an interesting move. After 10 a3 Bxc3 11 Bxc3 Rc8 12 0-0 d5 13 cxd5 Nxd5 14 Bxa6 Nxa6 15 Qe2 Nc5 both sides have chances.

10 0-0   d7-d6

Black could also contemplate 10 ... Nce4 11 Nxe4 Bxe4 12 Bd3 Bxd3 13 Qxd3 Bxd2 14 Qxd2 Rc8 with an equal position; Flohr-Unzicker, Sochi 1965; but not 10 ... Rc8? when 11 Nb5 gives White a sizeable advantage.

11 Rf1-d1   a7-a6

To prevent a possible 12 Nb5

12 b2-b3

12 a3 would be a mistake since after 12 ... Bxc3 13 Bxc3 is made un-playable by 13 ... Be4 followed by a

knight fork on b3 which wins the exchange for Black.

12 ... e6-e5

13 a2-a3   Bb4xc3

14 Bd2xc3   Qd8-e7

PARMA   15.1

KARPOV TO MOVE

This position offers equal chances. White has possibilities of a blockade of the d5 square together with his two bishops and potential Q-side pawn majority. Black has some tactical chances on the half-open c-file, good control of the central squares (in particular e4), and the possibility of a K-side attack.

15 Nf3-e1

After 15 b4 Be4 16 Qb2 Na4 17 Qb3 Nxc3 18 Qxc3 Rac8 19 Rac1 Rfd8 the chances are even. The text move aims for control of d5 by Bf3 and a white-squared bishop exchange.

15 ... Ra8-c8

16 Ra1-c1   Nf6-e4?!

The obvious 16 ... d5 was sufficient to maintain the balance. This logical freeing move would not only remove White's hold over the d5 square but also prevent him from establishing a Q-side pawn majority.

17 b3-b4   Ne4xc3

18 Qc2xc3   Nc5-e6

18 ... Ne4 would only lose time as

White can easily drive away the knight.

19 Qc3-d3

This prevents the threatened 19 ... d5 (or 19 ... b5) and strengthens White's grip on d5.

19 ... Rf8-d8

20 Be2-f3   Bb7xf3

21 Ne1xf3

Now White has achieved part of his aims as set out in the note after move 14. Although he has lost his two bishops he has managed to seize control of d5 and keep his potential majority. On the other hand Black has lost his central control and most of his tactical chances on the K-side and on the c-file. But so far White's advantage is only small. Karpov builds this up into a winning position with the clear and logical steps so characteristic of his style.

21 ... g7-g6

22 Nf3-d2   Ne6-c7

The alternative 22 ... f5 (to prevent 23 Ne4) would weaken the a2-g8 diagonal and after 23 Nb1 Qc7 (to hinder Nb1-c3-d5) 24 Qd5 Kf7 either 25 Rc3 or 25 f4 would give White excellent chances.

23 Nd2-e4   Nc7-e8

23 ... d5? would be a disaster because of 24 cxd5 Rxd5 25 Qxd5! Nxd5 26 Rxc8+ Kg7 27 Rxd5 when White has amassed two rooks and a knight for his queen. 23 ... f5? 24 Nxd6 Ne8 25 Nxc8! would win the exchange for White.

24 Qd3-d5   Kg8-g7

Black can only defend passively—any attempt to force matters would lead to disaster.

25 h2-h3   Ne8-f6

26 Ne4xf6   Kg7xf6!

The point of Black's 24th move. After 26 ... Qxf6 27 Qb7 White wins a pawn. The removal of the knights must increase Black's defensive prospects since it is the exchange of an aggressive piece for a defensive one.

27 Qd5-e4

Hoping for 28 Qh4+ and at the same time making way for a rook to come to d5.

27 ... Kf6-g7

28 Rd1-d5 Qe7-c7

An attempt to break free by 28 ... b5 would be unsuccessful as, after 29 c5, Black would be under severe pressure e.g.

(a) 29 ... dxc5? 30 Rxe5 and White wins a pawn.

(b) 29 ... f6 30 R1d1 dxc5 31 Rxd8 Rxd8 32 Rxd8 Qxd8 33 Qb7+! Kh6 34 bxc5 with excellent winning chances for White.

(c) 29 ... f5 30 Qd3 dxc5 31 bxc5 Rxd5 ,32 Qxd5 Rd8 33 Qc6 and the c-pawn should be a winning factor.

29 f2-f4!

PARMA TO MOVE   15.2

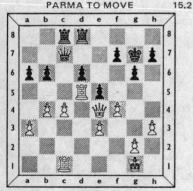

KARPOV

At last the Q-side majority begins to influence the game. After the exchange of his f-pawn for Black's d-pawn White can create a strong passed pawn which ultimately decides the issue.

Black would like to play 29 ... exf4 here but after the simple recapture 30 exf4 Black's game is highly uncomfortable. White threatens f4-f5-f6 and the dominating nature of his position makes this difficult to prevent. For example:

(a) 30 ... f5? 31 Qd4+ (or even 31 Qe6) Kf7 32 g4!

(b) 30 ... Re8? 31 Qd4+ and 32 Rxd6.

(c) 30 ... b5 31 c5 dxc5 32 Rxd8 Rxd8 33 bxc5 (This line is similar to the game continuation).

(d) 30 ... Rd7 31 f5 Re7 32 f6+! Kxf6 33 Qd4+ Ke6 34 c5!

In all these cases White's advantage is clear.

29 ... Rd8-e8

After 29 ... f6 30 fxe5 fxe5 31 c5! Black is in trouble. Thus:

(a) 31 ... bxc5 32 bxc5 dxc5 33 R1xc5! and White wins a pawn (33 ... Qxc5? 34 Qxe5+ or 33 ... Rxd5 34.Rxc7+)

(b) 31 ... bxc5 32 bxc5 Qe7 33 R1d1 Rxc5 34 Rxc5 dxc5 35 Rxd8 Qxd8 36 Qxe5+, followed by, 37 Qxc5 and again White wins a pawn.

30 f4xe5 d6xe5

31 c4-c5

White is now effectively a pawn ahead. The black K-side majority is useless, whilst the white c-pawn is the decisive factor. Suddenly White's strategy is complete and his advantage obvious.

31 ... Re8-e6

To blockade the c-pawn on c6.

32 Qe4-d3!

Preventing 32 ... Rc6 on account of 33 Rd7 Qb8 34 Rf1 with a winning K-side attack.

32 ... b6xc5

33 b4xc5

Not falling for 33 Rdxc5, Qd8! (but not 33 ... Rd8 34 Qxg6+ winning a pawn)

33 ... Qc7-c6

34 Rc1-b1 Qc6-c7

35 Rb1-f1 Rc8-f8

36 Kg1-h1 Qc7-c6

37 Rf1-b1 Qc6-c7

38 e3-e4 Rf8-b8

39 Rb1-f1 Rb8-b7

40 Qd3-c3   Rb7-b5

Black cannot free himself; so Karpov has played up to the time control at move 40. Now he begins again to strike home with his pawn.

41 a3-a4   Rb5-b8

42 Rf1-c1   Rb8-c8

43 Rc1-b1   Kg7-g8

44 Rb1-d1   Qc7-e7

45 Rd1-f1   Rc8-c7

46 a4-a5   Re6-c6

47 Rf1-c1   f7-f6

The alternative 47 . . . Re6 was no better. After 48 Rb1 Rec6 49 Rxe5 Qf6 (if 49 . . . Rxc5? then 50 Rxc5 Rxc5 51 Rb8+ wins) 50 Re8+ Kg7 51 e5 etc. and White will play 52 e6+ with decisive effect.

48 Qc3-d2

Keeping an eye on the a5 pawn and taking complete control of the d-file.

48 . . . Kg8-f7

48 . . . Rxc5? would lose to 49 R1xc5 Rxc5 50 Rd8+ followed by 51 Rd7, winning the queen.

49 Kh1-h2   Kf7-e8

Now, at last, Black is threatening to take the c-pawn.

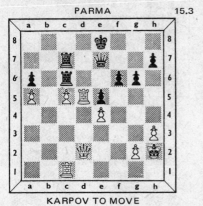

PARMA   15.3

KARPOV TO MOVE

50 Rd5-d6!

The point of 49 Kh2. Now 50 . . . Rxd6

is impossible (but with the white king on h1, 50 . . . Rxd6 51 cxd6 Rxc1 would be with check). The threat is 51 Qd5!

50 . . . Rc7-d7

51 Rc1-d1!   Rc6xd6

A neat point here is that 51 . . . Rdxd6 52 cxd6 Qd7 can be met by 53 Qd5! and if 53 . . . Kf8 then 54 Qxc6! Qxc6 55 d7 wins for White.

52 c5xd6   Qe7-e6

53 Qd2-d3

White wins the a6 pawn. The rest is a mopping-up operation with Black desperately seeking some K-side counterplay. After 53 . . . Ra7 54 Rb1 Qa2 (what else?) 54 Rb8+ Kd7 55 Qe3 wins the rook! or 54 . . . Kf7 55 Qc3 threatening 56 Qc6, 56 Qc7+!, or 56 Qc8.

53 . . . Qe6-a2

54 Qd3xa6   Qa2-c2

55 Qa6-a8+   Ke8-f7

If 55 . . . Rd8 56 Qd5! wins quickly.

56 Qa8-d5+   Kf7-g7

57 Rd1-d2   Qc2-c3

58 Rd2-a2   h7-h5

59 Ra2-d2!   h5-h4

60 Rd2-d1

Preventing a back-rank check by the black queen and thus removing any drawing chances.

60 . . . Qc3-c2

61 a5-a6   Qc2-a4

62 Qd5-d3   g6-g5

63 Rd1-b1   f6-f5

White could, of course, take this pawn but he prefers to finish the game more economically.

64 Rb1-b7   g5-g4

65 h3xg4   f5xg4

66 Qd3-e2   Black resigns

A beautiful example of a strong grandmaster being worn down and outplayed by an even stronger adversary.

Game 16

BLACK O'Kelly   Closed Ruy López, Breyer Variation
Caracas, 1970

Black sacrifices a pawn to obtain chances in the opening of this game. The position becomes unclear and Black certainly has some compensation for the sacrificed pawn but Karpov, playing move after move with great accuracy, forces a mistake from his opponent and swiftly pounces.

1 e2-e4   e7-e5

2 Ng1-f3   Nb8-c6

3 Bf1-b5   a7-a6

4 Bb5-a4   Ng8-f6

5 0-0   Bf8-e7

6 Rf1-e1   b7-b5

7 Ba4-b3   d7-d6

8 c2-c3   0-0

9 h2-h3   Nc6-b8

The Breyer Variation: very popular in grandmaster chess (see Games 44, 49, and 54). The idea is to transfer the queen's knight to d7, develop the queen's bishop on b7, and then support the e5 pawn by Re8 and Bf8. All these manœuvres are in preparation for an attack on the centre by c7-c5, or, more usually, by a tactical d6-d5.

10 d2-d4

Karpov chose 10 d3 against Spassky (Game 49) and against Gligorić at San Antonio (Game 44).

10 ... Nb8-d7

11 Nb1-d2   Bc8-b7

12 Bb3-c2   Rf8-e8

Gligorić here played 12 ... c5 against Karpov in the Leningrad Interzonal (Game 54).

13 Nd2-f1   Be7-f8

14 Nf1-g3   g7-g6

Both to transfer the bishop to g7 and to keep the white knight from f5.

15 a2-a4   Bf8-g7

Safer was 15 ... c5 e.g. 16 d5 c4 17 Be3 Qc7 18 Qe2 Nc5 with equal

chances. O'Kelly decides on a sharper line of play, involving the tactical break d6-d5.

16 Bc2-d3

Gipslis had played 16 d5! in this position against Stanciu at Lublin 1969. After 16 ... Qe7 17 b3! c6 18 c4 White had already achieved a substantial advantage.

16 ... d5?!

O'KELLY   16.1

KARPOV TO MOVE

After 17 exd5 (17 dxe5 is useless: after 17 ... Nxe4 18 Nxe4 dxe4 19 Bxe4 Bxe4 20 Rxe4 Nxe5 Black has the advantage.) 17 ... exd4 18 Rxe8+ (After 18 Nxd4 Rxe1+ 19 Qxe1 Nc5 20 Bf1 Qxd5 21 axb5 axb5 22 Rxa8+ Bxa8 23 Nxb5!? Nd3! the position is unclear.) Nxe8 19 Nxd4 Nc5 20 axb5 Bxd4! 21 cxd4 Nxd3 22 Qxd3 Qxd5 the game is level.

Karpov finds the only move to give
White any advantage.

17 Bc1-g5!   d5xe4

18 Bd3xe4   Bb7xe4

19 Ng3xe4   e5xd4

20 Nf3xd4

Black is now faced with the loss of
his b5 pawn. White also threatens
21 Nc6 Qc8 22 Nxf6+ Nxf6 23 Bxf6
Rxe1+ 24 Qxe1 Bxf6 25 Qe4 with a
spatial advantage and superior development; so Black plays a speculative pawn
sacrifice.

20 . . . c7-c5!?

21 Bg5xf6!   Nd7xf6

21 . . . Bxf6 would allow 22 Nc6 Qc7
23 Qxd7! winning at least a piece.

22 Ne4xc5   Re8xe1+

23 Qd1xe1   b5-b4!

It is important for Black to break up
White's solid Q-side pawn formation.

24 Ra1-c1

White could obtain a small advantage
here by 24 Rd1; if 24 . . . bxc3 25 Qxc3
But after 25 . .¹. a5! Black still has his
counterplay.
In his notes in *Informator 10*, Milić
shows that the aggressive try 25 . . .
Rc8 26 b4 Ne4 is doomed to failure
because of 27 Qe1! Nxc5 28 Nc6!
Qxd1 29 Ne7+ Kf8 30 Qxd1 Kxe7
31 bxc5 when White has a queen
against Black's rook and bishop. Note
that 28 . .¹. Nd3 here fails to 29 Ne7+
Kf8 30 Nxc8.

24 . . . b4xc3

25 b2xc3

After 25 Qxc3 Rc8 Black has many
tactical chances based on the pins on
the c-file and the a1-h8 diagonal.

25 . . . Qd8-d5!

The knight on c5 has no good square.
After 26 Nd3 Re8 27 Qd1 Ne4 Black
has plenty of counterplay.

26 Nd4-b3   Bg7-f8

27 Qe1-d1   Qd5xd1

28 Rc1xd1   Ra8-c8!

The exchange of queens has not
diminished the Black threats.

29 Nc5xa6   Rc8xc3

30 Rd1-b1   Bf8-d6!

Threatening 31 . . . Rc6 winning the
a6 knight.

31 Rb1-d1   Bd6-f8

32 Rd1-b1   Nf6-d7?

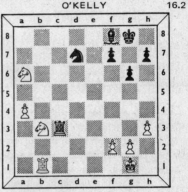

O'KELLY   16.2

KARPOV TO MOVE

This move, with the same idea as
Bd6—to trap the knight—is inadequate. After 32 . . . Bd6 33 Rd1
Black would be able to indicate the
move 33 . . . Bf8 and hence claim a
three-fold repetition of position.
It is difficult to see how Karpov
could have avoided this draw: e.g.

(a) 33 Na5 Ra3 and now 34 Nc4 Rxa4 or
34 Rb6? Ra1+ with mate to follow.

(b) 33 Na1? Rc6 34 Nb8 Rc8 35 Na6
Rc6 etc.

(c) 33 Nd4 Ra3 34 Nb5 Rxa4 winning
back the pawn.

(d) 33 Nd2 Ra3 34 Rb6 Ra1+ 35 Nf1
Ne4 36 f3 Bc5+ 37 Nxc5 Nxc5
regaining the pawn.

(e) 33 Nc1 Rc6 34 Nb8 (34 Nb4 Bxb4
wins a piece) Rc8 35 Na6 Rc6 etc.

33 a4-a5!   Rc3-c6

34 Rb1-d1

The point of 33 a5! Now 34 . . . Bd6

is met by 35 Nb4! Bxb4 36 Rxd7
Rc3 37 a6 Rxb3 38 a7 Ra3 39 Rd8+
Kg7 40 a8=Q Rxa8 41 Rxa8 with a
technically won ending for White.
Karpov makes the rest look simple.

34 ... Nd7-e5

35 Rd1-d5   Ne5-c4

36 Na6-b8   Rc6-c8

37 Nb8-d7   Bf8-e7

38 Nd7-b6   Rc8-c6

39 Nb6xc4   Rc6xc4

40 a5-a6   Rc4-a4

41 Rd5-a5   Black resigns

After 41 ... Rxa5 42 Nxa5 Bc5
43 Nc6 followed by 44 a7 leaves White a
piece to the good.

Game 17

WHITE Ivkov   Queen's Gambit Declined, Tartakover Defence
Caracas, 1970

This game was played in the eighth round of the seventeen-round tournament. The leading scores were Karpov 6, Kaválek 5½, Panno 5, Ivkov, Stein,
and Bisguier 4½, Parma, Barcza, Benko, and Addison 4. Karpov had already
played Bisguier, Barcza, Parma and Benko, and his next three games were
Black v. Ivkov, White v. Panno, and Black v. Kaválek.

In this game, he quickly gained the upper hand and so, when Ivkov
offered a draw, he declined. Ivkov then worked up a beautifully calculated
attack and beat Karpov. The result was not only a loss in this game but a
near loss against Panno (Karpov managed to save his position by accurate
passive defence), and another defeat at the hands of Kaválek. Even so he
managed to achieve the grandmaster norm.

1 Ng1-f3   Ng8-f6

2 c2-c4   e7-e6

3 Nb1-c3   d7-d5

4 d2-d4   Bf8-e7

5 Bc1-g5   0-0

6 e2-e3   h7-h6

The Tartakover Defence (in which
Black plays b6 to develop the queen's
bishop) is generally preceded by this
move, although 6 ... b6 is playable.

7 Bg5-h4   b7-b6

8 Bf1-d3

Also possible here is the exchange
8 cxd5 Nxd5 9 Bxe7 Qxe7 10 Nxd5
exd5 11 Rc1, or the passive 8 Be2
Bb7 9 Bxf6 Bxf6 10 cxd5 exd5
11 0-0.

8 ... Bc8-b7

9 0-0   c7-c5!

The quickest way to equalize. The
alternative is 9 ... N8d7 10 Rc1 c5
11 Qe2 Rc8 12 cxd5 Nxd5 13 Bxe7
Qxe7 14 Nxd5 Bxd5 15 Ba6 Rc7
with equal chances (Gligorić-Benko,
Hollywood 1963).

10 Qd1-e2

White can achieve nothing by the
simplifying exchanges 10 cxd5 Nxd5
11 Bxe7 Qxe7 12 Nxd5 exd5
13 dxc5 bxc5. The text move prepares
for occupation of the central files with
the rooks. By maintaining the tension
in the centre White keeps more chances
of achieving an advantage.

10 ... c5xd4

11 e3xd4

Although 11 Nxd4 is possible, it does not offer many dynamic chances. White is prepared to accept the isolating of his queen's pawn, a feature of the Queen's Gambit Declined.

11 ... Nb8-c6

Black could force the isolated pawn by 11 ... dxc4 12 Bxc4 Nc6. After the text move, White could equalize by 12 cxd5 Nxd5 13 Bxe7 Nxc3 14 bxc3 Qxe7, avoiding an isolated pawn. But nowadays most leading players prefer to play with the isolated pawn rather than against it. That is, theory suggests that with the isolated pawn set-up, as here, White has the better chances.

12 Ra1-d1?

A terrible mistake for such a player. He succumbs to a well-known type of combination which ought to have won the game.

12 ... Nc6-b4!

Now 13 cxd5 Nxd3 14 Qxd3 (or 14 Rxd3) Nxd5 would give Black an excellent position.

13 Bd3-b1   d5xc4

Winning a pawn, since if 14 Qxc4? Ba6, and Black wins the exchange.

14 Nf3-e5   Ra8-c8!

15 a2-a3

After 15 Nxc4 Ba6 16 b3 b5! Black wins a piece.

15 ... Nb4-d5

16 Bh4xf6

The pawn is still untouchable: 16 Nxc4 Ba6 17 Bd3 (17 b3? leaves the c3 knight en prise and 17 Nxd5 exd5 wins a piece) Nf4 followed by Nxd3 and Bxc4 wins at least a piece.

16 ... Be7xf6?   *(see Diagram 17.1)*

Karpov, most uncharacteristically, returns the compliment. Necessary to maintain an advantage was 16 ... Nxc3! so that 17 bxc3 Bxf6 18 Qc2 Re8 (if 18 ... g6 19 Nxg6 fxg6 20 Qxg6+ Bg7 21 Qh7+ Kf7 22 Qg6+ draws by perpetual check) 19 Qh7+

KARPOV   17.1

IVKOV TO MOVE

Kf8 and White has no further pieces with which to attack.

17 Qe2-c2   Rf8-e8

After 17 ... g6? 18 Nxg6 fxg6 19 Qxg6+ Bg7 20 Qh7+ Kf7 21 Bg6+ Kf6 22 Ne4+ and mates in two.

18 Qc2-h7+   Kg8-f8

19 Nc3-e4   Rc8-c7

In conjunction with his next move, this forms an excellent defensive plan for Black, and prevents White's immediate threat of 20 Nxf6 followed by:

(a) 20 ... gxf6? 21 Qxf7 mate.

(b) 20 ... Qxf6? 21 Nd7+.

(c) 20 ... Nxf6 21 Qh8+ Ng8 (or 21 ... Ke7 22 Qxg7) 22 Bh7 Ke7 23 Qxg7.

20 Rf1-e1!

Aiming for the manœuvre Ne4-g3-f5.

20 ... c4-c3!

A superb defence, as we shall see.

21 Ne4-g3

To take the c-pawn would remove White's aggressive e4 knight from its post. The threat now is 22 Nf5! and, meanwhile, Black's threat of 21 ... c2 is prevented.

21 ... Nd5-e7?!

A dubious move. Black could force matters with 21 ... g6: e.g.

(a) 22 Qxh6+ Bg7 23 Qh7 c2 wins a piece.

(b) 22 Ng4? Bg7 23 Nxh6? Nf6 wins the queen.

(c) 22 Bxg6 Bxe5 23 dxe5 fxg6 24 Qh8+ with perpetual check.

22 Qh7-h8+ Ne7-g8

23 Bb1-h7

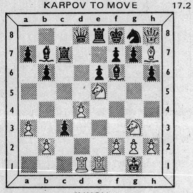

KARPOV TO MOVE   17.2

IVKOV

23 ... Bf6xe5?

This allows a brilliant finish by Ivkov. The last chance for Black was 23 ... Ke7! 24 Nf5+ exf5 25 Nc6+ Kd7 26 Nxd8 g6!! Now:

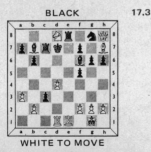

BLACK   17.3

WHITE TO MOVE

(a) 27 Rxe8? Bxh8 28 Rxg8 cxb2 and Black wins.

(b) 27 Qxg8! Rxg8 28 Bxg8 c2 29 Nxb7! (29 Rc1 Kxd8 30 Re2 Be4 and Black stands much better and has excellent winning chances) 29 ... cxd1=Q 30 Rxd1 Ke7 31 Bxf7! Kxf7 32 Nd6+

with a draw as the likely outcome.

24 Ng3-f5! e6xf5

25 Qh8xg8+ Kf8-e7

26 Re1xe5+ Ke7-f6

After 26 ... Kd7 27 Bxf5+ Kd6 28 Rxe8 the game would be over. Karpov tries for a last trick but Ivkov sees through it.

27 Re5xf5+!

The traps here are:

(a) 27 Qxe8 Qxe8 28 Rxe8 cxb2 29 Ree1 Be4 and Black stands better;

(b) 27 Rxe8 c2 28 Re6+ (28 Rf1 Qd5 or 28 Rc1 Qxd4 both win for Black) 28 ... Kxe6 (28 ... fxe6? 29 Qxd8+) 29 Re1+ Be4 (29 ... Kd7? 30 Bxf5+) 30 Qxd8 c1=Q 31 d5+ Ke5 32 f4+ Kd4! 33 Rxc1 Rxc1+ 34 Kf2 Rc2+ Now:

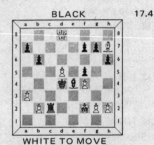

BLACK   17.4

WHITE TO MOVE

(b1) 35 Ke1 Ke3 36 Kd1 Rxb2! 37 Qc7 Rb1+ 38 Qc1 Rxc1+ 39 Kxc1 Bxd5 40 Bxf5 Bxg2 followed by 41 ... Kxf4 with three extra pawns in a bishop ending.

(b2) 35 Kf1 Ke3 36 Qh4 Rc1+ 37 Qe1+ Rxe1+ 38 Kxe1 Bxd5 39 Bxf5 Bxg2 with two extra pawns in a similar ending.

(b3) 35 Kg3 Rxg2+ 36 Kh4 (36 Kh3 Rg4! [threatening 37 ... Bg2 mate] 37 Bxf5 Bxf5 when Black will draw at least) 36 ... Rg4+ 37 Kh5 (37 Kh3 Bg2 mate) Rxf4! 38 Bxf5 (the only way to stop 38 ... Bf3 mate) 38 ... Bxf5 and 39 ... Bg6 mate is inevitable.

27 ... Kf6-e6

28 Rd1-e1+ Ke6-d7

29 Re1xe8
Now 29 ... Qxe8 is met by 30 Rxf7+ winning at least a rook. Thus:

(a) 30 ... Kd8 31 Qxe8+ Kxe8 32 Rxc7.

(b) 30 ... Qxf7 31 Qxf7+ Kd6 32 Qg6+ and 33 bxc3.

... Black resigns

Game 18

WHITE Stein   Closed Ruy López, Breyer Variation
38th USSR Championship, Riga 1970

We have already seen Karpov play White against the Breyer but now we see him play it as Black. He certainly plays resourcefully, and at times brilliantly, to achieve a creditable draw with his opponent. Although this was not to be another first for Karpov, he played some excellent chess and could well have finished higher than the 4th-6th place he reached.

1 e2-e4 e7-e5

2 Ng1-f3 Nb8-c6

3 Bf1-b5 a7-a6

4 Bb5-a4 Ng8-f6

5 0-0 Bf8-e7

6 Rf1-e1 b7-b5

7 Ba4-b3 d7-d6

8 c2-c3 0-0

9 h2-h3 Nc6-b8
The Breyer Variation

10 d2-d3
This move is almost as popular as the alternative 10 d4.

10 ... c7-c5
An interesting move. Karpov prefers not to follow the theoretical lines of 10 ... Nbd7 11 Nbd2 Bb7 12 Nf1 Nc5 13 Bc2 Re8 etc. The idea of 10 ... c5 is to bring the queen's knight back into play at c6 instead of d7.

11 Nb1-d2
After 11 a4 Bb7 12 axb5 axb5 13 Rxa8 Bxa8 14 Na3 Qb6 15 Ba2 Bc6 16 Nc2 Qa7 17 Bb1 Re8 18 Ne3 Bf8 19 Nf5 Nbd7 20 Nh2 d5 the game is equal (Keres-Scholl, IBM 1971).

11 ... h7-h6
In order to regroup by Re8 and Bf8 without allowing a possible Ng5 by White.

12 Nd2-f1 Nb8-c6

13 Nf1-g3
Also possible here is 13 d4 Re8 14 Ng3 Bf8 with equal chances. But 13 ... Bd7 (after 13 d4) is doubtful. In Tal-Tukmakov, Moscow 1971, Tal obtained an advantage after 14 dxc5 dxc5 15 Ne3 c4 16 Bc2 Be6 17 Qe2 Qc7 18 g4 Bc5 19 g5 hxg5 20 Nxg5 Rad8 21 Kh1 Bxe3 22 Qxe3 Bc8 23 b3 cxb3 24 Bxb3 Na5 25 Bd1 Nc4 26 Qg3.

13 ... Rf8-e8

14 a2-a4 Bc8-d7
Karpov must have thought hard about which diagonal was best for the queen's bishop. He decides on the c8-h3 diagonal in order to keep an eye on the f5 square. On b7 the bishop would help with a d6-d5 break and afterwards would give Black more threats against the white pawn on e4.

15 Bc1-e3
Stein is still preparing for his d3-d4.

15 ... Be7-f8

So that 16 d4 exd4 17 cxd4 Nxe4 wins a pawn for Black. Karpov has managed to develop and regroup his pieces on to their optimum squares and can now seek an advantage by the central push d6-d5.

16 Nf3-d2

The only logical way to bolster e4 for the coming d3-d4. The alternative move 16 Bc2 would allow 16 ...d5! with advantage to Black.

16 ...Nc6-a5

17 Bb3-c2

After 17 Ba2 bxa4 White will have great difficulty in ever regaining his pawn.

17 ...d6-d5!

KARPOV   18.1

STEIN TO MOVE

Black now holds a small advantage. He has achieved all his aims from this opening: he has the freer game, better co-ordinated development, and an obvious spatial advantage. On the other hand White's position is solid and free from any weakness, and he is now able to strike back immediately in the centre.

18 d3-d4

This move does not merit an ex-clamation mark as it is the only logical way to prevent Black's threat of 18 ...d4 winning a piece.

18 ...c5xd4

19 c3xd4   e5xd4

20 Be3xd4   Na5-c6!

After 20 ...Nxe4 21 N2xe4 dxe4 22 Bxe4 White's bishops dominate the board. So Karpov sacrifices a pawn for the bishop pair in an open position.

21 Bd4xf6   Qd8xf6

22 a4xb5

To 22 exd5 Black would simply reply 22 ...Rxe1+ 23 Qxe1 Nb4 threaten-ing the bishop, d-pawn, and b-pawn, and hence would regain the pawn with the better game.

22 ...Nc6-b4

The point of his 20th move. The recapture 22 ...axb5 would allow 23 Rxa8 Rxa8 24 exd5 when Black has not enough for the pawn.

23 b5xa6   Ra8xa6

After 23 ...Qxb2 24 Bb3 White will retain his extra pawn with comfort:

(a) 24 ...dxe4 25 Bxf7+! Kxf7 26 Nc4 regaining the piece.

(b) 24 ...Be6 25 exd5 Bxd5 26 Rxe8 Rxe8 27 Bxd5 Nxd5 28 a7 etc.

(c) 24 ...Be6 25 exd5 Nxd5 26 Nc4 Qf6 27 Ne4 etc.

(d) 24 ...d4 25 Nc4 Qc3 26 Ne2 Qd3 27 Nb6 Rad8 28 Nxd7 Rxd7 29 Ba4 winning the exchange.

24 Ra1xa6   Qf6xa6

KARPOV   18.2

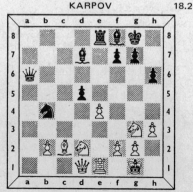

STEIN TO MOVE

Black has considerable compensation for the pawn. The d-pawn is a threatening weapon and cannot be removed (25 exd5 Rxe1+ 26 Qxe1 Nxc2). The immediate threat to the white bishop can easily be met but the menaces of Black's two bishops, passed pawn, and his general spatial advantage, force Stein to an ingenious and somewhat desperate defence.

25 Bc2-b1   d5-d4

26 Ng3-e2!

The start of an equalizing plan.

26 ...d4-d3

27 Ne2-f4   Bf8-d6

White appears to be in trouble, but he now reveals the point of his 26th move

28 Nf4xd3!

This leads, by a forced series of moves, to a drawn ending.

28 ...Nb4xd3

29 Bb1xd3   Qa6xd3

30 Nd2-f3   Bd7-b5

30 ... Qxd1 31 Rxd1 Re6 32 e5 would leave White with some winning chances.

31 Qd1xd3   Bb5xd3

32 Re1-d1   Bd3xe4?!

Better here was 32 ... Rd8 33 Rxd3 Bh2+ 34 Kxh2 Rxd3 when Black will win the b-pawn by force, but the resulting ending should still be a draw. After the text move a drawn rook-and-pawn ending is reached.

33 Rd1xd6   Be4xf3

34 g2xf3   Re8-b8

35 Rd6-d2   Kg8-h7

36 Kg1-g2   Kh7-g6

37 Kg2-g3   Kg6-f5

38 h3-h4   g7-g6

Draw agreed

Game 19

BLACK Bagirov   Alekhine's Defence, Modern Variation
38th USSR Championship, Riga 1970

The passed pawn in Karpov's hands is a deadly weapon. Black allows a harmless looking two-to-one Q-side majority and is then remorselessly crushed by it. Karpov plays the whole game with characteristic simplicity and ease.

1 e2-e4   Ng8-f6

2 e4-e5   Nf6-d5

3 d2-d4   d7-d6

4 Ng1-f3

The Four Pawns Attack 4 c4 Nb6 5 f4 is rather in the melting pot at the present time. The continuation 5 ...dxe5 6 fxe5 Bf5 7 Be3 e6 8 Nc3 Bb4 is double-edged, and theoretical improvements are often developed for both sides. The text move is the Modern Variation.

4 ...Bc8-g4

The alternative 4 ... g6 is equally popular. The move played is aimed at the classical development of the king's bishop on e7 and the knights on b6 and c6.

5 Bf1-e2   e7-e6

6 0-0   Bf8-e7

The move 6 ... Nc6 can lead to sharp play after 7 c4 Nb6 8 exd6 cxd6 9 d5 exd5 10 cxd5 Bxf3 11 gxf3! Ne5 12 Bb5+ N5d7 13 Qd4 Qf6 14 Re1+ with a clear advantage to

White. White can also choose to return to a continuation similar to the game by 9 b3 or 9 Nc3.

7 c2-c4   Nd5-b6

8 e5xd6   c7xd6

9 Nb1-c3

White may also try 9 b3 here. The point of this move is not necessarily to develop the queen's bishop on b2 but to meet a Black d6-d5 by c4-c5 without allowing the knight to come to the c4 square.

9 . . . 0-0

10 Bc1-e3   d6-d5

Black is afraid that 10 . . . Nc6 will be met by 11 d5 Bxf3 12 Bxf3 Ne5 13 dxe6 fxe6 14 Bg4! Bagirov played this line as Black and chose 14 . . . N5xc4 against Bichowski (USSR 1967) and 14 . . . Rf6 against Matanović (Beverwijk 1965), but in both cases he found himself with an inferior position.

11 c4-c5   Bg4xf3

12 Be2xf3   Nb6-c4

13 Be3-c1

This move is considered to be inferior to 13 Bf4 because of the game Corden-Timman, Hastings 1969-70, which continued 13 . . . b6 14 b3 Na5 15 b4? Nc4 16 Be2 bxc5 17 bxc5 Qa5 18 Bd2 Nxd2 19 Qxd2 Nc6 20 Rab1 Bf6 and White was already losing. Better was 15 cxb6 or 15 Na4, but in any event 13 . . . b6 is superior to the move chosen by Bagirov.

13 . . . Nb8-c6

14 b2-b3   Nc4-a5

15 Bc1-e3   *(see Diagram 19.1)*

The opening phase of the game is over. Black's strategy will be to try and attack the white pawns on d4 and c5 by Bf6 and b6. White meanwhile will be trying to advance his Q-side pawns without allowing the knight on a5 back to c4.

15 . . . b7-b6

16 Nc3-a4!   Ra8-b8

BAGIROV TO MOVE   19.1

KARPOV

To escape a pin on the h1-a8 diagonal. The exchanges 16 . . . bxc5 17 Nxc5 Bxc5? 18 dxc5 d4 19 Bd2 would be to White's advantage, because of his two bishops and Q-side majority.

17 Ra1-c1

White can now contemplate opening the c-file with 18 cxb6.

17 . . . b6xc5

After 17 . . . b5 18 Nb2 (or 18 Nc3) Black would have lost all his Q-side counterplay and would have to play very carefully to prevent White's winning with a direct attack on the Q-side.

18 Na4xc5   Be7-f6

White has weathered the Q-side break easily and now begins his majority advance.

19 a2-a3   Nc6-e7

Aiming for f5.

20 Bf3-e2

Preparing 21 b4 without allowing 21 . . . Nc4.

20 . . . Ne7-f5

21 b3-b4   Na5-b7

21 . . . Nc6 would lose a pawn to 22 Nxe6!

22 Be3-f4   Nb7-d6

23 Bf4-e5   Bf6xe5

A difficult decision for Black. This move removes White's weak pawn but establishes a supported passed pawn for Black.

24 d4xe5   Nd6-b7

25 Nc5-b3!
This piece will be useful for holding the Q-side until an advance can be arranged, and so it is removed from the range of the Black knights.

25 ... Qd8-b6

26 Be2-d3   Nf5-e7

27 Qd1-g4!
Threatening 28 Bxh7+ Kxh7 29 Qh4+ Kg8 30 Qxe7 winning a pawn.

27 ... f7-f5

28 Qg4-d4

31 Qd4-a1!   Qb6-b7
Going to g7 to put further pressure on e5.

32 Rf1-e1   Qb7-g7

33 Nb3-c5
Preventing 33 ... Nf7.

33 ... Rf8-f7

34 a4-a5   Rf7-e7
Note that the rook must come to e7 before the knight can come to f7. If Black had tried 33 ... Re8 and 34 ... Nf7 then 35 Nd7 would win the exchange owing to the threats of 36 Nxb8 and 36 Nf6+.

35 Nc5-a6   Rb8-a8
If 35 ... Rbb7 36 Rc8 is difficult to meet.

36 Bd3-f1!   Nd8-f7
Exactly the move Karpov was hoping for. By removing his bishop from possible attack by a knight on e5 he is now able to finish the game with characteristic economy.

37 Na6-c7   Ra8-d8
If 37 ... Rc8? 38 Nxd5! wins at least the exchange (38 ... Rxc1 39 Nxe7+).

38 Rc1-c6   Ng6-f8
On 38 ... N6xe5 (or 38 ... N7xe5) 39 Nxe6 wins the exchange. This is the point of 36 Bf1!

BAGIROV TO MOVE   19.2

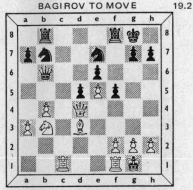

KARPOV

The secondary idea behind White's 27th move. With undisputed control of d4 White has now completed his preparations for a further advance. He has also prevented the break a7-a5 which Black might otherwise have tried.

28 ... Nb7-d8
Heading for f7.

29 b4-b5   g7-g5
And this move is to take away the natural support of the e5 pawn by f2-f4.

30 a3-a4   Ne7-g6
At last Black has a threat. Karpov simply removes his queen to support the advance.

BAGIROV   19.3

KARPOV TO PLAY

The pawn majority now has its say.
Black's attack on e5 has been refuted
and the game cannot go on much
longer.

39 b5-b6   a7xb6

40 a5-a6!

Much quicker than 40 axb6, although
this would win also.

40 ... Nf7-h6

41 Re1-c1   Nh6-g4

42 a6-a7   Ng4xe5

At last! But it is much too late.

43 Rc6-c2   Ne5-c4

44 a7-a8=Q   Rd8xa8

45 Nc7xa8   b6-b5

46 Rc2-a2   Re7-b7

This last move was sealed, but,
realizing that he had only three pawns
for a rook,

... Black resigned

The simplicity and logic of Karpov's
play make this game a superb example of
the power of a Q-side majority advance.

Game 20

BLACK Igor Zaitsev   Closed Ruy López
38th USSR Championship, Riga 1970

Once again Karpov establishes a Q-side majority from the opening, and
spends the rest of the game converting it into a winning advantage. The
opening is slightly unusual, although it is frequently played by Igor Zaitsev.

1 e2-e4   e7-e5

2 Ng1-f3   Nb8-c6

3 Bf1-b5   a7-a6

4 Bb5-a4   Ng8-f6

5 0-0   Bf8-e7

6 Rf1-e1   b7-b5

7 Ba4-b3   d7-d6

8 c2-c3   0-0

9 h2-h3   Qd8-d7

The idea of this move is to free the
d8 for the bishop and to enable
(after Bb7) the queen's rook to come
to e8.

10 d2-d4   Bc8-b7

Also possible here is 10 ... Re8 and
then:

(a) 11 Bg5 h6 12 Bh4 Bb7 13 Nbd2 g5!?
14 Bg3 Bf8 15 dxe5 dxe5 16 Qe2
Bc5 17 Rad1 Qe7 gives an equal game
(Smit-I. Zaitsev, USSR 1969)

(b) 11 Nbd2 Bf8 and now:

(b1) 12 Nf1 exd4 13 Nxd4 Bb7

14 f3 g6 15 Bg5 Bg7 16 Nxc6 Qxc6
with equality (Uitumen-I. Zaitsev,
Moscow 1970)

(b2) 12 Bc2 Bb7 13 d5 Ne7 14 c4 c6
15 b3 g6 16 Nf1 Bg7 17 Ne3 cxd5
18 cxd5 Nh5 with a level game
(Neikirch-I. Zaitsev, Riga 1968)

(b3) 12 d5! Ne7 13 Nf1 g6 14 c4
Bg7 15 c5 Nh5 16 a4 dxc5 17 axb5
Bb7 18 bxa6 Bxa6 19 Be3 with
advantage to White (Fischer-Wade,
Buenos Aires 1960)

11 Nb1-d2   Ra8-e8?!

This leaves Black weak on the Q-side,
and Zaitsev is planning 12 ... Bd8
which weakens him even further, since
it cuts off the black rooks. Preferable
here was 11 ... Rfe8 with 12 ... Bf8
in mind.

12 Nd2-f1   Be7-d8

13 Nf1-g3   h7-h6

14 Bb3-c2   Kg8-h8

15 b2-b3   Nf6-g8

IGOR ZAITSEV   20.1

KARPOV TO MOVE

Black's last three or four moves are based on the idea of a K-side attack. He intends to play the knight f6-g8-e7-g6 and thus not only bolster his e5 pawn but also prepare to put the knight on f4. This plan would be good if his Q-side pawns were not advanced but, since they are, the whole concept is dubious. With black pawns on, say, a7 and b6 White would have no immediate Q-side attack and so Black would be able to achieve his manœuvres without threats on the queen's wing. As it is, Karpov closes the centre and then exploits the lack of black pieces on the Q-side by a quick attack.

16 d4-d5!   Nc6-e7

17 c3-c4   c7-c6
Black is obliged to allow some opening up of the Q-side. 17 ... bxc4 18 bxc4 would give White uncontested use of the open b-file and 17 ... b4 18 c5! is unpleasant for Black.

18 d5xc6   Qd7xc6

19 c4xb5   a6xb5

20 b3-b4
So the result of White's Q-side attack is the creation of a two-to-one pawn majority. White's advantage here is clear: as well as the majority, he has weak black pawns to attack on b5

and d6, and a more harmonious development. Zaitsev plays cleverly to rid himself of the d6 weakness.

20 ... Bd8-b6

21 Bc2-d3   d6-d5!

22 Bc1-b2
The capture 22 Nxe5? would lead to disaster after 22 ... Qf6!, winning at least the exchange.

22 ... Ne7-g6

23 e4xd5
23 Qe2 is met by 23 ... Nf4.

23 ... Qc6xd5

24 Bd3-e4!
The tempting 24 Bxg6 is not so good. After 24 ... Qxd1 25 Raxd1 fxg6! 26 Nxe5 Rxf2! White is lost. Thus
(a) 27 Bd4 Rxg2+ 28 Kf1 Rf8+
(b) 27 Nxg6+ Kh7 28 Rxe8 Rxb2+ (the simplest way to win) 29 Kh1 (29 Kh2 Rxg2+ or 29 Kf1 Bxg2+ 30 Ke1 Bf2 mate) 29 ... Bxg2+ 30 Kh2 Be4+ etc.

24 ... Qd5xd1

25 Ra1xd1   Bb7xe4

26 Ng3xe4   Re8-a8

27 a2-a3

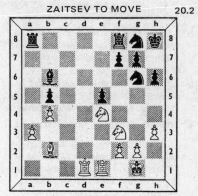

ZAITSEV TO MOVE   20.2

KARPOV

Black must now lose the b5 pawn. He cannot possibly move enough pieces to the Q-side in time to defend it. The white pieces are well co-ordinated for this ending, whereas Black's knights are still preparing for a K-side attack! Zaitsev, always a resourceful player, manages to force the win of the White a-pawn but this is not enough.

27 ... f7-f5

28 Ne4-d6   e5-e4

29 Nf3-d4   Bb6xd4

30 Rd1xd4   Ng6-f4

31 Nd6xb5   Nf4-d3

32 Re1-b1   Rf8-b8

33 Nb5-d6

33 Nc7? Ra7 would lead White nowhere.

33 ... Nd3xb2

34 Rb1xb2   Ra8xa3

35 Nd6xf5   Ng8-f6

36 b4-b5   Ra3-a1+

37 Kg1-h2   Ra1-a5

38 Nf5-d6   Rb8-b6

39 Rb2-c2!

Removing the blockader by Rc6.

39 ... Ra5-a8

40 Rc2-c6   Ra8-b8

41 Rd4-c4   Rb6xb5

If 41 ... Kg8 42 Rxb6 Rxb6 43 Rc6 and now:

(a) 43 ... Rxc6 44 bxc6 Nd5 (forced to prevent c7) 45 Nxe4 gives White a knight-and-pawn ending two pawns ahead.

(b) 43 ... Rb8 44 b6 Kf8 45 b7 Ke7 46 Rc8 Nd7 47 Rxb8 Nxb8 48 Nxe4 and again White wins a second pawn.

42 Nd6xb5   Rb8xb5 *(see Diagram 20.3)*

This ending is impossible for Black to defend. With a pawn on f7 instead of e4 Black could prolong the game considerably, but the pawn structure in the game ties the black knight to f6. First the white rooks tie the black pieces to defence, and then if necessary the white king can advance. Any exchange of rooks will instantly spell tragedy for Black, since White can then win by playing his king to

ZAITSEV   20.3

KARPOV TO MOVE

e3 or f4 and capturing the black knight with his rook, ensuring a won king-and-pawn ending: e.g. 43 R6c5 Rxc5? 44 Rxc5 Kh7 45 Kg3 Kg6 46 Kf4 Kf7 (what else?) 47 Rc6 Kg6 48 Rxf6+ Kxf6 49 Kxe4.

43 Rc4-c2

To prevent 43 ... Rb2.

43 ... Kg8-h7

44 Rc6-c7   Rb5-d5

45 Rc7-e7   Rd5-g5

46 Rc2-a2   Nf6-d5

Hoping for 47 Rxe4?? Nc3 with a drawn rook-and-pawn ending.

47 Re7-e8   Nd5-f6

48 Re8-b8

If Black plays passively the end will be achieved thus: 48 ... Kg6 49 Ra6 Kh7 50 Rb7 and now

(a) 50 ... Kg6 51 Re7 Kf5 (the threat was Rxe4) 52 Ra5+ followed by Rxg5.

(b) 50 ... Rg6 51 Kg1 Kg8 52 Re7! (threat Rxe4) 52 ... Kh7 53 g3 h5 54 h4 Kh6 55 Re5 and now 55 ... Rg4 56 Kf1 or 55 ... Kh7 56 Rg5.

(c) 50 ... Rf5 51 Kg1 h5 (51 ... Kg6 52 R6a7) 52 Re7 Kg8 53 Ra8+ Kh7 54 Rf8 Kg6 55 R8f7.

So Black decides to advance his K-side pawns, which unfortunately allows a pretty mating attack.

48 ...h6-h5

49 g2-g3   Rg5-f5

50 Kh2-g2   g7-g5

51 Rb8-b6

The threat now is 52 Ra7+ Kg6
(or 52 ...Kh8 53 Rb8+ Ng8
54 R7a8 winning the knight) 53 Re7
forcing the win of the e4 pawn.

51 ...g5-g4

52 h3-h4   Kh7-g6

53 Ra2-a7

Threat 53 Re7.

53 ...Rf5-f3

54 Ra7-e7   Kg6-f5

55 Rb6-b5+   Kf5-g6

56 Rb5-g5+   Black resigns

For 56 ...Kh6 is met by 57 Reg7!
and R5g6 mate.

5 1971 — Superb results

Karpov's first task in 1971 was to qualify for the 39th USSR Championship to be held later in the year. The semi-final tournament was played in May and June in Daugavpils. The final scores were Karpov 13/17, Vaganian 12, Djindjinhashvili and Karasev 11½, Alburt 9½, etc. Karpov's trainer Furman could score only 8½ and so was eliminated from the championship for that year. The game with Klovan (Game 21) is a classical example of the Ruy López Exchange Variation, although this opening is a rarity in Karpov's repertoire.

Following this success, Karpov joined the USSR team for the Student Olympiad in Mayaguez, Puerto Rico. He played behind Tukmakov and Balashov, with Podgaets, Kuzmin, and Razuvaev making up the rest of the team. As might have been expected Karpov was in a class of his own on the third board. He played quickly and confidently, beating opponents one after another, and it must have been slightly disappointing for him to have to concede a draw to a Colombian in the last round and so spoil a one hundred per cent record. His final score of 7½/8 was enough to give the Soviet team a comfortable victory. Games 22 and 23 show him in play against the USA and Canada.

Back in the USSR there next came two annual team championships. In the Soviet Team Championships at Rostov-on-Don in August Karpov scored 6½/7 to help his team, the Armed Forces, to second place. This result was on the junior board, but in the Army Team Championships in Leningrad later in the month Karpov played on first board for the Leningrad Army team. His score of 4/7 included a loss to Klovan (also a Ruy López, Exchange Variation) but this was counterbalanced by two fine wins over Dementiev (revenge for the loss in the previous USSR Championship) and Tukmakov. The game with Tukmakov (Game 24) is attractive because of the unusual nature of the winning manœuvre—a white Q-side attack in an open Sicilian.

The year's work was by no means over yet. September saw the beginning of the 39th USSR Championship in Leningrad. A bright start with a win against Taimanov (Game 25) in round one was marred by a loss to his old rival Vaganian in round two. In the next five rounds Karpov played four relatively short draws and beat Grigorian, before coming to life in an exciting win against Stein in round eight. Again the passed pawn proved to be the undoing of a strong grandmaster (Game 26). As with the win in round one, this was immediately followed by a loss, to Smyslov, in the next round. A series of draws came next, and then Karpov found a new lease of life in the long tournament. He won three of his next four games including a sharp little gem against Zeitlin (Game 27) and needed to beat Polugaevsky in the last round to tie for second place. It was not to be, and he had to be content with fourth place behind Savon, Smyslov, and Tal. His last round try against Polugaevsky is Game 28.

In November 1971 the Alekhine Memorial Tournament was held in Moscow. The competitors included four former world champions—Smyslov, Petrosian, Spassky, and Tal—and fourteen other grandmasters! This was the strongest chess tournament for many decades, rivalled in living memory only by the AVRO tournament of 1938.

After ten of the seventeen rounds Karpov had scored only one win, but he had drawn his other nine games. Most of these draws resulted from his playing a more solid game than usual and taking fewer risks, but an exception was the 103-move epic against Tal in round nine. From here onwards, Karpov's game began to take off. In round 11, Hort was on the receiving end of a precision attack and was forced to surrender (Game 29). Round 13 saw Bronstein caught in one of Karpov's favourite variations—6Be2 against the Najdorf Variation of the Sicilian. A nearly disastrous mistake by Karpov in the ending brought Bronstein to the brink of safety, but Karpov managed to hang on to his winning position (Game 30). In the next round it was Korchnoi's turn (Game 31). In the last round Karpov was matched with Savon. He was still half a point behind the leader Stein and so needed a win to have a reasonable chance of first place. This he achieved convincingly (Game 32). He then had to watch as the Tukmakov-Stein game progressed. For most of the game Tukmakov was one or two pawns ahead, but had the more exposed king position. After a tactical mêlée and a series of exchanges the deficit was reduced to one pawn, when the exposed nature of the white king forced Tukmakov to concede a draw. Thus Karpov had to be content with a shared first place—but even so this was the greatest achievement of his career so far.

Game 21

BLACK Klovan   Ruy López, Exchange Variation
39th USSR Championship (semi-finals), Daugavpils 1971

Karpov rarely plays the Exchange Variation, although he played it twice against Klovan in 1971. In this, the first game, Karpov won a classical knight-v.-bishop ending, but the second was a bishop-v.-knight win for Klovan! Since then Karpov has steered clear of the Exchange Variation.

1 e2-e4	e7-e5	3 Bf1-b5	a7-a6
2 Ng1-f3	Nb8-c6	4 Bb5xc6	d7xc6

5 0-0

The other options here are 5 Nc3 and 5 d4 but the text move, reintroduced into master chess by Fischer, is by far the most effective continuation.

5 ... f7-f6

Whilst this is the most popular move here there are many other possibilities:

(a) 5 ... Qf6 6 d4 exd4 7 Bg5 Qg6 8 Qxd4 Bd6 9 Nbd2 Be6 10 Re1 Ne7 11 Nc4 Rd8 12 Nxd6+ cxd6 13 e5! (Gipslis).

(b) 5 ... Qd6 6 d4 exd4 7 Nxd4 Bd7 8 Be3 Qg6 9 Nd2 0-0-0 10 Qe2 h5 11 f3 h4 12 Nc4 Qh5 13 Rfd1 with advantage to White (Gipslis).

(c) 5 ... Ne7 6 Nxe5 Qd4 7 Qh5 g6 8 Qg5 Bg7 9 Nf3! Qxe4 10 Re1 Qb4 11 b3! h6 12 Qg3!

(d) 5 ... Bd6 6 d4 exd4 7 Qxd4 f6 8 e5! fxe5 9 Nxe5 Qe7 10 Re1 Be6 11 Nf3 0-0-0 12 Bg5 Nf6 13 Bxf6 gxf6 with a small advantage to White (Strain-Roring corresp. 1972).

(e) 5 ... Bg4 6 h3 h5 7 d3! Qf6 8 Nbd2 Ne7 9 Re1 Ng6 10 d4 Bd6 11 hxg4! hxg4 12 Nh2 Rxh2! 13 Qxg4! Qh4 14 Qxh4 Rxh4 15 Nf3 Rh5 16 dxe5 Nxe5 17 Nxe5 Bxe5 18 c3 with a small endgame advantage (Barendregt-Zuidema 1965).

6 d2-d4   e5xd4

After 6 ... Bg4 White has the alternative plans

(a) 7 dxe5 when 7 ... Qxd1 8 Rxd1 fxe5 9 Rd3 Bxf3 10 Rxf3 Nf6 11 Nc3 Bb4 12 Bg5 Bxc3 13 bxc3 Rf8! 14 Bxf6 Rxf6 15 Rxf6 gxf6 gives an equal rook-and-pawn ending (Fischer-Smyslov, Monte Carlo 1967). or

(b) 7c3 Bd6 8 Be3 Qe7 9 Nbd2 0-0-0 10 Qc2 exd4 11 cxd4 Re8 12 e5 Bb4 13 h3 Be6 14 Ne4 Qf7 15 a3 Bb3 with equality (Smyslov-Geller 41st USSR Championship 1973).

7 Nf3xd4   Ng8-e7

The ending after 7 ...c5 8 Nb3 Qxd1 9 Rxd1 favours White. The continu-

ation 7 ... Bd6 8 Qh5+ g6 9 Qf3! Bxh2+ 10 Kxh2 Qxd4 11 Rd1 Qc4 12 Bf4 Qf7 13 Qb3! Qxb3 14 axb3 gave White a clear plus (Hecht-Gligorić, Teesside 1972).

8 Bc1-e3   Ne7-g6

9 Nb1-d2

In their game in the Army Team Championships later in the year Karpov played 9 Qh5. After 9 ... Bd6 10 Nf5 0-0 11 f4 Qe8 12 Nd2 Ne7?! Karpov played 13 Nxe7+? after which the position was no better than equal for him. Better would have been 13 Qxe8 Rxe8 14 Nxd6 cxd6 15 Nc4 with advantage to White.

9 ...Bf8-d6

10 c2-c3

More active is 10 Nc4. After 10 ...0-0 11 Qd3 Ne5 12 Nxe5 Bxe5 13 f4 Bd6 14 f5 Qe7 15 Bf4 Bxf4 16 Rxf4 Bd7 17 Re1 White has a substantial advantage: Fischer went on to win brilliantly against Unzicker at Siegen in 1970.

10 ...0-0

11 Qd1-b3+   Kg8-h8

12 Nd4-f5!

KLOVAN TO MOVE   21.1

KARPOV

The knight on f5 puts Black in a dilemma. He must either capture it or try to develop round it. Klovan elects to capture, but Gligorić in his

game with Mecking at Hastings 1971-2
chose 12 ... Ne5 13 Nxd6 cxd6
14 f4 Nf7 and went on to draw.

12 ... Bc8xf5

13 e4xf5   Ng6-h4
Gligorić recommends 13 ... Ne7
intending 14 ... Nd5. The capture
14 Qxb7 would then lead to a complex
situation with chances for both sides.

14 Qb3xb7   Qd8-d7
After 14 ... Rb8 15 Qxc6 Black has
insufficient counterplay for the
sacrificed pawn. His threat now is
15 ... Rfb8 winning the queen.

15 Qb7-b3   Nh4xf5

16 Nd2-c4
The knight is a tower of strength on
this square. It protects the e3 bishop
and the b2 pawn, and cannot be driven
away, since Black has no pawn with
which to attack it. The black bishop,
on the other hand, is a poor piece with
little scope. This minor-piece advantage
together with Black's weak, isolated
Q-side pawns, forms the basis of a
winning endgame for White. Karpov
concentrates on reducing the number
of major pieces on the board, and then
exploits his advantage in a simple
ending. Although it would be incorrect to say that Black is already
lost, his long-term prospects are poor,
and they never get any better.

16 ... Rf8-e8

17 Ra1-d1   Ra8-b8

18 Qb3-c2   Qd7-e6

19 b2-b3   Nf5xe3

20 Nc4xe3
So now the first part of Karpov's
plan has been achieved—the exchange
of black knight for white bishop. This
was not a mistake on Klovan's part,
since the bishop was at last threatening to escape from the knight's range
by 20 Bc1.

20 ... Rb8-b5

21 Rf1-e1   Rb5-e5

22 g2-g3!

So that 22 ... Bc5 could be answered
by 23 Ng2!

22 ... Kh8-g8

23 Ne3-g2!   Re5-e2

24 Re1xe2   Qe6xe2

25 Rd1-d2   Qe2-f3

26 Kg1-f1   Re8-e5

27 Qc2-d3   Qf3xd3

28 Rd2xd3

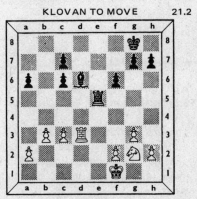

KARPOV

Karpov has thus managed to exchange
the queens without allowing any
deterioration in his position. This ending (or a similar one without the rooks)
has been Karpov's aim for the last
twelve or thirteen moves.
Black's position is bad, but not yet
lost. His weak Q-side pawns are
difficult to defend and his bishop is
inferior to White's knight. This might
be termed a classical Ruy-López-
Exchange-Variation ending.

28 ... Kg8-f7

29 Ng2-e3   Kf7-e6

30 Ne3-c4   Re5-h5

31 h2-h4   Bd6-c5

32 Nc4-b2!
Heading for d3, from where the knight
will dominate the bishop. Black cannot create any imbalance in the position
and so White's plan slowly develops.

32 ... Rh5-f5

33 Rd3-d2   h7-h5

34 Nb2-d3   Bc5-d6

35 Rd2-e2+   Ke6-d7

36 Re2-e3   g7-g5?
> Passive defence by 36 ... Rb5 would been better. After the text move the rook is trapped.

37 c3-c4!
> Removing the exit via b5.

37 ... c6-c5

38 Kf1-g2   c7-c6

39 f2-f3   g5xh4

40 g3xh4   Bd6-f4
> The threat of 41 Re4 and 42 f4 could not be prevented in any case.

41 Re3-e4   Bf4-d6

42 f3-f4!   **Black resigns**
> After 42 ... Be7 (what else?) 43 Kf3 Bd6 44 Re2 Be7 45 Ke4 Ke6 46 Rg2 White wins easily.

Game 22

WHITE Amos   Sicilian Defence
Students' Olympiad, Mayaguez, Puerto Rico, 1971

This brand of the Sicilian could well be called the Karpov Variation. The early manœuvering of the black knights causes White some embarrassment, since he is taken out of known theory and made to think for himself. By move 14 Karpov is already on top, and after a further 14 moves the game is over.

1 e2-e4   c7-c5

2 Ng1-f3   e7-e6

3 d2-d4   c5xd4

4 Nf3xd4   Nb8-c6

5 Nb1-c3   a7-a6

6 g2-g3
> So far Black has played a Paulsen or Taimanov set-up, and White is responding with normal developing moves. Now comes the 'Karpov system'.

6 ... Ng8-e7
> Karpov had tried a similar idea against Kholmov in the 38th USSR Championship in 1970, with 6 ... Nxd4 7 Qxd4 Ne7. But after the continuation 8 Bf4 Ng6 9 Bd6 Bxd6 10 Qxd6 Qe7 11 Qb6 White had the advantage. The idea of the text move is to delay the exchange on d4 and to continue after 7 Bg2 with 7 ... Nxd4 8 Qxd4 Nc6 9 Qd2 Bc5 with an excellent game for Black.

7 Nd4-b3
> A logical move. White withdraws his knight to prevent an exchange.

7 ... Nc6-a5!?
> The real point of Karpov's plan. The white king's bishop is destined for g2; so the c4 square will lack its support. 7 ... Na5 puts pressure on c4, and also makes room for the black king's knight to join in the Q-side operations.

8 Bf1-g2   Ne7-c6

9 0-0   d7-d6

10 Nb3-d2
> White decides to fianchetto his queen's bishop also. He is unable to develop this piece satisfactorily by 10 Bf4 on account of the reply 10 ... Nc4 when the defence of the b2 square will prove to be most difficult for White. The alternative (and probably superior) move is 10 Nxa5.

10 ... Bc8-d7

Black must develop his Q-side quickly so as to make the c4 square safe for his knight in case White should choose to undermine its position by a3 and b4.

11 b2-b3

11 a3 would seem to be more logical and in keeping with White's previous move.

11 . . . Bf8-e7

12 Bc1-b2 Ra8-c8!

So as to secure the c4 square. After 12 . . . 0-0 13 a3 b5 14 b4 Nc4 15 Nxc4 White has the advantage.

KARPOV   22.1

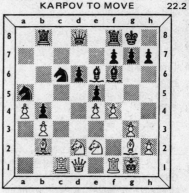

AMOS TO MOVE

Black has a solid position with no apparent weakness. He has won the fight for control of c4—for example 13 a3 b5 14 Qe2 Nd4 15 Qd3 e5 followed by 16 . . . Be6 gives Black a clear advantage. So instead of trying to exploit the position of the a5 knight White chooses to control the d5 and b5 squares more securely and thus prevent a black pawn break. Unfortunately this plan is doomed to failure: a break cannot be stopped.

13 Nc3-e2 0-0

14 c2-c4?

Preferable here was still 14 a3.

14 . . . b7-b5

Any other move allows 15 Nc3 when White has some grip on the position.

Black already has the advantage in initiative.

15 c4xb5 a6xb5

16 Nd2-f3

White's knights can only wander round aimlessly. The squares c3, d3, and e3 are already beginning to look weak. In particular the removal of the two bishops to their fianchettoed positions undermines White's control of his d3 and e3 squares.

16 . . . b5-b4

17 a2-a3 Rc8-b8

18 a3-a4

Black was contemplating the exchange sacrifice 18 axb4 Rxb4 19 Ba3 Rxe4 20 Nd2 Rb4 21 Bxb4 Nxb4. The resulting position offers Black good chances for the material sacrificed.

18 . . . e6-e5!

A move with a twofold objective. The white knights are further restricted in their movements and the square e6 is released for use of the bishop. To defend his weak b3 pawn White will have to go further back.

19 Nf3-d2 Be7-f6!

After 19 . . . Be6 20 f4 would be unpleasant, so Black paves the way for 20 . . . Be6.

20 Ra1-c1 Bd7-e6

21 f2-f4

KARPOV TO MOVE   22.2

AMOS

White is completely tied up and attempts to break for freedom. His downfall will occur on the a7-g1 diagonal and the weak squares d3 and e3.

21 ... e5xf4

22 Bb2xf6   Qd8xf6

23 Ne2xf4

23 gxf4 Bg4 would be no better for White.

23 ... Rf8-c8

24 Nf4-d5

The move 24 Nxe6 would give White no chances of a 'swindling' check on e7.

24 ... Qf6-d4+

25 Kg1-h1   Kg8-h8

Karpov removes White's last hope. White has no effective moves and cannot readily prevent the infiltration of the black knight from c6 to e5 and d3.

26 Qd1-e2   Nc6-e5

27 h2-h3   h7-h6

Also possible here was 27 ... Qb2 28 Rb1 Qa2 29 Ra1 Qc2 winning quickly.

28 Rf1-d1   Ne5-d3!

Now 29 Rxc8+ Rxc8 (threat 30 ... Nf2+) 30 Ne3, can be met by 30 ... Nb2 or 30 ... Rc1 with a winning position for Black. Of course White could prolong the struggle considerably, but decides he has had enough.

White resigns

Game 23

BLACK Rogoff   English Opening
Students' Olympiad, Mayaguez, Puerto Rico, 1971.

In this game Black plays a poor opening, reaches a bad position and is dealt with savagely in true Karpov style. Although Black is tied up it is instructive to see the speed with which the execution is carried out.

1 c2-c4   e7-e5

2 Nb1-c3   Ng8-f6

3 g2-g3   Bf8-b4

Also possible here are 3 ... d5, and 3 ... c6 (The Keres Variation).

4 Bf1-g2   0-0

5 d2-d3

Also possible are 5 Nf3, 5 e4, and 5 Qb3.

5 ... c7-c6

A logical move preparing the advance d5. However, preferable was 5 ... Re8 to give the bishop a retreat square on f8.

6 Qd1-b3!

Black is in a quandary. He is unwilling to part with his bishop by 6 ... Bxc3+

7 Qxc3, since the resulting position will leave him cramped and unable to achieve the freeing d5 break. Thus:

(a) 7 ... d6 8 Bg5 Nbd7 9 Nf3.

(b) 7 ... Re8 8 Bg5.

(c) 7 ... Qe7 8 e4 or again 8 Bg5.

On the other hand the bishop has no good square to fall back to. Black chooses the logical square but he is soon in trouble.

6 ... Bb4-a5

7 Ng1-f3   d7-d5

After 7 ... e4!? 8 dxe4 Nxe4 9 0-0 Nxc3 10 bxc3 White has a beautifully developed position and the threats to the black squares by Ba3 and on the semi-open b- and d-files give White a considerable advantage.

8 0-0

Of course not 8 Nxe5? d4, when Black wins a piece.

8 ... d5-d4

9 Nc3-a4!

Preventing support for the centre (at a later stage) by c6-c5 and also preparing a subtle counter.

9 ... Nb8-d7

10 e2-e3   d4xe3

After 10 ... c5 11 exd4 there follows:

(a) 11 ... exd4 12 Bf4 (threatening 13 Bd6) when White has an excellent position.

(b) 11 ... cxd4 12 c5! (one of the ideas of 9 Na4!) when White has a spatial advantage on the Q-side and Black's development is hampered.

11 Bc1xe3   Rf8-e8

12 a2-a3

ROGOFF TO MOVE   23.1

KARPOV

Black is in a bad way. He is unable to achieve co-operation between his pieces, which shows his opening was faulty. White is preparing to expand with d4 and b4; furthermore the opening of the d-file will increase his pressure.

It is difficult to suggest a constructive plan for Black. He decides to manœuvre his bishop from a5 to f8(!) to defend the weak points in his camp at c5 and d6.

12 ... Ba5-c7

13 Ra1-d1   Bc7-d6

14 d3-d4!

Black has chosen such an unfortunate plan that he must now allow the d-file to be opened. After 14 ... e4 15 Ng5 the threats of 16 c5 and 16 Nxf7 are already decisive: e.g.

(a) 15 ... h6? 16 Nxf7 wins at least a pawn (16 ... Kxf7 17 c5+).

(b) 15 ... Bf8 16 Nc3 and the e4 pawn falls.

(c) 15 ... c5 16 dxc5 wins at least a pawn.

14 ... e5xd4

15 Nf3xd4   Bd6-f8

White was threatening 16 Nxc6 bxc6 17 Rxd6 winning a pawn. But now Black can never develop his Q-side pieces.

16 Qb3-c3   Qd8-e7

17 Rf1-e1

We can now see a secondary point of 12a3—the black queen is dangerously short of squares. Black's Q-side is still locked in, and so he removes his queen to temporary safety.

17 ... Qe7-e5

18 b2-b4   Qe5-h5

19 h2-h3   Nd7-b6

At last Black achieves some Q-side freedom, but the noose is fast closing round the black queen.

20 Na4xb6   a7xb6

21 g3-g4   Qh5-g6

A piece-sacrifice here would be tantamount to resignation 21 ... Bxg4 22 hxg4 Nxg4 23 Bf4.

22 Be3-f4   Bc8-d7

The only move to prevent White's gaining control of the e-file. White now engineers a very pretty finish.

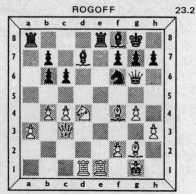

ROGOFF 23.2

KARPOV TO MOVE

23 Nd4-f3!
The immediate threats are 24 Nh4 trapping the queen and 24 Ne5 winning at least the exchange.

23 ... Re8xe1+
Apparently the only move. After 23 ... Ne4 24 Qc2! the threats of 25 Ne5 and 25 Rxd7 are just too much for Black!

24 Rd1xe1 Nf6-e8
With the possible exception of 24 ...

h6?! this is the only way to prevent loss of the queen by 25 Nh4. Other moves that fail are:

(a) 24 ... Ne4 25 Qd4 (threatening both the knight on e4 and the bishop on d7) 25 ... Nf6 26 Ne5 forking the queen and bishop.

(b) 24 ... h5 25 Nh4 Qh7 26 g5 Ne8 27 Qd4 and now

(b1) 27 ... Rd8 28 Qxb6 etc. winning several pawns.

(b2) 27 ... Be6 28 g6! Qh8 29 Rxe6 fxe6 30 Qd7 mating.

This last variation illustrates how defenceless Black's game really is.

25 Qc3-d2! Ra8-d8
Other tries that fail are:

(a) 25 ... Nf6 26 Nh4 winning the queen.

(b) 25 ... Bc8 26 Rxe8 winning a piece.

(c) 25 ... Be6 26 Nh4 Qf6 27 Bg5 winning the queen.

26 Nf3-h4
And now 26 ... Qf6 is met by 27 Bg5 winning a rook.

... Black resigns

Game 24

BLACK Tukmakov   Sicilian Defence, Scheveningen Variation
Army Team Championships, Leningrad 1971

Tukmakov is both positionally and tactically outplayed in a short, sharp exchange on the Q-side. The result of this is that he sacrifices a pawn to obtain some counterplay but, as always, a pawn in Karpov's hands is too large a handicap to overcome.

1 e2-e4	c7-c5
2 Ng1-f3	d7-d6
3 d2-d4	c5xd4
4 Nf3xd4	Ng8-f6
5 Nb1-c3	a7-a6
6 Bf1-e2	

So far a Najdorf variation. Black now has a choice of variations. He can opt for a Dragon Variation with 6 ... g6 (although in this case the move a7-a6 would not be particularly useful) or for Opocensky's Variation with 6 ... e5. The text continuation is the Scheveningen Variation.

6 . . . e7-e6

7 0-0   Bf8-e7

8 f2-f4   0-0

9 Bc1-e3

9 Qe1 would be premature on
account of the strong reply 9 . . . Qb6
10 Be3 Qxb2! and amazingly the
queen cannot be trapped:

(a) 11 a3 Qb6!

(b) 11 Na4 Qa3 12 Qa5? Bd7.

(c) 11 Rb1 Qa3 12 Rb3 Qc5 13 Nf5 Qc7,

although line (c) in particular offers
White plenty of attack for the sacrificed pawn.

9 . . . Nb8-c6

10 a2-a4

A good move and also typical of
Karpov's approach to such an opening.
He restricts the black counterplay
before pursuing his own attack with
Qd1-e1-g3.

10 . . . Qd8-c7

Also playable here is 10 . . . Bd7 so
that if 11 Qe1 Nxd4 12 Bxd4 Bc6,
and Black has counterplay against the
white centre.

11 Kg1-h1

A precautionary move that is common
in this variation. White avoids a possible pin on the a7-g1 diagonal.

11 . . . Nc6-a5?!

A dubious plan, as Karpov demonstrates. Correct is 11 . . . Bd7. It is
interesting to note that Tukmakov
played this opening as White against
Polugaevsky in the 39th USSR Championship shortly after this game
(Polugaevsky had played 10 . . . Bd7
in place of Tukmakov's 10 . . . Qc7).
That game continued 11 . . . Rc8
12 Nb3 (12 Bf3! is better) Na5!
13 e5?! Ne8 14 Nxa5 Qxa5 15 Qd2
Bc6 16 b4!? Qc7 17 b5 axb5 18 axb5
Bxg2+ 19 Kxg2 Qxc3 20 Qxc3 Rxc3
21 Bd3 dxe5 22 fxe5 Nc7 23 Bd2?
Ra3 and Black went on to win. With
23 Bd4 however White could have
maintained the balance.

12 Qd1-e1

Preparing to go to g3 and providing
the c3 knight with protection. 12 Qd3
was played in Tukmakov-Panno,
Buenos Aires 1970.

12 . . . Na5-c4

13 Be3-c1   Bc8-d7

14 b2-b3

Were the queen still on d1 this could
be met by 14 . . . Ne3 15 Bxe3 Qxc3
but now the knight must retreat.

14 . . . Nc4-a5

15 Be2-d3   Na5-c6

This knight has wasted four tempi
wandering to c4 and back, and is
now exchanged for the knight on d4.

16 Nd4xc6   Bd7xc6

17 Bc1-b2   e6-e5

In order to fix White's pawn on e4.
Black wishes first to prevent White
from attacking with 18 e5!? and
second to attack the immobilized
pawn on e4.

18 Qe1-e2

Interesting here is 18 Qg3!? If then
18 . . . Nh5 19 Qg4 Nxf4 20 Rxf4!
exf4 21 Nd5 and White wins.

18 . . . Ra8-d8

TUKMAKOV   24.1

KARPOV TO MOVE

Karpov's last move had a hidden point
which is now revealed.

19 b3-b4!

The idea is to gain control of d5 by first playing b4-b5 and then undermining the position of the black knight on f6. The point of 18 Qe2 is shown to be that 19 ... b5 is impossible (with the queen on e1 the c2 pawn would be en prise after 20 axb5 axb5 21 Rxa8 Rxa8 22 Nxb5 Bxb5 23 Bxb5). Now 19 ... b5 simply loses a pawn.
Also 19 ... exf4 20 b5 axb5 21 axb5 Bd7 22 Nd5! is very strong. After 22 ... Nxd5 23 exd5 Rfe8 24 Qe4 f5 25 Qxf4, White has a winning attack.

19 ... a6-a5

20 b4-b5 Bc6-d7

21 f4-f5
Also interesting here are:

(a) 21 Nd5 Nxd5 22 exd5 f6! and it is not clear how White should continue.

(b) 21 fxe5 dxe5 22 Rxf6!? and now:

(b1) 22 ... gxf6? 23 Nd5 Qd6 24 Ba3 Qxa3 25 Rxa3 Bxa3 26 Nxf6+ Kh8 (if 26 ... Kg7 27 Nxd7 Rxd7 28 Qg4+ winning the rook on d7) 27 Qh5 Kg7 28 Nxd7 as before.

(b2) 22 ... Bxf6 22 Nd5 Qb8 23 Rf1! with many chances for the sacrificed exchange.

As always Karpov prefers a safe positional advantage rather than a speculative sacrificial attack.

21 ... Bd7-c8
Threatening 22 ... d5.

22 Nc3-d1
With Bc4 and Ne3 coming, or even c4, Black decides on a speculative pawn sacrifice.

22 ... d6-d5?!

23 e4xd5 Nf6xd5
After 23 ... Rxd5 24 Ne3 R5d8 (if 24 ... Rc5 then 25 c4 e4 26 Bc2 and Black will not only lose a pawn, or the exchange to 27 Bd4, but also he will forego all control of the d5 square). 25 Nc4 and White wins the pawn in more favourable circumstances.

24 Qe2xe5 Qc7xe5

25 Bb2xe5 Rf8-e8

26 Nd1-b2!

TUKMAKOV TO MOVE 24.2

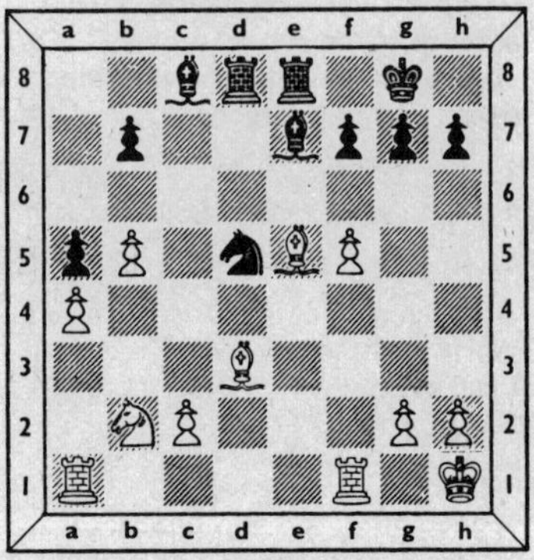

KARPOV

Black has little counterplay for the sacrificed pawn. Although White's pieces are temporarily disorganized, the plan of regrouping by Nd1-b2-c4 and Ra1-e1 is certain to relieve whatever pressure Black may have. Black still has problems in developing his queen's bishop. These can be satisfactorily solved only by b7-b6 and Bc8-b7, but this will leave Black with a weak pawn on b6 that will need constant attention. Black's next move is aimed at providing protection for the b6 pawn (so that the knight on d5 is free to move) but 26 ... Bb4 may have been better than the text move, since it would have prevented White from contesting the e-file.

26 ... Be7-c5

27 Nb2-c4 b7-b6

28 Be5-g3!
Preparing to increase the pressure against the b6 pawn by Bf2.

28 ... Bc8-b7

29 Ra1-e1
The game is almost decided. It is only a matter of time before Black's tactical threats are completely removed and White's extra pawn proves to be

enough to win.

29 ... Bc5-b4

30 Re1xe8+   Rd8xe8

31 h2-h4

White is in no hurry. He has plenty of time to secure his king's position before taking further action. This move and his next enable him to exchange black-squared bishops by Bf2 without allowing the uncomfortable reply Nf4.

31 ... g7-g6

32 Kh1-h2   Bb4-c5

33 Bg3-f2   Bc5xf2

34 Rf1xf2   Re8-e1

At first sight this looks quite dangerous. However White is well in control. His knight on c4 not only prevents the knight on d5 from moving but also as a result keeps the bishop locked on b7.

35 Kh2-g3   Nd5-b4

So that if 36 Nxb6 Nxd3 37 cxd3 Re3+ and Black regains the pawn and has some chance of saving the game.

36 Kg3-f4   Nb4-d5+

37 Kf4-g3   Nd5-b4

38 Rf2-d2!   Nb4-d5

The only logical way to defend the b6 pawn. Now comes a neat little combination to finish the game.

39 Nc4-d6   Bb7-a8

40 Bd3-e4   Nd5-c7

41 Be4xa8   Nc7xa8

42 f5-f6   h7-h6

The threat was 43 Ne4!

43 Nd6-c4   Re1-e8

44 Rd2-d6   Black resigns

Game 25

BLACK Taimanov   Sicilian Defence, Taimanov Variation
39th USSR Championship, Leningrad 1971

An apparently drawn game is suddenly brought to life by the introduction of mating threats. Taimanov can find no defence to these and his position is rapidly demolished. The early part of the game is noteworthy for the tactical traps set by both sides in a seemingly uncomplicated position.

1 e2-e4   c7-c5

2 Ng1-f3   e7-e6

3 d2-d4   c5xd4

4 Nf3xd4   Nb8-c6

The Taimanov variation.

5 Nd4-b5

This was played twice by Fischer against Taimanov in their world championship quarter-final match in Vancouver earlier in the year.

5 ... d7-d6

6 Bc1-f4   e6-e5

7 Bf4-e3   Ng8-f6

8 Be3-g5   Bc8-e6

Taimanov tried 8 ... Qa5+ against Fischer in the 2nd game of their match After 9 Qd2 Nxe4 10 Qxa5 Nxa5 11 Be3 White built up enough pressure to regain the pawn, and eventually went on to win.

9 Nb1-c3   a7-a6

10 Bg5xf6   g7xf6

11 Nb5-a3

TAIMANOV TO MOVE   25.1

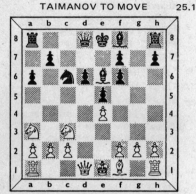

KARPOV

An interesting situation is reached. When Taimanov played the 6th game in his match with Fischer, he chose here 11 ... Nd4, but after 12 Nc4 f5 13 exf5 Nxf5 14 Bd3 Rc8 15 Bxf5 Rxc4 16 Bxe6 fxe6 17 Qe2 White had a clear advantage and went on to finish the match 6-0! The correct reply for Black is 11 ... d5! as first played in the first game of the world championship final between Fischer and Petrosian. This match began on 5 October 1971 in Buenos Aires, and it is quite possible that, although Taimanov was familiar with this move, he refrained from playing it in this game (which was played on 15 September) so as to increase the surprise value of the move when Petrosian played it against Fischer. Although Petrosian lost the game, there was no doubt that Fischer was surprised by the move and, indeed, achieved a poor opening position because of it.

After 11 ... d5! 12 exd5 (12 Nxd5 Bxa3 13 bxa3 Qa5+ 14 Qd2 Qxd2+ 15 Kxd2 0-0-0 gives Black a small advantage) 12 ... Bxa3 13 bxa3 Qa5 14 Qd2 0-0-0 15 Bc4 Rhg8 16 Rd1! Black can play 16 ... Rxg2! and thus keep his advantage. e.g.

(a) 17 Qe3 Nd4 18 Kf1 Nxc2 19 Qf3 Rxf2+ winning.

(b) 17 Ne4 Qb6! 18 Qe3 Nd4!∓

In the game Petrosian played 16 ... Bf5 17 Bd3 Bxd3? (17 ... e4!) 18 Qxd3 and lost only after a brilliant display by Fischer.

11 ... Nc6-e7

12 Na3-c4   d6-d5

13 e4xd5   Ne7xd5

14 Nc3xd5   Be6xd5

15 Nc4-e3   Bd5-c6

16 Bf1-c4!
With the unpleasant threat of 17 Qh5! So Black is obliged to exchange queens.

16 ... Qd8xd1+

17 Ra1xd1   Ra8-c8

18 Bc4-d5   Bc6xd5

19 Rd1xd5
White has a small advantage. The Q-side pawn majority, well-posted knight, and weak black K-side pawns, are worth more than Black's potentially dangerous bishop and half-open c- and g-files.

19 ... Ke8-e7

20 Ke1-e2   Ke7-e6
Threatening 21 ... Rxc2+ 22 Nxc2 Kxd5 winning a pawn.

21 Rh1-d1   f6-f5
White was unable to prevent this advance, since 20 g4? would have been met by 20 ... h5 when Black has completely freed his position.

TAIMANOV   25.2

KARPOV TO MOVE

22 g2-g3!?

An interesting and, as it turns out, good move. After 22 c3 f4 the chances are equal, because White has no good square for his knight. The text move initiates the first of the mating possibilities.

22 ... f5-f4

Black must accept the temporary sacrifice, since a passive move such as 22 ... f6 allows 23 c3, with clear advantage to White.

23 g3xf4   e5xf4

24 Ne3-g2   Rc8xc2+

25 Ke2-f3   Bf8-c5?!

Black would have been better to test out Karpov's idea by 25 ... Rxb2. After 26 Nxf4+ Kf6 27 Nh5+ (Best: Furman recommends 27 Re1 here, but the knight check appears to be stronger) 27 ... Kg6 (After 27 ... Ke6 28 Rd8 Ke7 29 Rc8 Rb5! [29 ... Bg7 loses a piece to 30 Rc7+] 30 Rc7+ Ke6 31 Nf4+ followed by 32 Rxf7 after 31 ... Ke5, 32 Rxf7+ after 31 ... Kf5, and 32 Rdd7 after 31 ... Kf6, gives White a dangerous attack) 28 Rg1+ Kh6 29 Ng3! Kg6 30 Ne4+ Kh6 Black's defences are amazingly resilient.

BLACK TO MOVE   25.3

WHITE

The move 31 ... Rb5! will answer most of White's threats: e.g.

(a) 31 Nf6 Rb5 32 Rd4 (32 Ng8+? Rxg8 33 Rxg8 Rxd5 34 Rxf8 leaves White a pawn down) 32 ... Rf5+ 33 Ke2! Rg5 34 Rh4+ Kg6 35 Rxg5+ Kxg5

36 Rxh7 Bg7! with equality.

(b) 31 Rg4 Rb5 32 Rxb5 axb5 33 Ng3 Bc5 34 h4 f6! and White has insufficient material to deliver mate.

(c) 31 Ng5 Kg6 32 Rd7 Rxf2+! 33 Ke4! (33 Kxf2 Bc5+ 34 Kg2 Bxg1 35 Nxf7 Rf8 36 Ne5+ Kf5 is equal) 33 ... f5+ 34 Kd3 Kf6 and Black is still alive.

Black has many resources in all of these lines and is far from lost. On the other hand, it is difficult, if not impossible, to visualize such possibilities at the board, and this is probably why Taimanov rejected the move 25 ... Rxb2. Also it is possible that in the above analysis may be concealed an obscure, quiet move or a tactical trick that would give White a winning position. Nevertheless, the unclear nature of these variations is surely sufficiently encouraging for Black (his defensive resources have been shown to be good). After the dubious text move, White is left with a well-posted knight against a poor bishop, and his rooks are the more active.

26 Ng2xf4+   Ke6-f6

27 Nf4-d3

Defending both the b2 and f2 pawns and menacing the c5 bishop. White stands better.

27 ... Rh8-c8

28 Rd5-d7   b7-b5?

Safer and better was 28 ... b6, as 29 Nxc5 R8xc5 30 R1d6+ Kg7 31 Rxb6 Rf5+ leaves White with no advantage at all.

29 Rd1-e1   Kf6-g7

30 Re1-e4   Rc2-c4

The threat was 31 Rf4 and the alternative defence of 30 ... Rc6 would lose to 31 Rf4 Rf6 32 Rxf6 Kxf6 33 Rc7.

31 Nd3-e5!

After 31 Rxc4 bxc4 32 Ne5 Kf6 White stands better although Black has managed to induce some tactical complications.

31 ... Rc4xe4

32 Kf3xe4   Kg7-g8!

33 f2-f4!
After 33 Rxf7 Bd6 reduces White's
advantage considerably.

33 ... Bc5-f8
After 33 ... Rf8 34 Kf5! White has
a dangerous attack!

34 Ne5xf7   Rc8-c2

35 Nf7-g5
Threatening 36 Rd8 and 37 Ne6
winning a piece.

35 ... Bf8-h6

36 Ng5-e6!   Rc2xh2
To capture the b-pawn would transpose back to the game continuation
after 36 ... Rxb2 37 Kf5 Bxf4
38 Kxf4 Rxh2 39 Rg7+ Kh8 40 Ra7,
except that Black's rook would be on
h2 instead of b2.

37 Ke4-f5   Bh6xf4
In view of the threat of 38 Kf6 and
39 Rd8 Black decides to give up a
piece. The alternative 37 ... Rg2 loses
quickly after 38 Rd8+ Kf7 39 Rh8!
trapping the bishop in a most unusual
manner.

38 Kf5xf4?
Far quicker would have been 38 Nxf4
Rxb2 39 Kf6 h6 40 Rg7+ Kf8
41 Ne6+ Ke8 42 Re7 mate. After
this blunder Karpov has to work
hard to redeem himself.

38 ... Rh2xb2

39 Rd7-g7+   Kg8-h8

40 Rg7-a7   h7-h5

41 Ra7xa6   b5-b4

42 Ne6-d4   Rb2-g2

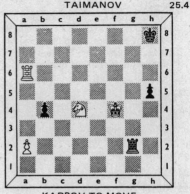

KARPOV TO MOVE

The only way for White to make progress is with a mating attack! There
appears to be no positional win possible (rook-and-knight v. rook alone is
a draw, except in special circumstances).
After a few king moves, Karpov comes
to the same conclusion.

43 Kf4-f3
Better was 43 Nf5 as we shall see.

43 ... Rg2-d2

44 Kf3-e3   Rd2-b2

45 Ke3-f4   Rb2-d2

46 Nd4-f5!   Rd2-b2
The only chance was 46 ... Kg8 but
after 47 Ke5! Black is surely lost.

47 Kf4-g5!   b4-b3
So Black achieves the exchange of
the last White pawn but in doing so
is mated himself.

48 Ra6-h6+!   Kh8-g8

49 Kg5-f6   Black resigns
The threat of 50 Ne7+ Kf8 51 Rh8
mate can be parried only by 49 ...
Rf2, after which 50 axb3 wins comfortably for White.

Game 26

BLACK Stein   Sicilian Defence, Sozin Attack
39th USSR Championship, Leningrad 1971

Stein becomes yet another victim of a Karpov outside passed pawn. This time, however, the pawn is advanced in the middle-game; although Stein induces many tactical possibilities into the position he cannot find one to prevent the pawn's progress.

1 e2-e4   c7-c5

2 Ng1-f3   Nb8-c6

3 d2-d4   c5xd4

4 Nf3xd4   Ng8-f6

5 Nb1-c3   d7-d6

6 Bf1-c4
The Sozin Attack. The major possibility other than the text move is 6Bg5—the Richter-Rauzer Attack.

6 ... Qd8-b6
Stein prefers to avoid the Velimirović Attack which occurs after 6 ... e6 7 Be3 Be7 8 Qe2 0-0 9 0-0-0 etc. The text move offers White a wide choice of 7th moves. The one chosen by Karpov is considered to be innocuous.

7 Nd4xc6
Other possibilities for White here:

(a) 7 Be3?! Qxb2 8 N4b5 Qb4! 9 Bd3 Qa5 and Black can maintain the extra pawn.

(b) 7 Ndb5 a6 8 Be3 Qa5 9 Nd4 e6* 10 0-0 Be7 11 Bb3 0-0 with a level game.
  *(If 9 ... Nxe4 then 10 Qf3! is very strong: e.g.

  (b1) 10 ... Nxc3 11 Nxc6 Qf5 12 Qxf5 Bxf5 13 Nd4 winning a piece.

  (b2) 10 ... Ne5 11 Bxf7+ Nxf7 12 Qxe4 with a small advantage.

  (b3) 10 ... f5 11 Nxc6 bxc6 12 0-0-0 with a promising attack.)

(c) 7 Nde2 e6 8 0-0 Be7 9 Bb3 0-0 and now either:

  (c1) 10 Ng3 a6 11 Be3 Qc7 12 f4

Na5 13 Qe2 b5 14 Rad1 Bb7 15 Bd4 Nxb3 16 axb3 Rac8 with equality, or

  (c2) 10 Kh1 Na5 11 Bg5 Qc5 12 f4 b5 12 Ng3 Bb7! (but not 13 ... b4 14 e5! Fischer-Benko, Candidates' 1959) and Black has at least equality.

(d) 7 Nb3 e6 8 0-0 (In later rounds of this event both Savon and Zeitlin chose 8 Bg5 against Stein here. After 8 Bg5 Bd7 9 Qe2 Rc8! 10 f4 Nd4! Savon was already in the worse position, and 8 Bg5 Bd7 9 0-0 Be7 10 Kh1 h6 11 Bxf6 gxf6 12 Be2 h5 gave Zeitlin an equal game only) 8 ... Be7 9 Be3 Qc7 10 f4 a6 11 Bd3 b5 12 Qf3 Bb7. This position can be reached in a number of different ways and offers about equal chances.

7 ... b7xc6

8 0-0   e7-e6

9 b2-b3
An interesting idea. White intends Bb2, Qe2, Bd3, Na4, and c4 thus restraining the black centre pawns and also preparing a possible c4-c5 or e4-e5 break.
Both 9 Bf4! and 9 Bg5 are possible here, since the White b-pawn is too hot to capture.

9 ... Bf8-e7

10 Bc1-b2   0-0

11 Qd1-e2   e6-e5
This move prevents 12 e5. Black cannot play 11 ... d5 as 12 exd5 cxd5 13 Bxd5! wins a pawn for White.

12 Kg1-h1   Qb6-c7

The black queen is exposed on b6; so she is removed to support e5 and also to create a masked threat against the white c2 pawn.

13 Ra1-e1   Nf6-d7

14 Nc3-a4   Bc8-b7

Furman suggested here 14 ... Bf6 in order to bolster the e5 point still further, but the text move is natural and cannot be bad.

15 Bc4-d3

Karpov immediately takes advantage of the fact that 14 ... Bb7 and not 14 ... Bf6 was played. After 14 ... Bf6 15 Bd3 d5! gives Black the edge. Now 15 ... d5? loses a pawn to 16 exd5 cxd5 17 Bxe5 etc.

15 ... Rf8-e8

16 c2-c4

STEIN TO MOVE   26.1

KARPOV

The assessment of this position depends upon the type of player involved. White has a semi-bind on the d5 square and chances of both a Q-side advance (as in the game) and a carefully built K-side attack. On the other hand, Black has a solid game with no apparent weaknesses. He has chances in the centre with a d6-d5 break and a possible Q-side attack by a7-a5, Nd7-b6, and a5-a4 etc. Karpov, being essentially a positional player, was no doubt happy here with his

Q-side prospects and Stein, a more aggressive type, with his chances of active counterplay.

16 ... Be7-g5

Aiming for 17 ... d5!

17 Qe2-c2!

With veiled threats against Black's h7 pawn and his queen.

17 ... h7-h6

18 b3-b4!

Now 18 ... d5? 19 cxd5 and the c6 pawn is pinned.

18 ... a7-a6

19 b5 was the threat, after which White would control d5. Black never gets a chance for d6-d5.

19 Qc2-b3   Ra8-b8

20 a2-a3   Bb7-c8

21 Qb3-c3   Bg5-f6

22 Qc3-c2   a6-a5?!

A dubious move, setting up a passed pawn for White. Stein must have been annoyed by Karpov's clever side-stepping. Although the threat of a black d5 has been in the air since move 11, White has not only avoided it but has managed to improve his position considerably since then. Meanwhile, without this break, Black's game remains cramped and he is unable to improve the positioning of his pieces. The logical move was 22 ... Nb6 (Note that 23 c5 is then impossible because of 23 ... Nxa4 24 cxd6 Qxd6 and the bishop on d3 is loose).

23 Bb2-c3   a5xb4

24 a3xb4

And now the White plan is becoming clear. The aim is for b4-b5-b6-b7-b8 =Q! Amazingly, Stein finds no answer to this plan.

24 ... Nd7-f8

Heading for e6 and then f4 or d4.

25 b4-b5   c6xb5?

Better was 25 ... Bd7. The opening of a further file on the Q-side can only improve White's chances of queening the pawn.

26 c4xb5   Bc8-d7
27 Re1-b1   Re8-c8

STEIN   26.2

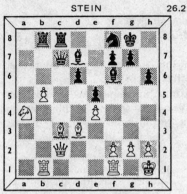

KARPOV TO MOVE

The white pawn now takes another
giant step forward.

28 b5-b6!
Based on an ingenious resource.

28 ... Qc7-b7
28 ... Bxa4? 29 bxc7 leaves Black
with no adequate move.

29 Bd3-b5   Rb8-a8

30 Qc2-b3
The hidden resource of 28 b6! Now
30 ... Bxb5 31 Qxb5 Rxa4 32 Qxa4
Rxc3 33 Qa7! wins instantly.

30 ... Bd7-e6

31 Qb3-b4   Bf6-e7

32 Rf1-c1   d6-d5
The long-awaited break, which
apparently wins the e4 pawn, but
Karpov has some tricks up his sleeve.
The dominating position of the white
b6 pawn takes care of any hopes that
Black may still possess.

33 Qb4-b2   d5-d4

34 Bc3-b4   Be7-g5
After 34 ... Bxb4 35 Qxb4 Black can
choose between 35 ... Qxe4 36 Nc5
(threatening 37 b7 as well as the
queen) and 35 ... Rxc1+ 36 Rxc1
Qxe4 37 Bc6 Qf4 38 Rb1. Both are
winning lines for White.

35 Rc1xc8   Ra8xc8

36 Qb2-e2   Rc8-a8

37 Bb4-d6
The bishop goes to c7 and then Na4-c5
followed by b6-b7 would win easily.

37 ... Nf8-g6

38 Qe2-c2   Ra8-c8

39 Bd6-c7
The threats of 40 Nc5 and 40 Bc6
(both followed by 41 b7) are unanswerable.

39 ... Bg5-d8

40 Na4-c5   Rc8xc7
It was impossible for Black to retreat
any further. Now 41 bxc7 Qxc7 gives
Black some hope of survival.
However ...

STEIN   26.3

KARPOV TO MOVE

41 Nc5xb7!   Rc7xc2

42 Nb7xd8
The passed pawn costs Black a piece
in all variations.

42 ... Be6-c8
A pretty finish would have been
42 ... Ba2 43 b7! Bxb1 44 h4.

43 g2-g3   Rc2xf2

44 Rb1-c1!   Rf2-f6

45 Rc1xc8   Rf6xb6

46 Bb5-c4   Kg8-h7

47 Nd8xf7   Black resigns

Game 27

BLACK Zeitlin   Ruy López, Schliemann Defence
39th USSR Championship, Leningrad 1971

This is a very sharp and unusual opening line. A white knight is imprisoned but manages to sacrifice itself for a mating attack.

After this win Karpov registered two more in the next two rounds, but he was unable to win any of his last three games—against Tal, Balashov, and Polugaevsky—and so had to be content with fourth place. Another half point would have put him equal second with Tal and Smyslov, behind Savon, who finished a convincing first.

1 e2-e4   e7-e5

2 Ng1-f3   Nb8-c6

3 Bf1-b5   f7-f5
  The Schliemann Defence.

4 Nb1-c3
  Generally considered to be the strongest move here. The other possibilities are:

(a) 4 exf5?! e4 5 Qe2 Qe7 6 Bxc6 dxc6 7 Nd4 Qe5 8 Nf3 Qe7 with repetition, or Black can try 8 ... Qxf5 9 Nc3 Nf6 10 d3 Bb4 11 Nd2 0-0 12 Ndxe4 Qg6 with an unclear position.

(b) 4 d3 fxe4 5 dxe4 Nf6 6 0-0 d6 7 Nc3 Be7 8 Qd3 Bg4 9 h3 Bxf3 10 Qxf3 0-0 11 Qd1 Kh8 12 Be3 with a small advantage to White (Pilnik-Rubinetti, Mar del Plata 1971).

(c) 4 d4 fxe4 5 Nxe5 Nxe5 6 dxe5 c6 7 Nc3! cxb5 8 Nxe4 d5 9 exd6 Nf6 10 Qd4 Nxe4 11 Qxe4+ Kf7 12 Bf4 with a small advantage to White.

4 ... Nc6-d4
  Rarely played. More common is 4 ... fxe4 5 Nxe4 d5 6 Nxe5 dxe4 7 Nxc6 and now

(a) 7 ... bxc6? 8 Bxc6+ Bd7 9 Qh5+ Ke7 10 Qe5+ Be6 11 f4 exf3 12 0-0 Rb8 13 d4 Nf6 14 d5 with a clear advantage for White (Gipslis-Tringov, Varna 1962).

(b) 7 ... Qg5 8 Qe2 Nf6 9 f4 Qh4+ 10 g3 Qh3 11 Ne5+ c6 12 Bc4 Bc5

13 c3 Ng4 14 d4 and again White's advantage is clear (Bagirov-Schatatinski, USSR 1966).

(c) 7 ... Qd5 8 c4 Qd6 9 Nxa7+ Bd7 10 Bxd7+ Qxd7 11 Qh5+ Kd8 12 Qa5 Ke8 13 0-0 Nf6 14 d3 exd3 15 Be3 with a small advantage to White.

5 Bb5-a4
  Again there are many moves that White can consider:

(a) 5 Nxe5 Qf6 6 Nf3 Nxb5 7 Nxb5 fxe4! 8 Qe2 Qe7 9 Nfd4 d6 gives equal chances.

(b) 5 exf5 Nf6 6 Nxe5 Bc5 7 0-0 0-0 8 Nf3 and Black has insufficient compensation for the sacrificed pawns.

(c) 5 Bc4 c6 6 0-0 d6 7 Re1 Nxf3+ 8 Qxf3 f4 9 g3 Qf6 10 d4 g5 11 dxe5 dxe5 12 Qh5+ with a small White advantage.

5 ... Ng8-f6

6 Nf3xe5
  Usually the order of White's 6th and 7th moves are reversed. By playing 6 Nxe5 Karpov allows the interesting possibility for Black of 6 ... Qe7 7 f4 b5!? 8 Nxb5 Nxb5 9 Bxb5 fxe4 or 7 Nf3 Nxf3+ 8 Qxf3 fxe4 9 Qg3 c6 10 0-0 b5 11 Bb3 d5 12 Re1 with a small advantage to White.

6 ... f5xe4
  6 ... Bc5 could be met by 7 Nd3! Bb6 8 e5 with advantage to White.

7 0-0 Bf8-c5

After 7 ... Bd6 White can reply with
8 Ng4 or 8 Nc4 Be7 9 d3 exd3
10 Qxd3 Ne6 11 Ne5 with advantage.

ZEITLIN 27.1

KARPOV TO MOVE

8 Nc3xe4!?

8 d3! is very strong here. After
8 ... exd3 9 Nxd3! Be7 10 Re1 0-0
11 Ne5 Black will have to play an
excellent game, even to escape from
the opening! So Black would do better
to sacrifice the e-pawn by 8 ... 0-0
9 dxe4 and play on with a pawn fewer
but with active pieces.

8 ... Nf6xe4

9 Qd1-h5+ g7-g6

9 ... Ke7? allows mate in two and
9 ... Kf8?? mate in one!

10 Ne5xg6

Now 10 ... hxg6? loses to 11 Qxh8+
Ke7 (11 ... Bf8 12 Qxd4) 12 Qe5+
and 13 Qxe4 when White is the
exchange and two pawns ahead.

10 ... Ne4-f6?

Losing the game virtually by force.
The only move to give Black real
chances of survival was 10 ... Qg5!
After 11 Qxg5 Nxg5 12 Nxh8 b5!
(not 12 ... Ne2+ 13 Kh1 Ne4
14 d3 Nxf2+ 15 Rxf2 Bxf2 16 Bh6
when White has an extra pawn and
with the threats to the black pieces
on e2 and f2 wins easily. White could,
if necessary, have avoided this line

ZEITLIN 27.2

KARPOV TO MOVE

altogether by playing 12 Re1+ Nge6
before 13 Nxh8) 13 Bb3 Nxb3
14 axb3 Bd4 15 c3 Bxh8 16 d4.
Although White's rook and two
pawns against Black's bishop and
knight is considered to be about
equal material, the disorganized black
pieces, White's superior pawn structure (in particular his three-to-one
K-side majority), and the open a-file,
give White the advantage in this
position.

11 Qh5-e5+

After 11 Qxc5? Ne6! 12 Qf5 hxg6
13 Qxg6+ Ke7 the position is unclear,
but Black, in my opinion, has the
better chances.

11 ... Bc5-e7

If 11 ... Kf7? 12 Nxh8+ Qxh8
13 Qxc5 gives White the exchange
and two pawns extra.

12 Ng6xh8

The alternative was 12 Re1 Nf3+!
13 gxf3 Rg8 14 Qxe7+ Qxe7
15 Rxe7+ Kd8 when, although
White is still winning, Black can put
up much resistance.

12 ... b7-b5

After 12 ... Nc6 both 13 Qg3 Kf8
14 d4 and 13 Bxc6 dxc6 14 Re1 Kf8
15 d4 win quickly.

13 Qe5xd4 b5xa4

14 Rf1-e1

Threatening the knight on f6.

14 ... Ke8-f8

15 d2-d3   Ra8-b8

16 Qd4-e5!
Now the threat is 17 Bh6+ Kg8 18 Qg5+ and mate next move (17 ... Ke8 would still allow 18 Qxf6).

ZEITLIN TO MOVE   27.3

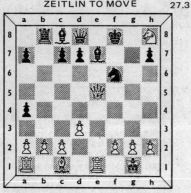

KARPOV

16 ... Nf6-g8
The only move 16 ... Kg8 leaves the e7 bishop en prise.

17 Qe5-h5   Kf8-g7

18 Nh8-f7   Qd8-e8
Now comes the final blow to Black's position.

19 Bc1-h6+!   Ng8xh6
19 ... Kf6? allows mate in two.

20 Qh5xh6+   Kg7xf7

21 Qh6xh7+   Kf7-f8
21 ... Kf6 is no better.

22 Re1-e3
Threatening 23 Rf3+, to which the only defence is as played.

22 ... Rb8-b6

23 Re3-g3   Black resigns
The threat of 23 Rg8 mate cannot be satisfactorily parried. 23 Rae1 Re6 24 Rf3+ would have been equally effective (24 ... Bf6 25 Rxf6+ Rxf6 26 Qh8+).

Game 28

WHITE Polugaevsky   English Opening
39th USSR Championship, Leningrad 1971

This game was included by Karpov chiefly because of the importance of its result. It was the last round of the twenty-one-round tournament, and Karpov was coming home very strongly. In the previous seven rounds he had scored four wins and three draws, and one more win would see him into third and possibly second place. The leading scores were: Savon 14½, Tal and Smyslov 13, Karpov 12½, Stein 12, and Balashov, Bronstein, and Polugaevsky 11. The pairings were Krogius v. Bronstein, Tukmakov v. Savon, Balashov v. Stein, Tal v. Smyslov, and Polugaevsky v. Karpov. Unfortunately Karpov could not force a win. Balashov beat Stein and the rest of the games were drawn.

Although this game is agreed drawn after only 23 moves it is an exciting and hard-fought encounter and not a 'grandmaster draw'.

1 c2-c4   c7-c5

2 Ng1-f3   Ng8-f6

3 Nb1-c3   d7-d5
Karpov seems to like this system

against the English Opening. For
further examples see his games with
Korchnoi (Game 31) and Stein (Game
36).

4 c4xd5   Nf6xd5

5 g2-g3

The most logical continuation—trying
to exploit the opened h1-a8 diagonal—
but also possible are 5 e3, 5 e4, and
5 d4 (Game 36).

5 ... g7-g6

Also playable are:

(a) 5 ... Nxc3 6 bxc3 g6 7 Qa4+ Nd7
8 h4 h5 9 Rb1 Bg7 10 Bg2 0-0 11 c4
e5 12 d3 Nb6 13 Qc2 Bd7 14 Be3
Qe7 15 Nd2 f5! 16 Nb3 Rac8
17 Bxb7 Rc7 18 Bg2 f4! with a strong
attack for the pawn (Petrosian-Szabo,
Bucharest 1953).

(b) 5 ... e6 6 Bg2 Nc6 7 0-0 Be7 8 Nxd5
exd5 9 d4 0-0 10 dxc5 Bxc5 with a
level position. This transposes into
the Queen's Gambit, Tarrasch Variation.

(c) 5 ... Nc7 (The Rubinstein System)
6 Bg2 Nc6 7 Qa4! Bd7 8 Qe4 g6
9 Ne5 Bg7 10 Nxd7 Qxd7 11 0-0 0-0
12 d3 Ne6 with approximately even
chances (Vaganian-Polugaevsky, 39th
USSR Championship 1971).

6 Bf1-g2   Bf8-g7

7 0-0   0-0

8 Nc3xd5

The logical way for White to develop
on the Q-side.

8 ... Qd8xd5

9 d2-d3   Nb8-a6!?

An interesting idea. Black is anxious
to prevent the development of the
white queen's bishop, but after the
natural 9 ...Nc6 10 Be3! is possible.
If then 10 ...Bxb2 11 Rb1 Bg7
(11 ...Qxa2? 12 Qc2 wins a piece)
12 Nd4! Qd6 (12 ...Qxa2 13 Nxc6
bxc6 14 Bxc6 Bh3 15 Bxa8 Bxf1
16 Qxf1 Rxa8 17 Bxc5 and White
stands slightly better) 13 Nxc6 bxc6
14 Qa4 Bd7 15 Rfc1 and White
regains the pawn with a much better

game. Also possible here is 11 Nd4!?
Qd6 12 Nb5 Qe5 13 Rb1 with advantage to White.

10 a2-a3

Naturally after 10 Be3 Bxb2 11 Rb1
Bg7 White has insufficient compensation for the sacrificed pawn. Thus:

(a) 12 Nd4 Qxa2.

(b) 12 Nd2 Qxa2 13 Bxb7 Bxb7 (or 13 ...
Rb8!?) 14 Rxb7 e6.

In each case Black holds the advantage.

10 ... Qd5-h5

Preparing to exchange the white-
squared bishops by 11 ... Bh3. This
move also takes the queen away from
the threat of the bishop on g2 to a
safer square.

11 Ra1-b1

Not necessarily with the idea of 12 b4
as this move also frees the bishop c1
from defending the weak b2 pawn.

11 ... Bc8-h3

The natural continuation. Now White
launches a dangerous Q-side attack.

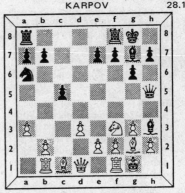

KARPOV   28.1

POLUGAEVSKY TO MOVE

12 Qd1-b3!

An unpleasant move for Black. The
b7 pawn cannot be defended easily
except by the text move. The alternative 12 b4 is not so strong: e.g.
12 b4 cxb4 13 axb4 Rfc8, when
Black's Q-side majority and lead in
development give him the advantage.

12 ...b7-b6

13 Qb3-c4   Na6-c7

The only way to defend the knight.

14 Bg2xh3

So that his next move will carry some extra force. After 14 b4 Bxg2 15 Kxg2 Ne6 the game is even.

14 ...Qh5xh3

15 b2-b4   Nc7-e6

Again the only logical defence.

16 Bc1-e3   Ra8-c8

After 16 ...cxb4 17 axb4 there is no way that Black can make anything of his Q-side majority. If the a-pawn advances the b6 pawn is lost, and otherwise the white queen will simply blockade at a6, thus immobilising the black pawns and gaining the advantage for White. e.g. 17 ...Rfc8 18 Qa6 Nc7 19 Qb7 Qd7 20 Rfc1 etc.

17 Qc4-a6!

Perhaps Karpov was expecting the inferior 17 Rfc1 when 17 ...Nd4! gives Black the advantage. Now however there is no satisfactory way to defend the a7 pawn. e.g. 17 ...cxb4 18 axb4 Rc7 19 Rfc1 Rfc8 20 Qxc8+ Rxc8 21 Rxc8+ Nf8 22 R1c1 with advantage to White.

17 ...Ne6-d4!

The only move to give Black any chances.

18 Be3xd4

18 Nxd4? would be a mistake. After 18 ...cxd4 Black has threats of either 19 ...Rc2 or 19 ...Rc7 and 20 ...R8c8 (note the black queen now covers c8) and thus holds a sizeable advantage.

18 ...c5xd4

19 Qa6xa7   Qh3-e6!

The point of the pawn sacrifice. The threat of Qxe2 followed by Qxd3 forces White into a defensive move.

20 Rf1-e1   Rc8-a8

Regaining the pawn.

21 Qa7-b7   Ra8xa3

At first sight it appears that this position is favourable to Black. The bishop is certainly superior to the white knight and the infiltration of the black rooks by Ra3-c3 and then Rf8-c8 would normally give Black the advantage. Unfortunately for Karpov, his queen is obliged to defend both the e7 and b6 pawns and this fact allows White a see-saw knight manœuvre to escape with a draw.

22 Nf3-g5   Qe6-e5

After 22 ...Qf5 23 Ne4 Qe6 White can still take the draw by 24 Ng5, or, since he now has the c3 square covered, can play 24 Rbc1 and 25 Rc7 (24 ... f5? 25 Ng5 Qf6 26 Qd5+ Kh8 27 Ne6 with a crushing position for White).

23 Ng5-f3

Now 23 ...Qd6 (to escape the repetition) loses a pawn to 24 Nd2! Since the coming 25 Nc4 cannot be adequately met (24 ...Ra2 25 Nc4 Qe6 26 Qxb6 Rxe2 27 Qxe6 Rxe6 28 Rxe6 fxe6 29 b5 etc.) On the other hand, the long-term prospects for White are poor (as outlined in the note to Black's 21st move).

Draw agreed

Game 29

BLACK Hort   Sicilian Defence, Scheveningen Variation
Alekhine Memorial Tournament, Moscow 1971

By choosing a sharp opening variation, Karpov brings about an unusual and complicated position, offering chances for both sides. In an obscure middle-game Karpov gains a pawn, but immediately returns it for a winning attack to score his second full point of the tournament. This game was played in round 11. Karpov had scored one win (against Lengyel) and nine draws before this game and went on to finish with four wins and three draws, and so tied for first place with Stein.

1 e2-e4   c7-c5

2 Ng1-f3   d7-d6

3 d2-d4   c5xd4

4 Nf3xd4   Ng8-f6

5 Nb1-c3   e7-e6

6 g2-g4

A dangerous move for Black. This line has become popular recently.

6 ... Nb8-c6

The idea 6 ... d5? is refuted by
7 exd5 Nxd5 8 Bb5+ Bd7 9 Nxd5
exd5 (if 9 ... Bxb5 10 Nxb5 exd5
11 Qxd5! wins a pawn) 10 Qe2+ when
White's advantage is clear. Thus:

(a) 10 ... Qe7 11 Be3 a6 12 Bxd7+
Nxd7 13 Nf5 Qe6 14 0-0-0 0-0-0
15 Qd3 Nf6 16 Rhe1 Qc6 17 Qd4.

(b) 10 ... Be7 11 Nf5 Kf8 12 Bxd7
Nxd7 13 Bf4 Qa5+ 14 c3 Re8
15 Nxe7 Qc5 16 Be3 Qxe7 17 0-0-0

But 6 ... h6 is possible: e.g. 7 g5 hxg5
8 Bxg5 Nc6 9 Qd2 a6 10 0-0-0 Bd7
11 h4 Qc7 12 Bh3 Be7 13 f4 Nxd4
14 Qxd4 0-0-0! (if 14 ... Bc6
15 Rhe1 and now 15 ... 0-0-0 can be
met by 16 Nd5! so Black chose
15 ... Kf8 [Gipslis-Jansa, Budapest
1970]) with an interesting game
offering chances for both sides.

7 g4-g5   Nf6-d7

8 f2-f4   a7-a6

If 8 ... h6 9 Nxe6 fxe6 10 Qh5+ is
a sacrifice worth considering.

9 Bc1-e3   Bf8-e7

9 ... h6!? would give White the opportunity to sacrifice on e6 as in the note
above but with an extra tempo. Both
10 gxh6 and 10 g6 are met by 10 ...
Qh4+!

10 Rh1-g1

Now 10 ... h6 11 g6 Bh4+ 12 Ke2!
is just one of the possibilities available.
Black chooses an equalizing plan
based on gaining control of the e5
square.

10 ... Nc6xd4

11 Qd1xd4   e6-e5

12 Qd4-d2   e5xf4

13 Be3xf4   Nd7-e5

14 Bf1-e2   Bc8-e6

HORT   29.1

KARPOV TO MOVE

Black has, to some extent, managed to equalize the position. He has control of the e5 square, but has lost both the d5 and f5 squares to White. He can seek some freedom by h7-h6 should the opportunity arise, and he can still castle on either side of the board. White, meanwhile, will be aiming to castle Q-side and will try to exploit the d5 and f5 squares. He can try for a central breakthrough or can use his spatial advantage to pin Black down to defence. For the time being, Karpov takes the two bishops and Hort replies by forcing h7-h6.

HORT TO MOVE   29.2

KARPOV

15 Nc3-d5   Be6xd5

15 ... Bf8? is too passive, and Black prefers to lose his white-squared bishop.

16 e4xd5   Ne5-g6

17 Bf4-e3

White could safely have continued 17 0-0-0 Nxf4 18 Qxf4 when despite the bishops of opposite colours White has the advantage owing to his spatial supremacy.

17 ... h7-h6!?

An interesting pawn sacrifice, leading to many complications and an unclear position. It would have been much safer to try and castle with 17 ... Qc7, for example 18 Rg3 (to meet 18 ... 0-0-0 by 19 Ba7!) 0-0 19 0-0-0 Rfe8 and although Black's game is a little cramped he has reasonable defensive chances. This alternative was also open to Black at move 16 and it is strange that Hort (very much a positional player) did not choose this line.

18 g5xh6   Be7-h4+

19 Ke1-d1   g7xh6

20 Be3xh6 *(see Diagram 29.2)*

20 ... Bh4-f6!

The best move. Both 20 ... Qf6 21 Be3! and 20 ... Qd7 21 Bg7 give White control of the a1-h8 diagonal. Black's immediate threat to the b-pawn is easily met, but the white h-pawn cannot be saved.

21 c2-c3   Bf6-e5

The idea of this move is to win back the h-pawn by 22 ... Qh4 (after 22 h3).

22 Rg1-g4!

After 22 Bg5 Qb6 23 Be3 Qc7 the h-pawn falls. The text move removes the threat of 22 ... Qh4 and gives the possibility of a central attack by Rg4-e4 or a Q-side 'prod' with Rg4-b4.

22 ... Qd8-f6?!

After this move Black cannot regain his lost pawn satisfactorily. After 22 ... Bxh2 23 Kc2! Ne5 24 Rb4 Qf6 the situation is very unclear. For example 25 Be3 Qf5+ 26 Kb3!? is possible. Black has excellent counter-chances against the black king to offset his inferior development and somewhat scattered forces.

23 h2-h4!

This pawn is untouchable on account of 23 ... Nxh4? 24 Bg5 winning a piece.

23 ... Qf6-f5

Preventing the threatened 24 h5 followed by 25 Bg7.

24 Rg4-b4!

This renews the threat of h5 and incidentally threatens the b7 pawn. It also frees the bishop on e2 which can now move to d3 and provide the c2 square for the king.

24 . . . Be5-f6

24 . . . Rg8 (threatening 25 . . . Nxh4
26 Rxh4 Rg1+ etc.) could be strongly
answered by 25 Bd3 Qf3+ 26 Kc2
and now the threat is simply 27 Be4
consolidating the extra pawn (26 . . .
Qxd5? allows 27 Bb5+!).

25 h4-h5 Ng6-e7

And not 25 . . . Ne5? when 26 Rf4
leaves Black's queen no square to
defend the bishop on f6.

26 Rb4-f4!

By a series of precise moves Karpov
is succeeding in driving home his extra
pawn advantage.

26 . . . Qf5-e5

Not 26 . . . Qxd5? 27 Rxf6 and White
wins a piece.

27 Rf4-f3!

HORT TO MOVE   29.3

KARPOV

The culmination of White's manœuvres.
The threats of 28 Bf4, 28 Re3, and the
simple 28 Kc2 give Hort no real chance
except to regain his lost pawn.

27 . . . Ne7xd5

28 Rf3-d3 Rh8xh6

The only move. After 28 . . . Ne7
29 Bf4 White is a pawn ahead with a
crushing position.

29 Rd3xd5!

After 29 Qxh6? Nf4 30 Rd2 0-0-0
the threat of 31 . . . Rh8 can be parried
only by 31 Qh7, when 31 . . . Re8

32 Bg4+ Kb8 gives Black excellent
counterchances. But even better is
29 . . . Bg5 30 Qh7 Ne3+ when Black's
chances are promising to say the least.
The text move is a Karpov crusher.

29 . . . Qe5-e4

Black could try 29 . . . Qe6 30 Rxd6
Qxd6 31 Qxd6 Rd8 32 Qxd8+ Kxd8
(or 32 . . . Bxd8). White's extra pawn
should prove decisive despite the
bishops of opposite colours, but Black
would retain some drawing chances.

30 Rd5-d3!

Now the threats 31 Re3 and 31 Qxh6
force Black's hand.

30 . . . Qe4-h1+

31 Kd1-c2 Qh1xa1

32 Qd2xh6 Bf6-e5

33 Qh6-g5

The threat is 34 Qg8+

(a) 34 . . . Kd7? 35 Qxe5 wins a piece.

(b) 34 . . . Kf8 35 Rf3 with 36 Bc4 coming.

(c) 34 . . . Rd8 35 Rf3 with 36 Qg8+
coming.

Black is lost in all variations. Hort
chooses the quickest way.

. . . Black resigns

A game that illustrates how a great
player is suited to all types of situation.
Every white move from 22 to 29 had to
be accurate to ensure the win. An excellent game by Karpov, and one which
Hort can consider himself unlucky to lose.

Game 30

BLACK Bronstein   Sicilian Defence, Najdorf Variation
Alekhine Memorial Tournament, Moscow 1971

Bronstein is trapped in an interesting, if highly theoretical, variation of the Najdorf. Karpov springs his improvement on move 21 (!) and Bronstein can find no adequate reply. In his notes to the game, Karpov showed that Black had a losing game in all variations, and so Bronstein's exchange sacrifice was Black's best practical choice. For once we see Karpov stumble a little on his way to victory, but the full point is always in his grasp.

1 e2-e4   c7-c5

2 Ng1-f3   d7-d6

3 d2-d4   c5xd4

4 Nf3xd4   Ng8-f6

5 Nb1-c3   a7-a6

6 Bf1-e2
As against Tukmakov in Game 24, Karpov allows Black to play a Scheveningen variation. Unlike Tukmakov, Bronstein chooses the Opochensky Variation.

6 ...e7-e5

7 Nd4-b3   Bc8-e6

8 f2-f4   Qd8-c7
So as to meet 9 f5 by 9 ... Bc4.

9 0-0   Nb8-d7

10 f4-f5   Be6-c4

11 a2-a4
Preventing the Q-side advance b5.

11 ...Bf8-e7

12 Bc1-e3   0-0

13 a4-a5
White's opening is aimed at dissuading Black from the advance b5 by indirect pressure on the a6 pawn and, in the long term, he is hoping for control of the d5 square. Black has counterplay against White's weak e4 pawn and hopes to use the c4 square, and possibly even the b4 square, to increase the pressure with his rooks and queen.

13 ...b7-b5
Although this move weakens the a6 pawn it is absolutely necessary. After (say) 13 ... Rfc8 14 Ra4! Bxe2 15 Qxe2 Black will have great difficulty in ever freeing his game.

14 a5xb6   Nd7xb6

15 Kg1-h1!
Threatening 16 Bxb6 Bxe2 17 Bxc7 Bxd1 18 Raxd1 winning a piece. The immediate 15 Bxb6 was played by Tal against Fischer at Curaçao in 1962, but after 15 ... Qxb6+ 16 Kh1 Bb5! Black already had the advantage. Note that now 15 ... Bxe2 16 Qxe2 Nc4 is strongly met by 17 Bg5! when White takes control of d5.

15 ...Rf8-c8

16 Be3xb6   Qc7xb6

17 Be2xc4   Rc8xc4

18 Qd1-e2   Rc4-b4
Better here is 18 ...Rac8! when 19 Ra2 Bd8 20 Rfa1 Qb7 21 Ra4 Rxa4 gives Black approximate equality. The game Karpov-R. Byrne, Leningrad Interzonal 1973, was agreed drawn here, but in the original game, Karpov-Stoica, Student Olympiad, Graz 1972, the continuation was 22 Rxa4 Rc6 23 Qd3 g6! 24 h3 Nh5 25 Ra1 Nf4 26 Qf3 Rc4! with equality.

19 Ra1-a2   *(see Diagram 30.1)*

The opening has come out in White's favour. His pressure against the a6 pawn outweighs the threats to his e4 pawn. Black's best try here appears to

BRONSTEIN TO MOVE   30.1

KARPOV

be, not 19 . . . Qb7 20 Na5 Qc7
21 Nd5 Nxd5 22 exd5 Rb5 23 Qd2
Qc5 24 c4 Rb6 (Geller-Fischer,
Curaçao 1962) when 25 Ra4! (and not
Geller's 25 Qe2) gives White a considerable advantage: e.g. 25 . . . Rab8
(the threat was 26 b4) 26 Nc6 R8b7
27 Ra5! and now 27 . . . Qxc4 is met
by 28 Nxe7+ Rxe7 29 Rc1 with mate
to follow; but 19 . . . Bd8 20 Rfa1
Qb7 (20 . . . a5 21 Rxa5 Rxa5 22 Nxa5
and now 22 . . . Rxb2 is met by 23 Nc4)
21 Rxa6 Rxa6 22 Qxa6 Qxa6
23 Rxa6 Be7! 24 Ra8+ Bf8 25 Kg1!
g6! (and not 25 . . . Nxe4 26 Nd5 Rb7
27 Na5 Rd7 28 b4) 26 fxg6 hxg6
27 Nd5 Nxd5 28 exd5 f5 when White's
extra pawn is of little significance in
the ending.
Bronstein's plan is to safeguard his
king by his next two moves and then
to proceed as in the second line above.
Karpov's solution is elegant and simple
and refutes Black's idea.

19 . . . h7-h6

20 Rf1-a1   Be7-f8
Now 21 Rxa6 Rxa6 22 Rxa6 (or
22 Qxa6 Qxa6 23 Rxa6 Nxe4
24 Nxe4 Rxe4) 22 . . . Qb7 23 Na5
Qc7 and Black's threats of 24 . . . Rxb2
and 24 . . . Qxc3! leave White with no
better than 24 Nb3 and a draw.

21 Ra2-a4!   Ra8-c8
After 21 . . . Rxa4 22 Rxa4 White has

complete control of the position and
Black has no adequate counterplay.

22 Ra4xb4!
After 22 Rxa6 Qd8 followed by
23 . . . Rxc3 etc. gives Black plenty of
play. By 22 Rxb4! White achieves a
clear advantage.

22 . . . Qb6xb4

23 Qe2xa6   Rc8xc3
A good practical try. After 23 . . . Rc4
24 Ra4 Rxe4! 25 Qf1! and now:

(a) 25 . . . Qxa4 26 Nxa4 Rxa4 27 g3
gives White queen against rook and
bishop.

(b) 25 . . . Rf4 26 Qxf4 Qxf4 27 Rxf4
exf4 gives White a much superior endgame.

24 b2xc3   Qb4xe4

25 Qa6-d3   Qe4-f4

26 Ra1-f1   Qf4-h4

BRONSTEIN   30.2

KARPOV TO MOVE

At the moment Black has for his exchange no pawns but several threats:
d6-d5 Nf6-g4 and Nf6-e4. White has
certain problems in converting his
extra material into a win, since he has
no convenient way of exchanging
queens. Karpov decides to give up a
pawn in order to force this exchange,
and from then on requires only a
winning technique.

27 Nb3-d2

Not 27 c4?! when 27 . . . Ng4 28 Qg3
Qxg3 29 hxg3 Ne3 wins a pawn for
Black. The game would then be almost
equal, although White would retain
a small advantage.

27 . . . e5-e4

28 Qd3-g3   Qh4xg3

29 h2xg3   d6-d5
Black's threats of Bd6, or e3 followed
by Ne4, are quite unpleasant, but
Karpov gives up the g3 pawn, frees
his pieces, and gives Black no further
chances.

30 Rf1-b1!   Bf8-d6

31 Kh1-g1   Bd6xg3
31 . . . Ng4 is met by 32 Rb5.

32 Kg1-f1   Bg3-f4

33 Kf1-e2
With his king centralized, Karpov can
now begin to work on the weak d5
pawn.

33 . . . Nf6-h5

34 Nd2-f1   Bf4-e5

35 Nf1-e3   Be5xc3

36 Rb1-b8+
The simple 36 Nxd5 was better.

36 . . . Kg8-h7

37 Ne3xd5   Nh5-g3+

38 Ke2-f2?
38 Ke3 was better. Black's hopes are
now briefly revived.

38 . . . Bc3-d4+!

39 Kf2-e1
And of course not 39 Kxg3 Be5+
winning the rook.

39 . . . Ng3xf5

40 Rb8-b4   Nf5-e3

41 Ke1-e2
White avoids 41 Rxd4?? Nxc2+
winning the rook.

41 . . . Bd4-c5

42 Rb4-b5   Ne3xd5

43 Rb5xc5   Nd5-f4+

44 Ke2-f2   Kh7-g6

45 g2-g3   Nf4-e6

46 Rc5-d5!

BRONSTEIN TO MOVE   30.3

KARPOV

Controlling the black knight and thus
preparing for the rapid advance of the
c-pawn. White has now succeeded in
regaining the ground he lost by his
inaccurate 36th and 38th moves. This
time he makes no mistake in seizing
the full point.

46 . . . f7-f5

47 c2-c4   f5-f4

48 c4-c5   e4-e3+

49 Kf2-f3   f4xg3

50 Kf3xg3   h6-h5

51 c5-c6   e3-e2
If 51 . . . h4+ 52 Kxh4 e2 53 Re5
Nd4 54 Rxe2 and now 54 . . . Nxe2
loses to 55 c7 and the pawn queens;
while 54 . . . Nxc6 loses the knight
after 55 Re6+.

52 Kg3-f2   Kg6-f6

53 Rd5-d7   Black resigns
The c-pawn costs Black a piece.

Game 31

WHITE Korchnoi   English Opening
Alekhine Memorial Tournament, Moscow 1971

After getting off to a poor start, Karpov seizes on an opportunity to equalize
the position, and thereafter goes from strength to strength. A passed pawn
plays a major part in Korchnoi's downfall, as in many other of Karpov's
victories.

1 c2-c4   c7-c5

2 Ng1-f3   Ng8-f6

3 g2-g3
> The Korchnoi-Karpov game from the
> 38th USSR Championship, Riga 1970,
> went 3 Nc3 d5 4 cxd5 Nxd5 5 d4
> cxd4 6 Qxd4 Nxc3 7 Qxc3 Nc6
> 8 e4 a6 9 Bc4 Qa5 10 Bd2 Qxc3
> 11 Bxc3 with advantage to White.
> Although 3 g3 cannot objectively be
> said to be a better move than 3 Nc3,
> it is certainly more effective if Black
> intends to play 3 . . . d5.

3 . . . d7-d5

4 c4xd5   Nf6xd5

5 Bf1-g2   g7-g6?!
> A dubious move. Far safer would
> have been 5 . . . Nc6 or even 5 . . . e6,
> when Black's position is sounder.

6 d2-d4!
> Now Black is faced with the threat
> of a massive pawn centre by 7 e4 and
> 8 d5, as well as the possible loss of a
> pawn to 7 dxc5.

6 . . . Bf8-g7
> After 6 . . . cxd4 7 Qxd4 Black has
> no convenient way to prevent 8 Qxh8
> —both 7 . . . Nf6 8 Qxd8+ Kxd8
> 9 Nc3, and 7 . . . f6 8 Ne5! and
> 9 Qa4+, are favourable to White.

7 e2-e4
> White could opt for a simple lead in
> development by 7 dxc5 Qa5+ 8 Nbd2
> Qxc5 9 0-0-0-0 10 Nb3! when White's
> threats against the d5 knight are
> awkward to meet. The aggressive 7 e4
> is more in Korchnoi's style.

7 . . . Nd5-c7!?
> The knight is headed for d4, where
> Black hopes it will provide an outpost
> in the enemy position and increase his
> hold on the a1-h8 diagonal. However,
> both 7 . . . Nf6 and 7 . . . Nb6 seem
> more logical, as in the analagous
> positions arising from the Neo-Grünfeld
> Opening.

8 d4-d5
> After 8 dxc5? Qxd1+ 9 Kxd1 Ne6
> White's extra pawn falls immediately.

8 . . . Nc7-b5

9 0-0 0-0
> Black could have increased his hold
> on d4 here by 9 . . . Bg4, and if 10 Qa4,
> then Qd7.

10 Qd1-c2   Nb8-a6

11 Bc1-f4   Bc8-g4

12 Nb1-d2

KARPOV TO MOVE   **31.1**

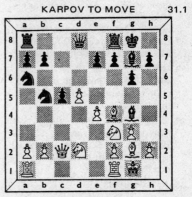

KORCHNOI

The position is favourable to White. He controls more squares in the centre and his pawns there are not easily attackable. His pieces co-ordinate well. The threat is simply 13 Qb3.

12 ... Nb5-d4

13 Nf3xd4   c5xd4

14 Nd2-f3

White is preparing to play Ne5, when the white-squared bishop will find itself very short of squares.

14 ... Qd8-b6

15 Nf3-e5?

Throwing away all his advantage. 15 Qd2 was a necessary preliminary to this move, as we shall see.

15 ... Bg7xe5!

The only move to keep Black's game alive: 15 ... Rac8 16 Qd2 gives White the move he wants, and 15 ... Bc8 is no move at all.

16 Bf4xe5   f7-f6

Now we see why 15 Qd2 was a necessary preliminary to Ne5—the black d-pawn is not en prise, and White is driven back in confusion.

17 Be5-f4   Ra8-c8

18 Qc2-a4

And not 18 Qd2? when 18 ... g5 wins the f4 bishop.

18 ... g6-g5

Black must prepare a square for his bishop before contemplating the capture of the b2 pawn. After 18 ... Qxb2 19 Rab1 Qc3 20 f3 Nc5 21 Qxa7, the situation is unclear.

19 Bf4-c1

After 19 Bd2, Black can take the b2 pawn in safety, since the bishop d2 is threatened.

19 ... Bg4-e2

Also possible here was 19 ... Nb4!? 20 f3 Bh5 and Black can occupy c2 as well as moving the bishop to e8 and then b5.

20 Rf1-e1   d4-d3

21 Bg2-f1

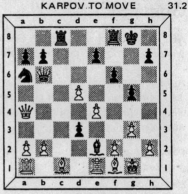

KARPOV TO MOVE   31.2

KORCHNOI

A remarkable transformation has come over the position. Black has pushed the white bishops to the back rank and has created a menacing passed pawn. Whatever advantage there is lies with Black, although White should be able to draw with best play, since the weakness of the d3 pawn compensates for Black's better development. However, Korchnoi is destined to commit a further inaccuracy.

21 ... Be2xf1

A tough decision: both 21 ... Nb4 and 21 ... Qb4 are tempting. In his notes in *Informator 12* Karpov gives the reason for rejecting 21 ... Nb4 as 22 Bxe2 Nc2 23 Bxd3 Nxe1 24 Be2, and now 24 ... Rc2 25 Be3 Qxb2 is refuted by 26 Bd4! winning the black queen; so Black must try 24 ... Nc2 25 Rb1 when White's two bishops and pawn, together with his threat of 26 Bg4, fully compensate for Black's rook and knight. Also 21 ... Qb4 22 Qxb4 Nxb4 23 Bxe2 Nc2 can be met by either 24 Bg4 Nxe1 25 Bxc8 Rxc8 26 Be3, or 24 Bxd3 Nxe1 25 Be2 Nc2 26 Rb1, and in both cases Black's advantage is minimal.

22 Re1xf1   Rc8-c2

23 Bc1-e3   Na6-c5

24 Qa4-d4?!

Probably better was 24 Qa3 Rc8
25 Rab1! Qa6 26 Qxa6 bxa6 (or
26 ...Nxa6 27 Rfd1) 27 Rfd1 Nxe4
28 Rxd3 when a draw is the likely
outcome.

24 ...e7-e5

25 d5xe6 e.p.   Qb6xe6

26 Ra1-c1?

After 26 b4 Nxe4 27 Qxd3 Rc3
Black's advantage is very small, but
now White never gets another chance
to capture the d3 pawn.

26 ...Rf8-c8

27 b2-b4   Nc5xe4

KARPOV TO MOVE   31.3

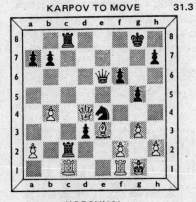

KORCHNOI

28 Rc1xc2

After 28 Qxd3 Nxf2! Black wins a
pawn and the White position falls
apart: e.g.

(a) 29 Qd4 Nh3+ 30 Kh1 Qc6+ and
mate in two.

(b) 29 Qxc2? Rxc2 30 Rxc2 Nh3+
31 Kg2 Qxe3 32 Kxh3 (or 32 Rc8+
Kg7 33 Rc7+ [33 Kxh3 Qe6+ wins
the rook] 33 ...Kg6 34 Kxh3 Qe2!
35 R7c1 g4+ 36 Kh4 h5 37 Rh1
Qe3 38 Rc5 Qg5+! 39 Rxg5 fxg5
mate) 32 ...Qe6+ 33 g4 (33 Kg2
Qe4+ wins the rook on c2) 33 ...
Qe3+ 34 Kg2 Qe4+ winning a rook.

(c) 29 Bxf2? Rxc1 winning the exchange.

(d) 29 Rxf2 Rxc1+ 30 Bxc1 Rxc1+
31 Rf1 (31 Kg2 g4! with a mating
attack e.g. 32 Re2 Qc6+ 33 Qe4 Rc2!!)
31 ...Rxf1+ 32 Qxf1 (32 Kxf1 Qxa2
33 Qd8+ Kg7 34 Qd7+ Qf7 with an
easy win because of the two extra
pawns) 32 ...Qe3+ 33 Kg2 Qe4+
34 Kg1 Kg7! and Black's queen
dominates the board, ensuring an easy
win.

28 ...d3xc2

Now the game is almost over. The
passed pawn is too much for White.

29 Rf1-c1   b7-b6

30 f2-f3   Ne4-d6

31 Qd4-d3   Rc8-c6!

White cannot capture the pawn
because his bishop would be en prise.
Black prepares for 32 ...Qc4—a move
that White is powerless to prevent,
since he must first defend his a-pawn.

32 a2-a4   Qe6-c4

33 Qd3-d2

33 Qxc4 Rxc4 would be equally hopeless. With queens on the board White
has some chance of exploiting the
slightly exposed black king.

33 ...Nd6-f7

34 f3-f4   g5-g4

35 b4-b5   Rc6-c8

36 Qd2-d7   h7-h5

The threat is now 37 ...Rd8
38 Qf5 Rd1+ 39 Kf2 Qf1 mate.

37 Kg1-f2   Qc4-c3!

Threatening 38 ...Rd8 39 Qf5
Rd2+.

38 Qd7-f5   Rc8-e8

White resigns

For after 39 Qg6+ Kf8 White is
powerless to prevent the loss of his
bishop (40 Re1 Qxe1+! 41 Kxe1
c1=Q+ etc.)

Game 32

BLACK Savon   Ruy López, Open Defence
Alekhine Memorial Tournament, Moscow 1971

When the seventeenth and last round of the Alekhine Memorial Tournament
was played, Karpov was still half a point behind the leader, Stein. The leading scores were Stein 10½, Karpov and Smyslov 10, Petrosian and Tukmakov 9½, and whereas Karpov had white against the USSR Champion
Savon, Stein was black against Tukmakov and Smyslov black against Hort.
Smyslov and Hort drew quickly and Tukmakov, although he was one or
two pawns up for the last fifteen moves of his game with Stein, drew.
Karpov, however, made no such mistake. Savon chose a rarely played opening line and was soon in trouble. He worked up a dangerous-looking attack,
but it was beaten off, and on move 24, Savon resigned. It must have been
disappointing for Karpov to see Stein survive against Tukmakov but nevertheless Karpov had still come equal first in the strongest chess tournament
for over twenty years.

This was a disappointing day for Savon also, for by losing to Karpov he
missed the grandmaster norm by half a point.

1 e2-e4   e7-e5
2 Ng1-f3 Nb8-c6
3 Bf1-b5 a7-a6
4 Bb5-a4 Ng8-f6
5 0-0   Nf6xe4
   The Open Defence to the Ruy López.
6 d2-d4   b7-b5
7 Ba4-b3 d7-d5
8 d4xe5   Bc8-e6
9 c2-c3   Bf8-c5
   The alternative is 9 ... Be7.
10 Nb1-d2 0-0
11 Bb3-c2 Be6-f5
   More popular here is 11 ... f5.
   Interesting is the move 11 ... Nxf2!?
   (The Dilworth Variation), but after
   12 Rxf2 f6 13 exf6 Qxf6 14 Qf1
   Bg4 15 h3 Bxf3 16 Nxf3 Ne5
   17 Bd1, White has the advantage.
12 Nd2-b3 Bf5-g6 *(see Diagram 32.1)*
   Again an unusual choice. 12 ... Bg4
   is more frequent, with the possibilities:
(a) 13 Qe1!? Bxf3 14 gxf3 Nxe5 15 Kg2

SAVON   32.1

KARPOV TO MOVE

Qf6 16 Qd1 Nxf2 17 Rxf2 Bxf2
18 Kxf2 with advantage to White.
(b) 13 Nxc5 Nxc5 14 Re1 Re8 15 Bf4
(15 Be3 Ne6 16 Qd3 g6 17 Bh6 Bf5
[17 ... Ne7 18 Nd4 Bf5 19 Nxf5
Nxf5 20 Bd2 Qh4 21 Qf1 Nc5 22 g3
Qc4 23 Qg2 Nd3 with an equal game:
Fischer-Larsen, Santa Monica 1966]
18 Qe2 Bxc2 19 Qxc2 Qd7 20 Rad1

Rad8 21 Qc1 Ne7 22 Bg5! with
advantage to White: Balashov-Karasev
39th USSR Championship 1971)
15 ... Bh5 (15 ... d4?! 16 h3! Bxf3
17 Qxf3 Ne7 18 Rad1 Ne6 19 cxd4
Nd5 20 Bc1 c6 21 Qe4 with a winning position for White: Robatch-
Zinser, Venice 1967) 16 Qd2 Bg6
17 Bxg6 hxg6 18 Rad1 Ne6 19 Ng5
with a small advantage for White:
Euwe-Eliskases, Mar del Plata 1947.

13 Nf3-d4   Bc5xd4

Also playable here is 13 ... Nxd4
14 cxd4 Bb6 15 f3 Ng5 16 Bxg5
followed by 17 f4 (Kostro-Pioch,
Poland 1973), but not 13 ... Nxe5?
when 14 f4 Nd7 15 f5 wins a piece
for White.

14 c3xd4

After 14 Nxd4 Nxd4 15 cxd4 c5
16 f3 cxd4 17 Qxd4 Ng3 18 Rf2!
White has the advantage.

14 ... a6-a5

Undermining the white d4 pawn, and
beginning a speculative Q-side attack.

15 Bc1-e3   Nc6-b4

16 Bc2-b1   a5-a4

17 Nb3-d2   a4-a3

Black's Q-side attack has reached its
logical conclusion. Black cannot bring
any more pieces into the offensive,
and since White can easily hold the

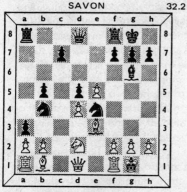

SAVON   32.2

KARPOV TO MOVE

situation, the idea behind Black's
Q-side attack must be considered
dubious. The remainder of the game
is thrust and counterthrust, as Savon
struggles desperately to avoid material
loss.

18 Qd1-c1!

The threat is 19 bxa3. Both 18 ... Nxd2
19 Qxd2 Nc6 20 Rc1 and 18 ... c5!?
19 dxc5 d4 20 Nxe4 dxe3 21 bxa3
exf2+ 22 Nxf2 are excellent for White
and, of course, 18 ... axb2 19 Qxb2
Nxd2 20 Qxd2 Nc6 21 Rc1 is no
better for Black. His position is poor
in all these variations; so Savon opts
for a tactical assault.

18 ... Ra8-a6

Karpov refutes this idea with his
customary ease, and after this move
Black's position can be considered lost.

19 b2xa3   Ra6-c6

After 19 ... Nxd2 20 Bxd2 Nc6
21 Bxg6 hxg6 22 Qc5 defends both
pawns (a3 and d4), threatens the
black b5 pawn, and prepares the way
for the white rooks to demolish Black's
Q-side pawns.

20 Qc1-b2   Nb4-c2

This meets with a neat refutation. No
better is 20 ... Nxd2 21 Bxd2 and
now 21 ... Nc2 is met by 22 Rc1!
and 21 ... Nd3 by 22 Qb3. In both
cases White wins a piece.

21 Rf1-c1!   Nc2xe3

The only try. After 21 ... Nxa1
22 Rxc6 or 21 ... Nxd2 22 Bxd2
Black loses a piece.

22 Rc1xc6   Ne4xf2

If 22 ... Qg5 23 Bxe4 Bxe4 24 g3
followed by 25 f4 and 26 Nxe4 wins.

23 Nd2-f1

And not (of course) 23 Kxf2 Nd1+.

23 ... Qd8-d7

Allowing a quick finish, but Black is
lost in any event.

24 Nf1xe3   Black resigns

After 24 ... Qxc6 25 Kxf2 Black is a
piece down without compensation.

6 1972 — Continued success

There were only ten days between the last round of the Alekhine
Memorial Tournament and the beginning of the Hastings International
Congress. Karpov began at Hastings where he had left off in Moscow, and
after ten rounds had scored seven wins and three draws. Three short draws
against Unzicker, Andersson, and Najdorf left him only half a point ahead
of Korchnoi. In the penultimate round the clash of the leaders produced a
decisive result in Korchnoi's favour, and so it was left to the author to
restore Karpov to his rightful first place by losing in the last round. Again
the first place had to be shared— this time with Korchnoi. The games from
this tournament are against Robert Byrne (Game 33), Hartston (Game 34),
and Mecking (Game 35). The first and last of these are remarkably similar
and together serve as a guide to endings with rooks, and bishops of opposite
colour. They are marked with the Karpov stamp of authority, unlike the
game against Hartston, who put up a brave fight and succumbed only under
time-pressure.

The follow-up to Hastings was yet another Soviet Team Championship.
This time Karpov was playing on a senior board for the first time—representing the RSFSR team on board two behind Polugaevsky. In the preliminaries
Karpov suffered a drastic reversal at the hands of Kjarner: he was two pieces
ahead at the time but blundered into a mating combination just three moves
deep. In the finals it was a different matter. He beat three of the best players in the whole competition, and despite a second loss, this time to Gipslis,
his score of 5½/9 helped his team to second place. The game with Stein
(Game 36) is a rare example of his defensive skill in beating off a dangerous
attack that follows a speculative piece sacrifice. Game 37 sees him outplaying the mighty Smyslov at his own game. Simply prodding, probing, and
quietly destroying, Karpov gets ample revenge for his defeat in the 39th
USSR Championship. The other game chosen from this event provides a
classical example of 'transference of advantage'. Karpov gives up a substantial positional advantage to buy time for a winning K-side attack.
Because of its devastating accuracy and simplicity, I consider this game
against Taimanov (Game 38) to be one of the finest in the collection.

After the Soviet Olympiad in March, Karpov had the chance of a short
rest before returning to the fray at the Student Olympiad held in Graz,
Austria, in July. Perhaps the lay-off affected his play, for in the preliminaries he managed only one win from four games. In the finals, however,
he shone again and brought his overall score up to 7/9. His best game was
a win over Hübner (Game 39) in which the domination of central squares
is a key factor.

At Skopje, Yugoslavia, in September and October the World Chess Olympiad saw Karpov representing the USSR on fifth board behind Petrosian, Korchnoi, Smyslov, and Tal, with Savon making up the team. His play seemed to be sharper than in previous events: he recorded win after win, and his final total of 13/15 was enough to give him first prize on board five. His one loss to Pădevski of Bulgaria was due solely to his aggressive tactics failing to pay off. In the game collection there are two examples of the aggressive Karpov winning by direct K-side attacks: against Enevoldsen who incidentally played only this one game throughout the whole Olympiad (Game 40), and against Ungureanu (Game 42). The other offering is a neat example of play against an isolated-queen's-pawn position. Bisguier (Game 41) is treated to a demonstration of active piece-play which completely destroys his defences. It is interesting to note that the Czech player Jansa drew against Karpov with black: he is thus the only player to have held Karpov with black in the Olympiads, Karpov having beaten his other fourteen opponents!

In the middle of November came the San Antonio (Texas) 'Fried Chicken' Tournament in which Karpov was to play. There were few weak players in this event and so Karpov spent enormous energy in the first half of the tournament beating the tail-enders. A 52-move win against Saidy was followed by a gem of a win against Browne (Game 43), although this too was a relatively long game, lasting 59 moves. A draw and a win were followed by a 60-mover against Suttles. Karpov scored a further 2½ in the next 3 rounds, which included completely outplaying Gligorić in round 8 (Game 44). So the leading scores after eight rounds were Karpov and Keres 7, Petrosian, Hort, and Gligorić 5. At this point both the leaders began to tire. Keres, who had already met most of the strong players, ended with five draws and two losses to finish in fifth place. For Karpov, however, the tournament was a little happier. He lost to Portisch from his favourite variation of the Nimzo-Indian in 26 moves, but managed to restore his confidence in time to grind out a 70-move win against Smith in the next round. His last five games were all drawn, not without incident. Against Kaplan in round 13 a draw was agreed in a position that was vastly inferior for Karpov, but Kaplan was in time-trouble. His poor finish allowed both Petrosian and Portisch to share first place with him: on the one hand a disappointment, but on the other another excellent tournament result.

Game 33

BLACK Robert Byrne   Sicilian Defence, Modern Rauzer
Hastings 1971-2

Karpov began the Hastings tournament in the same form he had shown at the Alekhine Memorial. After ten rounds he had seven wins and three draws, and looked all set for another convincing tournament win. But draws with Unzicker, Andersson, and Najdorf, and a loss to Korchnoi, left him half a point behind Korchnoi with only one round to go. At this point, however, I came to Karpov's rescue, and by losing an excellent game (on his part) I was able to ensure a joint first place for him.

   This game and Game 35 are two excellent examples of the attacking power of bishops of opposite colours, even when queens have been exchanged. Taken as a pair, they could well serve as textbook examples of endings with rooks, and bishops of opposite colour.

1 e2-e4   c7-c5

2 Ng1-f3   Nb8-c6

3 d2-d4   c5xd4

4 Nf3xd4   Ng8-f6

5 Nb1-c3   d7-f6

6 Bc1-g5   Bc8-d7
   The Modern Rauzer. It used to be considered that 7 Bxf6 was good here and, although this move is still played occasionally, it is generally thought that Black's two bishops and central pawn majority are adequate compensation for the weakened pawn-structure.

7 Qd1-d2   Ra8-c8
   Black aims at a rapid Q-side development with an exchange on d4 and Qa5 to follow.

8 0-0-0   Nc6xd4

9 Qd2xd4   Qd8-a5

10 f2-f4
   Black has more problems after 10 Bd2. His best try would appear to be 10 . . . a6 11 f3 (11 Kb1, Qc5 12 Qxc5 Rxc5 13 f3 with a small advantage to White) 11 . . . e5 12 Qe3 Be6 13 a3 Be7 14 g4 Qc7! with chances for both sides.

10 . . . h7-h6?!

A dubious move. Byrne was in an interesting situation here. The previous year, also at Hastings, he lost as White against the Yugoslav International Master Mestrović from this very variation. After 10 . . . h6 11 Bh4 g5 12 Be1 Bg7 13 g3 Bc6 14 Bh3 Mestrović chose the spectacular continuation 14 . . . 0-0!? 15 Bxc8 Nxe4? 16 Nxe4 Qxa2 and, after Byrne's 17 Qxg7+, was always winning. Byrne decides to test Karpov out in this line and is duly shown the way.

BYRNE   33.1

KARPOV TO MOVE

11 Bg5-h4   g7-g5

12 e4-e5!

The continuation is forced on Black. After 12 ... Ng4?! 13 exd6 e5 14 fxe5 gxh4 15 e6! White regains his piece with a winning attack, and 12 ... dxe5? 13 fxe5 gxh4 14 exf6 leaves the d7 bishop en prise.

12 ... g5xh4

13 e5xf6   e7-e6

14 Bf1-e2

White has already achieved a clear advantage. The black king is trapped in the centre for the rest of the game and White's central pressure with Bh5, Rhe1, and even Nd5 is strong.

14 ... Bd7-c6

15 Rh1-e1   Rh8-g8

After 15 ... Bxg2 16 Bb5+ Black is forced to play 16 ... Kd8, since 16 ... Bc6 17 f5! Bxb5 18 fxe6 is a winning attack for White:

(a) 18 ... fxe6 19 Rxe6+ Kd7 (or 19 ... Kf7 20 Qd5!) 20 Rxd6+ Kc7 (20 ... Bxd6 allows mate in two) 20 Qe5!

(b) 18 ... Bc6 19 e7.

(c) 18 ...h5 19 exf7+ Kd7 (19 ... Kxf7 20 Qd5+ wins the b5 bishop) 20 Qd5 or even 20 Re7+!?

After 16 ... Kd8 17 f5!? is an attractive possibility for White, and in any event, Black's position is highly suspect.

16 Be2-f3   Ke8-d7?!

More logical, and in keeping with his last move, was 16 ... Bxf3, but after 17 gxf3, because of the threats of a possible Rg1 (taking control of the g-file) and Kb1, followed by the direct Ne4 or Nd5, Black's game would still be much inferior.

17 Re1-e5   Qa5-b6

18 Qd4xb6   a7xb6

19 Bf3-h5!

Black is forced to exchange his f7 pawn for White's g2 pawn, since 19 ... Ke8? allows 20 Rxe6+.

19 ... Rg8xg2

20 Bh5xf7   Rg2xh2

21 Bf7xe6+   Kd7-c7

22 Re5-e3   Rc8-d8

23 Nc3-d5+!

Taking the game into a double rook and bishop ending.

23 ... Bc6xd5

Else the b6 pawn is lost.

24 Rd1xd5

BYRNE TO MOVE   33.2

KARPOV

We can now see the result of Karpov's idea. Black is tied up by White's control of the d5 point. His bishop on f8 is trapped by the f6 pawn. White can attack the black b6 and b7 pawns with his rooks, and Black's pieces are unable to prevent the Q-side invasion.

24 ... Rh2-f2

25 f4-f5   h6-h5

Threatening Bf8-h6-f4-e5.

26 Re3-c3+ . Kc7-b8

27 a2-a4   Rf2-f4?!

27 ... Bh6+ would activate the bishop and thus give Black better chances of survival.

28 Rc3-a3   Rf4-g4

29 a4-a5!

The Q-side attack does not take the expected form of Rb5, R3b3, etc., but is a short, sharp affair that decides the game rapidly.

29 ... Bf8-h6+

30 Kc1-b1   b6xa5

31 Rd5xa5

The threat is now 32 Ra8+ and
33 Rc3+ winning the d8 rook.

31 ... Kb8-c7

32 Ra5-b5   Rg4-g3

33 Ra3-a7   Rd8-b8

34 Be6-d5

Winning the b7 pawn. This is the
culmination of White's Q-side attack

begun by 29 a5! The rest of the game
is a neat rook-and-bishop mating
attack by White.

34 ... Rg3-g1+

35 Kb1-a2   Rg1-f1

36 Ra7xb7+   Rb8xb7

37 Rb5xb7+   Kc7-d8

38 Bd5-e6   h4-h3

39 Rb7-d7+   Kd8-e8

40 Rd7-c7   Black resigns

41 Rc8 mate cannot be prevented.

Game 34

BLACK Hartston   Sicilian Defence, Taimanov Variation
Hastings, 1971-2

After an opening in which Hartston manages to secure his K-side position
against Karpov's threats, the game is transformed by a well-timed black
pawn break. The resulting position should have been at best equal for
Karpov, but, with a little help from his opponent, he succeeds in forcing a
somewhat fortunate win.

1 e2-e4   c7-c5

2 Ng1-f3   e7-e6

3 d2-d4   c5xd4

4 Nf3xd4   Nb8-c6

5 Nd4-b5   d7-d6

6 c2-c4

The alternative to the 6 Bf4 played by
Karpov against Taimanov in Game 25.

6 ... Ng8-f6

7 Nb1-c3   a7-a6

8 Nb5-a3   Bf8-e7

9 Bf1-e2   0-0

10 0-0   b7-b6

The moves for both sides have been
natural, and it is only now that Black
has any other worthwhile possibilities:

(a) 10 ... Bd7 11 Be3 Qb8 12 f3 b6
13 Qe1 Ra7 14 Qf2 Rb7 15 Rfd1
Nb4 16 Rd2 Rd8 17 Rad1 Be8

18 f4 with a small advantage for
White (Kapengut-Balashov, 39th
USSR Championship 1971).

(b) 10 ... Rb8 11 Be3 (for 11 Bf4 b6
12 Qd2 Bb7 13 Rfd1 Ne5 14 f3
Qc7 15 Rac1 Rfd8 16 Kh1 and
now 16 ... Bc8 is best intending Bd7
but not 16 ...Bc6 17 Nd5! [Stein-
Taimanov, USSR 1970]) 11 ... Qa5
and now:

(b1) 12 Rc1 Bd7 13 f3 Rfd8 14 Qe1
Be8 15 Qf2 Nd7 16 Rfd1 Nc5 17 Bf1
Nb4 18 Nc2 Nxc2 19 Qxc2 b5!
(Kholmov-Taimanov, 37th USSR
Championship 1969).

(b2) 12 f3 Bd7 13 Qb3 b6 14 Rfd1
Rfc8 15 Bf1 Be8 16 Qc2 b5
(Drimer-Korchnoi, Luhačovice 1969).

(b3) 12 Qd2 Rd8 13 Rfd1 Bd7 14 f3
Be8 15 Rac1 Nd7 16 Bf1 Nc5
17 Nc2 Bf6 (Browne-Korchnoi,
Zagreb 1970).

(b4) 12 f4 Bd7 13 Qe1 Rfc8 14 Rd1
Be8 15 g4 Nd7 16 g5 Nc5 17 Rf3 f6
18 h4 Bf7 19 Qf2 with attacking
chances (Jansa-Korchnoi, Prague v.
Leningrad, 1970).

Although these lines are not totally
independent, they give the general
picture of the plans available for both
sides.

11 Bc1-e3 Bc8-d7

Black might also consider developing
the bishop on b7. By 11 . . . Bd7 and
a subsequent Rfd8 or Rfc8 Black can
manœuvre this piece to the excellent
square e8 from where it can support
the f7 pawn against a possible K-side
attack, and actively help in a b5 pawn
break. Furthermore on e8 the bishop
does not interfere with a black rook
on d8 and thus facilitates a d5 break.

After 11 . . . Bb7 12 f3 (if 12 Qd2?
Ne5 13 f3 d5 equalizes) then
12 . . . Re8 13 Qb3 Nd7 14 Rfd1
Nc5! 15 Qc2 Bf6 16 Rac1 Be5
17 Bf1 the game offers equal chances
(Jansa-Szabo, Budapest 1970).
The move 11 . . . Qc7 was played in
Matulović-Taimanov, Skopje 1970
and after 12 Rc1 Qb7 13 f3 Rd8
14 Qe1 d5! Black had already equalized. 13 f4 followed by 14 Bf3 is
however a stronger plan for White.

12 Ra1-c1 Qd8-b8

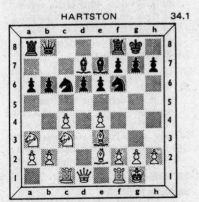

HARTSTON 34.1

KARPOV TO MOVE

13 g2-g4!?
A new idea. The black knight must
retreat to e8, since Black has no convenient way to clear the d7 square.
In the Fischer-Taimanov game White
played the more cautious 13 f3 but
after 13 . . . Ra7! 14 Nc2 Rd8 15 Qe1
Be8 16 Qf2 Rb7 17 a4 a5 Black had
an equal game.

13 . . . Rf8-c8
13 . . . b5!? is a fascinating possibility.
The threat of 14 . . . b4 forces White
to abandon his 14 g5 plans and
capture the sacrificed pawn (if 14 g5
b4 15 gxf6 Bxf6 Black has the advantage). After 14 cxb5 axb5 White can
try

(a) 15 Naxb5 Nb4 16 a3 (16 Na3?
allows 16 . . . Nxa2! 17 Nxa2 Qxb2
winning a pawn for Black) 16 . . . Na2!
17 Nxa2 Bxb5 with pressure on the
white Q-side pawns, as well as a direct
threat to the e-pawn.

(b) 15 Bxb5 Ne5 16 Bxd7 (16 g5 Nxe4!)
16 . . . Qxb2! with many chances for
both sides.

14 g4-g5 Nf6-e8

15 f2-f4
Black must now prepare the pawn
break d6-d5 (or possibly b6-b5) without allowing White any K-side chances.
This he does with a plan that is simple,
but nevertheless effective.

15 . . . Ra8-a7

16 Qd1-e1 Ra7-b7

17 Qe1-h4 g7-g6!
By bringing the knight to g7 Black
can beat off an f4-f5 pawn break and
be ready to answer an indiscretion
such as Qh4-h6 by Bf8 and Nh5,
trapping the queen. With the white
queen on h4 the possibility of h5 by
Black, blocking up the K-side, is
always in the air.

18 Rf1-f3 Ne8-g7

19 Rc1-f1
Of course 19 Rh3? would be a waste
of time, since Black would probably
play 19 . . . h5 for himself.

19 ... Rc8-e8

Both to prevent an f4-f5 break by
White (since Black would now have
useful e-file pressure) and to help with
the freeing d6-d5 push for Black.

20 Be2-d3

After 20 Nc2 b5 White has the unclear
piece sacrifice 21 Nd5!? exd5 22 cxd5.
After 22 ... Na5 23 f5! or 22 ... Nd8
23 Nd4 h5 24 f5 White has a dangerous attack.
Karpov prefers to keep the position
under control.

20 ... h7-h5

21 Qh4-f2 Nc6-b4!

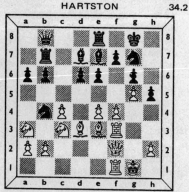

HARTSTON   34.2

KARPOV TO MOVE

Black strikes back in the centre. After
this and his next move, the pawn break
d6-d5 cannot be held back much longer.

22 Bd3-b1 Bd7-c6

23 Rf3-h3

Threatening 24 f5! After 23 Bd4 e5
24 fxe5 dxe5 25 Be3 (but not
25 Rxf7? exd4! 26 Rxg7+ Kxg7
27 Qf7+ Kh8 28 Qxg6 Bc5! winning
for Black) 25 ... Ne6! the game is
delicately balanced: e.g. 26 h4 Nf4!
or 26 Rxf7 Bxg5 (or even 26 ... Nf4!?).

23 ... Bc6-d7

24 Qf2-h4 Qb8-c8

Keeping control over f5.

25 Rf1-c1 Qc8-b8

26 Rc1-f1 Qb8-c8

27 Rh3-f3 d6-d5!

At last Black achieves the long-
planned pawn break. The position is
now equal: there is no way in which
White can seize the advantage.

28 c4xd5 e6xd5

29 f4-f5!?

Karpov is fighting to keep the
initiative. The d-pawn cannot be taken
since either 29 Nxd5 Nxd5 30 exd5
Nf5 31 Qf2 Nxe3 followed by 32 ...
Bc5, or 29 exd5 Nf5 30 Qf2 Nxe3,
wins at least the exchange.

29 ... Be7-c5

After 29 ... dxe4 30 Nxe4! Black can
try

(a) 30 ... gxf5? 31 Nf6+ and Black's
position is in ruins.

(b) 30 ... Nxf5 31 Rxf5 Bxf5 32 Nf6+
Bxf6 33 Bxf5 and Black is lost: e.g.
33 ... gxf5 34 gxf6 when mate cannot be averted. In this line 31 ... gxf5
is no better—32 Nf6+ Bxf6 33 gxf6;
and 32 ... Kf8 33 Bxf5 is just as bad.

(c) 30 ... Bxf5 31 Rxf5! gxf5 (if 31 ...
Nxf5 32 Nf6+ Bxf6 33 Bxf5 as in
(b) above) 32 Nf6+ Kf8 (or 32 ...
Bxf6 33 gxf6 with a winning attack
e.g. 33 ... Rxe3 34 Qg5 Kf8
35 Qxg7+ Ke8 36 Qg8+ Kd7
37 Bxf5+ Re6 38 Qxc8+ Kxc8
39 Bxe6+ fxe6 40 f7 or 33 ... Ne6
34 Rxf5 etc.) 33 Bxf5!? or simply
33 Nxe8 when White's advantage is
clear.

30 Be3xc5 Qc8xc5+

31 Qh4-f2 Qc5xf2+

32 Rf3xf2

White was obliged to offer the exchange of queens, since 31 Kh1 could
be met by 31 ... d4 32 fxg6 fxg6
when White has no compensation for
his weak e-pawn and Black's strong
d-pawn.

32 ... d5-d4

33 Nc3-e2 d4-d3

34 f5xg6 f7xg6

Black wisely avoids 34 ...dxe2 when 35 gxf7+ Kh7 36 e5+! wins at least the exchange for White.

35 Ne2-f4   Re8xe4

36 Nf4xd3

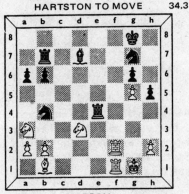

HARTSTON TO MOVE   34.3

KARPOV

Black has achieved complete equality. He should now have played 36 ...Bh3! and met 37 Rc1 or 37 Re1 by 37 ... Rbe7! after which he would have had excellent chances of winning. However, Black was under some pressure to reach the time control at move 40 and chooses a simple plan.

36 ...Re4-g4+?

37 Rf2-g2   Rg4xg2+

38 Kg1xg2   Nb4xd3?!

38 ...Nd5 would have left the game equal. The text move, although less good, should still have been sufficient to draw.

39 Bb1xd3   Ng7-f5

40 Bd3xa6   Bd7-c6+?

The final mistake, after which Karpov comes out a pawn ahead. 40 ...Ne3+ was now necessary to save the game. After 41 Kg1 (if 41 Kf2 Nxf1 42 Bxb7 Nxh2 equalizes) 41 ...Ra7 42 Bc4+ (if 42 Rf3 [or 42 Re1] 42 ...Rxa6 43 Rxe3 Ra5 44 Rg3 [44 h4 Ra4 45 Rd3 Bf5 etc.] 44 ...Be6! 45 b4 Ra4 and Black wins back his pawn) 42 ...Nxc4 43 Nxc4 Bb5 White can

retain his extra pawn by 44 b3 Rxa2 45 Rf6, but the rook ending is drawn.

41 Kg2-f2   Rb7-d7

42 Rf1-c1!

The bishop has only one reasonable square.

42 ...Bc6-e4

43 Ba6-e2   Nf5-d6?

After 43 ...Nd4 Black has more chances against the white king. The text move allows the knights to be exchanged, after which the win is merely a matter of time.

44 Na3-c4   Nd6xc4

44 ...Rc7? allows 45 Nxd6! Rxc1 46 Nxe4 with an easy win.

45 Rc1xc4   Be4-d5

46 Rc4-b4   Bd5xa2

47 Rb4xb6   Kg8-g7

48 Rb6-b4

Planning to consolidate the K-side pawns by h4 next move. Then the centralization of the king, and the advance of the b-pawn, will decide the game.

48 ...Ba2-b1

49 h2-h4   Kg7-f7

50 Kf2-e3   Rd7-e7+

51 Ke3-d2   Kf7-e6

52 Rb4-b5   Bb1-e4

53 b2-b4   Re7-c7

54 Kd2-e3   Be4-b1

55 Rb5-c5!   Rc7-e7

The bishop-and-pawn ending after 55 ...Rxc5 56 bxc5 Kd5 is lost for Black, even though he wins the c-pawn. Thus 57 Kf4 Kxc5 58 Ke5 Kc6 59 Kf6 Kd7 60 Bc4 Ke8 61 Bf7+ Kf8 62 Bxg6 etc. Or if 58 ...Bc2 59 Kf6 and now:

(a) 59 ...Kd6 60 Bc4 Kd7 61 Bf7 Kd8 62 Bxg6 Bd1 63 Bf7 Kd7 64 g6! Bc2 65 g7 Bh7 66 Bxh5 etc.

(b) 59 ...Kd4 60 Bb5 Ke3 61 Be8 Kf4 62 Bxg6 Bd1 63 Bf5! Kg3 64 g6 Kxh4 65 g7 Bb3 66 Be6.

56	Be2-f3	Ke6-d6+
57	Ke3-d4	Re7-f7
58	Rc5-c6+	Kd6-d7
59	Rc6-f6!	Rf7-e7

After 59 ...Rxf6 60 gxf6 the two white pawns cannot be stopped: e.g. 60 ...Ke6 61 b5 Kxf6 62 b6.

60 b4-b5   Black resigns
The pawn reaches b7 with decisive effect.

Game 35

BLACK Mecking   Sicilian Defence, Najdorf Variation
Hastings 1971-2

Whereas Byrne was mated on the Q-side in Game 37, Karpov's rooks and bishop this time turn to a K-side attack. The beauty of this game lies in the simplicity and directness of Karpov's plan, which completely immobilizes Black's position. Byrne chose to be mated on the back rank; Mecking plays his king up the board, but the result is still the same.

1	e2-e4	c7-c5
2	Ng1-f3	d7-d6
3	d2-d4	c5xd4
4	Nf3xd4	Ng8-f6
5	Nb1-c3	a7-a6
6	Bf1-e2	e7-e5
7	Nd4-b3	Bc8-e6
8	f2-f4	Qd8-c7
9	a2-a4	Nb8-c6?

A mistake, as Karpov illustrates. The correct procedure here is 9 ...Nbd7, as played by Bronstein in Game 34.

10 f4-f5
Now Black is obliged to exchange his bishop for the knight on b3.

10 ...Be6xb3
If the bishop were to retreat, 11 Bg5 gains immediate control of d5 for White.

11 c2xb3   Qc7-b6

12 Bc1-g5
White already has the advantage: Mecking's play on the a7-g1 diagonal and his control of the d4 square is inadequate compensation for the loss of the d5 point. This fact is illustrated by the following forced series of ex-

changes after which Black is left with a vastly inferior position.

12	...Bf8-e7	
13	Bg5xf6	Be7xf6
14	Nc3-d5!	Qb6-a5+
15	Qd1-d2	Qa5xd2+
16	Ke1xd2	Bf6-g5+
17	Kd2-d3	

MECKING TO MOVE   35.1

KARPOV

The game has swiftly transformed into a 'semi-endgame'. White's threat of Nc7+ can easily be met, but the grip exerted by his pieces is not so easy to deal with. Mecking decides, quite logically, to remove the d5 knight and hope for counterplay on the a7-g1 diagonal.

17 ... 0-0

18 h2-h4   Bg5-d8

19 Ra1-c1   a6-a5
Intending Nc6-b4 to rid himself of the d5 knight. If Black had tried 19 ... Nd4 then 20 Rc3 followed by b4 or by g3 and Rhc1 retains White's advantage.

20 Kd3-d2!
To meet Nb4 or Ne7 with 21 Bc4.

20 ... Ra8-b8

21 g2-g4
Black is so cramped and tied up that this K-side attack is already a near winner. The threat is Bc4 followed by g4-g5-g6!

21 ... Nc6-b4

22 Be2-c4
More accurate was 22 Nxb4, axb4 23 g5.

22 ... Nb4xd5

23 Bc4xd5   g7-g5
Hoping to blockade the K-side pawns on black squares but this attempt leads to a direct mating attack. Black has no time for both f7-f6 and h7-h6, and so can prevent 24 g5 only by the text move.

24 f5xg6   h7xg6

25 Kd2-d3
Preparing 26 h5.

25 ... Kg8-g7

26 h4-h5! *(see Diagram 35.2)*

The position is complex but amongst the possibilities are, for instance,

(a) 26 ... Bg5 when White can occupy c7 with strong attacks on b7 and f7, or

(b) 26 ... Rh8 when f7 can be attacked by 27 Rhf1. Now if

(b1) 27 ... Rf8 then 28 hxg6 Kxg6 29 Rf5 followed by 30 Rcf1 (or h1)

MECKING TO MOVE   35.2

KARPOV

(b2) 27 ... f6 then 28 g5! fxg5 29 h6+!! or 28 ... Rf8 29 hxg6 Kxg6 30 Rf5

Clearly, Black is in some trouble.

26 ... Bd8-b6

27 Rh1-h3   Bb6-c5
This manœuvre prevents infiltration of the white queen's rook.

28 Rc1-f1
Threatening 29 h6+ Kg8 30 Rxf7 Rxf7 31 h7+ Kg7 32 Bxf7 winning a pawn.

28 ... f7-f6

29 h5xg6   Kg7xg6

30 Rf1-h1
Black is powerless to prevent 31 Rh7.

30 ... Rb8-e8

31 Rh3-h7
The threat is 32 R1h5.

31 ... Kg6-g5

32 Kd3-e2   Kg5-f4
32 ... Kxg4 allows mate in two by 33 Rg7+ Kf4 34 Rh4.

33 Rh1-h3   Bc5-d4?
Overlooking the threat, but after 33 ... Kxg4 34 Rh1! Black must give up the exchange by 34 ... Rg8 (otherwise he will be mated).

34 Rh7-g7   Black resigns
There is no way to prevent 35 Rf3 mate.

Game 36

WHITE Stein   English Opening
Soviet Olympiad (finals), Moscow 1972

Stein tries an exciting piece-sacrifice in the early middle-game, but meets an excellent Karpov defence. For almost twenty moves the position offers tactical chances for White, but when Black surrounds and captures the advanced white pawns, the end is in sight.

Although Karpov likes to play with the initiative, this game, and Game 52 against Tal, show how capable he is in defence.

1 c2-c4   c7-c5

2 Ng1-f3   Ng8-f6

3 Nb1-c3   d7-d5

4 c4xd5   Nf6xd5

5 d2-d4   Nd5xc3

An improvement on his game with Korchnoi from the 38th USSR Championship, Riga 1970, which continued 5 . . . cxd4; see also Game 31.

6 b2xc3   g7-g6

7 e2-e4   Bf8-g7

This opening could equally well be called a Grünfeld Defence, Exchange Variation. With the white knight on f3 (and not on e2 as is usual for this variation) White is in some difficulties. Black can play 8 . . . 0-0 followed by 9 . . . Bg4 and thus seriously threaten the d4 pawn. The only ways to prevent this from happening are to play 8 h3 0-0 9 Bc4 Nc6 10 Be3 Qa5! 11 Qd2 cxd4 12 cxd4 Qxd2+ 13 Kxd2 Rd8 14 Bd5 as in Vidmar-Alekhine, Nottingham 1936, when 14 . . . e6! 15 Bxc6 bxc6 gives Black the advantage, or to play the text move.

8 Bf1-b5+

8 Be2 was played in Rubinstein-Alekhine, 1924 but after 8 . . . 0-0 9 0-0 b6 10 Be3 Bb7 11 e5 cxd4 12 cxd4 Na6 13 Qa4 Nc7 Black had the better game. After 9 . . . cxd4 10 cxd4 Nc6 11 Be3 Bg4 White must

play 12 d5! with the better game as 12 . . . Bxa1 13 Qxa1 Nb4 14 Bh6 regains the exchange.

8 . . . Nb8-d7

Other possibilities here are

(a) 8 . . . Bd7 9 Bxd7+ Qxd7 10 0-0 cxd4 11 cxd4 Nc6 12 Be3 0-0 13 Rc1 Rfc8 with equality (Kashdan-Alekhine, London 1932).

(b) 8 . . . Nc6!? 9 0-0 0-0 with advantage to Black.

9 0-0   0-0

10 a2-a4   a7-a6

11 Bb5-c4   Qd8-c7

12 Qd1-e2   b7-b6

Both sides have completed most of their development. Stein now envisages a sacrificial attack based on the weakness of the black K-side and, in particular, with the black queen's bishop likely to go to b7, on the possible exploitation of the a2-g8 diagonal.

13 e4-e5

Threatening 14 e5-e6.

13 . . . e7-e6

14 Nf3-g5

This knight can retreat to e4 after 14 . . . h6; so Karpov removes this possibility.

14 . . . Bc8-b7

15 f2-f4   h7-h6

KARPOV   36.1

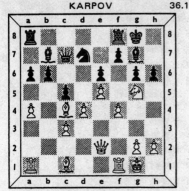

STEIN TO MOVE

White now has a difficult decision to
make. Karpov's 14th move has pre-
cluded the possibility of 16 Ne4?
since 16 ... cxd4 (17 cxd4 Bxe4
18 Qxe4 Qxc4) wins at least a pawn.
After 16 Nf3, White is under pressure
on the c- and d-files, as well as having
lost control of many of the white
squares. The game might continue
16 ... Rfc8 17 Bd3 c4 18 Bc2 b5
19 axb5 axb5 20 Be3 Nb6 when
Black's advantage is clear. Rather than
take a passive position, Stein prefers
to keep the initiative at the cost of a
piece.

16 Ng5xe6!?   f7xe6

17 Bc4xe6+   Kg8-h8

18 Qe2-g4
Threatening both the g6 pawn and the
d7 knight.

18 ... Rf8-d8

19 f4-f5
19 Qxg6 would be met by 19 ... Nf8
20 Qg4 cxd4.

19 ... Nd7-f8
And not 19 ... gxf5 20 Rxf5, when
the threat of 21 Rf7 is hard to meet
(20 ... Rf8 21 Bxd7 wins a piece).

20 f5-f6   Nf8xe6

21 Qg4xe6?
Overestimating his chances. Better
was 21 fxg7+ followed by 21 ... Nxg7
22 Qxg6 with chances for both sides.

21 ... Bg7-f8

22 Qe6-h3
Winning the h-pawn, but now White's
centre falls and his game collapses.

22 ... c5xd4!

23 c3xd4
23 Bxh6 can be met by 23 ... Bxh6
24 Qxh6+ Qh7   25 Qxh7+ Kxh7
26 cxd4 Rxd4 with the better
chances for Black.

23 ... Rd8xd4

24 e5-e6
24 Bxh6 transposes directly to the
note above.

24 ... Bf8-c5

25 Kg1-h1
If 25 Qxh6+ Qh7   26 Qxh7+ Kxh7
27 Be3 Rd2! or if 27 Kh1 Bd5!
28 e7 Rg4 Black has a winning
position.

25 ... h6-h5

26 Ra1-a2
The threat was 26 ... Rg4   27 Ra2
Bd5   28 Re2 and now either 28 ...
Bc4 or 28 ... Qc6.

26 ... Bb7-d5

27 Ra2-d2
If 27 Re2 then Bc4 wins the exchange.

27 ... Rd5xd2

28 Bc1xd2   Qc7-e5!

KARPOV   36.2

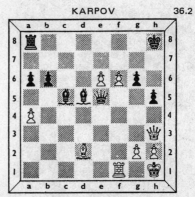

STEIN TO MOVE

This move spells the end of White's chances: with the fall of one of his advanced central pawns his position is hopeless. The rest of the game is a mopping-up exercise.

29 Qh3-d3

29 e7 is refuted by 29 ... Qe2! winning at least a piece.

29 ... Qe5xe6

30 Qd3xg6   Qe6-g4

31 Qg6-h6+   Kh8-g8

32 f6-f7+   Bd5xf7

33 Bd2-c3   Bc5-d4

34 h2-h3   Qg4-g7

Every move has an answer. White could safely resign here, but was probably in time-trouble and played through to move 40.

35 Qh6-c6   Ra8-d8

36 Bc3xd4   Qg7xd4

37 Qc6-b7   Rd8-d7

38 Qb7-c6

38 Qxa6? loses the exchange to 38 ... Bc4 39 Qa8+ (or Qc8+) 39 ... Rd8.

38 ... Kg8-g7

39 Qc6-c1   Qd4-e5

40 Rf1-e1   Qe5-f6

41 Re1-f1   Qf6-d4

White resigns

He is a piece down without compensation.

Game 37

BLACK Smyslov   Petroff Defence
Soviet Olympiad (finals), Moscow 1972

To beat a player of Smyslov's calibre is always a difficult job, and to beat him at his own game is well-nigh impossible; but Karpov achieves just that. Smyslov's innovation on move 8 leaves him with a cramped position, and Karpov, by pushing and probing all over the board, and by gaining better co-operation between his pieces, is able to outmanœuvre the former world champion to bring off a well-deserved victory.

1 e2-e4   e7-e5

2 Ng1-f3   Ng8-f6

The Petroff defence. Because of the symmetry of the pawn positions resulting from this opening, it is generally considered to be 'drawish'.

3 Nf3xe5

The alternative is 3 d4 and now:

(a) 3 ... Nxe4 4 Bd3 d5 5 Nxe5 Nd7.

(b) 3 ... exd4 4 e5 Ne4 5 Qxd4 d5 6 exd6 e.p. Nxd6 7 Nc3 Nc6 8 Qf4 g6 9 Bd2 Qe7+! 10 Be2 Be6 11 0-0-0 Bg7 12 h4 h6 13 Rhe1 Qf6 14 Bd3 Qxf4 15 Bxf4 0-0-0 16 Ne5 Nxe5 17 Bxe5 Bxe5 18 Rxe5 Bc4 with

equality (Keres-Trifunović, Bled 1961).

3 ... d7-d6

3 ... Nxe4? is an old trap that leads to the loss of a pawn for Black. 4 Qe2 Qe7 5 Qxe4 d6 6 d4 f6 7 Nc3 dxe5 8 Nd5 Qd6 9 dxe5 fxe5 10 Bf4. In this line 4 ... d5 is met by 5 d3 Qe7 6 dxe4 Qxe5 7 exd5 and 6 ... Nd7 by 7 Nc3 dxe5 8 Nd5 Nf6 9 Nxf6+ gxf6 10 Bb5+ Bd7 11 Bxd7+ Kxd7 12 0-0.

4 Ne5-f3   Nf6xe4

5 d2-d4   Bf8-e7

5 ... d5 is equally playable, with the intention of developing the bishop on d6.

6 Bf1-d3 Ne4-f6
Again 6 ... d5 is possible.

7 h2-h3 0-0

8 0-0 c7-c5
It is strange that Smyslov did not repeat the 8 ... Re8 of his exciting draw with Tal from the last round of the 39th USSR Championship, Leningrad 1971. The game continued 9 c4 Nbd7 10 Nc3 Nf8 11 d5! Ng6 12 Re1 Bd7 13 Bg5 Nh5! 14 Bd2 Nhf4 15 Bf1 Bf6 16 Rxe8+ Qxe8 17 Qc1 Be5 18 Qe1 Bf6 19 Kh2 Bf5 20 Qe3 Bd3! and was here agreed drawn.

9 Nb1-c3 Nb8-c6

10 Rf1-e1 a7-a6
After 10 ... cxd4 11 Nb5 White would regain the pawn with advantage, since the black d-pawn is isolated.

11 d4-d5 Nc6-a7
Aiming for a b7-b5 advance. 11 ... Nb4? would be strongly answered by 12 Bf1 Bf5 13 Re2 when the threat of 14 a3 is awkward for Black.

12 a2-a4
Threatening 13 a5. This cannot be satisfactorily prevented, since after 12 ...b6 the black bishop must be fianchettoed to avoid immediate loss of the a6 pawn, and then the advance b6-b5 will prove impossible.

12 ... Bc8-d7

13 a4-a5 Rf8-e8

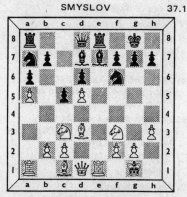

SMYSLOV 37.1

KARPOV TO MOVE

After 13 ...Nb5 14 Na4! is strong:
(a) 14 ...Qxa5?? 15 Rxe7.
(b) 14 ...Nxd5? 15 c4 winning a piece.
(c) 14 ...Re8 15 Nb6 Rb8 16 c4 Nc7 17 b4! with a huge spatial advantage for White.

The opening has been completely to White's advantage. He has a clear spatial advantage and, at the same time, has prevented any Q-side advance that Black may have had in mind. The thematic push b7-b5 would allow a5xb6, when the black a6 pawn is weak. On the other hand, White can afford a Q-side attack by c4 and then b4, or can play for a superior minor-piece ending by exchanging the major pieces on the e-file. Karpov chooses a combination of both these plans.

14 Bd3-f1 h7-h6

15 Bc1-f4 Be7-f8
Black can only defend passively and wait for White to attack.

16 Re1xe8 Qd8xe8

17 Bf4-h2 Qe8-d8

18 Nf3-d2 Qd8-c7

19 Nd2-e4
Exchanging Black's most effective piece for White's least active one (the f3 knight).

19 ... Nf6xe4

20 Nc3xe4 Bd7-f5

21 Ne4-d2 Ra8-e8

22 c2-c3 Qc7-d8

23 Qd1-b3 Qd8-d7

24 c3-c4
Smyslov is so far making the most of his position. He has occupied the open e-file and is preparing to put his f8 bishop to active use on the h8-a1 diagonal. His f5 bishop will shortly be exchanged by Bf1-d3, after which he will hope to reposition his a7 knight.

24 ... Na7-c8

25 g2-g4
White's next move will be 26 Bd3

so this is a free, space-gaining
manœuvre.

25 ... Bf5-g6

26 Bf1-d3
Again White exchanges an effective
black piece for a poorish one of his
own.

26 ... Bg6xd3

27 Qb3xd3   g7-g6

28 Ra1-b1   Bf8-g7

SMYSLOV   37.2

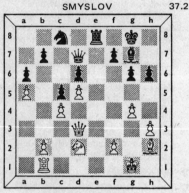

KARPOV TO MOVE

There is no need for White to rush
into a Q-side advance. First of all, he
took time to exchange his two worst
pieces, and only now does he set his
sights on an active plan. Black, on the
other hand, has played excellently in
defence. He has achieved the maximum
possible co-operation between his
pieces. His d6 pawn is well defended
and he has the weak a5 pawn to attack,
as well as seeking a further exchange of
pieces by Bg7-e5. The position is still
much superior for White, but Smyslov
is creating some real drawing chances.

29 b2-b4!
White cannot afford to waste any more
time, for 29 ... Qc7 will otherwise be
difficult to meet.

29 ... c5xb4
Black cannot allow a supported passed
pawn by 29 ... Be5 30 Bxe5 Rxe5

31 bxc5 dxc5, since either the c5 or
the b7 pawn will surely fall: e.g. 32 f4
Re8 33 Ne4! Qe7 34 d6! Qxe4
35 Qxe4 Rxe4 36 d7 winning. The
weakness of the f6 square also becomes
apparent.

30 Rb1xb4   Qd7-c7

31 Nd2-b3
Hoping for 32 c5!

31 ... Bg7-e5

32 Bh2xe5   Re8xe5

33 Kg1-g2   g6-g5?!
Black was anxious to prevent White
from gaining even more space by
34 f4. However, the weakening of the
f5 and h5 squares is serious for Black,
and so 33 ... Qe7 was preferable.

34 Qd3-d4
Again aiming to play 35 c5.

34 ... Qc7-e7

35 Nb3-d2
35 c5 dxc5 36 Nxc5 Nd6 gives the
black knight a beautiful post from
which to operate.

35 ... Re5-e1
The rook achieves nothing here, but
Black is at a loss for moves.

36 Rb4-b3!
An exchange of rooks will remove any
active counterplay that Black has.

36 ... Re1-e2

37 Kg2-f3
Threatening 38 Ne4!

37 ... Re2-e5

38 Rb3-e3!   f7-f6
After 38 ... Rxe3+ 39 fxe3 White's
threat is Nd2-e4-:f6. Black can try:

(a) 39 ... Qe5? 40 Qxe5 dxe5 41 c5
followed by 42 Ke4 with an easily
won ending.

(b) 39 ... f6 40 Ne4 Kf7 41 Qb2!
meeting 41 ... Na7 by 42 Qxb7! and
41 ... Kg7 by 42 Ng3.

(c) 39 ... Qc7! with some defensive
chances.

39 Nd2-e4   Kg8-g7

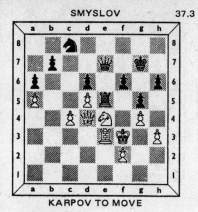

SMYSLOV   37.3

KARPOV TO MOVE

40 Kf3-g2!
A killer! The threat is simply 41 Ng3 followed by Nf5+, or Nh5+ and Rf3, as required. Black is restricted to queen or king moves (40 ... Na7 41 Ng3! or 40 ... f5? 41 gxf5 and the rook is pinned).

40 ... Qe7-c7

Other tries are:

(a) 40 ... Qe8 41 Ng3 Ne7 42 Nh5+ Kf7 43 Rf3 Ng8 44 Qd3 Ke7 45 Qh7+ Qf7 46 Qb1! winning.

(b) 40 ... Kf7 41 Ng3 Rxe3 42 fxe3 Qe5 43 Qxe5 dxe5 44 Nf5 Kg6 45 Kf3 with an easily won ending for White.

(c) 40 ... Kh7 41 Ng3 Rxe3 42 fxe3 Qe5 43 Qd3+ winning at least a pawn (43 ... Kh8 44 Qg6 43 ... Kg7 44 Nf5+ or 43 ... Kg8 44 Qg6+).

41 Re3-f3
Winning the f6 pawn.

41 ... b7-b5
After 41 ... Qxa5 42 Nxf6 White threatens both 43 Nd7, winning the exchange, and 43 Ne8+ followed by either 44 Nxd6 or 44 Qd3, according to the circumstances.

42 a5xb6   Black resigns
After 42 ... Qxb6 43 Qxb6 Nxb6 44 Nxd6 White will win the weak a-pawn also.

Game 38

BLACK Taimanov   Sicilian Defence, Paulsen Variation
Soviet Olympiad (finals), Moscow 1972

This game illustrates how one type of advantage can be converted into another, which decides the battle. This is most commonly achieved when an attack is used, not for mate, but to give a winning ending. In this game Karpov does it the other way round—he gives up his positional advantage, and so buys enough time to mate the black king in a most unusual and exciting manner.

1 e2-e4   c7-c5

2 Ng1-f3   e7-e6

3 d2-d4   c5xd4

4 Nf3xd4   a7-a6

5 Bf1-d3   Bf8-c5
The alternative way to play the Paulsen is 5 ... Nc6 6 Nxc6 bxc6

(or 6 ... dxc6).

6 Nd4-b3   Bc5-b6
Usual here is 6 ... Ba7. The idea behind Taimanov's move is to avoid the immediate exchange of bishops on move 9 (see Game 39).

7 0-0   Ng8-e7

8 Qd1-e2   Nb8-c6

9 Bc1-e3 Nc6-e5

The point of Taimanov's move 6.
With the bishop on a7, the exchange
is virtually forced, since Black would
have no convenient reply to 10 Bxa7:
thus 9 ... Bxe3 (if 9 ... Qc7?! 10 Bxa7
Rxa7 leaves Black awkwardly placed)
10 Qxe3 and now:

(a) 10 ... d6 11 c4 with a spatial advantage for White.

(b) 10 ... e5 11 c4 0-0 12 Nc3 d6
13 Rfd1 Be6 14 Bf1 Rc8 15 Rd2
Na5! so that 16 Nxa5 Qxa5 17 Rxd6
Bxc4 18 Rd7 Bxf1 19 Rxf1 Qb4
gives approximate equality. White
must try 17 b3 Rcd8 with a small
spatial advantage (Boleslavsky).

(c) 10 ... d5 11 e5 Qc7 12 Re1 Bd7
13 N1d2 f6 with equality (Parma-
Korchnoi, USSR-Yugoslavia match,
Zagreb 1964).

10 c2-c4!

After 10 f4?! either 10 ... Ng4
11 Bxb6 Qxb6+ 12 Kh1 h5! or
the simpler 10 ... Nxd3 11 Qxd3 d5
gives Black equality. Now Black must
watch out for 11 c5 or 11 Bxb6 and
12 c5 with some positional pressure
for White.

10 ... Bb6xe3

11 Qe2xe3 Qd8-c7

The exchange 11 ... Nxd3 12 Qxd3
would only help White but 11 ... d6
is a playable alternative. After either
12 Be2 (and 13 f4) or 12 Rd1, Qc7
13 Na3 White has a small advantage.

12 c4-c5! *(see Diagram 38.1)*

The positional pressure that this pawn
now exerts on the backward black
b- and d-pawns forces Black to free
his game as in the text. After 12 ...
Ng4? 13 Qg3 Qxg3 14 hxg3 Black
will be obliged to do some wriggling
to develop his queen's bishop: e.g.
14 ... Rb8! 15 N1d2 (threatening
16 Nc4) b5 16 cxb6 e.p. Rxb6
17 Nc4 Rc6 18 N3a5 Rc7 19 Nd6+
Kf8 20 Rac1 with a tremendous bind
on the position.

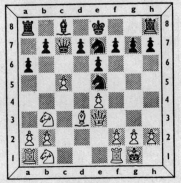

KARPOV

12 ... Ne5xd3

Because 13 Be2 and 14 f4 is now a
real threat.

13 Qe3xd3 b7-b6

14 c5xb6 Qc7xb6

Karpov now forces a further positional
gain, since Black must blockade the
centre with his pawns on squares the
same colour as his bishop.

15 Nb1-d2!

The threat of Nd2-c4-d6 leaves Black
no reasonable choice.

15 ... d7-d5

16 e4-e5!

16 exd5 would prove insufficient:

(a) 16 ... exd5 17 Rfe1 Be6 18 Nd4 0-0!

(b) 16 ... Nxd5 17 Nc4 Qb4 18 a3 Qe7

In each case Black has equalized.

16 ... Bc8-d7

17 Rf1-c1 0-0

18 Qd3-d4!

This position is similar to those arising
from the French Defence. White has
complete control of the squares d4
and c5; he is the first to occupy the
c-file with his rooks, and this, together
with the 'bad' black bishop, give him
a strong positional initiative. Black
must seek counterplay against the
White Q-side pawns, and must at all
cost try and prevent the exchange of

queens. It has often been shown that
a white knight at d4 against such a
bishop as this ensures White an easily
won ending. For example, the position:
White Kg1, Nd4, Pa2, b2, e5, f2, g2,
h2; Black Kg8, Bd7, Pa6, d5, e6, f7,
g7, h7, will prove difficult, if not
impossible, for Black to hold.
Taimanov, of course, is well aware of
this and thus seeks active play on the
Q-side.

18 ... Qb6-b8
Here 18 ... Qxd4? would give White
an advantageous ending after 19 Nxd4
Rfc8 20 N2b3 Nc6 21 Nxc6 Bxc6
22 Rc3! or even 22 Nd4.

19 Nd2-f3 Ne7-c6
If 19 ... Nf5 simply 20 Qf4 is sufficient
for a White advantage.

20 Qd4-e3 Rf8-c8
Abandoning all his K-side chances, but
20 ... f6? would allow 21 Nc5 with
many threats. This thematic pawn
advance would be extremely difficult
for Black to play as White's many
positional and tactical threats are
difficult to contain.

21 Rc1-c5 a6-a5

22 Ra1-c1 a5-a4

23 Nb3-d4

TAIMANOV TO MOVE   38.2

KARPOV

White's advantage is probably large
enough already to ensure a win. The

only problem remaining is the actual
winning plan. Karpov's beloved Q-side
majority will not help a great deal
here, as it will prove too difficult to
advance a passed b-pawn with all
Black's pieces so actively poised to
prevent it. A simple knight-v.-bishop
ending, as outlined in the note to
White's 18th move, is the easiest way,
but Taimanov will strive to keep the
major pieces on and thus avert this
possibility.
So Karpov closes up the Q-side for the
time being, and then launches out
with a K-side attack. The logic behind
this decision is quite simple: White
can easily bring two or three pieces
to attack the black king, whereas
Black will have to struggle to get more
than one piece to that side of the
board. The grip that White has on the
Q-side will ensure that Black's counterplay there will be too slow to be
effective.

23 ... Nc6-a5
Both 23 ... Nxd4, 24 Qxd4 (getting
White closer to his goal of a simple
ending) and 23 ... Qxb2? 24 Nxc6
(winning a piece) are inferior.

24 Rc5xc8+ Bd7xc8

25 b2-b3 Bc8-d7
25 ... axb3 26 axb3 Bd7 would meet
with the same idea.

26 h2-h4!
The threat is h4-h5-h6.

26 ... h7-h6

27 g2-g4 Qb8-b7
The queen might be more effective
on d8.

28 h4-h5
Now 29 g5 is extremely awkward for
Black.

28 ... Na5-c6
28 ... Rc8 29 Rxc8+ Qxc8 30 g5
would not help the Black cause.
The exchange of rooks does little
to stop the attack.

29 g4-g5 Nc6xd4

30 Nf3xd4 h6xg5

31 Qe3xg5   Kg8-h7
To prevent 32 h6 g6 33 Qf6 Kf8
34 h7!

32 Rc1-c3!

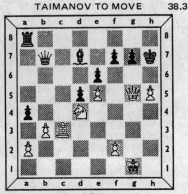

TAIMANOV TO MOVE   38.3

KARPOV

White's K-side attack cannot be
stopped. The immediate threat is
33 h6! and now:

(a) 33 ... g6 34 Qf6 Rg8 35 Qxf7+.

(b) 33 ... Rg8 34 Rh3 g6 35 Qf6 Be8
36 Nf3 and 37 Ng5+.

(c) 33 ... gxh6? 34 Rh3 and mate next
move.

32 ... Qb7-b4
With both Qe1+ and Qg4+ as well as
Qxd4 in mind.

33 Rc3-g3   Ra8-g8

34 Nd4-f3   a4xb3

35 a2xb3   Qb4xb3

36 Qg5-c1!
Not only threatening to win the queen
by 37 Ng5+ but also slowing down
Black's counterplay by preventing
the threatened 36 ... Qb1+ or
36 ... Qd1+.

36 ... Qb3-a2

37 Nf3-g5+   Kh7-h8

38 Ng5xf7+   Kh8-h7

39 Qc1-g5   Qa2-b1+

40 Kg1-h2   Black resigns
There is no way to prevent mate by
41 Qg6+! Qxg6 42 hxg6 without
allowing another mate in one.

Game 39

BLACK Hübner   Sicilian Defence, Paulsen Variation
World Student Olympiad (finals), Graz 1972

Karpov obtains a bind on the centre from the opening and maintains it
throughout the game. Hübner, as always, makes much of the running in
the middle-game but, after some mistakes from both sides, Karpov emerges
with the better prospects in the ending and succeeds in forcing the full
point.

1 e2-e4   c7-c5

2 Ng1-f3   e7-e6

3 d2-d4   c5xd4

4 Nf3xd4   a7-a6

5 Bf1-d3   Bf8-c5

6 Nd4-b3   Bc5-a7
For 6 ... Bb6 see Game 38.

7 0-0   Nb8-c6

8 Qd1-e2   d7-d6
More usual here is 8 ... Nge7, but the
text move, intending to develop the
king's knight at f6, is perfectly playable.

9 Bc1-e3   Ba7xe3

10 Qe2xe3   Ng8-f6

11 c2-c4

After 11 N1d2 e5 12 Rfd1 0-0
13 Bf1 d5 14 exd5 Nxd5 15 Qc5
Nf4 16 Ne4 Qh4 17 Nd6 Black has
comfortable equality (Stein-Polugaevsky,
31st USSR Championship, 1963).
Karpov prefers to keep a grip on the
black central pawns.

11 ... 0-0

12 Rf1-d1 Qd8-c7

The freeing 12 ... d5? would lose a
pawn after 13 cxd5 exd5 14 exd5
Nxd5 15 Bxh7+ Kxh7 16 Qe4+
followed by 17 Qxd5.

13 Nb1-c3 Nc6-e5

14 Ra1-c1 b7-b6

The exchanges 14 ... Nxc4 15 Bxc4
Qxc4 16 Rxd6 (but not 16 Nd5?
Nxd5 17 exd5 [17 Rxd5 exd5!] Qh4
when Black stands much better) favour
White, as the general opening of the
c- and d-files, together with the threat
of 17 e5 and 18 Nd5!, are difficult
for Black to deal with. Thus:

(a) 16 ... e5? 17 Rxf6! gxf6 18 Nd5
winning the queen, since a queen-move
is answered by 19 Nxf6+ Kg7 20 Qg5+
Kh8 21 Qh6 and mate.

(b) 16 ... Qc7 17 e5 (threatening 18 exf6
Qxd6 19 Qg5 g6 20 Qh6 mating)
17 ... Nd7 (if 17 ... Ne8 18 Ne4
Qb8 19 Rd8 wins at least a piece)
18 Na4 Qb8 (18 ... Qd8 19 Nb6
Rb8 20 Nxd7 Bxd7 21 Rcd1 wins
a piece) 19 Nb6 Nxb6 20 Qxb6 with
a dominating position.

(c) 16 ... Qb4 17 e5 Ng4 18 Qg3 (threat
19 Rd4) 18 ... h5 19 Rd4 Qe7
20 Ne4 with a dangerous attack.

15 Bd3-e2

15 f4? would be weak. After 15 ...
Neg4 16 Qf3 b5! Black threatens both
17 ... Qa7+ and 17 ... bxc4.

15 ... Bc8-b7

16 f2-f4 Ne5-g6

After 16 ... Nxc4 17 Bxc4 Qxc4
18 Qxb6 Qc6 (or 18 ... Bxe4 19 Na5)
19 Rxd6 White stands distinctly better.

KARPOV TO MOVE

White has a small advantage owing to
his spatial superiority. Black's counterchances will be based chiefly on the
advance e6-e5, followed by play on
the dark squares e5 and f4, and the
a7-g1 diagonal, but White must also
beware of a tactical b6-b5 or d6-d5
advance.

17 g2-g3 Rf8-d8

18 a2-a3

The game Ivkov-Hübner, Palma 1970,
continued 18 Rd2 Rab8 19 R1d1
Ba8 20 a4 Ne7 21 Nd4 e5? 22 fxe5
dxe5 23 N4b5! axb5 24 Nxb5 Rxd2
25 Nxc7 Rxd1+ 26 Bxd1 with a
winning position for White. This was
to be Hübner's tournament, however,
and Ivkov lost in time-trouble. Karpov's
idea is to be able to play 19 Nd4 and
then answer 19 ... Qc5 with 20 b4.

18 ... Ra8-c8?

This rook is much more useful on b8,
from where it can defend the b6 pawn
and prepare for a possible b6-b5
break.

19 Nb3-d4 Bb7-a8

20 b2-b3 Ng6-e7

Covering the f5 square, and thus
preparing for the e6-e5 advance. The
knight on d4 is denied the use of f5.

21 Be2-f3 Rc8-b8

After 21 ... e5 22 fxe5 dxe5 23 Nc2
followed by 24 Nd5 White has a useful

initiative; so Black awaits a more suitable moment.

22 a3-a4 Qc7-c5!
Once the b4 possibility has been ex-
cluded, the black queen takes up her
natural square. Black is beginning to
make use of the dark squares b4, d4,
e5, and the a7-g1 diagonal.

23 Rd1-d3!
The most economical way to defend
the queen against the threat of 23 ...
e6-e5.

23 ... e6-e5?!
According to Hübner this still leaves
White with some advantage, and Black
could have equalized here by 23 ...
Nc6.

24 Nd4-e2
The point of Karpov's 23rd move is
revealed. He wishes to avoid the exchange of pawns on e5 without losing
control of f4. For example, if White
were to play 24 Nc2? here then
24 ...exf4 25 gxf4 Ng6 would give
Black control of both e5 and f4, and
thus a sizeable advantage.

24 ... e5xf4
After 24 ... Nc6 25 Nd5 Nb4
26 Nxb4 Qxb4 27 Rcd1 Re8 28 f5
White has retained his spatial advantage
and can begin to try and exploit the
weakness of the black d-pawn.

25 g3xf4
25 Nxf4? would allow Black a knight
on e5 after 25 ... Nc6 and thus transfer the advantage immediately to Black.

25 ... Qc5xe3+

26 Rd3xe3 Ne7-g6? *(see Diagram 39.2)*

A poor continuation. After 26 ...
Re8! the game is about equal:

(a) 27 Rd1? Nf5! winning a pawn or the
exchange.

(b) 27 Kf2 Rbd8! 28 Rd1 Nc8 followed
by doubling rooks on the e-file,
although White has a slightly better
game.

(c) 27 Nd5? N7xd5 28 cxd5 Bxd5!
winning at least a pawn.

HÜBNER 39.2

KARPOV TO MOVE

27 Rc1-d1 Kg8-f8
Again a dubious move. Both 27 ...
Nf8 (and 28 ... Ne6) and 27 ... Re8!?
28 Rxd6 Nh4 29 Kf2 (29 Bh1? Nf5!)
29 ...Nxf3 30 Kxf3 Nxe4 31 Nxe4
f5 32 Nc3 fxe4+ 33 Kg4 give White
very little.

28 Re3-d3 Nf6-e8

29 Kg1-f2
So that 30 e5 Bxf3 can be answered
by 31 Kxf3

29 ... Rd8-c8

30 Kf2-g3 Ng6-e7

31 Ne2-d4 Rc8-c5

32 Rd1-d2
Intending 33 Nc2. If 32 Nc2 then b5!
is a strong reply.

32 ... Ba8-b7

33 Nd4-c2?
Better was 33 h4. Now Black gets
back into the game on the black
squares.

33 ... g7-g5

34 f4xg5 Rc5xg5+

35 Kg3-f2 Ne7-g6

36 Bf3-h1!
Bringing the rook across to g3 and
thus saving the bishop from exchange
by Ng6-e5xf3.

36 ... Rb8-c8

After 36 ... Ne5 37 Rg3 Rxg3
38 hxg3 f5 White retains the advantage
by 39 Nd4.

37 Rd3-g3 Rc8-c5

38 Nc2-e3 Ng6-e7

39 Bh1-f3 Rg5xg3?
Better was 39 ... Rg6. White now has
the h-file to work on, and he also
regains control of f4.

40 h2xg3 Rc5-e5
40 ... f5 fails to 41 exf5 Bxf3
42 Kxf3 Nxf5 43 Ne4 Re5 44 Nxf5
Rxf5+ 45 Kg4 winning a pawn, since
45 ... Re5 46 Nxd6 Re3 is met by
47 Rf2+! winning a piece (47 ... Ke7?
48 Nf5+).

41 g3-g4 a6-a5

42 Rd2-d1
42 Nf5 would not be so good: e.g.
42 ... Nxf5 43 exf5 Bxf3 44 Kxf3
h5 45 Nd5 Ng7! with counterplay.

42 ...Bb7-c6

43 Nc3-d5 Ne7-c8
If 43 ... Bxd5? 44 cxd5 followed by
45 Nc4 would win for White.

44 Ne3-f5

HÜBNER TO MOVE   39.3

KARPOV

44 ...Bc6xd5?
A terrible mistake. After 44 ... Bd7
45 Rh1 Kg8 46 Kg3 Be6 Black still
has some chances. 44 ... Bxd5 falls
into the same trap as at move 43.

45 c4xd5 Nc8-e7

46 Nf5-e3
The threat of 47 Nc4 cannot be
satisfactorily parried, and so Black
loses a pawn and thence the game.

46 ...Ne7-g8
After 46 ... Nf6 47 Nc4! Nxe4+
48 Kg2 Nc3 49 Nxe5! (49 Rd3
N3xd5! is still unclear viz. 50 Nxe5
Nf4+ 51 Kg3 dxe5 etc.) 49 ... Nxd1
50 Nd7+ Ke8 51 Nf6+ and 52 Bxd1
wins a piece for White.

47 Ne3-c4 Re5-e7

48 Nc4xb6 Re7-b7

49 Nb6-c4 Rb7xb3

50 Rd1-a1! Ng8-f6

51 Nc4xa5 Rb3-b2+

52 Kf2-e3 Nf6-d7

53 Na5-c6 Rb2-b3+

54 Ke3-f4?!
It was safer to retreat the king. Black
now gets some counterplay.

54 ...Nd7-e5

55 Nc6xe5 d6xe5+

56 Kf4-g3 Ne8-d6

57 Kg3-f2 Rb3-b2+

58 Kf2-g1 Rb2-b7

59 a4-a5 Rb7-a7

60 a5-a6 Kf8-e7
After 60 ... Nb7 either 61 Kf2, Nc5
62 Ra5, or 61 Be2 Nc5 62 Rb1 Nxe4
63 Rb7 Ra8 64 a7 Kg7 65 Rc7 wins
easily for White. Black could safely
resign here.

61 Kg1-f2 Ke7-d7	**62 Kf2-e3 Nd6-c4+**
63 Ke3-d3 Nc4-b6	**64 Bf3-e2 Kd7-d6**
65 Kd3-e3 Nb6-d7	**66 Ra1-h1 Nd7-f8**
67 Rh1-h6+ Kd6-e7	**68 d5-d6+ Ke7-d8**
69 Be2-b5 Ra7-a8	**70 Rh6-h5 f7-f6**
71 Rh5-h6 Ra8-b8	**72 Bb5-c6 Rb8-b3+**
73 Ke3-d2 Rb3-a3	**74 Rh6xf6 Ra3-a2+**

...Black resigns

Game 40

BLACK Enevoldsen   French Defence, Tarrasch Variation
Skopje Olympiad (A final) 1972

Karpov sacrifices a pawn in the opening for a lead in development and some attacking prospects. This investment is soon repaid when Enevoldsen allows a further sacrifice that breaks open his king's position. In spite of accurate defence the Danish player's position finally becomes untenable.

1 e2-e4   e7-e6

2 d2-d4   d7-d5

3 Nb1-d2   f7-f5?!
A dubious way to play against the Tarrasch. 3 ... Nf6, 3 ... Nc6, 3 ... dxe4, and 3 ... c5 are all better. The text move leads to a weakening of the f4 and e5 squares, together with the creation of a bad white-squared bishop for Black. In general, the positional drawbacks of this move far outweigh the attacking chances created by the hold on e4.

4 e4xf5
4 e5, although playable, is nowhere near as strong as the text move.

4 ... e6xf5

5 Nd2-f3
This knight is headed for e5 whilst the king's knight is going to e2 and then f4. Also possible here are:

(a) 5 Ngf3 Nf6 6 c4 Bd6 7 cxd5 0-0 8 Be2 Nxd5 9 0-0 Kh8 10 Re1 Be6 with equality (Geller-Benko, Curaçao 1962).

(b) 5 Bd3 Bd6 6 Ndf3 Nf6 7 Ne2 0-0 8 0-0 c6 9 Bf4 Kh8 10 c4 Na6 11 Bxd6 Qxd6 12 c5 with advantage to White (Rossolimo-Gudmundsson, Amsterdam 1950).

(c) 5 Qh5+ g6 6 Qe2+ and then:

(c1) 6 ... Qe7 7 Ndf3 Nf6 8 h4 Ne4 9 Nh3 Bg7 10 Nf4 c6 11 h5! with a small advantage to White.

(c2) 6 ... Be7 7 h4 Nf6 8 Ngf3 0-0 9 Ne5 Nc6 10 Ndf3 with a small

advantage to White (Bolbochan-Stahlberg, Mar del Plata 1944).

5 ... Ng8-f6

6 Bc1-g5
With this move Karpov must have decided to sacrifice a pawn, since White cannot easily avoid the following natural moves. The alternative was 6 Bd3 followed by Ne2 and 0-0.

6 ... Bf8-e7

7 Bf1-d3
After 7 Ne5 0-0 8 Ngf3 c5 Black has counterchances against the White centre.

7 ... Nf6-e4

8 Bg5xe7   Qd8xe7

9 Ng1-e2   Qe7-b4+
Black decides to accept the sacrifice After 9 ... 0-0 10 0-0 the threat of 11 c4 together with the control of f4 and e5 gives White a clear advantage.

10 c2-c3   Qb4xb2

11 0-0   0-0
After 11 ... Nxc3 12 Nxc3 Qxc3 13 Rc1 Qa5 14 Re1+ White's attack is already decisive as the e7 square cannot be adequately defended by Black: e.g.

(a) 14 ... Kf7 15 Qe2 Nc6 (or 15 ... Qb4 16 Rxc7+) 16 Rxc6 bxc6 17 Qe7+ Kg6 (or 17 ... Kg8 18 Qe8 mate) 18 Qg5+ Kf7 19 Re7+ and mate next move.

(b) 14 ... Kd8 15 Ng5 Rf8 16 Qe2 Qb4 17 Nf7+ and mate next move.

12 c3-c4

ENEVOLDSEN TO MOVE   40.1

KARPOV

White has ample compensation for
the sacrificed pawn. The open b- and
e-files, together with control of the
f4 and e5 squares, are strong factors,
but now White also seizes the a2-g8
diagonal for his bishop. The rook on
a1 can then swing into action with
gain of tempo.

12 ... d5xc4?!
It is easy to criticize this move, but
the other possibilities were far from
pleasant: e.g.

(a) 12 ... Be6? 13 Nf4 winning back
the pawn.

(b) 12 ... c6! 13 Nf4 and now 13 ...
Nf6 14 Re1 or 14 Rc1 leaves White
with an advantage but no clear continuation, but if Black tries to win a
piece by 13 ... g5? the move will re-
bound on him: e.g. 13 ... g5? 14 Bxe4
fxe4 15 Nxg5 Rxf4 16 Qh5 and now:

(b1) 16 ... Qxd4 17 Qxh7+ Kf8
18 Qc7 threatens both the rook on f4
and the bishop on c8.

(b2) 16 ... Bf5? 17 Qf7+ Kh8
18 Qf8 mate.

(b3) 16 ... Na6 17 Qxh7+ Kf8
18 Qh8+ Ke7 19 Qe5+ winning the
rook on f4.

(b4) 16 ... Nd7 17 Qxh7+ Kf8
18 Ne6+ followed by 19 Nxf4.

(b5) 16 ... Rf5 17 Qxh7+ Kf8

18 Qh8+ Ke7 19 Qxc8 Rxg5
20 Rab1.

(b6) 16 ... Rf6 17 Qxh7+ Kf8
18 Qh8+ Ke7 19 Qg7+ winning the
rook.

13 Bd3xc4+   Kg8-h8

14 Ra1-b1!
This is a much clearer way than either
14 Qd3 (threatening 15 Rab1 winning
the queen) 14 ... Qb6, or 14 Ne5 Nc6
15 Nf7+ Kg8! 16 Rb1 Qd2 17 Qb3
Na5 with an unclear position.

14 ... Qb2-a3

15 Nf3-e5
Threatening 16 Ng6+! hxg6 17 Rb3
winning the queen on account of the
threat of mate by 18 Rh3.

15 ... g7-g6
Providing the g7 square for the king.

16 Rb1-b3   Qa3-e7

17 Ne2-f4   Kh8-g7

18 Rb3-h3!
Threatening both 19 Rxh7+ and
19 Nfxg6.

18 ... Nb8-c6
Black's last chance was to try and
hold his position after 18 ... Ng5
19 Re3 Qd8 20 Rfe1 but White is
very much on top. 18 ... Qg5 is
strongly met by 19 Qc1! when White
adds the threat of 20 Ne6+ to his
attack.

ENEVOLDSEN   40.2

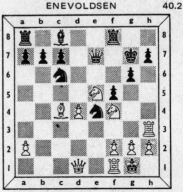

KARPOV TO MOVE

19 Nf4xg6
Although this sacrifice wins the game,
Black is, this way, left with a possible
defence. Correct was the alternative
19 Rxh7+! after which there are no
chances for Black. Thus 19 Rxh7+!
Kxh7 20 Nfxg6 (20 Nexg6 would
allow Black a defence by 20 ... Qd6
21 Nxf8+ Qxf8 22 Qh5+ Kg7)
20 ... Qd6 (20 ... Nxe5 21 Nxe7
Nxc4 allows mate in three by Qd1-h5-
g6-h6) 21 Nxf8+ and now:

(a) 21 ... Qxf8 22 Qh5+ Qh6 (or 22 ...
Kg7 23 Qg6+ Kh8 24 Nf7+ wins the
queen) 23 Bg8+! Kg7 24 Qf7+ Kh8
25 Ng6+ winning the queen.

(b) 21 ... Kg7 22 Qh5 (threat 23 Qf7+)
22 ... Nxe5 (22 ... Kxf8? 23 Qf7
mate or 22 ... Qxf8 23 Qg6+ Kh8
24 Nf7+ wins the queen) 23 Qh7+
Kxf8 24 dxe5 Qd7 (the only way to
prevent mate on f7 or g8 and save the
queen; if 24 ... Qe7? 25 Qg8 mate)
25 Qg8+ Ke7 26 Qf7+ Kd8 27 Qf8+
Qe8 28 Rd1+ Bd7 29 Qxf5 winning
at least a piece.

19 ...h7xg6

20 Ne5xg6 Qe7-f6!
Black is lost after 20 ... Qg5 21 Nxf8
Kxf8 22 Rh8+ Ke7 23 Re1, or
20 ... Kxg6? 21 Qh5+ and 22 Qh6
mate.

21 Ng6xf8
The alternative 21 Nf4 Qg5 22 Nh5+
Kg6 23 Bd3 Qd2 is unclear.

21 ...Kg7xf8

22 Rh3-h7 Nc6-e7?
Black would have had better chances
of beating off the attack by 22 ... Ng5!
23 Rh5 (if 23 Rxc7 Qd6 traps the R)
23 ... Be6 24 Bxe6 [(a) 24 Rxg5?
Bxc4 25 Qh5 Ne7; or (b) 24 d5? Bf7
25 dxc6 Bxc4 26 cxb7 Rb8 27 Qc1
Bxf1 28 Qxc7 Rxb7 29 Qxb7 Be2
and Black's bishop and knight are full
compensation for White's rook and
two pawns] 24 ... Nxe6 25 d5 Rd8
26 Qb3 Ned4 27 Qxb7 Rxd5
28 Qxc7 with the better chances for
White, although the game is still far
from over.

23 Rf1-e1
23 Rf7+ would also have been sufficient, but the black queen cannot
escape.

23 Qf6-g6
After 23 ... Be6 24 Bxe6 Qxe6
25 Nh8+ Ng8 26 Qh5 White has a
crushing position from which Black
can never hope to escape.

24 Rf7-h7+ Qg6xf7
The alternative is 24 ... Ke8 but after
25 f3 Be6 26 Bxe6 Qxe6 27 Rh7
White will win easily.

25 Bc4xf7 Kf8xf7

26 Qd1-h5+ Kf7-f8

27 Qh5-h6+ Kf8-f7
After 27 ... Ke8 the simplest win
is 28 f3 Nc3 29 Rxe7+ Kxe7 30 Qe3+
followed by 31 Qxc3.

28 Qh6-h7+ Black resigns
As 29 f3 will win a piece for White.

Game 41

WHITE Bisguier   English Opening
Skopje Olympiad (A final) 1972

This game serves as a powerful reminder of the result of losing control of
an isolated queen's pawn position. In Game 19 we saw Ivkov's attack come
storming through after an inaccurate defence by Karpov. This time we see
the other side of the story. White's attack never gets going, and Black is able
to exploit the weak central squares and the isolated pawn to force a convincing win.

1 c2-c4   c7-c5

2 Nb1-c3   g7-g6

3 Ng1-f3   Bf8-g7

4 e2-e3

For once Karpov has chosen a more
passive line than his favourite 2 . . .
Nf6 and 3 . . . d5. The alternative for
White here is 4 d4 cxd4 5 Nxd4 Nc6
6 Nc2 Bxc3+!? 7 bxc3 Nf6 8 f3 Qa5
9 Bd2 d5 with equality (Stein-
Matulović, Sousse 1967).

4 . . . Ng8-f6

5 d2-d4   0-0

6 Bf1-e2

After 6 dxc5 Na6, Black regains the
pawn with an equal game.

6 . . . c5xd4

7 e3xd4

If 7 Nxd4 Nc6 8 0-0 Nxd4 9 exd4
d5 Black has achieved equality.

7 . . . d7-d5

8 0-0

8 Bg5 could be met by 8 . . . dxc4
9 Bxc4 Bg4 followed by 10 . . . Nc6
with active development for Black.

8 . . . Nb8-c6

9 h2-h3

Black would meet 9 c5 by 9 . . . Ne4
with an e7-e5 break to follow. The
text move is necessary to prevent
9 . . . Bg4, after which Black would
exert great pressure on the white d4
pawn.

9 . . . Bc8-f5

The alternative was 9 . . . dxc4 10 Bxc4
Na5 11 Be2 Be6 when the game is
approximately equal.

10 Bc1-e3   d5xc4

11 Be2xc4   Ra8-c8

KARPOV   41.1

BISGUIER TO MOVE

Unlike a 'normal' isolated queen's
pawn position, Black has a fianchettoed
king's bishop. This has the advantage
that, from g7, the bishop can exert
greater pressure on the white d4 pawn
but, on the other hand, it makes it
more difficult for Black to control the
d5 square without allowing a weakening of the d6 square by e7-e6. The
chances in this position are about even.

12 Bc4-e2   Bf5-e6!

After 12 . . . Nb4 (to control the d5
square) the reply 13 Qb3 is unpleasant
for Black, as the b7 pawn is un-

defended. The alternative was 12 ...
Nd5 13 Qb3 when 13 ... Nxe3
14 fxe3 makes White happy but
13 ... Nxc3 14 bxc3 Na5 15 Qb4
Be6 gives Black control of both c4
and d5.

The text move is the best, however,
as Black precludes the possibility of
Qb3 and seizes control of d5 and, to
some extent, c4.

13 Qd1-d2
If 13 Ng5, Bd5 would be fine for
Black.

13 ... Qd8-a5
And 13 ... Na5 achieves nothing
after 14 b3.

14 Be3-h6?!
It is not in White's best interest to
exchange these bishops. His black-
squared bishop was needed for the
defence of d4, and, since White's
attacking chances are increased
negligibly by this manœuvre, it would
have been wiser to continue with
14 Rfe1 or 14 Rfd1.

14 ... Rf8-d8

15 Bh6xg7   Kg8xg7

16 Rf1-d1   Rd8-d6!
This move not only prepares for the
doubling of rooks on the d-file but
also increases the range of the d8
rook, so that it can take part in K-side
and Q-side operations along the third
rank.

17 Qd2-e3   Rc8-d8

18 a2-a3
Otherwise White would lose a pawn
to 18 ... Qb4, or possibly even more
after 18 ... Nb4 (threatening 19 ...
Nc2) 19 Rd2 N4d5, etc. The attack
18 Nb5 Rd5 19 Nc3 would lead
nowhere, since after 19 ... R5d7
20 Ne5 is unplayable on account of
20 ... Rxd4 21 Nxc6 Rxd1+ winning
a pawn.

18 ... Be6-b3!

19 Rd1-d2
If 19 Nb5 Bxd1 20 Nxd6 Bxe2
21 Nxb7 Qb6 22 Nxd8 Bxf3 Black

wins two pieces for a rook with considerable advantage.

19 ... Rd6-e6

20 Qe3-f4
After 20 Qd3 Black could continue
with the simple plan 20 ... a6
(preventing a Q-side sortie by White)
and then 21 ... h6, thus cramping
White's game even more.

20 ... Nf6-d5

21 Nc3xd5   Rd8xd5
With the threat 22 ... Rf5 23 Qg3
Rxf3 24 Bxf3 (24 Qxf3 Qxd2
25 Qxb3 Qxe2 wins a piece for Black)
24 ... Qxd2 25 Bxc6 Qxb2 winning
at least a piece.

22 g2-g4
If 22 Bd3 Rf6 23 Qe3 Rxf3! 24 gxf3
(24 Qxf3 Qxd2 wins a piece for Black)
24 ... Nxd4 is advantageous for Black.
After 25 Be4? Qxd2 26 Bxd5 Bxd5
27 Qe5+ Kh6! Black has a won
position, since 28 Qxd5 Ne2+ wins
the queen.

22 ... g6-g5!

23 Qf4-g3   Re6-f6

KARPOV   41.2

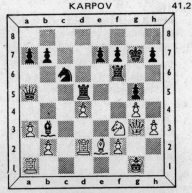

BISGUIER TO MOVE

White's position is in ruins, and it cannot be long now before the isolated
pawn falls. 24 Rd3 ? loses a pawn by
force to 24 ... Bc4 25 Re3 Bxe2
26 Rxe2 Rxf3 27 Qxf3 Nxd4 followed
by 28 ... Nxe2+.

24 Be2-d1   Bb3-c4!

After 24 ... Rxf3? 25 Qxf3 Qxd2
26 Bxb3 White wins owing to the
threats of 27 Bxd5 and, if the rook
moves, then 27 Qxf7+. The text move
is based on a tactical finesse that
Bisguier is powerless to prevent.

25 b2-b3

After 25 Rc2 Bd3 followed by 26 ...
Be4 forces the win of the pawn,
whilst 25 b4 Qd8 (but not 25 ...
Nxb4? when 26 Rc1 wins a piece for
White) is similar to the text continu-
ation.

25 ... Bc4-a6

Black carefully avoids the temptation
to try 25 ... Rxf3? as after 26 Bxf3
Qxd2 27 bxc4 (if 27 Rd1 then Qc3
28 bxc4 Rxd4 29 Rxd4 Nxd4
30 Qe5+ Kh6 wins for Black, as any
bishop move can be met by 31 ...
Nf3+ and 32 ... Qxe5) 27 ... Rxd4
28 Bxc6! bxc6 29 Qe5+ White has
equalized. In this line 27 ... Qc3!?
can be safely met by 28 cxd5! Qxa1+
29 Kg2 Nxd4 30 Qe5+ again with
equality.

26 b3-b4   Qa5-d8!

After 26 ... Nxb4 27 Bb3! the
position becomes unclear. Karpov's
move simply wins the d-pawn.

27 Bd1-b3   Nc6xd4!

The result of Black's manœuvres from
move 24. The game is now decided, for
not only does Black win a pawn but
also his pieces dominate the board.

28 Rd2xd4

After 28 Bxd5 Nxf3+ 29 Bxf3 Qxd2
30 Rd1 Qc3 Black is a clear pawn up
with the better position. Instead of
this Bisguier decides to liven things up
with an exchange-sacrifice, but as
always, Karpov refutes this with ease.

28 ... Rd5xd4

29 Nf3xg5   Rd4-d3

30 Qg3-h4

Threatening mate in two.

30 ... h7-h6

31 Ng5xf7   Qd8-d4

32 Ra1-e1   Rd3xh3!

White resigns

After 33 Qxh3 Qxf2+ 34 Kh1 Qxe1+
35 Kg2 Rf2+ 36 Kg3 Rxf7+ etc. White
will emerge at least a queen and rook
behind.

Game 42

BLACK Ungureanu   Sicilian Defence, Richter-Rauzer Attack
Skopje Olympiad ('A' final), 1972

Ungureanu chooses to play an old variation of the Richter-Rauzer attack
which follows theory for a considerable time. When the game finally diverges
from previous games it takes Karpov just two moves to gain the advantage,
and another four to achieve a winning position. The final assault is swift
and deadly.

1 e2-e4   c7-c5

2 Ng1-f3   Nb8-c6

3 d2-d4   c5xd4

4 Nf3xd4   Ng8-f6

5 Nb1-c3   d7-d6

6 Bc1-g5

The Richter-Rauzer Attack. 6 Bc4
would be the Sozin Attack, whilst
6 Be2, the Boleslavsky Variation, is

seldom met these days because of
the strong reply 6 ...e5, after which
Black has little difficulty in equalizing.

6 ...e7-e6

For an example of the Modern Rauzer
(6 ...Bd7) see Game 37.

7 Qd1-d2   Bf8-e7

Ungureanu plays the opening in an
old-fashioned manner. Nowadays the
rapid development of the Q-side by
7 ...a6 8 0-0-0 Bd7 9 f4 Be7 is more
common in master chess.

8 0-0-0   0-0

9 f2-f4

White can also try 9 Be2, 9 Kb1,
9 Bxf6, 9 N4b5, 9 Nb3, or 9 f3(!),
but the text is the most aggressive
continuation.

9 ...Nc6xd4

10 Qd2xd4   Qd8-a5

11 Bf1-c4

UNGUREANU TO MOVE   42.1

KARPOV

Although there are many possibilities
for White in this position the only
two that are regularly played are the
text move and 11 e5. After 11 e5
dxe5 12 Qxe5! Qxe5 (12 ...Qb6
fails to 13 Na4! Qc6 [13 ...Qb4
14 Rd4 or 13 ...Qf2 14 Rd2 Black
loses his queen] 14 Bb5 Qxg2 15 Rhg1
followed by 16 Bxf6, etc., winning a
piece) 13 fxe5 Nd5 14 Bxe7 Nxe7
15 Bd3 White has the better chances.

Ungureanu in his game with Matulović
from an earlier round of the A final
played 15 ...a6?! (15 ...Nc6 is better
here) 16 Be4 Ra7 17 Rd6 (better
would have been 17 a4! b5 18 axb5
axb5 19 Nxb5 Ra5 [or 19 ...Ra1+
20 Kd2 Ra5 21 c4 Ba6 22 Ra1 with
clear advantage to White] 20 c4 Ba6
21 Nd6 Rxe5 22 Rhe1 g6 23 b4 with
a winning ending for White) 17 ...b5
18 b4 Rc7 19 Kb2 f5 20 exf6. (The
last chance for a real advantage was
20 Bd3! Ng6 21 Re1 followed by
22 a4) 20 ...gxf6 21 g4 Ng6
22 Bxg6 hxg6 23 Re1 and here the
game was agreed drawn.

11 ...Bc8-d7

12 e4-e5!

Again the strongest continuation.
Others here are 12 Rhf1, 12 Rhe1,
12 Kb1, and 12 Bb3.

12 ...d6xe5

13 f4xe5   Bd7-c6

14 Bg5-d2!

The other tries are inferior:

(a) 14 Qf4 Nd5 15 Bxd5 Bxg5 16 Qxg5
exd5 with chances for both sides.

(b) 14 Bxf6 gxf6 15 Rhe1 f5 and Black
equalizes comfortably.

(c) 14 h4 Rad8 15 Qf4 Nh5 16 Qf2
Qb4! 17 Bxe7 Qxe7 18 Be2 g6
19 Bxh5 gxh5 with only a small
advantage for White.

14 ...Nf6-d7

If 14 ...Rad8? 15 Nd5! costs Black
at least the exchange (15 ...Rxd5
16 Bxa5).

15 Nc3-d5   Qa5-d8

16 Nd5xe7+   Qd8xe7

17 Rh1-e1   Rf8-c8

The alternative here is 17 ...Qc5 after
which 18 Qf4 offers White good
attacking chances (Kavalek-Benkö,
Netanya 1969) and 18 Qxc5 Nxc5
19 Bb4 b6 20 Re2 gives White a small
endgame advantage (Savon-Paoli,
Cienfuegos 1972).

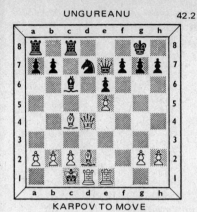

UNGUREANU   42.2

KARPOV TO MOVE

18 Qd4-f4

The move 18 Qg4 was played in the
game Tseshkovsky-Korensky, RSFSR
Championship 1973, and after 18 ...
Qc5 19 Bh6 g6 20 Re2! Rc7 21 Rf1
Re8 22 R2f2 Bd5 (22 ...Qe7 was
best) 23 Rxf7! Nxe5 24 Qd4! Bxc4
25 Qxc5 Rxf7 26 Re1 Ng4 27 Bd2
White had a winning position. Worth
considering, but as yet untested, is
18 h4!?

18 ...a7-a5

An interesting try; if followed up
correctly, this move leads to an unclear situation.

19 Kc1-b1   Nd7-b6?

After 19 ...b5 20 Bf1 (or 20 Bd3?!
Nc5 with an unclear position) White
has only a marginal advantage. The
text move is a mistake, for it allows
the white bishop to settle on d3 without interference.

20 Bc4-d3   Nb6-d5

21 Qf4-g4   Qe7-c5?!

Both 21 ...b5 and 21 ...Nb4 22 Bh6
Qf8 are better tries for Black.

22 Re1-e4!

Now 22 ...Nb4 is met by 23 Rc4!
and now:

(a) 23 ...Qe7 24 Bxb4 wins a pawn.

(b) 23 ...Qxe5 24 Bc3 h5 25 Qh4 with
a substantial advantage for White.

22 ...b7-b5

23 Qg4-h3!

Threatening both 24 Rh4 and
24 Qxh7+! Kxh7 25 Rc4+.

23 ...Nd5-b4

24 Bd2-e3!

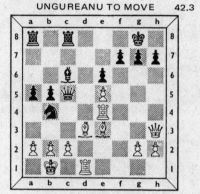

UNGUREANU TO MOVE   42.3

KARPOV

The winning move. 24 Bxb4 axb4
25 Qxh7+ Kxh7 26 Rc4+ wins a
pawn, and 24 Rxb4 axb4 25 Qxh7+
Kf8 26 Qh8+ Ke7 27 Qh4+ g5 gives
White excellent attacking chances for
the sacrificed exchange, but no clear
win in sight. The text move on the
other hand forces the win.

24 ...Bc6xe4

The only worthwhile try. The alternative 24 ...Qe7 (24 ...Qd5 loses to
25 Rxb4 axb4 26 Bxh7+ followed by
27 Rxd5) 25 Rxb4 Qxb4 (25 ...axb4
allows mate in two by Qh4xh7-h8)
26 a3!! and now:

(a) 26 ...Qe7 27 Qxh7+ Kf8 28 Qh8
mate.

(b) 26 ...Qa4 27 Qxh7+ Kf8 28 Bc5+
Ke8 29 Qg8+ Kd7 30 Qxf7+ Kd8
31 Qe7 mate.

25 Bd3xe4!

After 25 Bxc5 Bxd3 26 cxd3 Rxc5
the game would drag on for some time,
but the text move hastens the end.

25 ...Qc5xe5

26 Qh3xh7+ Kg8-f8

27 Be4xa8 Kf8-e7
    Both 27 ... g6 28 Rf1 winning easily
    for White and 27 ... Rxa8 28 Qh8+
    Ke7 29 Qxa8 Qxe3 30 Qd8 mate

are equally decisive.

28 Qh7-e4 Qe5-c7

29 Qe4-b7 **Black resigns**
    White comes out a piece ahead in all
    variations.

Game 43

BLACK Browne   English Opening
San Antonio, 1972

There could be no better example than this game of a simple strategical
idea being introduced in the opening and logically converted into a win.
Karpov's idea on move 2 (!) brings about a weakness in Black's pawn structure that proves decisive in the endgame.

1 c2-c4 c7-c5

2 b2-b3
    The underlying idea here is simple.
    The best development for the black
    pieces in the symmetrical English
    opening is Nb8-c6, g7-g6, and Bf8-g7,
    with the king's knight aimed for e7,
    f6, or even h6 and f5. Karpov's idea is
    to try and prevent Black from achiev-
    ing this harmonious development of
    his game. Browne immediately puts
    the idea to the test.

2 ... Ng8-f6

3 Bc1-b2 g7-g6?!
    The classical development of the bishop
    by 3 ... e6 would have been safer.

4 Bb2xf6!
    This move not only doubles Black's
    pawns but also ensures control of the
    d5 square.

4 ... e7xf6

5 Nb1-c3 Bf8-g7
    Black could try the same trick here,
    namely 5 ... b6 6 Nf3 Bb7 7 g3
    Bxf3! 8 exf3 Nc6 with equality. In
    view of this White would be obliged
    to develop his king's bishop on e2
    from where it would not have the
    same scope as in the game continu-
    ation. In the game Keene-Bellon,

Clare Benedict Cup 1974, Black tried
the idea 5 ...d6 6 g3, Nc6 7 Bg2 h5!
8 h4 Bh6 which, according to Keene,
is a superior way for Black to develop
his game.

6 g2-g3 Nb8-c6

7 Bf1-g2 f6-f5

8 e2-e3 0-0
    After 8 ... Bxc3?! 9 dxc3 White
    would have the open d-file to work
    on and, in particular, the backward
    black d-pawn.

9 Ng1-e2 a7-a6
    An interesting move. Black is pre-
    paring 10 ...b5 followed by Bb7,
    thus reducing the pressure from the
    white king's bishop. After 9 ...d6
    and 10 ... Be6 White would have the
    advantage, owing to his better-orga-
    nized pieces, better pawn-structure,
    and control of the d5 square.

10 Ra1-c1! b7-b5

11 d2-d3
    If White had tried 10 0-0?! then 10 ...
    b5 could not be met by 11 d3?
    (11 ...b4). After the text continu-
    ation White maintains his advantage.

11 ... Bc8-b7

12 0-0 d7-d6

13 Qd1-d2

BROWNE TO MOVE   43.1

KARPOV

Both sides have completed their basic development, and so now is a good time to assess the strength of Karpov's idea.

White has the more solid game owing, chiefly, to his superior pawn structure. His control of d5 is indisputable, and, with his last move, he both threatens the black b5 pawn (to have captured it previously would have left the a2 pawn en prise—13 cxb5 axb5 14 Nxb5 Rxa2), and prepares for a central thrust with 14 Rfd1 and 15 d4. Black on the other hand has the two bishops to compensate for his doubled pawns, and some attacking chances on the K-side by an eventual Nc6-e5 (exploiting the weakened f3 square). Also he has the possibility of a Q-side attack by 13 ...b4 and then a6-a5-a4. This second course of action is dangerous for White, as the black king's bishop would then be very powerful. It is, therefore, somewhat surprising that Browne does not choose the Q-side advance but instead opts for a queen exchange.

13 ...Qd8-a5?!

14 Rf1-d1   Ra8-b8

15 Nc3-d5   Qa5xd2

16 Rd1xd2

White has a clear advantage. Black's K-side and Q-side chances have both been drastically reduced by the queen exchange. Already it is difficult for him to find a satisfactory move: e.g.

(a) 16 ...bxc4? 17 dxc4 with a winning game, as the black d6 pawn will soon fall.

(b) 16 ...Rbc8 17 Ne7+ Nxe7 18 Bxb7 winning at least a pawn.

(c) 16 ...Rfe8 17 cxb5 axb5 18 Nc7 winning the b5 pawn.

(d) 16 ...Rfd8! 17 cxb5 axb5 18 d4! Bf8 (18 ...cxd4? 19 Rxc6 Bxc6 20 Ne7+ followed by 21 Nxc6 leaves White a piece ahead) 19 dxc5 dxc5 20 Nf6+ Kg7 21 Nd7 Ra8 with chances for Black to survive.

The text move is certainly no better than this last possibility.

16 ...b5-b4

17 d3-d4!   Rf8-d8

18 Rc1-d1

The threat now is 19 dxc5 dxc5 20 Ne7+! winning the exchange.

18 ...c5xd4

19 e3xd4   Kg8-f8

20 c4-c5

BROWNE TO MOVE   43.2

KARPOV

White intends 21 Nb6 (or possibly even 21 Nc7!?) followed by 22 d5 and 23 c6 etc. The creation of a passed

pawn is always a danger signal in
Karpov's games.

20 ... Nc6-a7

21 Nd5-e3!

And not 21 Nxb4? when 21 ... Bxg2
22 Nxa6 Bf3 23 Nxb8 Rxb8 leaves
Black with two bishops against rook
and two pawns, and excellent drawing
chances.

21 ... Bb7xg2

22 Kg1xg2   d6xc5

23 d4xc5   Rd8xd2

24 Rd1xd2

With this further reduction in material
Black's position is becoming serious at
the very least. The trouble lies in
White's Q-side majority. This, in itself,
can prove to be a decisive factor in a
single-piece ending and so Black should
be aiming to avoid any further piece
exchanges

24 ... Rb8-c8

25 Ne3-d5   Rc8xc5

After 25 ... a5 26 Nb6 Rc7 27 Rd8+!
Ke7 28 Rg8 the threats of 29 Rxg7
and 29 Nd5+ cannot both be parried.

26 Nd5xb4   a6-a5

27 Nb4-d5   Rc5-c6

28 Nd5-e3

The winning procedure here is to
bombard the weak black a-pawn by
Nc4 Rd2-d8-a8 etc. whilst the black
bishop remains out of play. The Q-side
majority is difficult to advance at the
moment, because there are too many
black pieces on the board. With his
next two moves, Browne shows that he
had either completely underestimated
the gravity of his position, or mis-
calculated the knight-and-pawn ending.

28 ... Rc6-c5?

28 ... Bh6 was more logical.

29 Ne2-f4   Bg7-h6

30 Rd2-d5!   Rc5xd5

31 Nf4xd5   Bh6xe3

32 Nd5xe3

KARPOV

The knight-and-pawn ending is hopeless for Black. He is in effect a pawn
down. His a-pawn is weak and he will
be tied to its defence after Nc4. White
will then centralize his king, blockade
the K-side pawns to remove Black's
tempi moves, and then infiltrate.

32 ... Kf8-e7

33 Kg2-f3   Na7-c6

If 33 ... Nb5 34 Nc4 Nc3 35 a4
wins a pawn.

34 Ne3-c4   Ke7-e6

35 Kf3-e3   Ke6-d5

36 a2-a3!

Now 36 ... Kc5 can be met by
37 Nxa5! Nxa5 38 b4+ with a
winning king-and-pawn ending, and
36 ... a4 by 37 Nb6+ and 38 Nxa4.

36 ... Kd5-e6

37 Ke3-d3   Ke6-d5

38 f2-f3   h7-h6

39 Kd3-c3   h6-h5

40 Kc3-d3   f7-f6

41 f3-f4   g6-g5

White will meet 41 ... Ke6 by 42 Ne3
and 43 Kc4 etc.

42 Nd5-e3+   Kd5-e6

43 h2-h4!

Threatening the g5 pawn. After

43 ... g4 44 Kc4 it would take Black
four moves to attack the white g3
pawn by which time the game would
be over: e.g. 44 ... Na7 45 Kc5 Nc8
46 Kb5 Nd6+ 47 Kxa5 Ne4 48 Nf1!
etc.

43 ... g5xh4

44 g3xh4 Nc6-e7

45 Kd3-c4
The decisive infiltration. Black could
resign.

45 ... Ne7-g6

46 Ne3-g2 Ke6-d6

47 Kc4-b5 Kd6-d5

48 Kb5xa5 Kd5-e4

49 b3-b4 Ke4-f3

50 b4-b5 Kf3xg2

51 b5-b6 Ng6-f8

52 Ka5-b5 Nf8-d7

53 a3-a4 Nd7xb6

54 Kb5xb6 Kg2-f3

55 a4-a5 Kf3xf4

56 a5-a6 Kf4-e3

57 a6-a7 f5-f4

58 a7-a8=Q f4-f3

59 Qa8-e8+ Black resigns

Game 44

BLACK Gligorić   Closed Ruy López, Breyer Variation
San Antonio, 1972

Karpov plays one of his favourite López manœuvering games and soon
gains a substantial spatial advantage. By probing and advancing he cramps
Gligorić's position still further, and the final breakthrough is both un-
expected and unanswerable.

1 e2-e4 e7-e5

2 Ng1-f3 Nb8-c6

3 Bf1-b5 a7-a6

4 Bb5-a4 Ng8-f6

5 0-0 Bf8-e7

6 Rf1-e1 b7-b5

7 Ba4-b3 d7-d6

8 c2-c3 0-0

9 h2-h3 Nc6-b8
The Breyer Variation.

10 d2-d3
For examples of 10 d4, see the games
with the black pieces against O'Kelly
(Game 16) and Gligorić (54) and with
white against Tal (52) and Tukmakov
(50).

10 ... Nb8-d7

Karpov here chose 10 ... c5!? against
Stein (see Game 18).

11 Nb1-d2 Bc8-b7

12 Nd2-f1 Nd7-c5

13 Bb3-c2 Rf8-e8

14 Nf1-g3
The knight stands better on g3 than
on e3. After 14 Ne3 Bf8 15 b4 Ncd7
16 Bb3 h6 17 g4 Black was able to
introduce complications by 17 ... d5!
18 Nxd5 Nxd5 19 exd5 a5! 20 bxa5
Nc5 21 c4 bxc4 22 dxc4 e4 with an
unclear position (Vasiukov-Razuvaev,
USSR Championship 1973).

14 ... Be7-f8
After 14 ... g6 15 Bh6 Bf8 16 Bxf8
Kxf8 17 Qd2 Kg7 18 d4 Ncd7
19 Rad1 h6 20 Nh2 Qe7 21 f4

White had a strong attack (Unzicker-Pădevski, Tel Aviv 1964).

15 b2-b4

More accurate than 15 Nh2 d5 16 Qf3 Ne6 17 Nf5 Kh8 18 exd5 Bxd5 19 Qg3 Nh5! 20 Qxe5 Qd7 21 Nd6 Bxd6 22 Qxh5 Qc6 when Black already had a small advantage, although a pawn down (Kurajica-Geller, Belgrade 1970).

15 ... Nc5-d7

Also possible is 15 ... Ne6!?

16 d3-d4

After 16 Bb3 d5 17 a3 c5 18 exd5 Bxd5 19 Bg5 Qc7 20 Nd2 cxb4 21 cxb4 Rac8 22 Bxd5 Nxd5 23 Qf3 Nf4 the game Petrosian-Portisch, Hamburg 1965, was agreed drawn.

16 ... h7-h6

Other possibilities here are:

(a) 16 ... a5 17 a3 axb4 18 cxb4 and now.

(a1) 18 ... exd4 19 Nxd4 d5 either 20 Bg5 (Ivkov-Lengyel, Amsterdam 1964) or 20 Bf4 give White the advantage.

(a2) 18 ... c5 19 bxc5 dxc5 20 dxe5 Nxe5 21 Nxe5 Qxd1 22 Rxd1 Rxe5 23 Bb2 Re6 24 e5 with advantage to White.

(b) 16 ... g6! 17 a4 Bg7 18 Bd3 bxa4 19 dxe5 Nxe5 20 Nxe5 Rxe5 with equality.

17 Bc1-d2

More active is 17 a4.

17 ... Nd7-b6

18 Bc2-d3 *(see Diagram 44.1)*

White's plan here is to build up his position with 19 Qc2 and 20 Rad1 and then to break open the centre with dxe5. The possibility of a c3-c4 break will always be in the air, and Gligorić's play is aimed at preventing this. In a later game Spassky chose to allow this Q-side advance (see Game 49) and was quickly beaten.

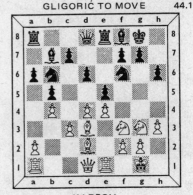

GLIGORIĆ TO MOVE   44.1

KARPOV

18 ... Ra8-c8

19 Qd1-c2   Qd8-d7

Heading for c6, in order to control c4. An interesting possibility was 19 ... exd4 followed by 20 ... c5. Thus:

(a) 20 cxd4 c5 21 d5 c4 22 Bf1 g6.

(b) 20 Nxd4 g6 followed by c5.

20 Ra1-d1   Qd7-c6

21 Bd2-e3   Nb6-a4

22 Rd1-c1

Threatening 23 c4 or 23 d5 followed by 24 c4.

22 ... Na4-b6

23 Qc2-b1

This move threatens 24 d5 Qd7 and now 25 c4!? or 25 Bxb6 cxb6 26 c4. In general, however, White will aim for c3-c4 supported by a knight on d2.

23 ... Qc6-d7

24 Nf3-d2

Now 25 c4 is a real threat. Black decides on a riposte that only weakens his position.

24 ... c7-c5?!

25 b4xc5   d6xc5

26 d4-d5   Nb6-a4

26 ... c4 was impossible, for 27 Bxb6 cxd3 28 Qxd3 leaves White a pawn ahead; thus Gligorić is unable to

prevent White's next move.

27 c3-c4   b5-b4
The pawn could not be defended on
b5, and 27 ... bxc4? 28 Nxc4 would
give White a clear plus.

28 Re1-f1
Preparing for f4.

28 ... Qd7-c7

29 f2-f4   Nf6-d7

30 Qb1-c2   Na4-c3

31 f4-f5!

GLIGORIĆ TO MOVE   44.2

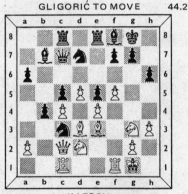

KARPOV

White has a considerable spatial
advantage. With control of e5, Black
was threatening 31 ... exf4 and
32 ... Bd6, Ne5 etc., with equality.
After the text move, he is condemned
to a passive and slightly cramped
position with no possible relief.
The next stage of the game sees
Karpov increase his spatial advantage
by a quick K-side advance which
Gligorić cannot prevent.

31 ... Nd7-f6

32 Ng3-e2   Nc3xe2+

33 Bd3xe2   Bf8-d6
More accurate was 33 ... a5.

34 g2-g4   Kg8-f8

35 h3-h4   Kf8-e7

36 g4-g5   h6xg5

37 h4xg5   Nf6-d7

Now comes the manœuvring for a
breakthrough. The possibilities are
obviously there. The c5 pawn is weak
and easily attackable, a bishop on g4
puts an f6 break in the air, and an
h-file infiltration is always possible.
Within a few moves Karpov has all
his pieces on their most effective
squares.

38 Be2-g4   Re8-g8

39 Kg1-f2   Rg8-h8

40 Rf1-h1   Rc8-g8

41 Qc2-d1   Ke7-d8

42 Qd1-g1   Nd7-b6

43 Rh1-h2   Qc7-e7

44 Nd2-b3   Kd8-c7

45 Kf2-f3   Nb6-d7

GLIGORIĆ

KARPOV TO MOVE

White has several possibilities now. He
can play for an h-file domination by
46 R1c2 and 47 Qh1 etc., or he can
try for a combination based on 46 f6
gxf6 47 Bxd7 Qxd7 48 Nxc5 etc.,
but much further preparation would
be needed for this. The third
possibility, almost certainly overlooked by Gligorić, decides the issue
in a few moves.

46 a2-a3!
After this quiet little move Black is
lost! The threat of 47 axb4 cxb4
48 c5 winning a piece cannot be

parried by 46 ... a5 because of
47 Nxa5. The text move therefore
is forced.

46 ... b4xa3

47 Rh2-a2

Black is unable to defend against the
Q-side pressure. His position falls apart.

47 ... Rh8-h4

48 Ra2xa3   Rg8-h8

49 Rc1-b1   Rh8-b8

50 Qg1-e1!

Threatening both 51 Qxh4 and
51 Qa5+.

50 ... Rh4xg4

51 Kf3xg4   Bb7-c8

52 Qe1-a5+   Black resigns

After 52 ... Rb6 53 Nxc5! Bxc5
54 Rxb6 Bxb6 55 Bxb6+ Nxb6
56 c5 White wins easily.

7   1973 — Interzonal year

The event at Budapest in February/March 1973 was the first international tournament since Caracas 1970 in which Karpov played but failed to achieve first place. It was a peculiar tournament as far as Karpov's play was concerned. In round 2 he beat Hort in a beautiful bishop-and-pawn ending (Game 45). In round 6 he allowed a drawing combination when in a winning position against Lengyel. Round 8 saw him take revenge on Sax, who had originally beaten him way back in 1969 in the RSFSR v. Hungary match. In round 9 he was left with an isolated queen pawn against Forintos, and had to scramble out with a draw. In the next round, he recovered to beat Adorjan (another of his old rivals) in an obscure game (46). In better form now, he pushed hard against Ribli but was finally held to a draw in the ending. The trio of wins against old rivals was completed in round 12, when he beat Vaganian in an excellent queen-and-pawn ending (Game 47). Overall, this was a poor tournament for Karpov. His play contained an element of hesitation and inaccuracy that was so clearly absent at Skopje and at San Antonio. Happily this did not last, and the old flair was back in time for his next event.

This was a novelty in the Soviet chess calendar: a double-round, triangular match between the USSR I, II, and Junior teams, held in Moscow in late April. Playing on board one for the junior team he scored 1½/2 against both Spassky and Taimanov. His win against Spassky (Game 49) contains an exciting example of a semi-positional exchange-sacrifice, after which Spassky was unable to cope with the problems of the position. The Taimanov game (48) features two positional sacrifices.

At last came Anatoly's chance to take part in the world championship series. The Leningrad Interzonal in June was one of the two qualifying tournaments for the final knock-out stages. Three players were to qualify from Leningrad—no easy task with Korchnoi, Larsen, Tal, Hübner, Gligorić, Robert Byrne, Kuzmin, and Smejkal also in the tournament. But Leningrad was to be yet another equal first place for Karpov. His play against the weaker competitors (including Quinteros, Uhlmann, and Tukmakov) was impressive—he conceded only one draw and won the other seven games— and this was the key to his victory.

The start of the tournament was slightly unsure for Karpov. Black in round 1, he beat Estévez in a long triple-piece ending, but in round 2 he overlooked a neat tactical resource in a winning position against Hübner, and had to be content with a draw. Round 3 produced his first good game. He beat Tukmakov in a Ruy López, Breyer Variation, by outplaying him in a seemingly innocuous sort of opening (Game 50). This game was full of tactical tricks, but Karpov was equal to them and came out an easy winner. In the next round Karpov chose an inferior line against Korchnoi's Pirc Defence and had to be satisfied with a short draw. Karpov had the black pieces in the next two games and increased his score by 1½—an interesting Nimzo-Indian draw against Taimanov and a comfortable win against Cuéllar. The Karpov-Kuzmin game in round 7 was a typical Botvinnik-influenced win (Game 51). Kuzmin was crushed by pawn advances first on the K-side, then on the Q-side, and could find no answer other than to reassemble his pieces on the back rank.

As usual in Interzonals the Soviet contingent was placed together in the draw, and Karpov's next opponent was Tal. The former world champion was already out of the running, after a disastrous start of 2/7, including losses to Korchnoi, Hübner, Estévez, and Torre! All the Karpov-Tal games have been exciting and this one was no exception. An ingenious exchange-sacrifice by Karpov was answered with a piece sacrifice by Tal; when the smoke cleared Karpov was left to draw a difficult ending. This he did, with his customary precision, to record his third draw against Tal (Game 52). The next game gave Karpov one of the three best-game prizes for the tournament. Quinteros was overwhelmed after a bold exchange sacrifice (Game 53). This put Karpov into second place behind Korchnoi, but half a point ahead of Robert Byrne, who had just lost his first (and only) game to Korchnoi. The leading scores at the half-way mark were Korchnoi 8, Karpov 7, Byrne and Larsen 6½, Smejkal 6. After careful shortish draws with Larsen and Byrne, Karpov beat the out-of-form Uhlmann, thus taking the joint lead with Korchnoi, who had just lost to the tail-ender Rukavina. Karpov's win against Gligorić in round 13 (Game 54) was a Q-side attack in a Breyer Variation, in contrast with their game at San Antonio (44) which Karpov won by a K-side offensive. In the next round Karpov made no mistake as Black against Rukavina reaching a winning position in a mere fifteen moves. Radulov had little difficulty in holding Karpov to a draw, and so Korchnoi moved back into the joint lead. The penultimate round saw Karpov as Black against Smejkal (Game 55). The leading scores were Karpov and Korchnoi 11½, Byrne 11, Smejkal 10½, and Hübner 9½, and so this game was the last chance for the Czech grandmaster to qualify. Karpov sprung a deeply-calculated innovation in the opening (the point did not become clear until move 25, although the innovation was played on move 13!) and reduced Smejkal's advantage to nil. During an interesting ending with queens, and bishops of opposite colours, Smejkal, in time-trouble, blundered away a pawn, after which Karpov won in exemplary fashion. The last-round win against Torre was a mere formality and ensured joint first place with Korchnoi. Karpov's overall play at Leningrad was most impressive. He made few mistakes, and no doubt Spassky and Petrosian, who both had byes to the finals of the Candidates' series, were already dreading the prospect of a match with him.

After the long, arduous struggle of the Interzonal Karpov took a break, playing on board 4 (!) for the USSR team in the European Team Championships held in Bath in July. His final score of 5/6 was bettered only by Geller, and helped the USSR to yet another team victory. Although Karpov chose none of the games from this tournament for inclusion, the finishes of his games with Ribli and Ghizdavu were given in Chapter 2.

The new-style Soviet Championship was held in Moscow in October 1973. The idea was to invite the top grandmasters, thus making it unnecessary for them to qualify, and then to start the championship on a league basis. Karpov was, of course, in the First Division, together with most of the top Soviet grandmasters. Karpov's results were somewhat like Jekyll and Hyde. He beat both Korchnoi and Kuzmin, who finished equal second, but scored only two wins against the last eight players in the tournament.

A win against Savon and a draw with Taimanov were followed by a somewhat disappointing draw with Sveshnikov. Karpov won a pawn but, in doing so, allowed all kinds of counterplay that proved ample compensation in the ending. In round 4, Karpov beat Beliavsky with a slice of luck from a lost position, and in round 5 came the customary draw with Tal. Rounds 6 and 7 produced Karpov's best chess in the tournament. A positional pawn-sacrifice led to Korchnoi's downfall (Game 56) although this was due mainly to Korchnoi's stubbornness in refusing to play for a draw. Round 7 was a most unusual game. Playing the Ruy López, Spassky chose the Chigorin defence after his loss with the Breyer earlier in the year. By a strong K-side advance, Karpov won a piece for two pawns in the middle-game, but somehow Spassky managed to conjure up sufficient counterplay to hold the position. This must have been a disappointing result for Karpov, and in the next round he lost a long game to Petrosian, after having been caught by a tactical trick in the opening that cost him the exchange. Karpov bounced right back after this loss and beat Kuzmin in the next round (Game 57). After this, Karpov won only one more of his remaining eight games. A brilliant defence against Tukmakov earned him only a draw. Although he was level with Spassky after ten rounds, his finishing run was bettered by the former world champion, who scored wins in rounds 11, 12, and 13 to win the first Soviet 'super-league' Championship. Karpov was left a point behind, in equal second place with Korchnoi, Kuzmin, Petrosian, and Polugaevsky.

The year was not quite over yet; in late November and early December Karpov played in the Madrid International tournament. He began with the same shaky form that had characterized his play at Moscow. He beat Pomar in round 1, but scored only one more win in the next six rounds. The second of these was indeed pretty and was Karpov's second win against Andersson in the collection (Game 58).

With half the tournament gone, Karpov was still trailing the leaders by half a point. Uhlmann, Furman, and Hort each had 5 to Karpov and Portisch on 4½. In the next four rounds Karpov scored 3 points—wins against Silvano Garcia and Kaplan, and draws with Furman and Hort. This was not good enough, however, to gain the lead, since Uhlmann had been beating everyone and now had 8½ points to Karpov, Hort, Furman, and Tukmakov on 7½. The crucial game, therefore, was the Karpov-Uhlmann encounter in round 12. Uhlmann was completely outplayed in the Karpov variation of the Tarrasch French—a struggle which earned Karpov the best-game prize for the tournament (Game 59). So now there was a tie on 8½ between Uhlmann, Karpov, Furman, and Tukmakov. Round 13 saw Uhlmann lose again—this time to Karpov's trainer Furman. Tukmakov could only draw with Andersson, but Karpov, now playing with real power, beat Calvo very easily (Game 60). Karpov and his trainer were thus left to battle out the last two rounds. Karpov tried hard against Portisch but, despite winning a pawn, was unable to achieve the win. This was no great setback, as it turned out, for Furman lost with white against Calvo, whom Karpov had so easily beaten in the previous round. This, at last, left Karpov clear of the field, and in his last-round game with Planinc (Game 51) he made no mistake. So Karpov achieved an unshared first place at last! He was also awarded the prize for the best score in the last four rounds.

At the meeting of chess journalists and writers held in Madrid at the same time as the tournament, a ballot was held to decide the 'chess player of the year', who would receive the World Chess Oscar. Previous winners were Larsen (1967), Spassky (1968 and 1969), and Fischer (1970, 1971, and 1972) but this year it was Karpov's turn to receive the trophy, thus improving on his fourth place in 1972.

The remainder of the year was spent in preparation for the Candidates' matches, which were to begin in January of the following year, and would show just how good the young grandmaster had become.

Game 45

BLACK Hort   French Defence, Tarrasch Variation
Budapest, 1973

The black queen's bishop is always a problem piece in the French Defence. Several systems involve devious manœuvres by Black aimed solely at the exchange of the white-squared bishops. For example:

(a) 1 e4 e6 2 d4 d5 3 e5 c5 4 c3 Qb6 5 Nf3 Bd7 6 Be2 Bb5 (Wade's Variation; (b) 1 e4 e6 2 d4 d5 3 Nc3 Bb4 4 e5 b6 5 a3 Bxc3+ 6 bxc3 Ne7 7 h4 Ba6; or (c) 1 e4 e6 2 d4 d5 3 Nd2 Nf6 4 e5 Nfd7 5 Bd3 c5 6 c3 b6 7 f4 Ba6.

The white-squared bishop is strategically bad because the central black pawns are by the nature of the opening, to be fixed on white squares. This game provides a good example of how the bad bishop can be exploited in the endgame.

1 e2-e4   e7-e6

2 d2-d4   d7-d5

3 Nb1-d2   Ng8-f6

For other lines see Games 12, 47, 51, and 59. (3 ...c5 by Black) and Game 40 (3 ...f5).

4 e4-e5   Nf6-d7

5 c2-c3   c7-c5

6 Bf1-d3

The alternative for White is 6 f4 Nc6 7 Ndf3 when 7 ...cxd4 8 cxd4 h5 9 Bd3 Nb6 10 Nh3 Bd7 11 0-0 g6 12 a3 a5 13 Qe2 Be7 14 Nhg5 a4 15 Qf2 Na5 16 Bd2 Nb3 17 Rad1 Nc4 18 Bc3 leaves White with a small advantage (Marić-Uhlmann, Skopje 1968); or 7 ...Qa5 8 Kf2!? b5 9 Bd3 b4 10 Ne2 Nb6 11 g4 bxc3 12 bxc3 with equality, according to Portisch.
This variation gives White a spatial advantage (in return for allowing Black more freedom on the Q-side) and a generally harmonious development.

6 ... Nb8-c6

7 Ng1-e2   Qd8-b6

8 Nd2-f3

The sacrifice 8 0-0!? cxd4 9 cxd4 Nxd4 10 Nxd4 Qxd4 11 Nf3 Qb6 offers approximately equal chances: e.g. 12 Qa4! Qb4! 13 Qc2 Qc5 14 Bxh7 b6 15 Bf4 Ba6 16 Rfc1 Qxc2 17 Bxc2 Nc5 18 Nd4 Be7 with equality (Furman-Uhlmann, Polanica Zdroj 1967).

8 ... c5xd4

9 c3xd4   f7-f6

The logical way to attack the centre.

10 e5xf6   Nd7xf6

11 0-0   Bf8-d6

HORT   45.1

KARPOV TO MOVE

White has many possible ways to develop from here, for example:

(a) 12 b3 0-0 13 Bb2 Bd7 14 Ng3 Kh8 15 Bb1 a5 16 a3 Rac8 17 Re1 Ne7 18 Ne5 Be8 19 Re3 Bxe5! 20 dxe5 Nd7 21 Bd4 Qd8 22 Bd3 Bg6 with equality (Florian-Uhlmann, Balatonfüred 1959).

(b) 12 Bd2 0-0 13 Bc3 Bd7 14 Ng3 Rae8 15 Ne5 Re7 16 Kh1 Be8 17 f4 Kh8 18 Bc2 Rc7 19 a3 Ne7 20 Qd2 Rc8 with equality.

(c) 12 Bf4 Bxf4 13 Nxf4 0-0 14 Rb1 Qc7 15 g3! e5 16 dxe5 Nxe5 17 Nxe5 Qxe5 18 Re1 with a clear advantage for White (Aronin-Kotkov Moscow 1960). Better here is 13 ... Qxb2! which with best play should equalize.

(d) 12 Re1 0-0 13 Nf4 Bd7 14 Nxe6 Rfe8 15 Bf5 Na5 (interesting here is 15 ...Bb4 16 Bd2 Bxd2 17 Qxd2 Ne7! 18 Nxg7 Kxg7 19 Qg5+ Ng6 20 Bxd7 Nxd7 with great complications and a totally unclear position)

16 Bg5 Bxe6 17 Rxe6 Bxh2+ 18 Nxh2
Rxe6 19 Bxe6 Qxe6 20 Bxf6 Qxf6
Agreed drawn (Gligorić-Schmid,
Dublin 1957).

According to theory the fifth possibility, chosen by Karpov, is the most
effective:

12 Ne2-c3!   0-0

13 Bc1-e3
White's idea is to complete his develop-
ment by Rc1 h3 etc. without allowing
Black any further freedom.

13 ...Qb6-d8
After the simple 13 ...Bd7 14 a3!
Qd8! 15 h3 Rc8 16 Re1 Kh8 17 Rc1
Qe8 18 Rc2 a6 19 Rce2 Rc7 20 Bc1
White has a small advantage (Geller-
Uhlmann, Skopje 1968). The traps
here are:

(a) 13 ...Ng4? 14 Bxh7+ winning a pawn.

(b) 13 ...Qxb2 14 Nb5 Be7 15 Rb1
Qxa2 16 Ra1 Qb2 17 Ra4! winning,
since the threat of 18 Bc1 cannot be
parried.

14 Be3-g5   Bc8-d7

15 Rf1-e1   Qd8-b8
15 ...Rc8 would be met by 16 Rc1
followed by 17 Bb1 and Qd3 with a
dangerous-looking attack, while
15 ...Qe8? would allow 16 Bxf6 and
17 Nxd5 winning a pawn.

16 Bg5-h4!
Karpov's idea of manœuvring the
bishop c1-g5-h4-g3 features also in
games 51 and 59.

16 ...a7-a6

17 Ra1-c1   b7-b5

18 Bd3-b1   Bd6-f4

19 Bh4-g3!   Bf4xg3

20 h2xg3 *(see Diagram 45.2)*

White has a clear advantage. He has
control over e5 and now f4 also. The
black bishop is badly hemmed in,
and so the endgame favours White.
White's next idea is to bring more
pressure to bear on the e6 pawn.

HORT TO MOVE   45.2

KARPOV

20 ...Qb8-b6
If 20 ...Qd6 then White could continue 21 Ne5 and 22 f4.

21 Nc3-e2
Heading for f4, to put more pressure
on the weak e6 pawn. But possibly
even stronger here was 21 Qd3! with
the idea of meeting 21 ...Rae8 by
22 Ne5! (a move which virtually wins
by force) e.g.

(a) 22 ...Bc8 23 Na4 Qxd4 24 Rxc6
Qxd3 25 Bxd3 bxa4 26 Bxa6 with
great advantage to White but possibly
23 Nxb5 (not 23 Nxd5? when 23 ...
exd5 24 Rxc6 Qxc6! gives Black
two rooks for queen and pawn)
23 ...Nxe5 24 dxe5 Qxb5 25 exf6
Qxd3 26 Bxd3 gxf6 27 Rc6 or
27 Rc7 is even better.

(b) 22 ...Nxe5 23 dxe5 Ne4 24 Nxe4
dxe4 25 Qe3! with a winning position
for White.

(c) 22 ...Qxd4? 23 Nxd7 wins a piece
(23 ...Qxd3 24 Nxf6+ or 23 ...
Nxd7 24 Qxh7+ Kf7 25 Bg6+ etc.).

21 ...Ra8-e8
Threatening 22 ...e5.

22 Ne2-f4   Nc6xd4?!
This combination is dubious and
should lead to an excellent position
for White. For once, however, Karpov's
reply is not the best.

23 Qd1xd4?!

After 23 Nxd4! e5 24 Nxd5! Black can choose between

(a) 24 ... Nxd5 25 Nf3 threatening both the d5 knight and the e5 pawn and hence giving White a glorious position.

(b) 24 ... Qxd4 25 Nxf6+ Rxf6 26 Qxd4 exd4 27 Rxe8+ Bxe8 28 Rc8 Kf7 29 Rd8 winning a pawn.

23 ... Qb6xd4

24 Nf3xd4   e6-e5

25 Nf4-e6!

Only by playing this move can White retain an advantage.

25 ... Bd7xe6

26 Re1xe5   Be6-d7

27 Re5xe8   Rf8xe8

28 f2-f3   Re8-c8

29 Rc1xc8+   Bd7xc8

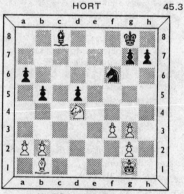

HORT   45.3

KARPOV TO MOVE

This series of exchanges has reduced White's advantage considerably. However, he still has a much better bishop and some weak black squares (e3, d4, e5, c5, etc.) on which to infiltrate with his king. The outcome should be a draw but the position is difficult for Black to defend.

30 Kg1-f2   Kg8-f7

31 Kf2-e3   Kf7-e7

32 b2-b4   g7-g6

33 g3-g4   Nf6-d7

34 f3-f4   Nd7-f8?

Hort is on the wrong track altogether. The correct way was not 34 ... Nb6, when 35 Nc6+! Kd6 36 Ne5 Nc4+ 37 Kd4! gives White good winning chances, but 34 ... Kd6! 35 g5! (not 35 Nf3 Nf6 36 g5 d4+ followed by 37 ... Nd5 forking the b4 and f4 pawns) 35 ... Nb6 36 Bd3 when White's advantage remains small.

35 g4-g5   Ke7-d6

36 Ke3-f3

Preparing for 37 g4 and 38 f5.

36 ... Nf8-e6?

Black's 34th move allowed White a substantial advantage; this further blunder allows him a winning position. Preferable was 36 ... Bb7 or 36 ... Nd7.

37 Nd4xe6   Bc8xe6

38 Kf3-e3   Be6-g4

39 Bb1-d3

To prevent the bishop from coming to e2 and c4 or f1.

39 ... Bg4-e6

40 Ke3-d4   Be6-g4

41 Bd3-c2!

Now 41 ... Be2 could be met by 42 f5!

41 ... Bg4-e6

42 Bc2-b3   Be6-f7

The only move to prevent a further king infiltration or the loss of a pawn.

43 Bb3-d1!   Bf7-e6

To prevent the threatened 44 Bg4.

44 Bd1-f3

Total zugzwang. Black has no moves.

44 ... Be6-f7

45 Bf3-g4   Black resigns

The threat of 46 Bc8 and 47 Bxa6 can be met only by 45 ... Be6, when 46 Bxe6 Kxe6 47 g4 Kd6 48 f5 wins easily for White.

Game 46

BLACK Adorjan   Grünfeld Defence
Budapest 1973

Although the Budapest tournament must have been a slight disappointment for Karpov after his brilliant results in 1972, he had the immense satisfaction of beating three old rivals. In his previous encounters with Adorjan he had three draws and one loss, with Sax a draw and a loss, and with Vaganian three wins, five draws, and three losses.

1 c2-c4   g7-g6

2 d2-d4   Ng8-f6

3 Nb1-c3   d7-d5
The Grünfeld Defence—a popular choice in master chess.

4 Ng1-f3
The Exchange Variation 4 cxd5 Nxd5 5 e4 Nxc3 6 bxc3 is the most crucial line in this opening. It is the favourite of Boris Spassky, who with it has twice defeated Bobby Fischer (Santa Monica 1966, and Siegen 1970).

4 . . . Bf8-g7

5 Bc1-g5   Nf6-e4
By far the best reply 5 . . . dxc4 5 , . . e6 and 5 . . . c6 all fail to equalize against best play by White.

6 c4xd5
An old trap is 6 Nxd5? when 6 . . . Nxg5 7 Nxg5 e6 wins a piece for Black.

6 . . . Ne4xg5
Although 6 . . . Nxc3 7 bxc3 Qxd5 is playable the text is superior.

7 Nf3xg5   e7-e6

8 Qd1-d2
The alternative here is 8 Nf3 exd5 9 e3 0-0 10 b4! with a minority attack giving White Q-side pressure.

8 . . . h7-h6
8 . . . exd5 is possible immediately: e.g. 9 Qe3+ Kf8 10 Qf4 Bf6 11 h4 h6 12 Nf3 Kg7 13 0-0-0 c6 14 e3 Be6 15 Bd3 Nd7 16 g4 Qb8 with equality (Stein-Spassky USSR Championship 1963).

9 Ng5-h3   e6xd5

10 Nh3-f4
After 10 Qe3+ Kf8 11 Nf4 c5! is strong and causes White some embarrassment.

10 . . . 0-0!

11 g2-g3
After 11 Nfxd5 c6 Black regains his pawn with the better game, and if 11 e3 c5! 12 dxc5 d4 13 exd4 (13 0-0-0? dxc3! 14 Qxd8 cxb2+ 15 Kb1 Bf5+ 16 Qd3 Bxd3+ 17 Nxd3 Na6 gives advantage for Black) 13 . . . Qxd4 14 Qxd4 Bxd4 15 Bb5 Na6 16 Nfe2 Bxc5 17 0-0 Nc7 18 Ba4 Bf5 leaves Black with a clear advantage (Pytel-Adorjan, Polanica Zdroj 1971).

11 . . . Nb8-c6!?
The alternative 11 . . . c6 12 Bg2 Bf5 13 0-0 Nd7 is safer and leads to an equal position.

12 e2-e3   Nc6-e7

13 Bf1-g2   c7-c5!
Black is aiming to exploit the fact that the white king is still uncastled.
(see Diagram 46.1)

14 d4xc5!
Other possibilities are:

(a) 14 0-0 cxd4 15 exd4 Nc6 with equality, but if White tries 16 Nce2?! then 16 . . . g5 17 Nh5 Bh8 18 f4 Bg7 19 Bf3 Bxf3 20 Rxf3 g4 gives Black the advantage.

(b) 14 Ncxd5 cxd4 15 0-0 with equality. 15 exd4 however is dubious on account

ADORJAN   46.1

KARPOV TO MOVE

of 15 ... Nxd5 16 Nxd5 Re8+ with
attacking chances for Black.

14 ...d5-d4

15 Nc3-d1
This leads to an exchange of queens
and a complicated position offering
chances to both sides. Both 15 Rd1 Bg4!
16 Nce2 dxe3 17 fxe3 (if 17 Qxe3
Qa5+ or 17 Qxd8 exf2+ Black has the
advantage) 17 ...Qc7, and 15 0-0-0
dxc3!? 16 Qxd8 cxb2+ 17 Kb1 Bf5+
18 Qd3 Bxd3+ 19 Nxd3 Rab8
20 Nxb2 Rfc8 21 Rc1 (21 Rd7 is
met by 21 ...Rxc5! 22 Rxe7 Rb5
regaining the piece) 21 ...Nc6 followed by 22 ...b6 with compensation
for the pawn, are unclear. Karpov
prefers a simpler type of game with
good prospects.

15 ...d4xe3

16 Nd1xe3 Qd8xd2+

17 Ke1xd2 Bg7xb2

18 Ra1-b1 Bb2-a3
The other options are:

(a) 18 ...Bd4 19 Rhc1

(b) 18 ...Rd8+ 19 Ke2 Ba3 20 Bxb7
(if 20 Nd3 then 20 ...Nf5 is strong)
20 ...Bxb7 21 Rxb7 Bxc5 22 Rc1
Bd6 (if 22 ...Bxe3 23 fxe3 Nf5
24 Rcc7 Nd6 25 Rxa7 Nb5 26 Rxa8
Rxa8 27 Rc2 gives White the advan-

tage of an extra pawn, since 27 ...
Rxa2? 28 Rxa2 Nc3+ 29 Kd2 Nxa2
30 Nd5 traps the knight) 23 Nd3.

In each case White has a slight plus.

19 Nf4-d3   Rf8-d8

20 Kd2-c3!
After 20 Ke2 or 20 Kc2 the reply
20 ...Nf5! is strong.

20 ...a7-a5!
The best way to prevent the threat of
21 Rb3. After 20 ...Be6 21 Rxb7
Nd5+ 22 Bxd5 Bxd5 23 Nxd5 Rxd5
24 Kc4 Rad8 25 Nb4 White retains
his extra pawn.

21 Rh1-d1   Bc8-e6

22 Bg2xb7

ADORJAN TO MOVE   46.2

KARPOV

The other possibilities here were also
interesting:

(a) 22 Nc2? would be a mistake, because
of the reply 22 ...Bxc5 23 Nxc5
Rxd1 24 Rxd1 Rc8 regaining the
piece with the better game.

(b) 22 Rxb7 Nd5+ 23 Nxd5 Bxd5
24 Bxd5 Rxd5 regaining the pawn
with equality.

(c) 22 Nc4 and now:

(c1) 22 ...Bb4+?! 23 Nxb4 axb4+
24 Kxb4 Rxd1 25 Rxd1 Rxa2 with
advantage for White.

(c2) 22 ...Rxd3+ 23 Rxd3 Bxc5
with some chances for the exchange.

22 ... Ra8-b8

23 c5-c6 Ba3-d6
White stands slightly better.

24 Ne3-c4 Ne7-d5+

25 Kc3-b2 Nd5-e7

26 Kb2-c3
If 26 Nxa5 then 26 ... Nxc6 27 Nxc6
Rxb7+ is advantageous for Black.

26 ... Ne7-d5+

27 Kc3-c2?!
White could have played safe and taken
the draw, but Black was under some
time-pressure.

27 ... Be6-f5

28 a2-a3
Preventing the threat of 28 ... Nb4+.

28 ... Bd6-c7

29 Rb1-b5 Nd5-e7

30 f2-f3
If 30 Nxa5 then 30 ... Rd4 followed
by Rbd8 is strong.

30 ... h6-h5
According to Adorjan 30 ... Rd4 is
strong e.g.

(a) 31 Ne3 Rbd8! with nasty threats.

(b) 31 Kc3 Rbd8 32 Ncb2 with an unpleasant pin on the d-file.

31 Kc2-c3 Ne7-d5+

32 Kc3-b2 Nd5-e7

33 Nd3-f2 Rd8xd1

34 Nf2xd1 h5-h4

35 g3xh4 Bf5-d3

36 Kb2-c3 Bd3-e2

37 Nd1-e3 Be2xf3

38 Nc4xa5

ADORJAN TO MOVE   46.3

KARPOV

38 ... Bc7xa5?
After 38 ... f5 White has the advantage, but the issue is still in doubt.

39 Rb5xa5 Ne7xc6?
This second blunder is more than
Black's position can stand, but even
after 39 ... Bxc6 40 Bxc6 Nxc6
41 Rc5 White is well on the way to a
win.

40 Ra5-a8!
Winning by force.

40 ... Rb8xa8

41 Bb7xa8 Nc6-e5

42 Ba8xf3 Ne5xf3

43 a3-a4 Nf3-e5

... Black resigns
The passed pawn will triumph soon.

Game 47

BLACK Vaganian   French Defence, Tarrasch Variation
Budapest, 1973

Vaganian gambits his isolated pawn in return for active piece-play, and only some fifteen moves later does the situation become clear. After a period of manœuvering for position, the game enters a queen-and-pawn ending in which Karpov demonstrates his flawless technique. This was Vaganian's only loss at Budapest.

1 e2-e4   e7-e6

2 d2-d4   d7-d5

3 Nb1-d2   c7-c5

4 Ng1-f3   Nb8-c6

5 e4xd5   e6xd5

6 Bf1-b5   Bf8-d6

7 d4xc5   Bd6xc5
  The move 7 ... Qe7+ is interesting here, but after 8 Qe2 Bxc5 9 Ne5 Bd7 10 Nxd7 Kxd7 11 Nb3 Qxe2+ 12 Kxe2 Re8+ 13 Kf3 Bd6 14 Be3 a6 15 Bxc6+ bxc6 White has a clear advantage (Portisch-Farago Hungary 1971).

8 0-0   Ng8-e7

9 Nd2-b3   Bc5-b6
  More usual is 9 ... Bd6 (see Games 51 and 59).

10 Rf1-e1   0-0

11 Bc1-g5!?
  Karpov tried 11 Be3 against Krogius in Game 12.

11 ... h7-h6

12 Bg5-h4
  After 12 Bxc6? hxg5 13 Bb5 g4 Black has the edge, but 12 Be3 Bf5 13 Bxb6 Qxb6 14 Bxc6 Nxc6 15 Nfd4 Be4 with equality is a possibility (Geller-Spassky match 1968).

12 ... g7-g5?
  Also playable is 12 ... f6 and 13 Bg3 Nf5.

13 Bh4-g3   Ne7-f5
  13 ... Bg4 would be adequately met by 14 Qd3 and 15 Nfd4.

14 Qd1-d2   Nf5xg3

15 h2xg3   Qd8-f6

16 c2-c3

VAGANIAN TO MOVE   47.1

KARPOV

The removal of White's bishop has done nothing to increase Black's K-side chances, since the white pawns are now impregnable. Black's two bishops are, at the moment, ineffective, and the d-pawn is difficult to defend. After 16 ... Be6 17 Rad1 Rad8 18 Nbd4 White has a clear advantage, but perhaps 16 ... a6!? is better. With his next move—a fine pawn sacrifice—Vaganian throws the game into a complex tactical mêlée whose outcome is difficult to foresee.

16 ... Bc8-f5!

17 Qd2xd5   Ra8-d8

18 Qd5-c4   Bf5-d3

19 Qc4-a4   Bd3xb5

20 Qa4xb5   g5-g4

21 Nf3-d4   Nc6xd4

22 c3xd4

White's previous five or six moves were forced, and so is this one—
22 Nxd4? a6 23 Qh5 Bxd4 wins back the pawn, since 24 Qxg4+!? Qg7 costs White a piece.

22 ...a7-a6

After 22 ... Bxd4? 23 Nxd4 Rxd4 24 Qxb7 Rd2 25 Qxa7 Rxb2 26 a4! White is left a clear pawn ahead.

23 Qb5-h5   Bb6xd4

This would also have been the reply to 23 Qe5.

24 Qh5xg4+   Qf6-g7

25 Qg4-f3!

After 25 Qxg7+ Bxg7 either 26 Re7 Rfe8 27 Rxb7 Re2 or 26 Re2 Rfe8 27 Rae1 Rxe2 28 Rxe2 b6 gives White only a minimal advantage.

25 ...Bd4xb2

26 Ra1-d1

If 26 Rab1 then 26 ...b5! 27 Re4 Kh8 is satisfactory for Black, but 26 ...b6 allows 27 Re4 Kh8 28 Qe2 winning a pawn.

26 ...b7-b6

27 Qf3-b7

27 Re4!? was an interesting try, but Karpov prefers to win a Q-side pawn.

27 ...Rd8xd1

28 Re1xd1   Qg7-g4

29 Rd1-b1   Rf8-d8

30 Qb7xa6   Rd8-d1+

31 Rb1xd1   Qg4xd1+

32 Qa6-f1

After 32 Kh2 Qh5+ 33 Kg1 Qd1+ White must try 34 Qf1 to avoid a three-fold repetition.

32 ...Qd1-c2

The knight-v.-bishop ending would almost certainly be lost for Black. His K-side pawns are weak, and the white king would aim for the Q-side via f1, e2, d3, etc.

33 Qf1-b5   Bb2-a3

After 33 ... Qd1+ 34 Kh2 Black has no further checks. The exchange of the Q-side pawns by 33 ...Qb1+ 34 Kh2 Qxa2 35 Qxb6 would be to White's advantage, for the knight would work better with pawns on one side only. The bishop is a long-range piece and is usually better with two groups of pawns on the board.

34 Qb5-d5

KARPOV

Of course the capture of the b6 pawn would leave Black a perpetual check on d1 and h5. White's advantage here is small. His main chance lies in a K-side attack with queen and knight against the black king and the weak black pawns on f7 and h6. In the meantime, however, he must watch for a Black attack on his f2 pawn and his weak a2 pawn. Karpov attains his objectives, but only after a little help from his opponent.

34 ...Ba3-f8?

34 ...Qxa2 would be met by 35 Qd8+ and 36 Qxb6, but 34 ... Bc5! is very strong. The threats of 34 ...Qxf2+ or 34 ... Qxa2 can be satisfactorily met only by 35 Nxc5 when bxc5 gives Black a strong passed pawn. A continuation might be 36 a4 (the only way to counter the advance of the black pawn) and now:

(a) 36 ...Qxa4 37 Qxc5 with some

winning chances.

(b) 36 ... c4 37 a5 c3 38 a6 Qd2! with advantage to Black.

So it seems that White would have had to play for a draw with 37 Qd8+ or 38 Qd8+.

35 Qd5-d2
If 35 a4? Qb1+ 36 Kh2 Qa2 threatens both the a4 and f2 pawns and 35 Nd2 Qd1+ both leave Black with a comfortable game.

35 ... Qc2-e4

36 Kg1-h2   Bf8-c5

37 Nb3-c1   Kg8-g7

38 Nc1-d3   Qe4-d4

39 Qd2-e2   Bc5-d6?!
There was no threat of 40 Nxc5 since the queen-and-pawn ending outlined in the note to Black's 34th move offers no winning prospects for White. Perhaps Black was hoping for 40 Qb2? Qxb2 41 Nxb2 Kf6 when his king comes deep into White's position. By his manœuvres of Kh2 and Nb3-c1-d3 Karpov has shown that he intends to keep the queens on, and so a passive defensive move such as 39 ... Qc4 was in order. White is now able to gain a little more initiative.

40 Kh2-h3!   Qd4-d5

41 Nd3-f4   Bd6xf4
If 41 ... Qf5+?? 42 Qg4+ leaves White with a winning knight-v.-bishop ending.

42 g3xf4   *(see Diagram 47.3)*

Although this is not yet a clear win, the transition into a queen-and-pawn ending has increased White's advantage enormously. Black's problem now is to avoid a queen exchange and at the same time prevent a general white K-side advance of f3, g4 and Kg3, f5, etc. The immediate threat is 43 Qe5+.

42 ... Kg7-f8

43 Kh3-g3   b6-b5

44 Qe2-b2   Qd5-d3+

VAGANIAN TO MOVE   47.3

KARPOV

45 Kg3-h4   Qd3-d8+

46 Kh4-g3   Qd8-d3+

47 Kg3-h2   Kf8-g8
Preventing the threat of Qh8+xh6.

48 a2-a3   Qd3-d6

49 Qb2-b4
If 49 Qxb5?? Qxf4+ gives Black an easy draw.

49 ... Qd6-f6

50 f2-f3!
A surprising move, as White's position is apparently weakened. In actual fact, Black can achieve no threats on the white king, and this move is the natural start of a K-side advance.

50 ... Qf6-h4+

51 Kh2-g1   Qh4-h5?
51 ... Qf6 was much better. After the text, Black is instantly paralysed.

52 Qb4-e7!   Kg8-h7
The other possibilities are no better:

(a) 52 ... Qg6 53 Qe8+ and 54 Qxb5 wins a second pawn for White.

(b) 52 ... Kg7? 53 Qe5+—see note (c).

(c) 52 ... Qf5 (or 52 ... Qd5) 53 Qe8+ Kg7 (if 53 ... Kh7 then 54 Qe4 wins) 54 Qe5+! Qxe5 55 fxe5 Kg6 56 f4 Kf5 57 g3 Kg4 58 Kf2 h5 59 Ke3! Kxg3 60 f5 h4 61 e6 fxe6 62 fxe6 h3 63 e7 h2 64 e8=Q h1=Q 65 Qg8+

Kh3 66 Qh8+ Kg2 67 Qxh1+ and
White wins the king-and-pawn ending
comfortably.

53 g2-g4   Qh5-h3
If 53 ... Qd5? 54 Qe4+ Qxe4 55 fxe4
wins easily for White, and 53 ... Qg6

54 Qe4 f5 55 Qd3! also wins quickly;
or if 54 ... Kg7 then 55 Qe5+ and
56 Qxb5 is the simplest way. Now
54 Qxf7+ Kh8 55 Qe8+ Kg7 56 Qe3!
wins for White.

... **Black resigns**

Game 48

WHITE Taimanov   Nimzo-Indian Defence, Rubinstein Variation
USSR II v. USSR Juniors Match Tournament, Moscow 1973

The so-called positional sacrifice is a most difficult idea to understand. This
game provides a beautiful example of such a sacrifice. A pawn is given up
for control of the white squares, and sixteen moves later it is recovered
with interest. Taimanov should have been able to draw, but under time-
pressure, and after a clever exchange-sacrifice, he was unable to cope with
the position and lost on time.

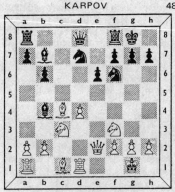

KARPOV   48.1

TAIMANOV TO MOVE

1 d2-d4   Ng8-f6

2 c2-c4   e7-e6

3 Nb1-c3   Bf8-b4

4 e2-e3   c7-c5

5 Bf1-d3   0-0

6 Ng1-f3   d7-d5

7 0-0   d5xc4

Karpov prefers to avoid the older
continuation 7 ... Nc6 8 a3! The
text move allows Black to develop
his queen's knight on d7 and to
fianchetto his queen's bishop.

8 Bd3xc4   c5xd4

9 e3xd4

Both 9 Qxd4 and 9 Nxd4 leave an
equal and somewhat uninteresting
position.

9 ... b7-b6

10 Qd1-e2   Bc8-b7

11 Rf1-d1   Nb8-d7   *(see Diagram 48.1)*

The double pawn exchanges on moves
7 and 8 typify Karpov's approach to
this variation of the Nimzo-Indian.
In his match with Polugaevsky in 1974
he chose the more solid 8 ... Nc6, and

thus drew every game with the black
pieces. It is interesting to notice that
Karpov completed his bishop's fianchetto before developing his queen's
knight. Against Portisch at San
Antonio in 1972 he had tried 9 ...
Nbd7 10 Qe2 b6 but, after 11 d5
Bxc3 12 dxe6 Bb4 13 exd7 Qxd7
14 a3!, White already had the advantage and went on to win.
The key position has now been
reached. White must choose between
several possibilities:

(a) 12 Bg5 Bxc3 13 bxc3 Qc7 14 Nd2
Rfe8 15 Bb5 a6 16 Bxd7 Nxd7 is
equal (Rabar-Karaklaić, Yugoslavian
Championship 1961).

(b) 12 Ne5 Rc8 13 Bg5 Bxc3 14 bxc3
Qc7 leaves Black with no problems
(Najdorf-Pădevski, Moscow Olympiad
1956). If 13 Rd3 then 13 ... Bxc3
14 bxc3 Rxc4! 15 Nxc4 Ba6 16 Nd6
Nb8 17 Ne4 Nxe4 18 Qxe4 Bxd3
19 Qxd3 Nc6 gives equality (Gligorić-
Toran, Torremolinos 1961).

(c) 12 Bd3 Rc8 13 Bd2 Be7 14 Rac1
Nd5 15 Ba6 Nxc3 16 Bxc3 Bxa6
17 Qxa6 and now 17 ... Nf6!
(18 Qxa7 Ra8) gives equality (Kozma-
Holmov, Kislovodsk 1972).

(d) 12 d5 (the best try) 12 ... Bxc3
13 dxe6 Bxf3 14 gxf3 (14 Qxf3 Ne5
15 exf7+ Kh8 16 Rxd8 Nxf3+ 17 gxf3
Raxd8 18 bxc3 with approximately
equal chances: Portisch-Donner,
Hamburg 1965) 14 ... fxe6 15 bxc3
Qc7 16 Bxe6+ Kh8 17 Be3 Nc5
18 Bd5 Nxd5 19 Rxd5 Ne6 with
approximate equality (Gligorić-
Unzicker, Leipzig Olympiad 1960).

Taimanov's move aims at a variation
similar to (c) but with an extra tempo.

12 Bc1-d2   Ra8-c8
In Smyslov-O'Kelly, Havana 1965,
the continuation was 12 ... Bxc3
13 Bxc3 Qc7 14 Ne5 Ne4 15 Bb4
Nxe5 16 dxe5 Rfd8 17 f3 Nc5
with a solid position for Black.

13 Bc4-a6   Bb7xa6

14 Qe2xa6   Bb4xc3

15 b2xc3
In his book on this opening, Taimanov
gives 15 Bxc3 Qc7 16 Rac1 Nd5
17 Bd2 Qb8 with equality. The pawn
recapture looks better, but here again
Black has no trouble in equalizing.

15 ... Rc8-c7!
This move brings equality at once.
The point is that after 16 c4?! Qc8!
is strong.

16 Ra1-c1   Qd8-c8

17 Qa6-a4

After 17 Qxc8 Rfxc8 Black takes
control of the c4 square and thus has
the advantage. After the text move
White threatens to gain control of
c4 by 18 c4; so Black must act quickly
to retain the initiative.

KARPOV TO MOVE   48.2

TAIMANOV

17 ... Rc7-c4!
A brilliant idea, logically exploiting
the white-squared weaknesses in
White's position. Black is prepared to
sacrifice a pawn in order to keep control of c4 and d5.

18 Qa4xa7   Qc8-c6
Threatening both 19 ... Ra8 and
19 ... Ra4.

19 Qa7-a3   Rf8-c8

20 h2-h3   h7-h6

21 Rc1-b1   Rc4-a4

22 Qa3-b3   Nf6-d5

23 Rd1-c1   Ra4-c4

24 Rb1-b2
After 24 Qb5 Qxb5 25 Rxb5 Ra8
Black has at least equality.

24 ... f7-f6!?
Black can, of course, regain the
sacrificed pawn now by 24 ... Nxc3
25 Bxc3 Rxc3 26 Rxc3 Qxc3
27 Qxc3 Rxc3 but the position
would be devoid of winning chances
for either side. Karpov prefers to
keep some tension, to increase his
grip on the position, and to recapture

the c-pawn at a more advantageous
moment.

25 Rc1-e1 Kg8-f7

26 Qb3-d1 Nd7-f8

27 Rb2-b3 Nf8-g6

28 Qd1-b1 Rc8-a8

29 Re1-e4

An interesting possibility here was
29 Qd3!? in order to meet 29 ... Rxa2
by 30 Rxe6!? with a totally obscure
situation. Karpov has at last achieved
the best positions for his K-side pieces,
and now begins to think about regaining the sacrificed pawn. The knight
on g6 will then spring into action on
f4 or h4 against the white king.

29 ...Rc4-a4

30 Rb3-b2 Ng6-f8

31 Qb1-d3 Ra4-c4!

Again 31 ... Rxa2 32 Rxa2 Rxa2
would regain the pawn but after 33 c4
White would have the better chances.

32 Re4-e1 Ra8-a3

32 ... Ng6?! could be met by 33 Rxe6!
when

(a) 33 ... Qxe6 34 Qxc4, with advantage
to White.

(b) 33 ... Kxe6 34 Qxg6, with compensation for the sacrificed exchange.

33 Qd3-b1 Nf8-g6

34 Re1-c1?!

KARPOV TO MOVE   48.3

TAIMANOV

Better was 34 Qd3! threatening
35 Rxe6. The point is that 34 ... Nxc3
would then be met by 35 Rb3! leaving
Black in great difficulties.

34 ...Nd5xc3

Not only does Black regain his pawn,
but also his remaining pieces exert
some pressure on the white king, and
this ensures a small advantage for
Black. In addition, Taimanov was
under some time-pressure.

35 Qb1-d3

After 35 Bxc3 Raxc3 36 Rxc3 Rxc3
Black has a substantial advantage, for
37 Rxb6? Rc1+ 38 Kh2 Qc7+.

35 ...Nc3-e2+

The resulting simplification of the
position leaves Black with a clear
advantage.

36 Qd3xe2 Rc4xc1+

37 Bd2xc1 Qc6xc1+

38 Kg1-h2

The alternative is 38 Ne1 but after
38 ...Nf4 39 Qd2 Rc3 Black stands
much better.

38 ...Ra3xf3!?

39 g2xf3

39 Qxf3? leaves the rook on b2 en
prise.

39 ...Ng6-h4

White lost on time

The position is difficult for White in
any case. For example:

(a) 40 Kg3? Qg5+ and mate next move.

(b) 40 Rxb6? Qc7+ wins the rook.

(c) 40 Rb3 Qg5 41 Qf1 Qf4+ 42 Kh1
Nxf3 winning back the exchange
(43 Qg2? Qc1+ and mate next move
or 43 Kg2 Nd2 44 Qc1 Qe4+ 45 f3
Qe2+)

(d) 40 d5! (the only real chance, but this
is a difficult move to find) 40 ...Qf4+
41 Kh1 exd5 42 Qe3 (if Rxb6? Qc1+
43 Kh2 Qc7+ wins the rook) 42 ...
Qf5 43 f4 Qg6 with a very strong
position (44 Qg3 Qe4+ 45 f3 Nxf3
or 44 f3 Qg3).

Game 49

BLACK Spassky   Closed Ruy López, Breyer Variation
USSR I v. USSR Juniors, Match Tournament, Moscow 1973

Spassky attempts to improve on Gligorić's play from Game 48, but after accepting a nicely judged exchange-sacrifice, succumbs to a devastating K-side attack: his first loss to Karpov.

1 e2-e4   e7-e5

2 Ng1-f3   Nb8-c6

3 Bf1-b5   a7-a6

4 Bb5-a4   Ng8-f6

5 0-0   Bf8-e7

6 Rf1-e1   b7-b5

7 Ba4-b3   d7-d6

8 c2-c3   0-0

9 h2-h3   Nc6-b8

10 d2-d3   Bc8-b7

11 Nb1-d2   Nb8-d7

12 Nd2-f1   Rf8-e8

13 Nf1-g3   Nd7-c5

14 Bb3-c2   Be7-f8

15 b2-b4   Nc5-d7

16 d3-d4   h7-h6

17 Bc1-d2   Nd7-b6

18 Bc2-d3   g7-g6

At last the game varies from the Karpov-Gligorić encounter. Whereas Gligorić tried to prevent the advance c3-c4 Spassky allows it.

19 Qd1-c2

Intending 20 c3-c4.

19 ... Nf6-d7

20 Ra1-d1   Bf8-g7

21 d4xe5   d6xe5?!

Safer was 21 ... Nxe5.

22 c3-c4!   b5xc4

23 Bd3xc4   Qd8-e7?   *(see Diagram 49.1)*

After 23 ... Nxc4 24 Qxc4 White has only a small advantage. After the text move, however, he is able to keep the two bishops.

SPASSKY   49.1

KARPOV TO MOVE

24 Bc4-b3!   c7-c5

25 a2-a4

The threat of 26 a5 gives White an advantage. If 25 ... cxb4 then 26 a5 and now:

(a) 26 ... Rac8   27 Qa2 Na8   28 Bxb4! Qxb4!   29 Bxf7+ Kf8   30 Rxd7 leaves White a pawn up with a winning position.

(b) 26 ... Nc8   27 Bxb4 Qxb4   28 Rxd7 Re7   29 Rd8+ or 29 R1d1 gives White a clear positional plus.

The text involves a long-range exchange sacrifice.

25 ... c5-c4

26 Bb3-a2

If 26 Bxc4? Rac8 costs White a piece.

26 ... Bb7-c6

27 a4-a5   Bc6-a4

28 Qc2-c1

For the sacrificed exchange White

gets the h-pawn, and should get the
c-pawn also. However, before the
real point of the sacrifice is revealed,
Spassky blunders.

28 ... Nb6-c8
The rook cannot escape.

29 Bd2xh6   Ba4xd1

30 Re1xd1   Nc8-d6?
The decisive mistake. Either 30 ...
Kf8 or 30 ... Ra7 31 Bxg7 Kxg7
32 Qxc4 would have been better.

31 Bh6xg7   Kg8xg7

SPASSKY   49.2

KARPOV TO MOVE

32 Qc1-g5!
Winning immediately. The defensive
tries are:

(a) 32 ... Nf6 33 Rxd6! Qxd6 34 Nf5+
wins the queen.

(b) 32 ... Kf8 33 Qh6+ Kg8 34 Ng5
Nf8 35 Nh5! with a winning attack.

(c) 32 ... Qxg5 33 Nxg5 f6 34 Rxd6
winning a piece.

32 ... f7-f6

33 Qg5-g4!
Threatening 34 Rxd6 and 35 Nf5+
winning the queen.

33 ... Kg7-h7

34 Nf3-h4!   Black resigns
There is no satisfactory defence:

(a) if 34 ... Rg8 35 Bxc4! Rg7 (35 ...
Nxc4 loses to 36 Rxd7) 36 Rxd6!
Qxd6 37 Nhf5! mates by 38 Qh4, or
if 37 ... gxf5 by 38 Qh5.

(b) if 34 ... Nf8 35 Nxg6! Nxg6
36 Qh5+ Kg7 37 Rxd6! followed by
38 Nf5+ wins easily.

Game 50

WHITE Tukmakov   Ruy López, Breyer Variation
Leningrad Interzonal 1973

Karpov has shown himself to be a master of both sides in the Breyer
Variation. Tukmakov tries a rare, if not new, line in the opening, and soon
loses control of the black squares in his camp. Karpov's positional attack
wins the exchange, and thereafter he merely has to avoid a series of devious
tactical tricks to secure the win.

1 e2-e4	e7-e5	5 0-0	Bf8-e7
2 Ng1-f3	Nb8-c6	6 Rf1-e1	b7-b5
3 Bf1-b5	a7-a6	7 Ba4-b3	d7-d6
4 Bb5-a4	Ng8-f6	8 c2-c3	0-0

9 h2-h3   Nc6-b8

10 d2-d4   Nb8-d7

11 c3-c4

An unusual, but by no means bad, choice. The common move is 11 Nbd2, as played by Tal against Karpov later in the same tournament (see Game 52)

11 ... c7-c6

The alternative is 11 ... b4 (11 ... Bb7 is met by 12 Nc3!) 12 c5 Bb7 13 Qc2 exd4 14 c6 d3 15 Qc4 Nb6 16 cxb7 Nxc4 17 bxa8=Q Qxa8 18 Bxc4 Nxe4 19 Bxd3 d5 20 a3 Nc5 (20 ... a5 21 Be3 Nc5 22 Bf1 b3 23 Nbd2 with advantage to White: Geller-Filip, Amsterdam Candidates' 1956) 21 Rxe7! (21 Bf1? Nb3! gives Black the edge: Kotov-Korchnoi USSR 1958) 21 ... Nb3 22 Rxc7 Nxa1 23 axb4 Qb8 24 Bf4 Qxb4 25 Be5 with advantage to White according to Suetin.

12 Bc1-g5

This move is very rare in tournament play, and after Karpov's handling of the variation in this game will probably disappear from master chess. With this and his previous move White has weakened himself on the black squares. The following exchange of black-squared bishops is greatly to Black's advantage, since his whole position is freed, and he immediately exerts strong pressure on the White centre.
The other possibilities here are:

(a) 12 c5 Qc7 13 cxd6 Bxd6 14 Bg5 exd4 15 Bxf6 gxf6 16 Nxd4 (or 16 Qxd4) with an unclear position.

(b) 12 a3 bxc4 13 Bxc4 Nxe4 14 Rxe4 d5 15 Re1 dxc4 16 Qe2 Re8 with equality (Matanović-Barcza, Yugoslavia v. Hungary match 1963).

(c) 12 cxb5 axb5 13 Nc3 Ba6! 14 Bg5 h6 15 dxe5 Nxe5! with equality (Geller-Unzicker, Kislovodsk 1972).

(d) 12 Nc3 b4 13 Nb1 c5 14 dxe5 dxe5 15 Nbd2 Bb7 16 Ba4 Qc7 17 Bxd7 Nxd7 18 Nf1 Rfe8 19 b3 Nf8 with equal chances (Geller-Darga, Havana 1963).

(e) 12 Qc2 a5 13 a4 bxc4 14 Bxc4 d5 15 Bd3 dxe4 16 Bxe4 Nxe4 17 Qxe4 Nf6 (and not 17 ... Bb4? 18 Bd2 Bxd2 19 Nbxd2 exd4 20 Qxd4 with advantage to White: Geller-Portisch, Portoroz 1973) 18 Qxe5 Bd6 with compensation for the sacrificed pawn.

12 ... h7-h6!

The most aggressive option open to Black, and the most logical, since it aims for control of the black squares c5, d4, and e5, as we shall see.
12 ... Bb7 was played in Gheorghiu-Portisch, Hamburg 1965, and after 13 Nbd2 c5 14 dxe5 Nxe5 15 Nxe5 dxe5 16 Qe2 b4 17 Rad1 Qc7 18 Bc2 Rfd8 19 Nf1 Rxd1 20 Rxd1 Rd8 21 Bxf6 Bxf6 22 Ne3 Rd4 the game was equal.
According to Keres the simplest way for Black to equalize is by 12 ... bxc4 13 Bxc4 Nxe4 14 Bxe7 Qxe7 15 Rxe4 d5.

13 Bg5-h4?!

Better was 13 dxe5 as in the analagous variation (c) given above.

KARPOV TO MOVE   50.1

TUKMAKOV

13 ... Nf6-h5!

The forced exchange of black-squared bishops highlights the weaknesses in White's position. Black takes control of the black central squares c5 and e5 and, later, d4.

14 Bh4xe7   Qd8xe7

15 c4xb5

Whilst 15 Nxe5 dxe5 16 Qxh5 exd4
offers White no advantage, either
15 Nc3 b4 16 Ne2 or 15 g3 is
playable.

15 ... a6xb5

16 Nb1-c3?!

Two more-logical developments were
available here. Either 16 Nbd2 or the
more enterprising 16 Qc1, Bb7 17 Qc3
Nf4 18 Nbd2 was safer.

16 ... b5-b4

17 Nc3-b1

The alternative was 17 Ne2, but after
17 ... Ba6 Black has a small advantage
and the freer position.

17 ... Nh5-f4

18 Nb1-d2   e5xd4!

19 Nf3xd4   Nd7-e5

Black has established a grip on the
central black squares and already has
an advantage. The immediate threat
is 20 ... Bxh3 21 gxh3 Qg5+ followed
by mate on g2.

20 Nd2-f3   Qe7-f6

So as to renew the threat of 21 ...
Bxh3, this time to be followed by
22 ... Qg6+.

21 Nf3xe5   d6xe5!

22 Nd4-f5!

The other two possibilities are:

(a) 22 Nf3? Rd8 23 Qc2 Nxh3+ winning
at least a pawn.

(b) 22 Ne2 Rd8 23 Qc2 when

(b1) 23 ... Nxh3+ 24 gxh3 Qf3
25 Bxf7+! gives Black an endgame
advantage after 25 ... Kxf7 26 Qb3+
Qxb3 27 axb3 Bxh3 although White
could try 26 Qc4+ with an unclear
situation.

(b2) 23 ... Qg5 24 Nxf4 exf4 25 Kh2
f3! yields clear advantage for Black.

22 ... Bc8xf5

23 e4xf5   Ra8-d8! *(see Diagram 50.2)*

To capture the f5 pawn immediately
by 23 ... Qxf5 would allow 24 Qd6

KARPOV   50.2

TUKMAKOV TO MOVE

Qg6! 25 Qxg6 Nxg6 26 Rac1 when
White regains the pawn in the ending.
After the text move Black increases
the pressure relentlessly.

24 Qd1-f3

After 24 Qc2 Rd2!! 25 Qxd2 Qg5
the double threat of 26 ... Qxg2
mate and 26 ... Nxh3+ is decisive.

24 ... Rd8-d2

25 Re1-e3!

The only chance to survive. After
25 Rab1 R8d8 White has a hopelessly
passive position, while if 25 Rac1
Qxf5 26 Rxc6 Nxh3+! 27 Qxh3
Qxf2+ wins the exchange.

25 ... Rd2xb2

The alternative way to increase the
pressure was 25 ... Qxf5 26 R1e1
Qg6! when 27 Rxe5 loses the exchange
to 27 ... Nd3.

26 Ra1-e1   Rf8-e8

27 Re3-e4

Threatening 28 Rxf4.

27 ... Nf4-d5

28 Qf3-g3!

This exchange sacrifice is the only
way to prolong the game.

28 ... Nd5-c3

29 Re4xb4

29 Rxe5 is met by 29 ... Ne2+! and
29 Rg4 by 29 ... Kh8! (not 29 ...
Ne2+ 30 Rxe2 Rxe2 31 Rg6 when

White has counterplay).

29 ... Nc3-e2+

30 Re1xe2   Rb2xe2

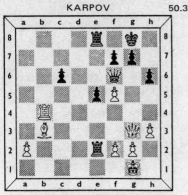

KARPOV   50.3

TUKMAKOV TO MOVE

31 Rb4-b7?

The losing move. The only chance left was 31 Qg6! when:

(a) 31 ... Kf8 32 Qh7.

(b) 31 ... Rf8 32 Rb7.

(c) 31 ... Qe7? 32 Rg4 Qf8 33 f6 and White is winning.

(d) 31 ... e4! and now either

(d1) 32 Rb7 Qa1+ 33 Kh2 Qe5+ 34 g3 Rxf2+ 35 Kg1 e3 wins for Black, or

(d2) 32 Qxf6 gxf6 33 Kf1 Rd2 34 Rb7 Rf8 35 Rc7 with an unclear position.

31 ... Re8-e7

32 Rb7-b8+   Kg8-h7

33 Kg1-f1!

A well-disguised final trap. Both 33 ... Re4 and 33 ... Rb2 are met by the surprising 34 Qg6+!! In the first case, 34 ... Qxg6 (34 ... fxg6 35 Bg8+ draws by perpetual check) 35 fxg6+ Kxg6 36 Bc2 wins back the exchange; in the second, 34 ... Qxg6 35 fxg6+ Kxg6 36 Bxf7+ followed by 37 Rxb2 leaves a level rook-and-pawn ending.

33 ... Re2-d2!

White resigns

Game 51

BLACK Kuzmin   French Defence, Tarrasch Variation
Leningrad Interzonal 1973

This is another of Karpov's favourite openings. Here he tries out his patent manœuvre Bc1-g5-h4-g3 against Kuzmin, and the result is a pretty and unusual win. The ease with which Kuzmin is confined and then strangled leaves an impression of almost frightening power in Karpov's game.

1 e2-e4   e7-e6

2 d2-d4   d7-d5

3 Nb1-d2 c7-c5

4 e4xd5   e6xd5

5 Ng1-f3 Nb8-c6

6 Bf1-b5 Bf8-d6

7 d4xc5   Bd6xc5

8 0-0   Ng8-e7

9 Nd2-b3 Bc5-d6

Both Krogius (Game 12) and Vaganian (Game 47) preferred to retreat the bishop to b6. The text move is more aggressive and it is only by Karpov's manœuvre that the black-squared bishops can now be exchanged.

10 Bc1-g5 0-0

11 Bg5-h4!

The old tries were:

(a) 11 Qd2 Qc7 12 h3 h6 13 Be3 Bf5
with equality (Pogacs—Portisch,
Hungarian Championship 1958).

(b) 11 Re1 and now

(b1) 11 ...h6 12 Be3 Bg4 13 h3
Bh5 14 Be2 Re8 15 Nbd4 a6
16 Qd2 with a slight edge for White
(Larsen-Andersson, Siegen Olympiad
1970).

(b2) 11 ...Qc7 12 h3 h6 13 Bd2
Bf5 14 Nbd4 Be4 15 Bc3 Rad8
16 Bd3 with advantage to White
(Toran-Kramer, Beverwijk 1957).

(b3) 11 ...Bg4 12 Be2 (12 h3!? Bh5
13 Bxc6 bxc6 14 Nbd4 gives White
the advantage according to Keres)
12 ...Qc7 13 h3 Be6 with equality.

11 ...Qd8-c7?!
A waste of time. Balashov-Uhlmann
from the Moscow 1971 tournament
went 11 ...Bg4 12 Re1 Re8 13 Bg3
Bxg3 14 hxg3 Qb6 15 Bd3 with a
small advantage to White. Balashov's
suggestion of 11 ...f6!? also merits
consideration.

12 Bh4-g3 Bd6xg3

13 h2xg3

KUZMIN TO MOVE   51.1

KARPOV

White already has the advantage. He
has a firm grip on the d4 blockade
square and has achieved the exchange
of black-squared bishops—an important step in the exploitation of the

isolated pawn, for it removes Black's
most dangerous attacking piece.

13 ...Bc8-g4

14 Rf1-e1 Ra8-d8

15 c2-c3 Qc7-b6

16 Bb5-d3 Ne7-g6

17 Qd1-c2 Bg4xf3

18 g2xf3 Rd8-d6
Safer were 18 ...Rfe8 or 18 ...d4
when 19 c4 Nb4 20 Qd2 Nxd3
21 Qxd3 White has some chances
against the isolated d-pawn.

19 f3-f4 Rf8-d8

20 a2-a3!
So as to be able to meet 20 ...d4 by
21 c4 without allowing 21 ...Nb4.

20 ...h7-h5?
Kuzmin overestimates his chances and
should instead have transferred his
wayward king's knight from g6 by
Nf8-e6-c5.

21 Kg1-g2 h5-h4

22 Re1-e2 Ng6-f8

23 Nb3-d2!
The knight will exert a great deal of
pressure from its new post on f3.

23 ...Rd6-h6

24 Nd2-f3 h4xg3

25 f2xg3 Nf8-d7

26 Ra1-e1 Kg8-f8

KUZMIN   51.2

KARPOV TO MOVE

How is White to increase his advantage? Karpov solves the problem in an unusual and enterprising fashion and soon forces the win of a pawn.

27 g3-g4!

Not only gaining space on the K-side but also illustrating the lack of cohesion in the black camp. Black's pieces are so poorly co-ordinated that he is unable to prevent the rout of his whole position.

27 ... Qb6-c7

28 g4-g5   Rh6-h8

29 Kg2-g3!

The real point to White's 27th move. The spatial advantage renews pressure on the d-pawn. Black also has to cope with infiltration along the h-file or e-file.

29 ... Nd7-c5

30 Bd3-f5   g7-g6

31 b2-b4!   Nc5-e4+

After 31 ... Nd7 32 Bxg6 fxg6

33 Qxg6 Black is helpless, whilst 31 ... gxf5 32 bxc5 Qd7 33 Nd4 is also very good for White.

32 Bf5xe4   d5xe4

33 Qc2xe4

The rest is easy and quick, since White has maintained his positional advantage.

33 ... Kf8-g7

34 b4-b5!   Nc6-a5

35 Qe4-e7

Winning a second pawn, since 35 ... Qxc3 loses to 36 Re3! Qb2 37 Re5 (but not the immediate 36 Re5? when 36 ... Rh3+! draws at least).

35 ... Qc7xe7

36 Re2xe7   Rd8-d3

37 Re7-c7   Na5-b3

38 Kg3-g4   Rh8-f8

39 Re1-e7   Black resigns

Either 40 Rxf7+! or 40 Ne5 would be sufficient.

Game 52

WHITE Tal   Ruy López, Breyer Variation
Leningrad Interzonal 1973

After an uncharacteristic opening inaccuracy, Karpov finds himself under considerable positional pressure. A clever exchange-sacrifice relieves the situation and, even though Tal breaks through on the Q-side with a piece-sacrifice, he is unable to convert his advantage into a win. Karpov remains cool throughout and his precise defence justifiably earns him a draw.

1 e2-e4   e7-e5

2 Ng1-f3   Nb8-c6

3 Bf1-b5   a7-a6

4 Bb5-a4   Ng8-f6

5 0-0   Bf8-e7

6 Rf1-e1   b7-b5

7 Ba4-b3   d7-d6

8 c2-c3   0-0

9 h2-h3   Nc6-b8

10 d2-d4   Nb8-d7

11 Nb1-d2   Bc8-b7

12 Bb3-c2   Rf8-e8

The alternative is 12 ... c5 as played by Gligorić in Game 56.

13 b2-b4

Two other moves are regularly played here (although the text move is the most promising continuation for White):

(a) 13 b3 Bf8 14 Bb2 g6 15 a4 Bg7
16 Bd3 c6 17 Qc2 Rc8 18 Bf1 is
equal according to Portisch.

(b) 13 Nf1: see Game 16.

13 ...Be7-f8
Either 13 ...d5?! 14 Nxe5 Nxe5
15 dxe5 Nxe4 16 Nxe4 dxe4 17 Qg4
(Kavalek-Robatsch, Sarajevo 1968)
or 13 ...exd4 14 cxd4 a5 15 bxa5
c5 16 Bb2 Qxa5 17 a4 (Ciric-
Robatsch, Beverwijk 1967) gives White
a clear advantage, but 13 ...a5 is an
interesting try.

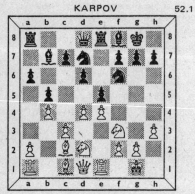

KARPOV   52.1

TAL TO MOVE

14 Bc1-b2
A more promising idea is 14 a4, when
Black can try:

(a) 14 ...Nb6 15 a5 Nbd7 16 Bb2 Qb8
17 c4 bxc4 18 Ba4 c6?! (better is
18 ...Rd8) 19 Nxc4 exd4 20 Qxd4
d5 21 exd5 Rxe1+ 22 Nxe1 followed
by 23 Nd3. White has a clear advantage (Kavalek-Reshevsky, USA 1973).

(b) 14 ...a5 15 bxa5 Rxa5 16 Rb1 Ba6
and now:

(b1) 17 d5 Qa8 18 Ba3 c5 19 dxc6
Qxc6 20 Bb4 Rxa4 with a small edge
for White (Beliavsky-A. Petrosian,
USSR 1973).

(b2) 17 axb5 Rxb5 18 Ra1 Rb6
19 Bb3 h6 20 Ba3 c5 21 dxc5 Nxc5
22 Bxc5 dxc5 23 Bc4 Bb7 and again
White stands a little better (Matanovic-

Smejkal, Ljubljana-Portoroz 1973).

(c) 14 ...d5!? 15 dxe5 Nxe4 16 Nxe4
dxe4 17 Bg5 f6 18 Bxe4 Bxe4
19 Rxe4 Nxe5 20 Rd4 Nxf3+
21 Qxf3 Qc8 22 Be3 c5 23 Qd5+
Kh8 24 Rh4 cxb4 with equality
(Vasjukov-Zuidema, Wijk aan Zee
1973). Possibly a better move was
17 e6!?

14 ...a6-a5?!
Safer is 14 ...Nb6 15 a3 h6 16 c4
Nxc4 17 Nxc4 bxc4 18 dxe5 dxe5
19 Nxe5 c5 20 Nxc4 cxb4! with
equality (Parma-Unzicker, Berlin
1971). Also playable is 14 ...g6
15 c4 exd4 16 cxb5 axb5 17 Nxd4
d5 18 exd5 Rxe1+ 19 Qxe1 Bxd5
20 a3 c6 21 Ne4 with a small advantage for White (Dueball-O'Kelly,
West Germany 1970).
The text move is dubious on two
counts. Firstly, it gives White good
chances to capture the a5 square in
an advantageous manner, and secondly,
after White's reply the black queen's
bishop is forcibly hemmed in.

15 Bc2-d3!
A far superior continuation than
occurred in Gufeld-Dely, Keskemet
1968, where White played 15 a3 and
after 15 ...Qb8 16 dxe5 dxe5 17 Nb3
axb4 18 cxb4 c5 19 bxc5 Nxc5
20 Nxc5 Bxc5 the game was equal.
Now Black must shut in his own
queen's bishop in order to protect his
b5 pawn.

15 ...c7-c6

16 a2-a3
Preparing either the advance c3-c4,
or the manoeuvre Nd2-b3-a5 embarrassing the black queen's bishop.

16 ...Nd7-b6

17 Ra1-c1
Both aimed at c3-c4 and providing an
escape square for the bishop on b2 in
case of 17 ...Na4.

17 ...e5xd4

18 Nf3xd4
18 cxd4 would be weak on account
of 18 ...axb4 19 axb4 d5! 20 e5

Nfd7! when Black's control of c4
and attack on the White b4 pawn
give him at least equality.

18 ...Nf6-d7!
Karpov is preparing an original exchange sacrifice to relieve his somewhat cramped position. In return for
the material he will obtain a pawn
and a solid position.

19 Nd2-b3   Nd7-e5
The alternative way to sacrifice here
was 19 ...Nc4! 20 Bxc4 bxc4
21 Nxa5 Rxa5 22 bxa5 Ne5 with
counterplay.

20 Nb3xa5   Ra8xa5

21 b4xa5   Nb6-c4

22 Rc1-c2   Qd8xa5

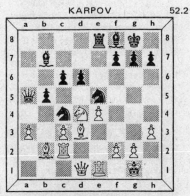

KARPOV   52.2

TAL TO MOVE

For the sacrificed exchange Karpov has
a grip on the central e5, c4, and d3
squares, and immediately wins a pawn.
Tal must decide which bishop to keep
and chooses to keep the white-squared
one. The alternative to the text move
is 23 Bc1 when 23 ...Nxd3 24 Qxd3
d5 25 Rce2 c5 26 Nb3 still leaves
White with a slight advantage.

23 Bd3-f1   Nc4xb2

24 Rc2xb2   Qa5xc3

25 Rb2-b3   Qc3-a5

26 Qd1-b1
Threatening 27 Nxb5! cxb5 28 Rxb5

followed by 29 Rxb7. Tal must try to
take advantage of Black's Q-side
pawns; so he engineers a sacrifice.

26 ...Qa5-a7
Threatening the exposed knight and
hence preventing the white pawn
advance 27 a4! which would be strong
after 26 ...Qa8 e.g. 27 ...Qxa4
28 Nxb5! etc.

27 Re1-d1   Ne5-d7

28 Nd4-f5   Re8-e6

29 Nf5-d4   Re6-e8

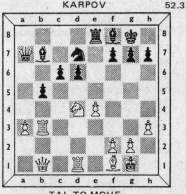

KARPOV   52.3

TAL TO MOVE

30 Bf1xb5!
An excellent sacrifice, which represents Tal's only winning chance.
The a4 coup has been prevented by
Karpov's 27th move: 30 a4 Nc5!
31 Rb4 (31 axb5!? Nxb3 32 Qxb3
gives an unclear position with chances
for White) 31 ...Nxa4, and Black has
equalized.

30 ...c6xb5
If 30 ...Nc5 then 31 Nxc6 ensures
White an extra pawn at least.

31 Nd4xb5   Qa7-c5

32 Nb5xd6!   Bf8xd6

33 Rb3xb7   Nd7-f6

34 Qb1-b3   Bd6-c7?!
With 34 ...Re6! Black could have
immediately equalized. After 35 Rb6
(threatening 36 R6xd6 followed by

37 Qb8+) Black could reply 35 ...
Kf8! with excellent counterchances
in the complications. The text move
allows the exchange of queens.

35 Qb3-b5!   Qc5-c2

36 Qb5-b1!

Now 36 ...Qc5 37 Rc1 wins a piece
for White. Although this queen
exchange loses a pawn for White, it
is in the long run a beneficial manœuvre. In the ensuing ending White's
outside passed pawn is strong and
offers winning chances.

36 ...Qc2xb1

37 Rd1xb1   Bc7-d6

Both the a3 and e4 pawns are now
attacked.

38 a3-a4   Re8xe4

39 Rb1-d1

Stronger was 39 a5! Then 39 ...Ra4
could be met by 40 Rb8+! Bf8
41 Rd1 h6!. 42 R1d8 Nh7 43 Ra8
with a winning position for White.
The text move was played in some
time-trouble.

39 ...Nf6-e8

40 a4-a5   Kg8-f8

41 a5-a6

KARPOV TO MOVE   52.4

TAL

This was the sealed move. The alternative 41 Ra7 would probably have trans-
posed back into the game continuation
after 41 ...Ra4 42 a6. Black needs

exact defence and even then there are
some chances of a win for White.

41 ...Re4-a4

42 Rb7-a7!

42 a7, although apparently a crushing
move, can be met by the ingenious
42 ...Bc5 43 R1d7 f6! after which
White is completely movebound.

42 ...g7-g5!

The obvious 42 ...Be5 loses to
43 g3 Nd6 44 Re1! f6 45 Rb1.

43 Ra7-a8   Bd6-e5

44 g2-g3?

After this the ending is drawn. Karpov
was expecting 44 f4! when 44 ...
Rxf4 (44 ...Bxf4 or 44 ...gxf4 lose
to 45 R1d8) 45 R1d8 (But not 45 a7
when 45 ...Ra4 46 R1d8 Kg7
47 Rxe8 Rxa7! 48 Rxa7 Bd4+ gives
Black an easy draw) Bd4+ 46 Kh2
Re4 47 a7 Bxa7 48 Rxa7 leads to an
ending in which White still has winning
chances. For example, the classic ending in this situation was Vidmar-
Alekhine, San Remo 1930 (White:
Kg3, Ne6, pawns f3, g2, h2;
Black: Kg8, Ra2 pawns g7, h7.)
Neither Alekhine in his book nor
Fine in *Basic chess endings* give a draw,
and so the position must be considered
lost for White. It is true that the Tal-
Karpov ending has extra rooks but
this can work for either side—Tal has
more attacking chances, and Karpov
has better chances of achieving a
blockaded position. In general, a
knight loses against a rook with level
pawns on one side of the board only,
while a bishop has good chances of a
draw. With a pawn more for the
defending side, as is the case here,
the bishop would draw easily whereas the knight might not.

44 ...Kf8-e7

45 Rd1-e1   f7-f6

46 a6-a7   Ne8-c7

47 Ra8-h8   Ra4xa7   Draw agreed

48 f4 can be answered by 48 ...gxf4
49 gxf4 Ra1! 50 Rxh7+ Kd8 with an
easy draw for Black.

Game 53

BLACK Quinteros   Sicilian Defence, Najdorf Variation
Leningrad Interzonal, 1973

In this game Karpov chooses the sharpest continuation against the Najdorf, namely 6 Bg5. He switched from 6 Be2 after his game with Stoica (Student Olympiad, Graz 1972) since it appears that Black can equalize in the main line (for detailed discussion see Game 30), yet two rounds later at Leningrad he was content to play 6 Be2 against Robert Byrne and agree to a quick draw. He also tried 6 f4 against Kuzmin (Game 57) before eventually returning to a modified variation of 6 Be2 in his match with Polugaevsky (see Games 63 and 64).

This battle is a gem, and was awarded one of the three best-game prizes. Karpov breaks open the way to the black king with a fine exchange-sacrifice and shows us the full range of his attacking talents.

1 e2-e4   c7-c5

2 Ng1-f3   d7-d6

3 d2-d4   c5xd4

4 Nf3xd4   Ng8-f6

5 Nb1-c3   a7-a6

6 Bc1-g5   e7-e6

7 f2-f4   Qd8-b6

This 'Poisoned Pawn Variation' was very popular in the late sixties and early seventies but has gone out of fashion since the 11th game of the Spassky-Fischer match.

8 Nd4-b3

A typical Karpov reply. The pawn sacrifice 8 Qd2 Qxb2 9 Nb3 Qa3 10 Bxf6 gxf6 11 Be2! was played in the Spassky-Fischer game and after 11 ...h5 12 0-0 Nc6 13 Kh1 Bd7? 14 Nb1! Black's queen was already in trouble and was trapped on move 24. The text move leads to a much simpler life and is by no means inferior to the aggressive 8 Qd2.

8 ...Bf8-e7

The exchange of queens 8 ...Qe3+ 9 Qe2 Qxe2+ 10 Bxe2 does nothing to ease Black's position, but either 8 ...h6 or 8 ...Nbd7 is playable.

9 Qd1-f3   h7-h6?!

A dubious move that merely helps the White bishop to h4 and g3 from where it can support the advance e4-e5. (One move earlier 8 ...h6 9 Bh4 would have been met by 9 ...Qe3+ and 10 ...Qxf4 winning a pawn.) Better here was 9 ...Nbd7 as played by Quinteros against Szabo (Amsterdam 1973) less than a month later.

10 Bg5-h4   Nb8-d7

The exchanges 10 ...Nxe4 11 Bxe7 Nxc3 12 Qxc3 Kxe7 13 Qxg7 are very much in White's favour.

11 0-0-0   Qb6-c7

QUINTEROS   53.1

KARPOV TO MOVE

12 Bh4-g3!

Both 12 Bd3 and 12 g4 are met by
12 ...g5! but 12 Be2 (to meet 12 ...
g5 by 13 fxg5 Ne5 14 Qe3 Nfg4
15 Bxg4 Nxg4 16 Qf4) is a good
alternative. The text move is the
strongest, however, and already
threatens the advance 13 e4-e5.

12 ...b7-b5

13 e4-e5   Bc8-b7

14 Qf3-e2   d6xe5?

Better was 14 ...Nd5! with the
following possibilities:

(a) 15 exd6 Nxc3! 16 dxc7 Nxe2+
17 Bxe2 Rc8 18 f5 e5! when White
has only a small advantage.

(b) 15 Nxd5 Bxd5 16 exd6 (16 f5 Nxe5
17 fxe6 Bxe6 18 Nd4 0-0 19 Bxe5
dxe5 20 Nxe6 fxe6 21 Qe4 with an
unclear position, but better for Black
is 18 ...Bg4!) 16 ...Qxd6 17 f5 e5!
and now:

(b1) 18 Qd3 Nf6 19 Qc3 Ne4
20 Qxe5 Qxe5 21 Bxe5 Nf2 22 Rxd5
Nxh1 23 Bxg7 is unclear.

(b2) 18 h4! 0-0 19 Rh3! Rac8
20 Bh2 Qc6 21 Na5 when 21 ...
Qa8 22 Rhd3 and 21 ...Qc5 22 Rc3
are both very strong for White.

(c) 15 Ne4 dxe5 16 fxe5 Nxe5 17 N4c5
Bxc5 18 Bxe5 Bd6 19 Bxg7 Rg8
20 Bxh6 Bxh2 with approximate
equality.

15 f4xe5   Nf6-h7

Naturally 15 ...Nd5? loses to
16 Nxd5 Bxd5 17 Rxd5! exd5 18 e6.

16 Nc3-e4!   Be7-g5+?!

After this move Black is always in
difficulty, but it is hard to find a
worthwhile alternative. The three
obvious tries are:

(a) 16 ...0-0 17 Nf6+! with a winning
attack.

(b) 16 ...Nxe5 17 N4c5 Bxc5 18 Bxe5
with a large plus for White.

(c) 16 ...Ng5 17 Nf6+! gxf6 18 exf6
Qc4! 19 Qd2! when White has a clear
advantage.

17 Kc1-b1   0-0

18 h2-h4   Bg5-e7

19 Ne4-d6

Of course 19 Nf6+? is no longer
possible, for the bishop on g3 is loose
after 19 ...Ndxf6 20 exf6 Qxg3
21 fxe7 Rfe8 22 Rd7 Bc6, and Black
wins a pawn.

19 ...Bb7-d5

Both 19 ...Bc6 and 19 ...Rad8 are
better. The text move allows a powerful exchange-sacrifice.

QUINTEROS   53.2

KARPOV TO MOVE

20 Rd1xd5!   e6xd5

21 Nd6-f5

Both 22 Nxe7+ and 22 e6 are threatened. So Black's hand is forced.

21 ...Qc7-d8

22 Qe2-g4   g7-g6

23 Nf5xh6+   Kg8-g7

24 Nh6-f5+?!

According to the masters present at
Leningrad, 24 Nd4! was a winning
move here. After 24 ...Kxh6 25 Nf5+!
gxf5 26 Bf4+ Ng5 27 Qxf5 Kg7
28 hxg5 Rh8 29 Rh6! White has a
winning attack in view of the threats
of 30 e6, g6, or Bd3.

24 ...Kg7-h8

25 Bf1-d3!   Rf8-g8

After 25 ... gxf5? 26 Qxf5 Ndf6
27 exf6 Nxf6 28 Be5 Black is powerless to prevent a speedy mate.

26 Nf5-h6   Rg8-g7

27 h4-h5   Qd8-e8

28 e5-e6!   Nd7-f6
28 ... fxe6 29 hxg6 is fatal for Black.

29 e6xf7   Qe8-d8
The alternative of 29 ... Qf8 (29 ...
Nxg4? loses a piece to 30 fxe8=Q+
and 31 Nxg4) allows 30 hxg6!! Nxg4
31 Nxg4 Bd6 (to prevent 32 Be5 and
33 Rxh7 mate) 32 Nf6! Bxg3
33 Nxh7 Qd6 34 Nf6+ Bh2 35 Ne8!
Rxg6 36 Bxg6! winning for White.

30 Qg4-d4   Nf6xh5

31 Bg3-e5   Be7-f6

32 Rh1-e1
An alternative win was 32 Ng4! Rxf7
33 Bxg6 etc.

32 ...Bf6xe5

33 Re1xe5   Nh5-f6

34 g2-g4!   Qd8-f8

35 g4-g5   Nf6-e4

36 Bd3xe4   d5xe4

37 Qd4xe4   Black resigns
The f7 pawn is uncapturable, since
the a8 rook is loose. An excellent
example of Karpov's attacking play—
this was his best game at Leningrad.

Game 54

BLACK Gligorić   Ruy López, Breyer Variation
Leningrad Interzonal, 1973

Gligorić loses control of the a-file in the opening, and his two bishops prove
to be insufficient compensation. After a tough struggle he loses a pawn and
cannot conjure up enough counterplay to justify the loss. The ending is
always in White's favour because, as was pointed out in Chapter 2, a knight
is often better than a bishop when the play is on one side of the board only.

1 e2-e4   e7-e5

2 Ng1-f3   Nb8-c6

3 Bf1-b5   a7-a6

4 Bb5-a4   Ng8-f6

5 0-0   Bf8-e7

6 Rf1-e1   b7-b5

7 Ba4-b3   d7-d6

8 c2-c3   0-0

9 h2-h3   Nc6-b8

10 d2-d4   Nb8-d7

11 Nb1-d2   Bc8-b7

12 Bb3-c2   c7-c5
Gligorić has often played this move
recently. More popular however is
12 ... Re8, as played by Karpov
against Tal in Game 52.

13 d4-d5
Karpov prefers to play the López in
this manner, and in most of his games
he plays this advance at an early stage.
Whilst 13 b3 and 13 a4 are playable
the only good alternative is 13 Nf1
Re8 14 Ng3 (14 d5 g6 15 Be3 Bf8
16 N1h2 Bg7 17 Ng4 Nxg4 18 hxg4
Nf6 Agreed drawn: Spassky-Gligorić,
Bath 1973) 14 ...Bf8 (14 ...g6
15 Bh6 Bf8 16 Qd2 Qe7 17 a4 with
a small advantage to White: Keres-
Gligorić, San Antonio 1972) 15 d5
(15 b3 g6 16 Bb2 Bg7 17 Qd2 Qc7 is
equal: Westerinen-Spassky, Tallinn
1973; but 15 dxe5 dxe5 16 Nf5
merits consideration) 15 ...g6 16 b3
(16 Bg5 Bg7 17 Qd2 Nb6 18 Bd3 c4
19 Bc2 Nbd7 20 Nh2 Qe7 21 Ng4
Qf8 22 Nh6+ with a slight edge for

White: Geller-Ivkov, USSR v. Yugo-slavia 1973) 16 ... Nb6 17 Be3 Bc8 18 a4 bxa4 19 bxa4 Nc4 20 Bg5 Bg7 21 Qe2 Na5 22 Qd2 Rb8 23 Rab1 Rxb1 24 Rxb1 Bd7?! 25 c4! with advantage to White (Tal-Gligorić, Leningrad Interzonal 1973). Better according to Gligorić was 24 ... Re7 intending 25 ... Rb7,

13 ... Nf6-e8!

Intending 14 ... g6 and 15 ... Ng7, thus removing all K-side attacking chances for White. Gligorić tried 13 ... Nb6 against Ciocaltea at Ljubljana-Portoroz in 1972, with the continuation 14 Nf1 Re8 15 Ng3 g6 16 b3 Bf8 17 Bg5 h6 18 Be3 Bg7 19 Qc1 h5?! (better was 19 ... Kh7 with an equal game) 20 Bg5 with a slight advantage for White.

14 Nd2-f1   g7-g6

15 Bc1-h6   Ne8-g7

16 Nf1-e3

It is now clear that Black cannot hope to play the freeing advance f7-f5 at any time and that White has virtually exhausted his K-side attack. Thus the action is switched to the weakened black Q-side pawns.
Against Hartston at Bath in 1973 Gligorić played 13 ... g6, 14 ... Nh5, and now 15 ... Re8, whence 16 b3 Bf6 17 a4 Bg7 18 Bg5 Qc7 gave equality.

16 ... Nd7-f6!

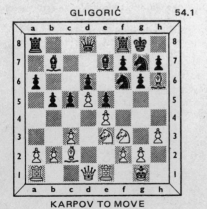

GLIGORIĆ   54.1

KARPOV TO MOVE

This is the last step in refuting any idea of a White K-side attack. The idea is to remove the White queen's bishop by Kh8 and Ng8.

17 a2-a4!

A logical place to strike: White's chances are on the Q-side now.

17 ... Kg8-h8

18 b2-b3

The immediate 18 Qe2 would be met by 18 ... c4! with probable equality. White can meet 18 ... Ng8?! by 19 Bxg7+ Kxg7 20 Qe2 when the b5 pawn is difficult to hold: e.g. 20 ... Qb6 21 axb5 axb5 22 Bd3 etc.

18 ... Ra8-b8

19 Qd1-e2   Bb7-c8

The natural 19 ... Qb6 seems better, but Gligorić was obviously happy with the text move, for he played it against Gheorghiu at Bath a few weeks later.

20 a4xb5   a6xb5

21 Ra1-a7   Nf6-g8

The logical outcome of Black's K-side manœuverings. Black gains the two bishops in return for the a-file.

22 Bh6xg7+   Kh8xg7

23 Re1-a1   Ng8-f6

24 Bc2-d3   Bc8-d7

25 Qe2-a2

Hoping to exchange queens by the sortie 26 Qa5.

25 ... Nf6-e8?!

This leaves Black weak on his second rank. Better was 25 ... Qb6! as played by Gligorić against Gheorghiu in the aforementioned game. After 26 Ng4 Rfd8 27 Nxf6 Bxf6 a draw was agreed!

26 Qa2-a6

After the immediate 26 Qa5 Qc8 27 Qa6 Bd8! Black has consolidated his position.

26 ... Rb8-b6?!

The alternative 26 ... Nc7 would be no better, since after 27 Qa5 Ra8! (27 ... Rc8? 28 Qb6 followed by 29 Rb7 étc. is strong) 28 Rxa8 Qxa8 29 Qxc7! Qxa1+ 30 Kh2 Rd8 31 Bxb5 Bxb5

32 Qxe7 Rd7 33 Qh4 (threatening
34 Ng4) 33 ...f6 34 c4 Ba6 35 g4,
White with his solid king position and
good attacking chances would have
ample compensation for the sacrificed
exchange.

27   Qa6-a5

The threat is 28 Rxd7! Qxd7
29 Qxb6.

27 ...Ne8-f6

After 27 ...Rb8 28 Qxd8 Rxd8
29 Rb7 White wins a pawn and, more-
over, maintains control of the a-file.

GLIGORIĆ   54.2

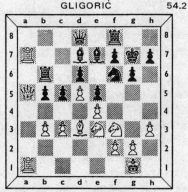

KARPOV TO MOVE

28 Ne3-g4!

This brings much greater scope to the
White attack by removing the key
defender of the second rank.

28 ...Rb6-b8

The threat was 29 Nxf6 Bxf6
30 Rxd7! as before, and the obvious
28 ...Nxg4 would be met by
29 Rxd7! Qxd7 30 Qxb6 when White
rapidly infiltrates on the Q-side.

29 Ng4xf6

After 29 Qc7 Karpov gives 29 ...Bxg4
30 hxg4 Qxc7 31 Rxc7 Bd8 32 Rc6
c4! 33 bxc4 bxc4 34 Rxc4 Nxg4
when the weakness of White on f2 will
soon be exploited. Black stands no
worse in this variation.

29 ...Be7xf6

30 Qa5-c7   Qd8xc7

31 Ra7xc7   Rf8-d8

32 Ra1-a7   Bd7-e8

33 Ra7-b7!

This eventually leads to the win of a
pawn. The threat is 34 Bxb5 Bxb5
35 Rxf7+ Kg8 36 Rxb8, when 36 ...
Kxf7 37 Rxb5 (or 36 ...Rxb8
37 Rxf6) leaves White a couple of
pawns ahead.

33 ...Kg7-g8

34 g2-g4   h7-h6

35 h3-h4

Gligorić now tries to break out, with
fatal consequences. If 35 ...Kh8
36 g5 hxg5 37 hxg5 Bg7 38 Nh2 Kg8
39 Ng4 Kh7 40 Kg2! or if 36 ...Bg7
then 37 gxh6 Bxh6 38 Ng5 Bxg5
39 hxg5 Kg8 followed by Kg1-g2-g3
and f2-f4. White has a clear advantage.

35 ...Rb8xb7

36 Rc7xb7   c5-c4!

37 b3xc4   b5xc4

38 Bd3-e2!

After 38 Bxc4 Bd7! 39 g5 Bg4!
(39 ...hxg5 40 Nxg5 leaves White a
clear pawn ahead) 40 gxf6 (40 Nh2
Bc8 wins back the pawn) 40 ...Bxf3
41 Bd3 g5! Black has many counterchances against the white king.

38 ...Rd8-a8

39 Be2xc4   Be8-a4

The alternative was 39 ...Rc8, when
Karpov gives 40 Be2 Ba4 (40 ...
Rxc3 41 g5! hxg5 42 hxg5 and now
42 ...Bg7 loses to 43 Rb8 Kf8
44 Bb5 Rxf3 45 Rxe8 mate, and
42 ...Rxf3!? to 43 Bxf3 Bxg5 44 Bg4,
when White should win the ending;
but there appears to be no obvious
refutation of 42 ...Bh8!? e.g. 43 Rb8
Kf8 44 Bb5 Rxf3 45 Rxe8+ Kg7
46 Rd8 Rf4 or 43 Rb8 Kf8 44 Nd2!?
Rc2 45 Nc4 Rxe2 46 Nxd6 Ke7!)
41 g5 (the simplest; although 41 c4
Bc2 42 g5 hxg5 43 Nxg5 Bxg5
44 hxg5 Bxe4 45 Rd7 wins a pawn)
41 ...hxg5 42 Nxg5 Bxg5 43 hxg5
Rxc3 44 Rb6 and White wins the d6
pawn.

40 Bc4-b3   Ba4xb3

41 Rb7xb3   Ra8-c8
   41 ... Ra4 allows 42 Rb4.

GLICORIĆ   54.3

KARPOV TO MOVE

42 Kg1-g2
This was the sealed move. Gligorić
was expecting 42 h5 (fixing the h6
pawn on a black square) after which
he analysed the following win for
White: 42 ...Bd8 43 Ra3 Kg7
44 Kf1 gxh5 45 gxh5 f5 46 exf5
Kf6 47 Nd2 Kxf5 48 f3 e4!
49 Nxe4 Ke5 50 Ra6 Kxd5 51 Rxd6+
Ke5 52 Rxh6 Ba5 53 Rg6 Bxc3
54 Nxc3 Rxc3 55 Kg2 Kf5 56 Rg4!
with a winning ending.
Karpov on the other hand was more
concerned with the exchange of his
pawn on c3 for Gligorić's on d6.

42 ...h6-h5
If 42 ... Be7, Gligorić gives 43 Kg3
followed by 44 Nd2: e.g. 43 Kg3 f5
44 gxf5 gxf5 45 Nd2 Kf7 46 Kh3!
and Black has no counterchances.

43 g4xh5   g6xh5

44 Rb3-b6
Threatening not only 45 Rxd6 but
also 45 Rc6!

44 ...Rc8xc3

45 Rb6xd6   Kg8-g7

46 Rd6-c6   Rc3-d3

47 Rc6-c7   Kg7-g6?
A blunder, after which Black's position
collapses with a bang! Black still had
some drawing chances with 47 ...Ra3.
The text move loses to a simple trick.

48 Rc7-c8!
Now 48 ...Ra3 49 Re8 Ra4 50 Nxe5
is check; so Black must play for f6,
after which he is hopelessly lost.

48 ...Bf6-g7

49 Rc8-c6+   Kg6-h7
Other moves allow 50 Nxe5+.

50 Nf3-g5+   Kh7-g8

51 Rc7-c8+   Bg7-f8

52 Rc8-c7   f7-f6

53 Ng5-e6   Bf8-h6

54 Rc7-d7   Rd3-d2

55 Kg2-f1   Rd2-d1+

56 Kf1-e2   Rd1-d2+

57 Ke2-e1   Rd2-c2

58 d5-d6   Rc2-c1+

59 Ke1-e2   Rc1-c2+

60 Ke2-f1   Rc2-c6

61 Kf1-g2   Rc6-b6

62 Ne6-c7   Rb6-b7

63 Nc7-d5!   Black resigns
After 63 ...Rxd7 64 Nxf6+ Kf7
65 Nxd7 Ke6 66 Nxe5! wins a third
pawn.

Game 55

WHITE Smejkal   Sicilian Defence, Taimanov Variation
Leningrad Interzonal, 1973

This game was a tragedy for Smejkal. He held the edge until move 33 but, after a small mistake, was forced to lose a pawn and eventually the game. The queen-and-bishop ending can have few equals for its beauty and the precision with which Karpov executes the win. The broader reason that this was a tragedy for Smejkal was that after 15 of the 17 rounds the leading scores were Karpov and Korchnoi 11½, Byrne 11, Smejkal 10½, Hübner 9½. With only three to qualify Smejkal had to score at least 1½ from his last two games.

1 e2-e4 c7-c5

2 Ng1-f3 e7-e6

3 d2-d4 c5xd4

4 Nf3xd4 Nb8-c6

5 Nb1-c3 a7-a6

6 Bf1-e2 Qd8-c7

7 0-0 Ng8-f6

8 Bc1-e3 Bf8-b4

9 Nc3-a4!

Aiming to exploit the weak black squares.

9 ... 0-0

Not 9 ... Nxe4 when 10 Nxc6 Qxc6 (10 ... bxc6 loses a piece to 11 Qd4) 11 Nb6 Rb8 12 Qd4 gives White a substantial initiative.

10 Nd4xc6 b7xc6!

11 Na4-b6 Ra8-b8

12 Nb6xc8 Rf8xc8!

A great improvement on the 12 ... Qxc8 of Mecking-Portisch, Sousse 1967, which continued 13 e5 Nd5 14 Bd4 c5 15 c4 cxd4 16 cxd5 Qc5 17 Bf3 with advantage to White.

13 Be2xa6

Thus reaching the starting point for theoretical discussion. Black will, of course, always regain his pawn. The threat to the white e4 pawn must be met (assuming a move by the black rook) when the retreat 14 ... Bd6 will

attack the h2 and b2 pawns simultaneously.

KARPOV TO MOVE   55.1

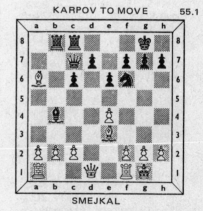

SMEJKAL

13 ... Rc8-d8!

An improvement on the old line of 13 ... Re8 when 14 Bd3 Bd6 gives White the following options:

(a) 15 f4 e5 16 f5 Rxb2 17 g4 h6 18 h4 and now:

(a1) 18 ... Nd5!? 19 exd5 e4 20 Be2 Bc5! draws, since 21 Bxc5 allows 21 ... Qg3+ etc. (Shamkovich-Doda, Polanica Zdroj 1970).

(a2) 18 ... Bf8 19 g5 Nd5! 20 Bc1! (20 exd5 e4 gives advantage to Black) 20 ... Qb6+ 21 Kh1 Ne3 22 Bxe3 (22 Qf3?! Nxf1 23 Bxb2 Nd2 24 Qg2

Qxb2 25 Rg1 should lead to Black's
advantage after 25 ...Nxe4! 26 Bxe4
d5 27 gxh6 Qd4! but in Sivohin-
Letunov, USSR 1973, White won
after 25 ...hxg5? 26 Qxd2 gxh4
27 f6! g6 28 Bc4 d5 29 exd5 etc.)
22 ...Qxe3 23 Rf3 Qd4 24 gxh6 d5!
25 hxg7 dxe4 26 gxf8=Q+ Kxf8
27 Bxe4 Qxe4 with equality
(Djindjihashvili-Taimanov, Leningrad
1971).

(a3) 18 ...h5!? 19 gxh5 Qa5? (better
is 19 ...Bf8! followed by 20 ...d5).
20 Kh1 Bc5 21 Bg5 d5 22 h6! dxe4
23 hxg7 Be7 24 Bxf6 Bxf6 25 Qh5
Kxg7 26 Bc4 Rb7 27 Rab1! Reb8
28 Rg1+ Kf8 29 Qh7 winning (Ribli-
Matulović, Helsinki 1972).

(b) 15 g4 h6 (15 ...h5!? is an interesting
reply) 16 f4! (16 Kh1? Be5! 17 Rb1
Bxb2 18 Rg1 Be5 19 Rxb8 Rxb8
20 h4 was played in Geller-Tal, Leningrad 1971. Black would have had the
advantage after 20 ...d5!) 16 ...e5
17 g5!? (17 f5 Rxb2 transposes to
line (a)) 17 ...exf4! (17 ...Nxe4?
18 gxh6! exf4 19 Qg4 gives advantage
to White, but not 18 Bxe4? exf4
19 Qf3 Rb4! with equality: Klovan-
Furman USSR 1972) 18 gxf6 fxe3
19 Qg4 g6 with a small edge for Black
in view of his plan of Re8-e5-g5.

(c) 15 Kh1 Be5! (either 15 ...Bxh2
16 f4 or 15 ...Rxb2 16 Bd4! gives
White the advantage) 16 c3 Rxb2
17 Qc1 Qb7! (the game continuation
would lose if the rook were on e8,
since at move 25(!) the black rook
would be en prise) 18 f4 Bc7 19 e5
Nd5 20 Bc5 Qb8? (20 ...Ba5! is
necessary) 21 c4 Ne7 22 Ba7! Qb7
23 Bd4 Rb4 24 Bc5 Ra4 25 Bxh7+
winning (Kochiev-Ruderfer USSR
1972).

13 ...Rd8 was at the time a new
move, and was aimed specifically at
the variation that occurred in the
game.

14 Ba6-d3   Bb4-d6

15 Kg1-h1!   Bd6-e5!

Both 15 ...Bxh2 16 f4 Bg3 17 Qf3
and 15 ...Rxb2 16 Bd4 R2b8
17 Bxf6 gxf6 18 Qh5 leave White
with a comfortable advantage.

16 c2-c3

After 16 f4 Bxb2 17 Rb1 e5! Black
has equalized, but 17 ...d5?! 18 e5
Nd7 19 Qg4 is to White's advantage.

16 ...Rb8xb2

17 Qd1-c1

KARPOV TO MOVE   55.2

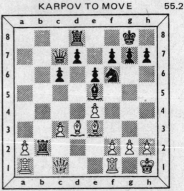

SMEJKAL

The aim of Karpov's 13th move will
not become apparent until move 25.
His choice here is an exchange-
sacrifice.

17 ...Nf6-g4!

White was threatening both the rook
and 18 f4 winning a piece. The alternative was 17 ...Qb7 18 f4 Bc7, when

(a) 19 e5 Nd5 20 Bc5 d6!

(b) 19 e5 c5!? 20 Rf3 Ng4 21 Bxc5 d6!

(c) 19 Bd4 d5! 20 e5 Ne4 21 c4 dxc4!
22 Qxb2 Qxb2 23 Bxb2 cxd3,

all lead to unclear complications.

18 f2-f4

18 Qxb2? would lose after 18 ...Bxc3!

18 ...Ng4xe3

19 Qc1xb2

19 ...Qb6 would be an adequate reply
to 19 fxe5.

19 ...Be5xf4

20 Qb2-f2!

The return of the exchange is White's most promising continuation.

After 20 Rf3 Ng4 Black has a dangerous attack: e.g.

(a) 21 h3? Bc1! wins.

(b) 21 g3 Ne5! gives Black an extra pawn.

(c) 21 Qe2 Be3! 22 g3 Bb6 with good chances for the sacrificed exchange.

20 ... Ne3xf1

21 Ra1xf1   e6-e5?!

Better was Taimanov's suggestion 21 ... g5! when 22 g3 Qd6 23 Bc2 Be5 24 Qxf7+ Kh8 25 Kg2 (25 Rd1 Rf8!) 25 ... Qd2+ 26 Rf2 Qd6 27 a4 g4! 28 a5 c5 gives White a minimal edge, and 23 Be2 Be5 24 Qxf7+ Kh8 25 Rd1 Qf8 26 Qxf8+ Rxf8 27 Rxd7 Bxc3 28 Bc4 with a small advantage, but again 25 ... Rf8! is better.

22 g2-g3   Qc7-d6

The only move to save the piece.

23 Bd3-e2!

Best, according to Shamkovich and Kotov. The alternative was 23 Bc4 Bg5 24 Qxf7+ Kh8 25 a4 Bf6 26 a5 Rf8 27 Qh5 when:

(a) 27 ... Qd2 28 Qxe5 h6 29 Qc5 wins for White.

(b) 27 ... Qc5! 28 Bf7 Bd8 is unclear.

Also playable was 25 ... h6 26 a5 Qc5 27 a6 d5 28 Bd3 Qxc3.

23 ... Bf4-g5

24 Qf2xf7+   Kg8-h8

25 a2-a4!

The point of Karpov's improvement becomes clear: on d8 the rook is not en prise, whereas with the rook on e8 this whole line would have been unplayable. Dangerous for Black was 25 Bg4 Be7 26 Rd1 Qa3 27 Rxd7: e.g. 27 ... Qc1+ 28 Kg2 or 27 ... Rxd7 28 Qe8+ both win for White.

25 ... Bg5-e7!

After 25 ... h6 26 Bh5! Qd3 27 Bg6 is strong for White.

26 a4-a5   Rd8-f8

27 Qf7-c4   Rf8xf1+

28 Be2xf1

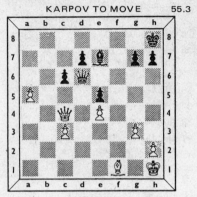

KARPOV TO MOVE   55.3

SMEJKAL

White has a slight advantage in this ending. His passed a-pawn is potentially dangerous and Black has no compensation, save that his king has a safer position.

28 ... Qd6-f6

29 Kh1-g2   Qf6-f8!

Threatening 30 ... Bc5 and then 31 ... Qf2+ etc.

30 Bf1-e2   Be7-c5

31 Be2-g4!   Qf8-f2+

Stronger than 31 ... Qd6 32 Qf7 Qd2+ 33 Kh3 Qh6+ 34 Bh5 when 34 ... Qe6+ 35 Qxe6 is a highly advantageous ending for White, whilst 34 ... g6 35 Qe8+ wins for him.

32 Kg2-h3   d7-d6

Other possible defences were:

(a) 32 ... d5!? 33 exd5 cxd5 34 Qxd5 Qf1+ 35 Qg2 Qa6.

(b) 32 ... g6! 33 Bxd7 Qe3 (Shamkovich).

In each case White has a small advantage.

33 Bg4-d7?!

Although this wins a pawn directly it is vastly inferior to 33 Qe6! e.g. 33 ... Qf1+ 34 Kh4 Qf6+ 35 Qxf6 gxf6 with a winning ending for White. This is the turning point of the game.

Karpov succeeds in wresting the
initiative, and soon wins a pawn.

33 ...g7-g6!
Already the game is equal.

34 Bd7xc6   Kh8-g7

35 Bc6-b5   Qf2-b2
The threat of 36 ...Bg1 wins back
the lost pawn.

36 a5-a6   Bc5-g1

37 Qc4-e2   Qb2xc3

38 Bb5-c4   Qc3-c1

39 Qe2-f1?
A blunder in time-trouble. After
39 Kg2 the game is still equal.

39 ...Qc1-h6+

40 Kh3-g2   Qh6xh2+

41 Kg2-f3   Qh2-h5+

42 Kf3-g2   Qh5-h2+

43 Kg2-f3   Bg1-d4

44 Bc4-d5?!
The bishop is better left on the f1-a6
diagonal.

44 ...Bd4-c5

45 Bd5-c6   Bc5-d4

46 Bc6-b7?
It is vital that the bishop should be
able to reach the f1-a6 diagonal. Now
White has great difficulty in defending
against the mating threats from the
K-side pawns.

KARPOV TO MOVE   55.4

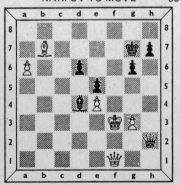

SMEJKAL

46 ...g6-g5!
After 46 ...h5 47 Qg2 is playable.
Now 47 Qg2 loses to 47 ...g4+. The
threatened mate by 47 ...h5 and
48 ...g4 forces White's king into the
open.

47 Kf3-g4   h7-h5+!

48 Kg4-f5
After 48 Kxg5 Qxg3+ 49 Kxh5 Bf2
White must give up his queen to
avoid mate.

48 ...Qh2xg3
The win of this second pawn is
decisive.

49 Kf5-e6   Qg3-f2!
Were the white bishop able to reach
the f1-a6 diagonal, White could draw
by 50 Qxf2 Bxf2 51 Kf5 g4 52 Bc4
when the Black passed pawns could
be blockaded. After the text move
only a little effort and care is needed
to promote one of the K-side pawns.

50 Qf1-b5   Qf2-f6+

51 Ke6-d5   g5-g4

52 Bb7-c8   Qf6-e7

53 Bc8-f5   Kg7-h6

54 Qb5-f1   Qe7-c7

55 Qf1-e2   Qc7-c5+

56 Kd5-e6   Kh6-g5

57 Qe2-f1   Qc5-a3

58 Qf1-e2   Bd4-c5

59 Qe2-d2+   Qa3-e3

60 Qd2-a5
The ending after 60 Qxe3+ Bxe3
61 Kxd6 is lost for White: 61 ...Bd4
followed by h5-h4-h3-h2-h1=Q wins
comfortably.

60 ...Bc5-b6

61 Qa5-a2   Qe3-f2

62 Qa2-b1   g4-g3

63 Bf5-h3   Kg5-h4

64 Bh3-g2   Qf2-g1
The queen-and-pawn ending after
64 ...Qxg2 65 Qxb6 is also won for
Black, but the text move makes life
much simpler.

65 Qb1xg1 Bb6xg1	68 Kd6xe5 Kh4-g4
66 Ke6xd6	69 Ke5-d5 h5-h4
After 66 Kf5 Bd4 White is in	70 e4-e5 h4-h3
zugzwang, 67 Bf1 being met by	71 Bg2xh3+ Kg4xh3
67 ...g2! 68 Bxg2 Kg3 followed by	72 e5-e6 Ba7-c5!
the advance of the h-pawn.	
66 ...Bg1-d4	**White resigns**
67 a6-a7 Bd4xa7	73 Kxc5 g2 74 e7 g1=Q is now check.

Game 56

WHITE Korchnoi   Polish Defence
41st Soviet Championship, Moscow 1973

This game has a peculiar similarity to Karpov's win over Taimanov (Game 52). Black sacrifices a pawn at an early stage for control of some central white squares. Whereas in the Taimanov game Black regained the pawn and won by the more aggressive positioning of his pieces, here the threat to regain the pawn leaving a good-knight-v.-bad-bishop ending is sufficient to force Korchnoi's resignation.

This result brought Karpov up to 4½ from 6 games, but in the next two rounds his chances slipped away. In round seven he drew with Spassky (the eventual winner) after a long game in which he won a piece for two pawns, and in round eight he lost to Petrosian. Karpov's opponents in rounds 5 to 9 were respectively Tal, Korchnoi, Spassky, Petrosian, and Kuzmin, who together with Karpov formed the USSR team in the 1974 Nice Olympiad.

1 Ng1-f3 Ng8-f6

2 g2-g3 b7-b5

3 c2-c3

Karpov's interesting second move meets with an interesting reply. Korchnoi is aiming for 4 a4 and a direct attack on the b5 pawn. The 14th match game of the 1966 World Championship match between Petrosian and Spassky continued 3 a4 b4 4 d3 Bb7 5 e4 d6 6 Bg2 Nbd7 7 0-0 e6 8 a5 Rb8 9 Nbd2 Be7 10 Nc4 0-0 with equality. Korchnoi's plan of fixing the b5 pawn first seems more logical.

3 ...Bc8-b7

The alternative was 3 ...e6, in order to meet 4 a4 by 4 ...b4.

4 a2-a4 a7-a6

5 e2-e3 Nb8-c6!

Far superior to the alternative 5 ...e5?! when 6 d4 is good for White.

6 d2-d4

After an attempt to win a pawn by 6 axb5 axb5 7 Rxa8 Qxa8 8 Bxb5 the reply is 8 ...Nd4! 9 Nxd4 Bxh1 10 f3 e5 winning for Black.

6 ...e7-e6

7 b2-b4

Korchnoi's opening plan is to fix the b5 pawn and then attack it until it falls. Karpov meets this by a nicely-timed counterthrust.

7 ...Bf8-e7

8 Nb1-d2 Nc6-a7

White was at last threatening to take the b5 pawn.

9 Bf1-d3   0-0

10 e3-e4   d7-d6

11 0-0   c7-c5!

KARPOV   56.1

KORCHNOI TO MOVE

This break gives Black a small advantage. He is thus able to exploit his lead in development, bringing some pressure to bear on the White centre. The weakness of the white c3 pawn is evident in some of the possible variations:

(a) 12 e5? dxe5 13 dxe5 (13 dxc5 e4 wins a piece) 13 ...Nd5 threatening both c3 and b4.

(b) 12 axb5 Nxb5! 13 Bb2 (13 Bxb5 gives Black the two bishops, while 13 bxc5 dxc5 leaves White with an exposed centre) 13 ...cxd4 14 cxd4 d5! (threatening the b4 pawn) 15 e5 Ne4 with a winning position for Black.

Korchnoi opts for a safer continuation.

12 b4xc5   d6xc5

13 Bc1-b2   Na7-c6!?

This move offers the b-pawn in return for some positional pressure. However, safer and sufficient to retain the advantage was 13 ...c4.

14 e4-e5

After 14 axb5 axb5 15 Bxb5 Black can choose either 15 ...cxd4 16 cxd4 Qb6 17 Qe2 (17 Bxc6 Bxc6 leaves Black ample compensation for the pawn) 17 ...Na7 18 Bd3 Qxb2 19 Rab1 with advantage to White, or 15 ...Qb6! 16 c4 (16 Qe2 Na7 17 Bd3 Qxb2 18 Rab1 Qxc3 gives advantage to Black) 16 ...Nxd4 17 Nxd4 cxd4 18 e5! Nd5! with compensation for the eventually lost d-pawn.

14 ...Nf6-d5

15 a4xb5   a6xb5

16 Qd1-b1   c5xd4

17 c3xd4

After 17 Bxh7+ Kh8 18 cxd4 g6 19 Bxg6 fxg6 20 Qxg6 Qe8 21 Qxe6 Qf7 Black has the advantage even though White has four pawns for his piece and five connected passed pawns.

17 ...h7-h6

18 Bd3xb5   Qd8-b6

19 Bb5-e2

The manœuvre 19 Bd3 intending 20 Be4 also had its merits. On e2 the bishop cannot deal with the threats on the a8-h1 diagonal.

19 ...Ra8xa1

20 Bb2xa1   Qb6-a7

21 Nd2-c4

Botvinnik in *Informator 16* recommends 21 Ne4! intending to return the pawn by 22 Nc5! after which the game would be equal.

21 ...Rf8-b8   *(see Diagram 56.2)*

Now is a good time to assess the strength of Karpov's sacrifice. His Q-side counterplay is not particularly strong, but his long-range prospects are excellent. All his pieces are actively placed, whereas all of White's could be better employed. The possible attack along the a8-h1 diagonal coupled with White's bad bishop on a1 make it difficult for Korchnoi to play for more than a draw. As in the game with Taimanov (52),

KARPOV   56.2

KORCHNOI TO MOVE

Black bides his time and is in no hurry
to regain the sacrificed pawn: first he
improves even further the positioning
of his pieces.

22 Ba1-b2   Bb7-a6

23 Qb1-c2   Qa7-b7

24 Bb2-a1
After 24 Bc1 Qb1! 25 Qxb1 Rxb1
the pin on the a6-f1 diagonal is
difficult to break: e.g.

(a) 26 Ncd2 Bxe2 27 Nxb1 Bxf3 wins
two pieces for the rook.

(b) 26 Be3 Nc3! 27 Bd3 Rb4 with
pressure.

24 ... Nc6-b4

25 Qc2-d2   Rb8-c8

26 Nc4-e3
After 26 Rc1 Qc7 27 Bb2 then
27 ... Na2! 28 Rc2 Ndb4 wins
material.

26 ... Nd5xe3

27 Qd2xe3
If 27 Bxa6 then 27 ... Nxf1 wins the
exchange.

27 ... Ba6xe2

28 Qe3xe2   Rc8-c2

29 Qe2-d1   Qb7-c6

30 h2-h3?!
The exchanges of bishops and knights
have in no way reduced Black's advan-

tage. Korchnoi would have been wise
to strike out for a draw here by 30 d5!
Qxd5 (if 30 ... Nxd5?? then 31 Nd4
wins a rook) 31 Qxd5 Nxd5 32 Bd4!
after which Black's advantage is
minimal.

30 ... Nb4-d5

31 Qd1-d3   Qc6-a4

32 Nf3-d2   Rc2-a2

33 Nd2-b3
Now 33 ... Ra3 can be met by 34 Rb1.

33 ... Nd5-b4

34 Qd3-b1   Nb4-d5

35 Rf1-c1   Qa4-a8

36 Rc1-c8+   Qa8xc8

37 Qb1xa2   Qc8-c4

38 Qa2-b1   Qc4-e2

KARPOV   56.3

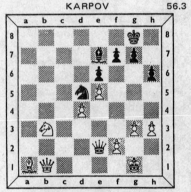

KORCHNOI TO MOVE

Even the exchange of rooks has not
lessened Black's initiative. The white
bishop is still weak, and the threats
to the white king are growing serious.
Korchnoi appears to underestimate
the dangers in the position and loses
quickly. The only hope for White here
is 39 Nc5! when:

(a) 39 ... Bxc5 40 dxc5 Qc4 41 Qd1
Qxc5 42 Bd4 gives White some
defensive chances.

(b) 39 ... Bg5 40 Ne4! Be3! 41 fxe3
Nxe3 42 Nf2 Qf3 43 Qe4 winning.

(c) 39 . . . Qf3 40 Qd3 forcing the exchange of queens.

Instead Korchnoi blunders into a lost position.

39 Qb1-c1?　Be7-g5

40 Qc1-f1

The last chance was 40 Qb2, but after 40 . . . Qd1+ 41 Kg2 h5 White is movebound and would soon lose.

40 . . . Qe2-f3

41 h3-h4

The threats were 41 . . . Qxb3 and 41 . . . Ne3!

White resigns

The winning line is 41 . . . Be3! (threatening 42 . . . Qxg3+ and meeting 42 fxe3 by 42 . . . Qxg3+! 43 Kh1 Nxe3! when 44 Qg1 allows 44 . . . Qf3+ 45 Kh2 Ng4+ winning the queen and 44 Qe2 allows 44 , , , Ng4! [followed by 45 . . . Nf2+] 45 Qg2 Qxh4+ 46 Kg1 Qe1+ 47 Qf1 Qe3+ followed by 48 . . . Qxb3 with two extra pawns) 42 Qg2 and now:

(a) 42 . . . Qd1+ 43 Kh2 Qxb3 44 fxe3 Nxe3.

(b) 42 . . . Bxf2+ 43 Qxf2 Qxb3 44 Kh2 Qd3! 45 Bb2 Ne3 46 Kh3 h5! 47 Qf3 Qd2.

In either case the queen and knight form an effective mating net.

Game 57

BLACK Kuzmin　　Sicilian Defence, Najdorf Variation
41st Soviet Championship, Moscow 1973

With impressive ease Karpov converts a spatial advantage and safer king-position into a win—a good recovery after his loss to Petrosian in the previous round. Having already played seven of the best ten participants, Karpov should have had an excellent chance, but once again he faltered, and could score only one more win in his last eight games to finish in joint second place.

1 e2-e4　c7-c5

2 Ng1-f3　d7-d6

3 d2-d4　c5xd4

4 Nf3xd4　Ng8-f6

5 Nb1-c3　a7-a6

6 f2-f4

Karpov rejects the 6 Be2 with which he beat Bronstein in Game 34 and Mecking in Game 39. He reverted to this move in his match with Polugaevsky (see Game 67 and 68).

6 . . . Qd8-c7

Usual here is the immediate 6 . . . e5, although the text move is by no means inferior. Kuzmin is playing a Dragon-like line.

7 a2-a4!

Otherwise Black will complete his Q-side development before castling.

7 . . . g7-g6

8 Nd4-f3　Bc8-g4

9 Bf1-d3　Nb8-c6

10 h2-h3　Bg4xf3

11 Qd1xf3

The opening is similar to the variation of the Pirc defence with 1 e4, d6 2 d4 Nf6 3 Nc3 g6 4 f4 Bg7 5 Nf3 0-0 6 Be2 c5 7 dxc5 Qa5 8 0-0 Qxc5+ 9 Kh1. The pawn structure is identical, but the black pieces are in slightly different places.

11 . . . Bf8-g7

12 0-0   0-0

13 Bc1-d2   e7-e6

KUZMIN   57.1

KARPOV TO MOVE

White has a small advantage. His pieces
are effectively developed and his pawns
grip the central squares, in particular
d5. Black's last move threatens 14 ...
Nb4 followed by 15 ...d5 or 15 ...
Nxd3. The weakening of the black
square f6 is not, as yet, significant.

14 Nc3-e2
Preparing to bring the knight to g3
or even f4 and preventing the threatened 14 ...Nb4. Or does it?

14 ...Ra8-c8
Kuzmin misses 14 ...Nb4! 15 Bxb4
Qb6+ regaining the piece with at
least an equal game. 15 Kh1 is met
by 15 ...Nxd3.

15 Kg1-h1   e6-e5
Seemingly a strange move, but having
missed the boat at his last turn this is
his only remaining central break.
15 ...d5 is answered by 16 e5 with
control of d4.

16 Ne2-c3
Karpov switches back to control d5.

16 ...e5xf4

17 Bd2xf4   Nc6-b4

18 Bf4-d2!
There is no point in playing 18 Bg5,
for Black intends Nf6-d7-e5. The text
move defends the c3 knight which

will be en prise after 18 ...Nd7.

18 ...Nf6-d7

19 Qf3-g3   Qc7-c6

20 Bd2-g5
Now 20 ...Bxc3 21 bxc3 Qxc3
22 Be7 Rfe8 23 Bxd6 is greatly to
White's advantage.

20 ...Rc8-e8

21 Ra1-d1   Nd7-e5?!
Karpov now takes a grip on the black
squares. Preferable was 21 ...h6
22 Bc1 Ne5.

22 Qg3-h4   Ne5xd3
This strengthens White's centre. More
logical was 22 ...Re6, intending
23 ...f6.

23 c2xd3   Qc6-d7

24 Bg5-f6   a6-a5

25 d3-d4!

KUZMIN TO MOVE   57.2

KARPOV

White has now built up his position to
give a clear advantage. His control of
the dark squares and his spatial advantage give him a strong initiative.

25 ...Re8-e6

26 e4-e5   d6-d5?
Better was 26 ...dxe5 27 dxe5 Qc6
when Black rids himself of his weak
d-pawn.

27 Bf6xg7   Kg8xg7

28 Rf1-f6   h7-h6

29 Rd1-f1   Re6xf6

30 Rf1xf6!

Much more effective than 30 Qxf6+.
The rook infiltrates along the sixth
rank.

30 ...Rf8-e8

31 Nc3-e2!

So as to meet 31 ... Re6 with 32 Nf4!
Rxf6 33 Qxf6+ followed by 34 e6!
winning at least a pawn (33 ... Kh7
34 e6 fxe6 35 Qxg6+ or 33 ... Kg8
34 e6 Qe8 35 exf7+ Qxf7 36 Qxg6+).

31 ...Nb4-c6

This leads to the loss of a pawn, but

there was no superior move.

32 Rf6-d6   Qd7-f5

33 Ne2-g3!   Qf5-d3

If 33 ...Qb1+ 34 Kh2 Qxb2 then
Black is mated by 35 Nf5+! gxf5
36 Qxh6+ Kg8 37 Qg5+ Kf8
38 Rh6!

34 Rd6xd5   Re8-e6

35 Qh4-f4   Re6-e7

36 Kh1-h2   Kg7-g8

Probably a miscalculation in time-
trouble, but Black is lost in any case.

37 Qf4xh6   Qd3-c4

38 Ng3-e4!   Black resigns

Mate is imminent.

Game 58

BLACK Andersson   Queen's Indian Defence

Madrid 1973

The passed pawn strikes yet another grandmaster down! After going wrong
in the opening, Andersson is always struggling to keep in the game. Karpov
trades his positional advantage for his beloved Q-side majority and goes on
to queen a pawn. This game follows the same theme as Karpov's win over
Parma (Game 17) in which he made a similar exchange of advantages.

1 d2-d4   Ng8-f6

2 c2-c4   e7-e6

3 Ng1-f3   b7-b6

It is strange to see Andersson reject
his favourite 3 ...Bb4+ (Bogolyubov
Opening), with which he has won
many games, including two against
Korchnoi (Wijk aan Zee 1970—1 and
Hastings 1971—2).

4 g2-g3   Bc8-b7

5 Bf1-g2   Bf8-b4+

6 Nb1-d2

Whereas this move is the best reply to
3 ...Bb4+ it is now generally considered to be inferior to 6 Bd2.

6 ...0-0

Capablanca played 6 ...Ne4 against
Reti at Bad Kissingen in 1928, and

after 7 0-0 Nxd2 8 Bxd2 Bxd2
9 Qxd2 d6 10 Rfd1 0-0 11 Rac1
Qe7 12 Ne1 Bxg2 13 Nxg2 Nd7
14 e4 Rfd8 15 Ne3 g6! had already
equalized. The text move is more
ambitious.

7 0-0   c7-c5?!

This was playable a move earlier
(6 ...c5 7 a3 Bxd2+ 8 Qxd2
[8 Bxd2 cxd4 9 Bb4 Nc6] 8 ...cxd4
9 Qxd4 Nc6 10 Qh4 Rc8! with
equality: Uhlmann-Portisch, Moscow
1967) but is now dubious. Safer was
7 ...d5 8 a3 Be7 9 b4 c5! 10 bxc5
bxc5 11 dxc5 Bxc5 12 Bb2 Nbd7
13 Ne5 Nxe5 14 Bxe5 Ng4! 15 Bc3
Rb8 with approximate equality
(Rubinstein-Alekhine, Semmering
1926).

8 a2-a3   Bb4xd2

9 Bc1xd2!   c5xd4?!
Better was 9 ...d6, 9 ...d5, or 9 ...
Ne4.

10 Bd2-b4!
After 10 Nxd4 Bxg2 11 Kxg2 Black
has no problems.

10 ...Rf8-e8
If 10 ...d6 then 11 Qxd4 gives White
pressure down the d-file.

11 Bb4-d6

ANDERSSON TO MOVE   58.1

KARPOV

Black must strike quickly to relieve
the cramped nature of his position.
Andersson chooses the wrong plan
and this soon leads him into a desperately passive situation, in which
White's advantage is clear. The
correct way to minimize White's
edge was 11 ...Bxf3! 12 Bxf3 Nc6
when

(a) 13 b4 Rc8 14 Rc1 e5 leaves Black
a clear pawn up.

(b) 13 Bxc6 dxc6 14 Qxd4 Ne4 (if 14 ...
c5 then 15 Qf4 is strong) 15 Rfd1
Nxd6 16 Qxd6 with only a small
advantage to White.

11 ...Nf6-e4?

12 Qd1xd4   Nb8-a6

13 b2-b4   Ra8-c8

14 Ra1-c1   Ne4xd6

15 Qd4xd6   Na6-c7
After 15 ...Qc7 16 Qd3 the threat
of 17 Ng5 is awkward for Black.

16 Rf1-d1
White's advantage is indisputable. He
has strong pressure on the d-file and
with his next move he also obtains
bishop-v.-knight advantage.

16 ...Re8-e7

17 Qd6-d3!
Threatening 18 Ng5. After 17 ...h6
18 Ne5 Bxg2 19 Kxg2 White wins a
pawn: for example

(a) 19 ...Qe8 20 Nxd7 Rd8 21 Nf6+!

(b) 19 ...d5 20 Nc6.

After 17 ...d5 18 e4! is strong.

17 ...Bb7xf3

18 Bg2xf3   Nc7-e8

19 Bf3-b7!   Rc8-c7
If 19 ...Rb8 then 20 Bc6! Nf6 21 e4!
Rc8 22 Bb5 leaves Black completely
tied up.

20 Bb7-a6!   Rc7-c6
Aiming to exchange a pair of rooks
by 21 ...Rd6.

21 Qd3-b3   Qd8-b8
After 21 ...Rd6 22 Rxd6 Nxd6
23 c5 bxc5 24 Rxc5 White has
established a two-to-one Q-side
majority.

22 Qb3-a4
Threatening 23 Rxd7! Rxd7 24 Qxc6.

22 ...Rc6-c7

23 Qa4-b5
Now the establishment of a Q-side
majority cannot be adequately
prevented.

23 ...Ne8-f6

24 f2-f3
Threatening 25 e4! restraining the
black d-pawn. Andersson seizes his
opportunity to rid himself of his
backward pawn, but at the same
time releases Karpov's Q-side majority.
24 ...Qe8 could be met by 25 Rd6!
with a bind.

24 ...d7-d5

ANDERSSON   58.2

KARPOV TO MOVE

25 c4-c5!   h7-h5

26 a3-a4!   Re7-e8

27 c5xb6   a7xb6

28 a4-a5!   Rc7xc1

29 Rd1xc1   Qb8-e5
   The b-pawn cannot be saved. After
   29 ... bxa5 30 Qxb8 Rxb8 31 bxa5

the bishop-and-knight ending following (say) 31 ... Nd7 32 Rc8+ Rxc8
33 Bxc8 is won for White, since the
a-pawn costs Black his knight.

30 Qb5xb6
   The rest of the game is technique.
   White's position is overwhelming.

30 ... d5-d4

31 Kg1-h1   Qe5-e3

32 Rc1-f1   e6-e5

33 Ba6-d3   h5-h4

34 g3xh4   Qe3-f4

35 Rf1-g1   Qf4xh4

36 a5-a6   g7-g6
   Or 36 ... e4 37 fxe4 Nxe4 38 Qc6
   winning easily.

37 a6-a7   Kg8-g7

38 Bd3xg6!   Black resigns
   After 38 ... fxg6 either 39 a8=Q
   Rxa8 40 Qb7+, or 39 Qb7+ Kh6
   40 Qf7! (threatening both 41 Qxg6
   mate and 41 Qxe8 followed by
   42 a8=Q) wins easily.

Game 59

BLACK Uhlmann   French Defence, Tarrasch Variation
Madrid 1973

This game was the real decider at Madrid. It was played in round 12, when
the leading scores were: Uhlmann 8½, Karpov, Furman, Tukmakov, and
Hort 7½. Not only did Karpov beat Uhlmann, and, incidentally, win the
best-game prize in the process, but also he went on to beat Calvo and
Planinc (Games 64 and 65) and draw with Portisch to take first place in
the tournament, and win a special prize for the best score in the last four
rounds.

   The game itself is superb. Karpov takes control of an open file with his
rooks, transfers them to the seventh rank and ploughs through Uhlmann's
weak pawns. The opening also is of some interest, for Karpov's variation is
tested by the best French-Defence player in grandmaster chess.

1 e2-e4   e7-e6
2 d2-d4   d7-d5
3 Nb1-d2 c7-c5

4 e4xd5   e6xd5
5 Ng1-f3 Nb8-c6
6 Bf1-b5 Bf8-d6

7 d4xc5 Bd6xc5

8 0-0 Ng8-e7

9 Nd2-b3 Bc5-d6

Examples of the alternative 9 ... Bb6 are to be found in Games 13 and 51.

10 Bc1-g5

'Karpov's Variation.'

10 ... 0-0

11 Bg5-h4! Bc8-g4

In Game 55 Kuzmin chose 11 ... Qc7.

12 Bb5-e2

Browne tried the immediate 12 Bg3 against Uhlmann, with the continuation 12 ... Bxg3 13 hxg3 Qb6 14 Bd3 Nf5 (threatening 15 ... Nxg3). The game Balashov-Uhlmann (Moscow 1971) went 12 Re1 Re8 13 Bg3 Bxg3 14 hxg3 Qb6 15 Bd3 with a small advantage to White.

12 ... Bg4-h5

At the Leningrad Interzonal in 1973 Uhlmann tried 12 ... Re8 here against Robert Byrne, and 12 ... Qb6?! against Kuzmin.

13 Rf1-e1 Qd8-b6

14 Nf3-d4 Bh5-g6

15 c2-c3

UHLMANN TO MOVE 59.1

KARPOV

White has successfully blockaded the isolated black d-pawn and at the same time he is poised to remove Black's most dangerous attacking piece (his king's bishop) by Bh4-g3. As in all such variations White's advantage, although only slight, is obvious. Uhlmann now tries, with eventual success, to lift the blockade by exchanges on d4.

15 ... Rf8-e8

If 15 ... Nxd4 16 Qxd4 Qxd4 (or 16 ... Nf5!? 17 Qxb6 axb6 18 Bg3 Nxg3 19 hxg3 with advantage to White) 17 Nxd4 Nf5 18 Nxf5 Bxf5 19 Bf3 gives White a winning position, since the d-pawn cannot be adequately guarded.

16 Be2-f1 Bg6-e4

This is a part of Uhlmann's idea conceived on move 12.

17 Bh4-g3 Bd6xg3

18 h2xg3 a7-a5?!

This move weakens the key b5 square, as we shall see. Possibly it was based on the idea that Karpov's next move was unplayable. Both 18 ... a6!? and 18 ... Rad8 were better.

19 a2-a4! Nc6xd4

20 Nb3xd4!

After 20 cxd4 the game would be equal.

20 ... Ne7-c6

If 20 ... Qxb2? then 21 Nb5! threatens both 22 Nc7 winning the exchange, and 22 Re2 trapping the queen. Uhlmann must have overlooked this when playing his 18th move.

21 Bf1-b5 Re8-d8

Now at last Uhlmann is threatening to break the blockade by 21 ... Nxd4.

22 g3-g4!

There are two reasons why this move merits an exclamation mark. First, it is another good example of transference of advantage, as illustrated in Game 42. Karpov allows the blockade to be broken in return for control of the open e-file, and consequently a clear endgame advantage. Second, the actual move played prevents the bishop from manœuvring via f5 to e6 or d7 and this, as we shall see, is a key factor.

UHLMANN   59.2

KARPOV TO MOVE

22 ... Nc6xd4
Uhlmann plays the logical move, but
it was probably better to avoid these
exchanges.

23 Qd1xd4   Qb6xd4

24 c3xd4   Ra8-c8
This allows a rook to the seventh
rank, but even 24 ... Kf8 fails to
prevent infiltration (25 Re2 Rac8
26 f3 Bg6 27 Rae1 and now 27 ...
Rc7? is met by 28 Re8+ and mate
next move).

25 f2-f3   Be4-g6
As we shall see Karpov's 22nd move
was the beginning of K-side operations aimed at embarrassing the
position of the black queen's bishop.

26 Re1-e7   b7-b6
Better than 26 ... Rc2 27 Rae1 h6
28 Rxb7 Rxb2 29 R1e7.

27 Ra1-e1   h7-h6
The immediate 27 ... h5 would have
been better here.

28 Re7-b7   Rd8-d6?!
After this move Black is lost. The last
chance was 28 ... Rc2 29 R1e7 Kf8!
(29 ... Rxb2 30 Be8! Rc8 31 Kh2!
R8c2 32 Kg3! and although White
loses two pawns the position is
winning for him) 30 Red7 when
White has the advantage but no clear
winning plan.

29 Re1-e7
Threatening 30 f4 followed by 31 f5
and carnage along the seventh rank.

29 ...h6-h5

30 g4xh5   Bg6xh5

31 g2-g4!   Bh5-g6

32 f3-f4!
Winning. The threat of 33 f5 cannot
be satisfactorily prevented.

32 ...Rc8-c1+

33 Kg1-f2   Rc1-c2+

34 Kf2-e3!

UHLMANN TO MOVE   59.3

KARPOV

White is even willing to allow 34 ...
Re6+, for then 35 Rxe6 fxe6
36 Rxb6 Rxb2?! 37 f5! wins easily.

34 ...Bg6-e4

35 Re7xf7   Rd6-g6

36 g4-g5   Kg8-h7

37 Rf7-e7!
White's next move cannot be stopped.

37 ...Rc2xb2

38 Bb5-e8   Rb2-b3+

39 Ke3-e2   Rb3-b2+

40 Ke2-e1   Rg6-d6
If 40 ... Rb1+ then 41 Kd2 Rb2+
42 Kc3 Rc2+ 43 Kb3 escapes from
the checks.

41 Re7xg7+   Kh7-h8

42 Rg7-e7   Black resigns

Game 60

WHITE Calvo   King's Indian Attack
Madrid 1973

Karpov defeats Calvo in all departments. Firstly, he wins the central battle of the opening. Then he ties up Calvo on the K-side, prevents any Q-side counterplay, and finally crashes through with a neat piece-winning man-œuvre. Despite this drastic reversal, Calvo was awarded the prize for the best score by a Spanish player against the grandmasters and tied with Pomar for the prize for the best overall score by a Spanish player.

1 e2-e4   c7-c5

2 Ng1-f3   e7-e6

3 d2-d3

Calvo seems to be more at home in open Sicilians. His victories over Kaválek (Las Palmas 1973) and Jansa (Nice 1974) bear this out.

3 ... Nb8-c6

4 g2-g3   d7-d5

5 Nb1-d2   Bf8-d6

Karpov's sole aim in the opening stages is control of the e5 square.

6 Bf1-g2   Ng8-e7

7 0-0   0-0

8 Rf1-e1?!

It is better here to play for 9 f4 by 8 Nh4.

8 ... Qd8-c7!

9 b2-b3?

And now 9 c3! is essential if White is to contest the centre. An interesting idea here is 9 exd5 and if 9 ... exd5 (9 ... Nxd5 10 Nc4) then 10 c4!?

9 ... Bc8-d7

10 Bc1-b2   d5-d4!

Although White now has the opportunity to gain the two bishops (by Nd2-c4xd6) this is insufficient compensation for the dominating black pawn centre.

11 Nd2-c4   e6-e5

The threat was 12 e5 winning a piece.

12 a2-a4

Preventing the undermining of the knight's position by 12 ... b5.

12 ... b7-b6

13 Qd1-d2?

KARPOV TO MOVE   60.1

CALVO

This move achieves nothing. It was better to continue with 13 Nxd6 Qxd6 14 Nd2 when White gains the two bishops and has some chances of an eventual f2-f4 break. The text move blocks the way of the f3 knight.

13 ... f7-f6

14 h2-h4?!

White cannot hope for a K-side attack and so this move is both illogical and weakening. Better is 14 c3!? or even 14 Qe2.

14 ... Qc7-b8

Preparing to remove the bishop. This is White's last chance to retain the two bishops.

15 Bb2-a3   Bd6-c7

16 Re1-b1   Bd7-e6

This move aims at preventing a b3-b4 advance. Calvo decides that such an advance would be premature and concentrates on regrouping.

17 Kg1-h2   Qb8-c8

18 Qd2-e2   Be6-g4

19 Qe2-f1   f6-f5!

20 Nc4-d2

After 20 exf5? Qxf5 21 Ncd2 Nd5! Black has a bind on the whole position that White is unable to break.

20 ...f5-f4!

21 Bg2-h3

White's regrouping is complete. He thus achieves the exchange of white-squared bishops.

21 ...h7-h5!

22 Qf1-g2   Ne7-g6

23 Nf3-g5?

KARPOV TO MOVE   60.2

CALVO

After the text move White is driven back and his position cramped still further. Better was b3-b4.

23 ...Bc7-d8!

Now 24 b4 loses a pawn to 24 ...cxb4 25 Bxb4 Nxb4 26 Rxb4 Bxg5

27 hxg5 f3 28 Qf1 Qd8 or simply 28 ... Qxc2.

24 Ng5-f3   Bd8-e7

25 Rb1-g1   Qc8-e6

There is no way for White to avoid the approaching onslaught. No Q-side breaks are playable and any attempt to play on the K-side by gxf4 would quickly lose after Rxf4 R8f8 etc.

26 Ra1-f1   Rf8-f7

27 Rg1-h1   Ra8-f8

28 Kh2-g1

There is nothing else left. White is virtually in zugzwang.

28 ...Qe6-d6

29 Kg1-h2   a7-a6

30 Kh2-g1   Rf7-f6!

With further passive play the end might be 31 Kh2 Nd8! 32 Kg1 Nf7 33 Kh2 Nh6 34 Kg1 Qd7 35 Kh2 fxg3+ 36 fxg3 Bxh3 37 Qxh3 Ng4+ 38 Kg1 Qc6! 39 Ng5 Ne3 40 Rxf6 Qxf6 41 Qe6+ Qxe6 42 Nxe6 Rf6 followed by 43 ...Nxc2 etc.

This plan of Nc6-d8-f7-h6 cannot be prevented because, as pointed out in the note to Black's 25th move, any active play by White will lead only to a quicker loss.

31 Bh3xg4   h5xg4

32 Nf3-g5   f4-f3

33 Qg2-h2

KARPOV TO MOVE   60.3

CALVO

To unravel his K-side pieces White would have to play his king to d2(!) by which time, of course, a Black Q-side attack would have demolished his game. Karpov sets a little trap into which Calvo obligingly falls.

33 ... Ng6-h8!

34 Rf1-c1?
The way to continue the struggle was 34 Rb1, but still 34 ... Rh6 35 Nc4 Qc7 36 Bc1 b5 37 axb5 axb5

38 Nb2 Qa5 wins (threats are 39 ... Qe1 mate and 39 ... Qa2 winning the rook).

34 ... Rf6-h6

35 Nd2-c4   Qd6-c7

White resigns
Although he was beaten so comprehensively, this game did not demoralize Calvo. In the next round he had the black pieces and beat Furman, ensuring first prize for Karpov!

Game 61

WHITE Planinc   Sicilian Defence, Paulsen Variation
Madrid 1973

It must have become clear to Tukmakov at an early stage of the last round that he was not going to tie for first place. After twenty moves Planinc could have resigned, for he was a pawn behind in an inferior position. This was a result of Karpov's deep opening preparation, which led to a position from which Planinc had no escape.

1 e2-e4   c7-c5

2 Ng1-f3   e7-e6

3 d2-d4   c5xd4

4 Nf3xd4   Nb8-c6

5 Nb1-c3   a7-a6

KARPOV   61.1

PLANINC TO MOVE

Although Karpov has employed an unfashionable move-order this is the basic set-up of the Paulsen Variation.

6 f2-f4
This move is unusual but by no means bad. White has a wide choice of development plans here:

(a) 6 g3 Qc7 7 Bg2 Nf6 8 0-0 Be7 9 Re1 d6 (after 9 ...0-0 10 Nxc6 is strong and gives White the advantage—10 ... dxc6 11 e5 Nd5 12 Qg4, or 10 ... bxc6 11 e5 Nd5 12 Na4 f6 13 c4 Nb6 14 Bf4, so as to meet 14 ... fxe5 by 15 Bxe5 d6 16 c5!) 10 Nxc6 bxc6 11 e5 dxe5 12 Rxe5 0-0 13 Bf4 Qb7 14 Re3 Rd8 15 Qe1 Bd7 16 Be5 Be8 17 Ne4 with advantage to White (Boleslavsky).

(b) 6 g3 Qc7 7 Bg2 Nf6 8 0-0 Nxd4 9 Qxd4 Bc5 10 Bf4! d6 (if 10 ... Bxd4 11 Bxc7 Bxc3 12 bxc3 d5 13 exd5 Nxd5 14 Be5 f6 15 c4! Nb4 16 Bc3 gives White an endgame advantage Honfi-Kozma, Wijk aan Zee 1969) 11 Qd3! Nd7 12 Na4 e5 13 Bd2 b5 14 Nxc5 Nxc5 15 Qa3 Bb7 16 Ba5 Qc6 17 Rad1! 0-0 18 Rd5 f5 19 Rfd1 Nxe4 20 Qb3! Kh8 (Matulović-Vasyukov, Skopje 1970) and now White maintains his advantage by 21 Rxd6!.

(c) 6 g3 Qc7 7 Bg2 Nf6 8 0-0 d6 9 Re1 Bd7 10 Nxc6 bxc6 11 Na4 e5 12 c4 Be7 13 c5! 0-0 14 cxd6 Bxd6 15 Bg5 Be7 with a positional advantage to White (Tal-Najdorf, USSR v. Rest of World match, 1970).

(d) 6 Be2 Qc7 and now:

(d1) 7 Be3 b5 8 Nxc6 Qxc6 9 e5 Bb7 10 Bf3 Qc7 11 0-0 Rd8 12 Bxb7 Qxb7 13 Bg5 Be7 14 Bxe7 Nxe7 15 Qd3 0-0 White has the freer game.

(d2) 7 f4 (This is different from the text, since Planinc intends to develop his bishops on d2 and d3) 7 ... b5 8 Nxc6 dxc6 9 Be3 Bb7 10 0-0 Nf6 11 e5 Nd5 12 Nxd5 cxd5 13 Bd3 White stands better.

(d3) 7 a3 b5 8 Nxc6 Qxc6 9 0-0 Bb7 10 Bf3 Qc7 11 e5 Rc8 12 Bxb7 Qxb7 13 Bf4! Ne7 14 Qe2 Nf5 (Kholmov-Suetin, 30th USSR Championship 1962) is also to White's advantage.

(e) 6 Be3 Qc7 7 Bd3 Nf6 8 0-0 when Black can choose between

(e1) 8 ... Ne5 9 h3 b5 10 f4 Nc4 11 Bxc4 Qxc4 12 e5 Nd5 13 Nxd5 Qxd5 14 Qe2 Bb7 15 Nb3 Rc8 16 c3 Qc4 17 Qf2 Bd5 18 Rad1 Be7 19 Rd4 Qc7 20 Qg3 with a strong attack for White.

(e2) 8 ... Nxd4 9 Bxd4 Bc5 10 Bxf6 gxf6 11 Qg4 Kf8 12 Kh1 h5 13 Qh4 Be7 14 f4: White stands better (Tolush-Matulović, USSR v. Yugoslavia 1965).

6 ... Qd8-c7

7 Nd4xc6 Qc7xc6

8 Bf1-d3
After 8 Be3 b5 9 Be2 Ba3!? 10 bxa3

Qxc3+ 11 Kf2 Nf6 12 Bf3 Bb7 13 Bd4 Qxa3 14 Qd3 Qxd3 15 cxd3 0-0 16 Rhc1 Rfc8 White has compensation for his sacrificed pawn and the chances are roughly equal (Matanović-Vasyukov, USSR v. Yugoslavia 1966).

8 ... b7-b5

9 Qd1-e2   Bc8-b7

10 Bc1-d2?!
Better was 10 0-0. The text move is aiming at Q-side castling.

10 ... Bf8-c5!

11 Qe2-g4?!
Preferable was 11 a3, but Planinc is still following the course of an earlier game of his against Suetin.

11 ... g7-g6

12 a2-a3

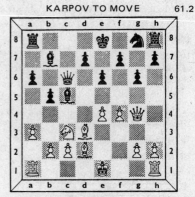

PLANINC

At last the game diverges from Planinc-Suetin, Ljubljana-Portoroz 1973. This ended 12 Qh4 b4! 13 Nd1 Be7 14 Qh3 Nf6 15 Nf2 d5 16 exd5 Qxd5 17 0-0-0 18 Rae1 Rfe8 19 b3 Bc5 20 Re5 Qc6 21 Kh1 Qb6 22 Qh4 Be7 23 Be3 Qc6 24 Qh3 Rad8 25 Bc1 Nd7! 26 Ng4! Bf8 27 Bb2? f5! 28 Re3 fxg4 29 Qxg4

Nc5 30 Rh3 Nxd3 31 cxd3 Bg7
32 Bxg7 Kxg7 33 Qg5 Kg8 and
White resigned. The weakness on the
a7-g1 and a8-h1 diagonals in White's
position is illustrated both in the
Suetin game and in this one.

12 ...f7-f5!

13 e4xf5?
Better was 13 Qh4 (to prevent
13 ... Nf6) when the position is still
a little unclear according to Minic,
but after 13 ... Be7 14 Qg3 Nf6!
Black stands much better.

13 ...e6xf5

14 Qg4-e2+
Planinc's resource, but this loses a
pawn, as do all other moves.

14 ...Ke8-f7!
The double threats of 15 ... Re8
and 15 ... Qxg2 cannot be answered
satisfactorily. After 15 Kf1, Re8 wins
instantly; so White is obliged to lose
a pawn.

15 0-0-0   Ra8-e8

16 Qe2-f1   Ng8-f6!
The pawn cannot escape, and after
16 ... Qxg2 17 Bc4+ gives White
some hopes.

17 a3-a4   Qc6xg2

18 Qf1xg2   Bb7xg2

19 Rh1-e1   b5-b4

20 Nc3-a2   a6-a5

White is lost, and could resign here.
Apart from being a pawn behind, his
remaining K-side pawns are weak and,
to add to this, Black has complete control of the central squares e4, d5, and
d4. The rest of the game is a simple
technical exercise for Karpov.

21 Kc1-b1   Bg2-f3

22 Rd1-c1   Nf6-e4

23 Bd3xe4
The bishop on d2 had no square!
23 Be3? loses to 23 ... Bxe3 24 Rxe3
Nd2+

23 ... Bf3xe4
Simpler was 23 ... fxe4, when the
passed pawn, together with an attack
along the f-file, would soon have
ended the game.

24 Kb1-a1   d7-d5

25 Bd2-e3   Bc5xe3

26 Re1xe3   d5-d4

27 Re3-e2   Be4-c6

28 Re2-d2   Re8-e4

29 Rc1-d1   Bc6xa4

30 b2-b3   Ba4-c6

31 Rd2xd4   Re4xd4

32 Rd1xd4   Rh8-e8

33 Rd4-c4   Re8-e1+

34 Ka1-b2   Bc6-e4

35 Na2-c1   Re1-h1

36 Rc4-c7+   Kf7-g8

37 Nc1-e2   Rh1xh2

38 Ne2-d4   h7-h5

39 Nd4-e6   h5-h4

40 Ne6-g5   h4-h3

41 Rc7-c8+   Kg8-g7

42 Rc8-c7+   Kg7-f8

White resigns
Having avoided both 42 ... Kh6??
and 42 ... Kf6?? Black wins easily.

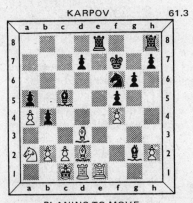

KARPOV   61.3

PLANINC TO MOVE

8   1974 — The candidates' matches

1974 was a relatively quiet year for Karpov in terms of the number of games played, but he succeeded in establishing himself as the challenger for Bobby Fischer's world championship title.

He began in January with a quarter-final match against Polugaevsky in Moscow—to be decided as soon as one of the two contestants scored three wins. (The new rules for the candidates' matches in the world championship were based on number of wins scored rather than number of points accumulated, but with a maximum number of games to be played, in case neither contestant reached the required number of wins.) The first three games were relatively uneventful, but in the fourth a fluctuating struggle went Karpov's way late in the game to give him a 1-0 lead. The fifth game was the key to the whole match. Polugaevsky won the exchange, but Karpov, with a little luck and great defensive skill, managed to save the game and thus retain his lead. After this Polugaevsky was shattered, and lost two of the next three to give Karpov a 3-0 win after only eight games. The best games of the match—the fifth, sixth, and eighth—are the first three of this chapter (62, 63, and 64).

The semi-final against Spassky provided a different kind of challenge. The very first game saw Karpov lose with the white pieces—a thing that had not happened since mid-1972! Karpov equalized in the third game and then struck a decisive psychological blow when he chose to defend against Spassky's king's-pawn opening with the Caro-Kann. Spassky had experienced great difficulty in breaking down this defence when he played Petrosian in the 1966 world championship match. Against Karpov he fared even worse, and Karpov played a beautiful ending to win his second game in the sixth encounter (Game 65). The eighth game (66) saw Karpov at his defensive best, refuting and repulsing Spassky's attack to achieve a hard-earned draw. In the next game (67) a brilliant positional victory by Karpov virtually assured him of the match, since he then required only one more victory to give him a place in the final. The time was now over for experimenting with the Caro-Kann and Karpov quite rightly switched to his solid and reliable Breyer Defence of the Ruy López. Spassky was given no chance to break through and score the win he so desperately needed. Karpov wrapped it all up with a nicely judged piece-sacrifice in the eleventh game (68) to give himself a 4-1 win.

The month of June saw the 21st chess Olympiad played in Nice. This was the fiftieth anniversary of the formation of the international chess organization *Fédération Internationale Des Echecs*, and so this Olympiad was held in the country where FIDE was founded.

In his first appearance on board one for the USSR Karpov was completely unplayable. He won all of his seven games with white and three of his seven with black. Only against Hartston was he ever in trouble and here he managed to draw. His best two wins, against Unzicker and Kaválek, are Games 69 and 70. The first is a complete positional strangulation, and the second a further demonstration of Karpov's technique in endings with rooks, and bishops of opposite colours. Needless to say the Soviet team finished first.

After the Leningrad match with Spassky, the candidates' final against Korchnoi, played in Moscow, proved to be a much sterner test of Karpov's all-round ability. He was soon in the lead (Game 71) when he produced a gem of an attack against Korchnoi's Dragon Variation. The sixth game saw him increase his lead in a rather scrappy Petroff Defence (Game 72). The outstanding feature of this match was the determination shown by both players in their attempts to win. Every single game was fiercely contested and most were of very high standard. The thirteenth game (73) was just one such encounter. Karpov seized the initiative, but lost it in time-trouble, and thereafter had to produce a superb defence in order to hold the position.

When Karpov increased his lead to 3-0 in the seventeenth game (74) not even the most ardent Korchnoi supporter could have predicted what an upheaval was about to take place. Korchnoi surged back into the match by winning the nineteenth and twenty-first games (the latter in only nineteen moves!) to make the score 3-2 with only three more games to play. But Karpov's technique stood firm and he comfortably drew the last three games (the crucial twenty-third game is Game 75) to take the match, and with it the right to challenge Bobby Fischer for the world championship.

Game 62

WHITE Polugaevsky   Nimzo-Indian Defence
Candidates' Match (quarter-final, fifth game) Moscow 1974

This was the most important game of the Karpov-Polugaevsky match. Games 1 and 2 had both been favourable for White, although both ended in draws. The third game was a quick draw, but in the fourth Karpov, after playing a near-disastrous opening, came back strongly to win. In such circumstances the next game is always crucial, since the defeated player must strive to even the score. Polugaevsky should have achieved this, but was denied the chance by a couple of inaccuracies and a brilliant defence by his opponent. After this game Karpov wound up the match (the first to three wins) by winning his next two games with white.

1 d2-d4   Ng8-f6

2 c2-c4   e7-e6

3 Nb1-c3   Bf8-b4

4 e2-e3   0-0

5 Bf1-d3   c7-c5

6 Ng1-f3   d7-d5

7 0-0

This position is the starting point for theoretical discussion. Black's plans here are many and varied.

7 ...d5xc4

The general preference in this position is to develop the queen's knight to d7 rather than c6. So the old variation of 7 ...Nc6 8 a3! is less common now than it was in the forties, fifties, or even early sixties.

8 Bd3xc4   Nb8-c6

It is strange that Karpov chose this move in all four of his match games with Polugaevsky. His favourite variation involves a second pawn-exchange followed by a Q-side fianchetto, as in Game 48 against Taimanov. The line played in this game is more solid and reliable.

9 a2-a3   Bb4-a5

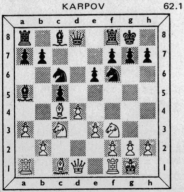

KARPOV   62.1

POLUGAEVSKY TO MOVE

10 Bc4-a2

Polugaevsky chose this move in the third and seventh games of the match

also, the idea being to build up a battery on the b1-h7 diagonal, by Ba2-b1 and Qd1-d3 (or c2), without allowing Black to threaten the d4 pawn.

An interesting try here is 10 Qd3 (with basically the same idea, although both 11 Ne4 and 11 Rd1 are also possible now) 10 ...a6 when Taimanov gives the main lines as

(a) 11 Rd1 b5 12 Ba2 Bb6! 13 Qc2 c4 14 Qe2 Qe8 15 b3 cxb3 16 Bxb3 Bb7 17 e4 e5 18 dxe5 Nxe5 19 Nxe5 Qxe5 20 Bb2 Bd4! (to meet 21 Rxd4 Qxd4 22 Nd5 by 22 ...Qxe4! winning for Black) 21 Bd5! (In a Portisch-Polugaevsky game from the 1970 Palma de Mallorca Interzonal, White played 21 Rxd4 Qxd4 22 Re1 but had insufficient compensation for the sacrificed exchange and lost quickly) 21 ...Bxc3 (21 ...Bxd5 22 Rxd4! Bc4 [if 22 ...Qxd4 23 Nxd5 Qc5 24 Rc1 Qd6 25 Rc6!] 23 Qd2 with advantage to White or 21 ...Nxd5 22 Rxd4 Nxc3 [again 22 ...Qxd4 23 Nxd5 Qc4 24 Qg4 is good for White] 23 Bxc3 and White stands better) 22 Bxc3 Qxc3 23 Bxb7 Ra7 with chances for both sides.

(b) 11 Ne4 b5 12 Nxf6+ Qxf6 13 Qe4 Bb7 14 Bd3 g6 15 dxc5 Nb4! 16 Qe5! (after 16 Qxb7 Nxd3 Black stands better despite a temporary pawn minus) 16 ...Qxe5 17 Nxe5 Nxd3 18 Nxd3 Rfd8 19 Ne5 Bc7 20 Nf3 a5 21 Nd4 Rd5! 22 c6 Bc8 23 Bd2 e5 24 Nf3 Bg4 25 e4 Rd6 Black regains the pawn and thus reaches an equal position (Gligorić-Unzicker, Ljubljana 1969).

(c) 11 dxc5 Qxd3 12 Bxd3 Bxc3 13 bxc3 Na5 14 Rb1 Rd8! 15 Bc2 Bd7 16 Ne5 Rac8 regaining the pawn when the two black knights are a match for the two white bishops owing to the weakness of the white Q-side pawns.

Polugaevsky tried 10 Bd3 in the first game of the match, but after 10 ...

cxd4 11 exd4 Bb6 12 Be3 Nd5
13 Bg5 (Gligoric tried 13 Nxd5 exd5
14 h3 against Karpov in the Hastings
1971—2 tournament, and after
14 ...Ne7 15 Bg5 f6 16 Bd2 Bf5
17 Bb4 Bxd3 18 Qxd3 Re8 19 Rfe1
Qd7 20 Bc5 Bc7 21 Bxe7 Rxe7
22 Rxe7 Qxe7 23 Qb5 Qf7 24 Kf1
Bd6 the game was agreed drawn)
13 ...f6 14 Be3!? Karpov could have
tried 14 ...Nxe3 15 fxe3 e5! After
his 14 ...Nce7 15 Qc2 Nxe3
16 fxe3 g6 17 Bc4 White had a small
advantage.

10 ...a7-a6
In the seventh game of the match
Karpov chose the 'inferior' 10 ...Bb6
when 11 dxc5 Bxc5 12 b4 Bd6
13 Bb2 Qe7 14 Qc2 Bd7 15 Rfd1
Ne5! gave an equal game.

11 Ba2-b1
Polugaevsky got nowhere with his
11 Na4 in game 3. After 11 Na4 cxd4
12 exd4 h6! 13 Bf4 Bc7! 14 Bxc7
Qxc7 15 Qe2 Rd8 16 Rfd1 Bd7
17 Rac1 Be8 18 Nc3 Rd6! Black had
already equalized. The text move aims
at an interesting pawn sacrifice.

11 ...Ba5-b6

12 Qd1-c2! g7-g6
Acceptance of the gambit by
12 ...cxd4 13 exd4 Nxd4 14 Nxd4
Bxd4 would give White a strong
initiative after 15 Bg5.

13 d4xc5 Bb6xc5

14 b2-b4 Bc5-e7
A possible improvement for Black
was 14 ...Bd6, intending 15 ...Qe7.

15 Bc1-b2 e6-e5

16 Rf1-d1 *(see Diagram 62.2)*
Black's opening play has been refuted
by White's clever twelfth move.
Already Black's situation is uncomfortable, and his queen is embarrassed. The choice of the e8 square
for the queen is neither better nor
worse than the c7 square. 16 ...Qc7
would allow the strong continuation
17 Ba2 Bg4 18 Nd5 Nxd5 19 Bxd5
with eyes on the weak e5 pawn.

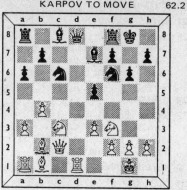

KARPOV TO MOVE   62.2

POLUGAEVSKY

16 ...Qd8-e8
A fork on c7 is now difficult to
prevent.

17 b4-b5
White could also have improved his
position by the simple move 17 h3.
The text move allows a drawing
chance for Black.

17 ...a6xb5

18 Nc3xb5 Bc8-f5

19 Qc2-e2 Bf5xb1?
This loses the exchange. The correct way, according to Polugaevsky,
was 19 ...e4! 20 Nh4 Bg4 21 f3
exf3 22 gxf3 Bh5 23 Nc7 Qc8
24 Nxa8 Qh3 when Black has some
chances. After the text move he has
a losing position.

20 Nb5-c7! Qe8-b8

21 Nc7xa8 Bb1-f5
After 21 ...e4 22 Raxb1 exf3
23 Qxf3 the f6 knight is en prise,
and so White retains his extra
exchange.

22 Na8-b6 e5-e4

23 Nf3-d4 Nc6xd4

24 Bb2xd4 Bf5-g4

25 f2-f3
If 25 Qb2 then 25 ...Bxd1 26 Bxf6
Bxf6 27 Qxf6 Qd8! equalizes.

25 ...e4xf3

26 g2xf3 Bg4-e6

27 Ra1-c1 Rf8-d8

28 Qe2-b2!

Black's position is hopelessly lost, but even in such adverse circumstances Karpov continues to play the best moves.

28 ...Nf6-e8

29 Bd4-e5 Be7-d6

After 29 ...Qa7 30 Qb5! Ng7 31 Rxd8+ Bxd8 32 Bd4 Qxa3 33 Ra1 White wins comfortably.

30 Be5xd6 Rd8xd6

31 Qb2-b4?

Better was 31 Qb5! Qd8 32 Rxd6 Nxd6 33 Rd1.

31 ...Qb8-d8!

32 Rd1xd6 Ne8xd6

33 Rc1-d1 Qd8-g5+

At last Black achieves some counterplay. This is due solely to White's slip at move 31. With his queen on b5 White would prevent such counterplay.

34 Kg1-f2 Nd6-f5

35 Qb4-f4 Qg5-f6

36 Nb6-a4!

The alternative 36 Nd7 allows 36 ...Bxd7 37 Rxd7 Qb2+

36 ...Be6-b3!

37 Rd1-d2?

After this move White can only draw. Better was 37 Re1 when White retains winning chances.

37 ...g6-g5!

38 Qf4-b8+

If 38 Qb4 then 38 ...Bxa4 39 Qxa4 Qe5 wins a key pawn.

38 ...Kg8-g7

39 Na4-b2 Bb3-d5

40 Nb2-d3

Taking the bishop would lose the e3 pawn after 40 ...Qxb2+ 41 Ke1 Qc1+.

40 ...Nf5-d6!

41 Nd3-f4!

Opting for the draw. By now Black has dangerous attacking chances.

41 ...g5xf4

42 Rd2xd5 Qf6-b2+

43 Kf2-f1 f4xe3

The winning tries 43 ...Qc1+ (to take the e3 pawn with check) and 43 ...Qb1+ (to win the rook by 44 ...Qa2+) are adequately met by 44 Kg2 and 44 Ke2 respectively.

44 Rd5-g5+ Draw agreed

After 44 ...Kh6 45 Qxd6+ Kxg5 46 Qe7+ a level queen-and-pawn ending is reached.

KARPOV TO MOVE   62.3

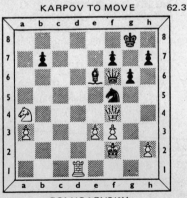

POLUGAEVSKY

Game 63

BLACK Polugaevsky   Sicilian Defence, Najdorf Variation
Candidates' Match (quarter-final, sixth game) Moscow 1974

Karpov at last plays the opening correctly (which he had failed to do in the second and fourth games) and quickly reaches an advantageous position. A two-pawn sacrifice leads to some complications, but on regaining the material Karpov has a winning position.

1 e2-e4   c7-c5

2 Ng1-f3   d7-d6

3 d2-d4   c5xd4

4 Nf3xd4   Ng8-f6

5 Nb1-c3   a7-a6

6 Bf1-e2

So after some tries with 6 f4 and 6 Bg5 (see Games 57 and 53 respectively) Karpov returns to his trusty 6 Be2.

6 . . . e7-e5

7 Nd4-b3   Bf8-e7

8 0-0   Bc8-e6

9 f2-f4   Qd8-c7

10 a2-a4   Nb8-d7

11 Kg1-h1!

Karpov's improvement on his games with Bronstein (Game 30), Robert Byrne at the 1973 Leningrad Interzonal, and Stoica at the Student Olympiad, Graz 1972, which all continued (with move transposition) 11 f5 Bc4 12 Be3 0-0 13 a5 b5 14 axb6 Nxb6 15 Kh1 Rfc8 16 Bxb6 Qxb6 17 Bxc4 Rxc4 18 Qe2. White achieved nothing after the 18 . . . Rac8! of the last two of these games.

11 . . . 0-0

12 Bc1-e3

The threat now is to take control of the c4 square. After for example 12 . . . Rac8 13 f5! Bc4 14 a5 Rfd8 15 Ra4! White's advantage is clear. So Black is obliged to exchange on f4.

12 . . . e5xf4

13 Rf1xf4

POLUGAEVSKY TO MOVE   63.1

KARPOV

Nimzo-Indian Defences were played in all the odd-numbered games of the match (where Karpov had black). Najdorf Sicilians were played in all four even games. This position was reached four times. In the second match game Polugaevsky chose 13 . . . Rfe8, but after 14 Nd4 Ne5 15 Nf5! Ng6 16 Rf1 Bf8 17 Qd4 (17 Bd4! is better) Black was already in trouble. The other three games all contained Polugaevsky's improvement.

13 . . . Nd7-e5

14 a4-a5!

Improving on the fourth match game, where Karpov played the inaccurate 14 Nd4 Rad8! 15 Qg1 Rd7 16 Rd1 Re8 and then the mistake 17 Nf5, when 17 . . . Bd8! gave Black the edge.

14 ...Nf6-d7?!

For 14 ... Rfe8 see Game 64.

15 Rf4-f1

Preventing the threat of 15 ... Bg5.

15 ...Be7-f6

16 Nc3-d5! Be6xd5

17 Qd1xd5!

Initiating a brilliant two-pawn sacrifice.

17 ...Qc7xc2

18 Nb3-d4 Qc2xb2

19 Ra1-b1 Qb2-c3

20 Nd4-f5

POLUGAEVSKY TO MOVE   63.2

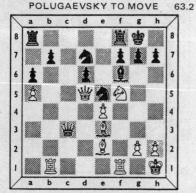

KARPOV

Now is the time to assess White's sacrifice. He is bound to regain the d6 pawn and thus maintain pressure on the b7 and f7 pawns also. Polugaevsky's strategy is to attack the exposed white bishops and at the same time bring his d7 knight via c5 to the excellent post d3, where it will overlook e5, f2, c1, and e1. In effect he will sacrifice the extra pawn to achieve this aim. The continuation is most interesting—each player is striving to fulfil his own ideas and to fore-stall his opponent.

20 ...Qc3-c2!

Removing the queen, with tempo, to a safer square. The immediate 20 ... Nc5 is bad on account of 21 Bd4 Qc2 22 Nxd6.

21 Rb1-e1?!

More logical would have been 21 Rfe1: e.g. 21 ... Nc5 22 Nxd6 Ncd3 23 Bxd3 Nxd3 24 Red1 Nf2+ 25 Bxf2 Qxf2 26 e5 when White has a clear and substantial advantage. The text move allows an ingenious defence overlooked by Polugaevsky at the board.

21 ...Nd7-c5?!

Better was 21 ... Rad8! 22 Nxd6 Nb8! 23 Qc5 Qxc5 24 Bxc5 Rd7! or 22 Qxb7 Nc5 23 Bxc5 dxc5 and in both cases Black has the initiative.

22 Nf5xd6 Nc5-d3

23 Be2xd3 Ne5xd3

24 Re1-d1 Nd3-b4

25 Qd5xb7

Interesting is 25 Qh5!? threatening 26 e5 or 26 Rxf6: e.g.

(a) 25 ... Rad8? 26 Rxf6 gxf6 27 Bh6 Kh8 28 Nxf7+ wins for White.

(b) 25 ... Qc3 26 Bd2 followed by 27 Rxf6 gives the same result: 26 ... Qb2 27 Rxf6 gxf6 28 Bh6 Kh8 29 Nxf7+! Rxf7 (29 ... Kg8 allows mate by 30 Qg4+ Kxf7 31 Qg7+ Ke6 32 Qd7+ Ke5 33 Qf5) 30 Qxf7 Rg8 31 Bg7+! and mate in two.

(c) 25 ... Be7 26 Rxf7!! Bxd6 27 Rxg7+! Kxg7 28 Bd4+ Kg8 29 Qg4+! Kf7 30 Qd7+! and now:

(c1) 30 ... Be7 31 Rf1+ Kg6 32 Qe6+ Bf6 (32 ... Kg5 33 Be3+ Kh5 34 Qh6+ and 32 ... Kh5 33 g4+ allow quick mates) 33 Bxf6! and White, although a rook down, has a winning attack (33 ... Qc6 34 Qf5+ Kf7 35 Qxh7+! and 36 Qe7 mate).

(c2) 30 ... Kg6 31 Qxd6+ when Black, without the help of his bishop, is quickly mated: 31 ... Kg5 32 Be3+ with mate in two, or 31 ... Kh5 32 g4+ with mate in four.

Black's best defence appears to be 25 ... Qb2 when 26 Rb1 can be met by 26 ... Qe5! or 26 Nc4 by 26 ... Qb3! In the first of these lines White

can win a pawn by 27 Qxe5 Bxe5
28 Nxf7 Rxf7   29 Rxf7 Kxf7
30 Rxb4 Rd8!   31 Rxb7+ Ke6, but
the win is still far from clear.

25 ... Ra8-b8

26 Qb7-a7
The continuation 26 Qd7 Rbd8
27 Qf5 Nd3!? is unclear according
to Polugaevsky.

POLUGAEVSKY TO MOVE   63.3

KARPOV

The only reasonable way for Black to
deal with White's K-side offensive is
to bring his queen across to the
defence by 26 ... Qe2! 27 Rde1 Qh5.
Instead of this Polugaevsky allows the
white queen to come tearing back to
the K-side and demolish the remains
of his defences.

26 ... Qc2-c6?

27 Be3-f4!
The exchange sacrifice on f6 is
promising, but the text move is even
stronger.

27 ... Rb8-a8

28 Qa7-f2   Ra8-d8

29 Qf2-g3   Qc6-c3

30 Rf1-f3   Qc3-c2

31 Rd1-f1
White has a winning position as Black
is unable to defend both the f7 and g7
pawns simultaneously.

31 ... Bf6-d4

32 Bf4-h6   Nb4-c6

33 Nd6-f5   Qc2-b2
A prettier finish would have been
33 ... Be5   34 Bxg7!! Bxg3   35 Rxg3
h5   (the only move) 36 Bf6+ Kh7
37 Rg7+ Kh8   38 Rxf7+ Kg8   39 Nh6
mate.

34 Bh6-c1!
Winning the exchange and a pawn.

34 ... Qb2-b5

35 Nf5-h6+   Kg8-h8

36 Nh6xf7+   Rf8xf7

37 Rf3xf7   Bd4-f6

38 Qg3-f2   Kh8-g8

39 Rf7xf6   g7xf6

40 Qf2xf6   Black resigns
Besides being two pawns behind
Black has a fatally weak king position.

Game 64

BLACK Polugaevsky   Sicilian Defence, Najdorf Variation
Candidates' Match (quarter-final, eighth game) Moscow 1974

This proved to be the final game of the match, for Karpov won his required
third game. As in his later match with Spassky, the best was saved until the
last. Karpov allows a dangerous-looking exchange of queen and pawn for
two rooks, but thereafter his bishops dominate the board in a few moves
and the end is inevitable.

1	e2-e4	c7-c5
2	Ng1-f3	d7-d6
3	d2-d4	c5xd4
4	Nf3xd4	Ng8-f6
5	Nb1-c3	a7-a6
6	Bf1-e2	e7-e5
7	Nd4-b3	Bf8-e7
8	0-0	Bc8-e6
9	f2-f4	Qd8-c7
10	a2-a4	Nb8-d7
11	Kg1-h1	0-0
12	Bc1-e3	e5xf4

The Soviet player Klovan (see Game 21) has experimented with this variation since this match. In Klovan-Gutman, USSR 1974, the continuation was 12 ... Bc4 13 a5 Rac8 14 Bxc4 Qxc4 15 Ra4 Qc6 16 Qf3 (16 f5 Rfd8 17 Qf3 h6 18 Raa1 Nc5 19 Nd5 gives White the advantage) 16 ...Bd8 17 Nd2 b5 18 axb6 Bxb6 19 Bxb6? (19 Rxa6! Qb7 20 Ra2 is correct and gives White the advantage) 19 ...Qxb6 and Black went on to draw, although he still stands worse at this point.

13	Rf1xf4	Nd7-e5
14	a4-a5	Rf8-e8!

Polugaevsky's improvement on the sixth game. Tukmakov tried 14 ... Rac8 against Klovan but ran into trouble after 15 Nd4 Rfe8 16 Nf5 Bf8 17 Qd2 Nfd7 18 Bd4 g6 19 Raf1!?

15	Be3-b6

Klovan tried to improve on Karpov's play here by 15 Nd4 against Kirpičnikov. After 15 ... Qd7 16 Rf1 Rac8 17 Nf5 Bxf5 18 Rxf5 Nc4 19 Bd4 Nxe4 20 Bg4 Nxc3 21 bxc3 Bf8 22 Qd3 g6 23 Raf1 Ne5 24 Bxe5 Rxe5 25 Rxe5 Qxg4 26 Re4 White stood better but the game was eventually drawn.

15	...Qc7-d7
16	Ra1-a4!?	Ra8-c8!
17	Ra4-d4

KARPOV

The critical point is reached. Polugaevsky should act swiftly by 17 ... Rxc3! 18 bxc3 Qc6 when not only would he threaten the c3 pawn, and soon the e4 pawn too, but also he would reduce the scope of the white rooks and bishop on b6. The threat is 19 ... Nfd7 winning a pawn. White must provide a square for the bishop and at the same time keep the e4 pawn protected. The continuation might be 19 Rb4 Qxc3 20 Ra4! when the game is to say the least unclear.

After his actual choice Black's position remains horribly cramped, and because he cannot free his game the decisive combination is not far off.

17	...Qd7-c6?
18	Rd4-d2!

Completing a most unusual rook manœuvre (a1-a4-d4-d2). This move allows the bishop on b6 a retreat square, and at the same time keeps up the pressure on the d-file. But the main point of the move is the win of the queen as occurred in the game.

18	...Be6xb3

After 18 ...Ng6 19 Nd4 would force Black even further back and at the same time save the menaced e4 pawn. The immediate 18 ...Nfd7 would lose the queen to 19 Nd4.

19	c2xb3	Nf6-d7

20 Bb6-g1 Be7-g5
This series of exchanges turns out
badly for Black, but after the alternative 20 ... Rcd8 White can play either
21 b4?! Bg5 22 Rxd6 Bxf4 23 Rxc6
Nxc6, or simply 21 Rf1.

21 Rd2xd6 Bg5xf4

22 Rd6xc6 Rc8xc6

POLUGAEVSKY   64.2

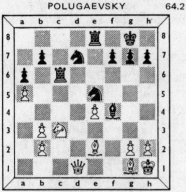

KARPOV TO MOVE

At first sight Black appears to have
good value for his queen. He has two
rooks and a secure blockade of the e5
square, and White's bishops are at the
moment ineffective; but with a few
blows in the right places Karpov unleashes the full power of the bishops,
and thus establishes a winning advantage.

23 b3-b4!
The b4-b5 advance cannot be prevented, and so Black tries to arrange
his pieces in their most constructive
fashion.

23 ... Nd7-f6
The alternative was 23 ... Rcc8, but
even in that case White stands better
after 24 b5 axb5 25 Bxb5 Red8.

24 b4-b5 Rc6-e6

25 b5xa6 b7xa6

26 g2-g3 Bf4-g5

27 h2-h4 Bg5-h6

28 Bg1-b6!
The bishops have a target: the end is
in sight.

28 ... Ne5-d7

29 Be2-c4 Re6-e5

30 Qd1-b3!
Now 30 ... Rf8 loses the exchange to
31 Bc7: e.g. 31 ... Nc5 32 Qa3! Rh5
33 Be2, or 31 ... Ree8 32 Bd6. So
Black must lose the f7 pawn also.

30 ... Re8-b8

31 Bc4xf7+ Kg8-h8

32 Qb3-c4!
Accurate to the last. Now 32 ... Nxb6
33 axb6 Re7 loses to 34 e5! Rxe5
35 b7.

32 ... Bh6-d2

33 Bb6-c7
Decisive. White wins back the two
rooks for his queen, and comes out a
pawn up.

33 ... Re5-c5
After 33 ... Rc8 34 Qxa6 wins
comfortably.

34 Qc4xc5 Nd7xc5

35 Bc7xb8 Bd2xc3

36 b2xc3 Nf6xe4

37 c3-c4
Of course the two knights are useless
against two such powerful bishops.

37 ... Nc5-d7

38 Bb8-c7 g7-g6

39 Bf7-e6 Ne4-c5

40 Be6xd7! Nc5xd7

41 Bc7-d6 Black resigns
The advance of the c-pawn will cost
Black a piece. An excellent game by
Karpov, who must have assessed
Black's queen 'sacrifice' before his
rook manœuvre on move 16!

Game 65

WHITE Spassky   Caro-Kann Defence
Candidates' Match (semi-final, sixth game) Leningrad 1974

Spassky had had great difficulties in breaking down the Caro-Kann Defence in the world championship match with Petrosian in 1966. Karpov played this opening in the second, fourth, sixth, and eighth games of this match: from four games he scored one win and three draws. In the tenth game he resorted to his favourite Breyer Variation, Ruy López, but by then he had a commanding 3-1 lead.

1 e2-e4   c7-c6

2 d2-d4   d7-d5

3 Nb1-c3   d5xe4

4 Nc3xe4   Bc8-f5
The other possibilities here are 4 ... Nf6 and 4 ... Nd7. All three variations are solid and reliable.

5 Ne4-g3   Bf5-g6

6 Ng1-f3   Nb8-d7

7 Bf1-d3
Spassky got nothing from his pet variation 7 h4 against Karpov in the fourth game, and so reverts to this solid line. In the eighth game (66) he switched back to 7 h4 once more.

7 ...e7-e6

8 0-0   Ng8-f6

9 c2-c4
According to Schwarz the most accurate move order is 9 Re1! Be7 10 c4. By this means White prevents the black bishop from developing on its aggressive d6 square (as 9 ... Bd6 is met by 10 Nf5).

9 ...Bf8-d6

10 b2-b3   0-0

11 Bc1-b2   Qd8-c7
Karpov chose the freeing line 11 ...c5 in game 2 of the match. After 12 Bxg6 hxg6 13 Re1 Qc7 14 dxc5 Bxc5 15 Qc2 Rfd8 16 Ne4 Nxe4 17 Qxe4 that game was agreed drawn.

12 Bd3xg6   h7xg6

13 Qd1-e2   Rf8-e8

14 Ng3-e4   Nf6xe4

15 Qe2xe4   Bd6-e7

16 Ra1-d1   Ra8-d8

17 Rf1-e1

KARPOV TO MOVE   65.1

SPASSKY

Now that the rooks are centralized we can assess the position. Black's position is cramped but solid. His bishop on e7 is well placed to prevent a white K-side attack by Ng5 Qh4 etc.; it can neutralize the white queen's bishop by Bf6 at a suitable moment; and as in the game it can help with the undoubling of the g-pawns by g6-g5-g4. Nevertheless it is White who holds the advantage. He can plan for a central pawn-break by d4-d5 and thus put pressure on the black pieces.

17 ... Qc7-a5!

The beginning of an ingenious combination of moves.

18 a2-a3   Qa5-f5

19 Qe4-e2

The exchange of queens would seriously lessen White's central pressure.

19 ...g6-g5

20 h2-h3

The immediate 20 d5! was better.

20 ...g5-g4

21 h3xg4   Qf5xg4

22 d4-d5!   c6xd5

23 c4xd5

Black is in some difficulty, and it is only by accurate play that he can hold White to a small advantage only.

23 ...e6-e5!

The only move. After 23 ...exd5 24 Rxd5 Black is in great difficulty.

24 d5-d6

To capture the e-pawn does not help White:

(a) 24 Nxe5 Qxe2 25 Rxe2 Bxa3! 26 Bxa3 Rxe5 27 Rxe5 Nxe5 and Black can blockade the dangerous passed pawn.

(b) 24 Nxe5 Qxe2 25 Rxe2 Bd6! 26 R1e1 Nxe5 27 Bxe5 Bxa3 with advantage to Black.

24 ...Be7-f6

25 Nf3-d2?

This seemingly strong plan of exchanging queens and at the same time bringing the knight to e4 is in fact a near-losing blunder, as Karpov brilliantly demonstrates. The correct plan was 25 Qb5, with eyes on the weak Q-side pawns. After 25 ...e4! 26 Nh2 Qe6 27 Bxf6 Nxf6 28 Qxb7 Rd7 29 Qb4 Red8 30 Qa4 Rxd6 31 Rxd6 Rxd6 32 Qxa7 Qxb3 33 Nf1 White stands a little better, owing to his outside passed pawn.

25 ...Qg4xe2

26 Re1xe2 *(see Diagram 65.2)*

Now comes a brilliant concept. The d6 pawn is weak, so Karpov wins it!

SPASSKY

26 ...Rd8-c8!

Making way for the bishop.

27 Nd2-e4   Bf6-d8

28 g2-g4   f7-f6

The king is to be posted to e6. Note also that the bishop, previously so useless on f6, finds an excellent diagonal on a7-g1.

29 Kg1-g2   Kg8-f7

30 Rd1-c1   Bd8-b6

31 Re2-c2   Rc8xc2

32 Rc1xc2   Kf7-e6

Black stands much better now. It is difficult for White to hold on to his d6 pawn without seriously compromising his position.

33 a3-a4   a7-a5

34 Bb2-a3   Re8-b8

35 Rc2-c4   Bb6-d4

The threat of 36 ...b5! is yet another embarrassment for White.

36 f2-f4?!

Better was 36 Nc3 Bxc3 37 Rxc3, when Black has only a slight edge.

36 ...g7-g6

Naturally 37 f5+ could not be allowed. With his next move White renews this threat, but the exchange of knight for bishop increases Black's chances.

37 Ne4-g3   e5xf4

38	Rc4xd4	f4xg3
39	Kg2xg3	Rb8-c8
40	Rd4-d3	g6-g5
41	Ba3-b2	b7-b6
42	Bb2-d4?!	

In view of the fact that all Black's pawns are on black squares White should have tried the bishop-v.-knight ending after 42 Rc3! Rxc3 43 Bxc3 Kxd6 44 b4 axb4 45 Bxb4+ Kd5 46 a5! with a likely draw. But Black's best try here is 43 ... Nc5! 44 Kf3 Nxb3 45 d7 Kxd7 46 Bxf6 Nc5 47 Bxg5 Nxa4, when his chances of winning are better.

42	...	Rc8-c6
43	Bd4-c3	

Hoping for 43 ... Nc5 44 Re3+ Kf7 (if 44 ... Kd5? 45 Bxf6! and if then 45 ... Ne4+ 46 Rxe4 Kxe4 47 d7 wins for White) 45 Re7+ Kg6 46 Bd4! Rxd6 47 Bxc5 bxc5 when White has good drawing chances in the rook ending.

43	...	Rc6-c5

Karpov now sets about exchanging his knight for the white bishop before capturing the d6 pawn. In this way he obtains a favourable rook ending, unlike the one in the note above.

44	Kg3-g2	Rc5-c8
45	Kg2-g3	Nd7-e5
46	Bc3xe5	

Clearly 46 Re3 Kxd6 would leave Black in an excellent position.

46	... f6xe5	*(see Diagram 65.3)*

With accurate play (47 Kf3! Rd8 48 b4! Rxd6 49 Rb3) Black would be held to a small advantage, and the outcome would still be very much

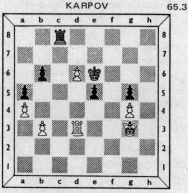

KARPOV   65.3

SPASSKY TO MOVE

in the melting pot. Spassky, however, commits a second blunder, after which he is lost.

47	b3-b4?	

47 Kf3! Rd8 48 Ke4 loses to 48 ... Rxd6 49 Rxd6+ Kxd6 50 Kf5 Kd5 51 Kxg5 e4 52 Kf4 Kd4 53 g5 e3 54 g6 e2 55 g7 e1=Q 56 g8=Q Qf1+ followed by 57 ... Qg1+.

47	... e5-e4!	
48	Rd3-d4	Ke6-e5
49	Rd4-d1	a5xb4

The rest is easy, for Karpov.

50	Rd1-b1	Rc8-c3+
51	Kg3-f2	Rc3-d3
52	d6-d7	Rd3xd7
53	Rb1xb4	Rd7-d6
54	Kf2-e3	Rd6-d3+
55	Ke3-e2	Rd3-a3

White resigns

Infiltration by 56 ... Kf4 cannot be prevented.

Game 66

WHITE Spassky   Caro-Kann Defence
Candidates' Match (semi-final, eighth game) Leningrad 1974

Although he had taken the lead by winning the sixth game of the match, and come close to increasing it in the seventh, Karpov sticks to the Caro-Kann Defence. This time Spassky tries his 7 h4 line and the result is an exciting game in which Karpov is called upon to defend in an unusual and brilliant manner.

1 e2-e4   c7-c6

2 d2-d4   d7-d5

3 Nb1-c3   d5xe4

4 Nc3xe4   Bc8-f5

5 Ne4-g3   Bf5-g6

6 h2-h4   h7-h6

7 h4-h5   Bg6-h7

8 Ng1-f3   Nb8-d7

9 Bf1-d3   Bh7xd3

10 Qd1xd3   Ng8-f6

11 Bc1-d2

It is only here that theory takes an interest in the position. This variation has become popular since the 1966 Spassky-Petrosian match in which Spassky showed the potential of the plan 12 Qe2, intending 13 Ne5, as distinct from the old plan of developing the king's rook via h4. Karpov has played to avoid the 'old variation', since 10 ... Qc7 could be met by 11 Rh4 e6 12 Bf4 Bd6 13 Bxd6 Qxd6 14 Ne4 Qe7 15 Qa3!? with chances for both sides (Browne-Pomar, Siegen 1970). Should White play 11 Bf4, to try to take advantage of the move order, Black could safely reply 11 ... Qa5+ 12 Bd2 Qc7 when the text position is reached but with both sides having lost a tempo. In the fourth game of the match Karpov played 10 ... e6 and met Spassky's somewhat old-fashioned treatment of 11 b3 Ngf6 12 Bb2 by 12 ... Qa5+ 13 Bc3 (13 c3 Ba3! 14 0-0-0 Bxb2+ 15 Kxb2 0-0 equalizes) 13 ... Bb4

14 Bxb4 Qxb4+ 15 Qd2 Qxd2+ 16 Kxd2 with an equal game.

11 ... Qd8-c7

12 c2-c4   e7-e6

13 Qd3-e2!

Generally this move is preceded by 12 0-0-0, but it is the strongest continuation here.

13 ... Bf8-d6

14 Ng3-f5

This idea is one of the latest in Caro-Kann theory. With 12 0-0-0 (in place of 12 c4) the game Westerinen-Rytov, Tallinn 1973, continued 14 ... Bf4 15 Ne3 b5 16 Rh4 0-0-0 17 c4 Bxe3 18 fxe3 bxc4 19 Kb1 Kb7 20 Rc1 Nb6 21 Ne5 Rd5 22 a4 a5 23 b3 Rxe5 with chances for both sides and a complicated position. Also interesting is the piece-sacrifice 15 Nxg7+ Kf8 16 Nxe6+ fxe6 17 Qxe6.

14 ... Bd6-f4

15 Bd2xf4

Now the piece-sacrifice is unsound because of Spassky's choice of 12th move. The continuation 15 Nxg7+ Kf8 16 Nxe6+ fxe6 17 Qxe6 would lose outright to 17 ... Re8.

15 ... Qc7xf4

16 Nf5-e3   Qf4-c7

17 0-0-0   *(see Diagram 66.1)*

As in the sixth game White completes the opening with a spatial advantage, while Black's position, though cramped, is perfectly sound. Karpov yet again solves this problem by tactical means, ensuring a lively game ahead.

KARPOV TO MOVE   66.1

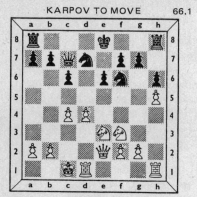

SPASSKY

KARPOV   66.2

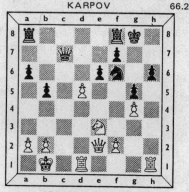

SPASSKY TO MOVE

17 ... b7-b5!
Taking immediate control of the white squares at c4, d5, and e4.

18 c4xb5   c6xb5+

19 Kc1-b1   0-0

20 g2-g4
To take the b5 pawn would allow Black excellent attacking chances.

20 ... Nf6-e4
Keeping one eye on g5 and one on c3. Now 21 Qxb5? loses to 21 ... Nc3+ 22 bxc3 Rab8.

21 Rh1-g1?!
This natural move was criticized by Kotov in his notes to the game. He recommended the far-from-obvious move 21 Ng2! with the continuations:

(a) 21 ... Ndf6 22 Ne5!

(b) 21 ... f5 22 Nfh4!

(c) 21 ... Ng5 22 Nxg5 hxg5 23 Qe3 Rac8 24 Rc1.

In each case White has the advantage.

21 ... Ne4-g5

22 Nf3xg5   h6xg5

23 d4-d5
After 23 Qxb5? Rab8 24 Qxg5? Rxb2+ wins immediately.

23 ... a7-a6!

24 h5-h6   g7xh6

25 Rg1-h1   Nd7-f6!

Suddenly White's attack fades away. Black still requires care to level the position, but Karpov plays every move with the utmost precision.

26 Rh1xh6   Kg8-g7

27 Rh6-h1
The obvious 27 R1h1 is satisfactorily met by 27 ... Rh8.

27 ... Ra8-d8

28 d5xe6   f7xe6

29 Ne3-c2   Qc7-f4!
To meet 30 Qxe6 by 30 ... Rxd1+ 31 Rxd1 Qxg4 etc.

30 f2-f3   Kg7-f7
Black's king is now perfectly safe, and so White's only chance is to play on the weakened pawns on g5, a6, and e6.

31 a2-a3   e6-e5

32 Nc2-b4   e5-e4!
Even though this costs Black a pawn, the removal of the e5 weakness is adequate compensation.

33 f3xe4   Rd8xd1+

34 Rh1xd1   Rf8-e8!

35 Nb4xa6   Qf4xe4+

36 Qe2xe4   Re8xe4

37 Na6-c7   b5-b4

38 a3xb4   Re4xb4

39 Rd1-f1   Rb4-f4   Draw agreed

Game 67

BLACK Spassky　Sicilian Defence, Scheveningen Variation
Candidates' Match (semi-final, ninth game) Leningrad 1974

This game is decided by one of the most unlikely looking winning moves
on record. Thus Karpov increased his lead to 3-1 and virtually settled the
match. This is the best of all Karpov's games in the candidates' matches
and even surpasses his defeat of Korchnoi in Game 71.

1 e2-e4　c7-c5

2 Ng1-f3　e7-e6

3 d2-d4　c5xd4

4 Nf3xd4　Ng8-f6

5 Nb1-c3　d7-d6

6 Bf1-e2

> Karpov plays the main-line Scheveningen; for this match he has also given
> up the Keres attack, 6 g4, with which
> he beat Hort in Game 29.

6 ... Bf8-e7

7 0-0　0-0

8 f2-f4　Nb8-c6

9 Bc1-e3　Bc8-d7

> Spassky prefers this modern treatment to the older lines with 9 ... a6
> and 10 ... Qc7. He chose 9 ... e5 in
> the first game of the match and later
> developed his queen's bishop on e6.

SPASSKY　67.1

KARPOV TO MOVE

10 Nd4-b3

> The two other moves here are 10 Qe1
> and 10 Kh1. After 10 Qe1 Black has
> two playable replies:

(a) 10 ... Qc7 11 Qg3 Nxd4 12 Bxd4
Bc6 13 Kh1 (after 13 Bd3 Rad8
14 Rae1 b6 15 Kh1 e5 16 fxe5 Nh5
17 Qh3 dxe5 18 Bxe5 Qxe5 19 Rf5
Nf4! the complications are over and
the position is equal) 13 ... Rad8
14 e5 (possibly better is 14 Rae1 b6
15 Bd3 Ne8) 14 ... dxe5 15 Bxe5
Qb6 16 f5 exf5 17 Rxf5 Bd6
(Suetin-Bagirov, 31st USSR Championship 1963). Now the queen sacrifice
18 Qxg7+ is incorrect, and 18 Rg5 g6!
is level. Boleslavsky suggests 16 ...
Bd6! 17 fxe6 fxe6 when Black has
excellent counterchances.

(b) 10 ... Nxd4 11 Bxd4 Bc6; now
White has a choice between:

(b1) 12 Qg3 g6! 13 Bd3 Nh5!
14 Qf2 Nxf4 15 Qxf4 e5 16 Qf2
exd4 17 Qxd4 Qa5 18 Kh1 Qe5
with equality (Shdanov-Kapengut,
USSR 1966).

(b2) 12 Bd3 Nd7 13 Rd1 e5!
14 fxe5 dxe5 (Matanović-Korchnoi,
European Team Championship 1965,
went 14 ... Nxe5 15 Kh1 Bf6
16 Qe2 Nd7 17 Bc4 [17 Bxf6 Nxf6
18 e5 is met by 18 ... Re8 19 Rxf6
gxf6 20 Qg4+ Kf8 21 Bxh7 Rxe5
when White has insufficient compensation for the sacrificed exchange]
17 ... Bxd4 18 Rxd4 Qb6 19 Rxd6
Qxb2 20 Qd2 with advantage to
Black) 15 Bf2 Bc5 16 Bc4 Qb6
17 Bb3 (the line 17 Nd5 Qxb2

18 Bxc5 Nxc5 19 Ne7+ Kh8
20 Nxc6 bxc6 is unsound—White has
no compensation for the sacrificed
pawn) 17 ... Nf6 18 Bxc5 Qxc5+
19 Qf2 Qxf2+ 20 Rxf2 with equal
chances (Parma-Udovicić, Zagreb
1965).

After 10 Kh1 Nxd4 11 Bxd4 Bc6
12 Bd3 (Better than the alternative
12 Bf3) 12 ...Nd7 13 Qe2 Black can
chose one of the three equalizing
attempts:

(a) 13 ...e5 14 Be3 exf4 15 Bxf4 Qb6
(also possible is 15 ...Ne5) 16 Rab1
Rac8 17 Bc4 with control of the d5
square and thus the advantage
(Neshmetdinov-Jansa, Sochi 1965).

(b) 13 ...Nc5 14 Bxc5 dxc5 15 e5 Qe8
(15 ...Qb6 may be better) 16 Ne4 b6
17 Nf6+ Bxf6 18 exf6 g6 White has
K-side attacking chances and stands
better (Szabo-Lehmann, European
Team Championship 1965).

(c) 13 ...a6! 14 Rad1 b5 (Liberzon-
Boleslavsky, USSR Team Championship 1966 went 14 ...Qc7 15 Rf3
e5 16 Be3 exf4 17 Bxf4 Bf6
18 Rh3 g6? 19 Bc4 Ne5 20 Nd5
Bxd5 21 Bxd5 Rac8 22 c3 with
advantage to White. Better for Black
is 18 ...Be5! 19 Nd5 Bxd5 20 exd5
Bxf4!) 15 Rf3 e5 16 Be3 Bf6 17 Nd5
(17 Rh3 is adequately answered by
17 ...exf4 18 e5 g6!) 17 ...Bxd5
18 exd5 Re8! when Black stands no
worse.

10 ...a7-a5
The alternative is 10 ...a6 11 Bf3
Rb8 12 g4 Be8! 13 g5 Nd7 14 Bg4
b5 15 h4 Nb6 when despite the
cramped nature of Black's position
his defensive resources are adequate
(Nikitin).

11 a2-a4
A good reply to Black's tenth move is
11 a3, when 11 ...a4 12 Nd2 d5
13 exd5 Nxd5 14 Nxd5 exd5 15 Nf3
leaves White with the advantage.

11 ...Nc6-b4
Intending Bd7-c6 and then a d6-d5
or e6-e5 break.

12 Be2-f3   Bd7-c6
The move 12 ...e5 was played in the
Portoroz play-off 1973 in a Geller-
Polugaevsky encounter. After 13 Kh1
Bc6 14 fxe5 dxe5 15 Qe2 White
stood a little the better.

13 Nb3-d4   g7-g6?!
To prevent Nd4-f5 after a Black
e6-e5 advance. Safer was 13 ...Qd7
intending 14 ...Rfc8.

14 Rf1-f2   e6-e5

15 Nd4xc6   b7xc6
If 15 ...Nxc6 then 16 f5! is uncomfortable for Black.

16 f4xe5   d6xe5

SPASSKY   67.2

KARPOV TO MOVE

17 Qd1-f1!
The exclamation mark here should
perhaps have been given to White's
14th move. This system of development highlights the weaknesses in the
black camp: a5 c5, and e5 are weak;
the queen prepares to come to c4,
exerting pressure along the a2-g8
diagonal; and the f- and d-files are
cleared for use by the rooks.

17 ...Qd8-c8

18 h2-h3   Nf6-d7

19 Bf3-g4
The white-squared bishop is of little
use to White, and so he is happy to
exchange it for a knight.

19 ...h7-h5?!

20 Bg4xd7   Qc8xd7

21 Qf1-c4   Be7-h4

22 Rf2-d2   Qd7-e7

23 Ra1-f1

Compare the relative developments:
White has pressure on the f- and d-files,
as well as on the a2-g8 diagonal. His
bishop is well-placed and only his
knight is poorly situated. Black, on
the other hand, has a poor development and a position riddled with weaknesses. White could win the exchange
here by 23 Bc5 Qg5 24 Rd7 Nxc2
25 Bxf8 Rxf8 but this would give
Black counterplay.

23 ... Rf8-d8

The winning move here is far from
obvious.

SPASSKY   67.3

KARPOV TO MOVE

24 Nc3-b1!

The immediate threat is to the black
Q-side pawns after 25 c3, but the long-
term threat to bring the knight to d2,
and then c4 or f3 (from where it would
menace e5, h4, and indirectly f7) is
much more serious and difficult to
meet.

24 ... Qe7-b7

25 Kg1-h2!

Threatening simply 26 g3 winning the
bishop.

25 ... Kg8-g7

26 c2-c3   Nb4-a6

27 Rd2-e2!

The extra pair of rooks will give White's
attack more bite.

27 ... Rd8-f8

28 Nb1-d2   Bh4-d8

29 Nd2-f3   f7-f6

In keeping out the knight Black has
fatally weakened his white squares. It
is now only a short time before the
final blow can be delivered.

30 Re2-d2   Bd8-e7

31 Qc4-e6   Ra8-d8

32 Rd2xd8   Be7xd8

The alternative recapture 32 ... Rxd8
allows 33 Nxe5 winning a pawn.

33 Rf1-d1   Na6-b8

Black's position is in ruins, and it is
not surprising to find that White has
a winning continuation.

34 Be3-c5   Rf8-h8

35 Rd1xd8!   **Black resigns**

After 35 ... Rxd8 36 Be7 Black can
chose between

(a) 36 ... Re8 37 Qxf6+ Kh7 38 Qf7+
and mate next move.

(b) 36 ... Rf8 37 Bxf8+ Kxf8 38 Qxf6+
winning at least two pawns.

A brilliant display by Karpov. The
17 Qf1 and 24 Nb1 manœuvres
indicated precisely the weaknesses in
the black position and a series of
positional ideas allowed Karpov to
destroy Black's defences by tactical
means in a swift and vicious attack.

Game 68

BLACK Spassky   Queen's Gambit Declined, Tartakover Defence
Candidates' Match (semi-final, eleventh game) Leningrad 1974

Karpov's brilliant display in the ninth game is all but repeated in this, the last game of the match. Once again a series of quiet positional moves build up the white position and a quick sacrificial stab is sufficient to bring about Black's collapse.

1 d2-d4

Karpov played this move in the third, fifth, and seventh games of the match. Spassky chose to defend with a King's Indian Defence in the third, a Nimzo-Indian Defence in the fifth and a Stonewall Defence in the seventh. Now he tries yet another defensive formation.

1 ... Ng8-f6

2 c2-c4 e7-e6

3 Ng1-f3

Spassky came close to winning the fifth game; so Karpov avoids the Nimzo-Indian this time.

3 ... d7-d5

4 Nb1-c3 Bf8-e7

5 Bc1-g5 h7-h6

6 Bg5-h4 0-0

7 e2-e3 b7-b6

The Tartakover Defence. An interesting choice by Spassky, for Karpov is also a devotee of this opening (see Game 17).

8 Bf1-e2

Ivkov in Game 17 preferred 8 Bd3.

8 ... Bc8-b7

9 Bh4xf6 Be7xf6

10 c4xd5 e6xd5

11 0-0 *(see Diagram 68.1)*

In return for the loss of the two bishops White has a solid position free from weaknesses. His first aim will be to conduct a minority attack—a Q-side pawn advance—in the hope of further weakening the black pawn structure.

SPASSKY TO MOVE   68.1

KARPOV

11 ... Qd8-d6

This move temporarily prevents the advance 12 b4, and prepares for the development of the knight to d7. Another idea is to play for the advance c7-c5 by 11 ... Qe7 12 Qb3 Rd8 13 Rad1 c5 14 dxc5 Bxc3 15 Qxc3 bxc5 16 Rc1 Nd7 with an unclear position (Korchnoi-Geller match 1971). Against Botterill at Hastings 1971-2 Karpov played 11 ... Re8 here, and after 12 b4 a6 13 Qb3 Qd6 14 Nd2 Nc6 15 a3 Ne7 16 Bf3 Rad8 17 g3 Nf5 18 Qc2 g6 19 Nb3 the position was about level.

12 Ra1-c1 a7-a6

13 a2-a3 Nb8-d7

14 b2-b4

The advance b4-b5 will soon become a powerful threat, and so Spassky at a small positional cost prevents it for ever.

14 ...b6-b5
Black loses control of c5, but has
compensation in the gain of c4. Both
players rapidly occupy their outposts.

15 Nf3-e1
Heading via d3 for c5.

15 ...c7-c6

16 Ne1-d3 Nd7-b6

17 a3-a4!
Gaining more space. Black cannot
contemplate capturing the pawn on
a4, since he would then lose his
control of c4; so he must allow a4-a5.

17 ...Bf6-d8
Hoping perhaps for a tactical a6-a5
break, and bringing the bishop to a
more active post on the b8-h2 diagonal.

18 Nd3-c5 Bb7-c8

19 a4-a5 Bd8-c7

20 g2-g3 Nb6-c4

21 e3-e4!

SPASSKY TO MOVE   68.2

KARPOV

A further spatial increase. Black is
obliged to capture this pawn, for he
cannot allow 22 e5; but after this
capture not only does he lose his
control of the c4 square but also his
pieces are severely harassed.

21 ...Bc8-h3

22 Rf1-e1
Also interesting was 22 e5. The text
move retains this threat and also lays

plans for persecution of the black
queen.

22 ...d5xe4

23 Nc3xe4 Qd6-g6
So as to meet 24 Bxc4 bxc4 25 Rxc4
by 25 ...f5 26 Nd2 f4 with a strong
attack.

24 Be2-h5! Qg6-h7
Better was 24 ...Qf5 25 f4 Qc8!
followed by 26 ...Bf5 when White
has no clear win; although he has
an advantage, and 26 Nf2! Bf5
27 Bf3 Bd6 28 N2e4 leaves Black in
all sorts of difficulties.

25 Qd1-f3!!
Threatening 26 g4. This move also
pressurizes the weak c6 pawn, and
prepares the decisive sacrificial breakthrough.

25 ...f7-f5

26 Ne4-c3 g7-g6
Winning a piece, but Karpov has fore-
seen all this and now unleashes his
winning combination.

SPASSKY   68.3

KARPOV TO MOVE

27 Qf3xc6! g6xh5

28 Nc3-d5!
There is no defence to the threats of
29 Qxc7, 29 Re7, and 29 Nf6+.
Spassky could resign here, but since
this would cost him the match, he
plays on for a few more moves.

28 ...f5-f4

After 28 ... Bd6 White could play
29 Nd7 regaining the exchange, or
29 Rxc4 bxc4 30 Qxd6 when he has
the added threat of 31 Nf4 Bg4
32 Qd5+ and 33 h3. In either case
White wins comfortably. The text
move allows Black same temporary
hopes based on the tactical tricks of
this advanced pawn.

29 Re1-e7!
Nicely calculated. Now 29 ... fxg3
would lose to 30 Nf6+! Rxf6 31 Qxa8+
Rf8 32 Qxf8+ Kxf8 33 Rxh7.

29 ... Qh7-f5
The only available square, but in view
of the fork on e7 Black must waste
another tempo.

30 Re7xc7   Ra8-e8

31 Qc6xh6   Rf8-f7

32 Rc7xf7   Kg8xf7

33 Qh6xf4
A third pawn goes, but Spassky still
hopes for counterplay.

33 ... Re8-e2

34 Qf4-c7+
Far stronger than the exchange of
queens.

34 ... Kf7-f8

35 Nd5-f4   Black resigns
The threats are just too numerous to
meet.

Game 69

BLACK Unzicker   Ruy López, Chigorin Defence
Nice Olympiad (A Final) 1974

Karpov won all seven of his games with the white pieces in Nice: this was
perhaps the most instructive. Unzicker gives up a file and a diagonal, after
which Karpov sweeps over the board. Karpov's mastery of this type of
position in general, and the López in particular, make 1 ... e5 almost a
losing blunder in reply to his 1 e4.

1 e2-e4   e7-e5

2 Ng1-f3   Nb8-c6

3 Bf1-b5   a7-a6

4 Bb5-a4   Ng8-f6

5 0-0   Bf8-e7

6 Rf1-e1   b7-b5

7 Ba4-b3   d7-d6

8 c2-c3   0-0

9 h2-h3   Nc6-a5
The Breyer Variation 9 ... Nb8
features in Games 16, 18, 44, 49, 50,
52, and 54. The unusual 9 ... Qd7
was played in Game 20.

10 Bb3-c2   c7-c5

11 d2-d4   Qd8-c7

12 Nb1-d2   Na5-c6
More reliable than Andersson's

12 ... Bb7 in Game 8.

13 d4-d5!?

UNZICKER TO MOVE   69.1

KARPOV

Karpov's liking for this central advance is so great that he prefers this unusual continuation to the more-common lines arising after 13 dxc5 dxc5 14 Nf1 Be6 15 Ne3 Rad8 16 Qe2.

13 ... Nc6-d8

The retreat 13 ... Nb8 is poor on account of 14 a4 Bb7 15 c4 b4 16 Nf1 Nbd7 17 g4, when White has the advantage on both sides of the board (Ceskovski-Henry, Dresden 1969). The other playable move was 13 ... Na5 14 b3! (14 Nf1 is met by the equalizing 14 ... Nc4) 14 ... Bd7 15 Nf1 Nb7 16 Ng3 (16 c4 would by transposition be the Karpov-Andersson game mentioned above) 16 ... c4 17 b4 Rfc8 18 Nf5 Bf8 19 Nh2 a5 20 Re3 axb4 21 cxb4 Bxf5 22 exf5 c3 23 Ng4 Be7 24 Nxf6+ Bxf6 25 Re4! when White has a clear plus (Geller-Mecking, Palma 1970).

14 a2-a4!

The most effective continuation. Other tries such as 14 b3, 14 Nf1, and 14 c4 are less threatening.

14 ... Ra8-b8

An attempt to close the Q-side by 14 ... b4 was strongly met by 15 Nc4 a5 16 Nfxe5! in Capablanca-Vidmar, New York 1927.

15 a4xb5

The alternative was 15 b4 c4 (15 ... Nb7 is no better) 16 Nf1 Ne8 (16 ... Bd7 is more promising) 17 axb5 axb5 18 N3h2 when White has chances on both wings.

15 ... a6xb5

16 b2-b4

The move 16 c4?! was played in Schmid-Smyslov, Havana 1967 but after 16 ... b4 17 Nf1 Ne8 18 Kh2 g6 19 g4 Ng7 20 Ng3 f6 21 Be3 Nf7 22 Rg1 Kh8 23 Nd2 Bd7 24 Ba4 Ra8 the position was level.

16 ... Nd8-b7

17 Nd2-f1 Bc8-d7

18 Bc1-e3!

In a Spassky-Korchnoi match game 1968, Spassky chose 18 Bd2 here (with the idea of bringing the f1 knight to e3). The game progressed 18 ... Ra8 19 Ne3 Rfc8 20 Kh2 Rxa1 21 Qxa1 Qd8 22 Qa7 Ra8 with approximate equality. Geller suggested 20 Rc1 after the game, claiming advantage for White. Karpov's system of development with Nf1-g3, Bc2-d3 and Qd1-e2 or d2 is much more effective in this position.

18 ... Rb8-a8

19 Qd1-d2 Rf8-c8

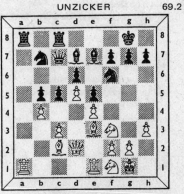

UNZICKER   69.2

KARPOV TO MOVE

White has the advantage. It is difficult for Black to contest the a-file, and at the same time he is embarrassed by the threat of 20 Bd3, followed in due course by Qe2 or Ra2! White also has chances on the K-side, and his forthcoming Ng3 will keep an eye open for any possibilities in that area. Unzicker decides to start his defence by securing his K-side position.

20 Bc2-d3

The threat was 20 ... cxb4.

20 ... g7-g6

21 Nf1-g3 Be7-f8

22 Ra1-a2!

Black has no way to combat this idea. His next move however releases a new avenue of attack for the white pieces.

22 ...c5-c4?

The temporary discomfiture to the d3 bishop is insufficient compensation for the opening of the g1-a7 diagonal. Black's position was already difficult in any case, for example: 22 ...Bg7 23 Rea1 and now 23 ...Qd8 can be met by 24 Rxa8 Rxa8 25 Rxa8 Qxa8 26 bxc5 Nxc5 27 Bxc5 dxc5 28 Nxe5 Nxe4 29 Nxe4 Qa1+ 30 Kh2 Bxe5+ 31 f4 Bg7 32 Nxc5 Bxc3 33 Qe2 when White's advantage is already substantial, or simply by 24 Qe2 c4 25 Bb1 with advantage.

23 Bd3-b1   Qc7-d8

No better was 23 ...Rxa2 24 Qxa2 Qd8 25 Qa7! Qc7 26 Bc2 and 27 Ra1.

24 Be3-a7!

Behind this piece White can build up effectively on the a-file. The bishop cannot be dislodged because the black pieces are so badly placed, particularly the knight on b7.

24 ...Nf6-e8

25 Bb1-c2   Ne8-c7

26 Re1-a1   Qd8-e7

27 Bc2-b1   Bd7-e8

Having for the moment achieved the best positioning of his Q-side pieces Karpov now switches to the K-side for the final assault. Notice that White's pieces are far better placed for a K-side attack than are Black's for a K-side defence.

28 Ng3-e2   Nb7-d8

29 Nf3-h2   Bf8-g7

30 f2-f4!

30 ...f7-f6?

Preferable was 30 ...exf4, but Black's lack of control of the key black squares f6 and d4 would soon tell.

31 f4-f5   g6-g5 *(see Diagram 69.3)*

A sad move to have to make. After this Black is completely lost, but even passive defence by 31 ...Bf7 would lose to a general assault such as 31 ... Bf7 32 Ng3 Ne8 33 Qf2 when the threats along the f-file, a-file and g1-a7 diagonal together with the possibilities of infiltration by the white

UNZICKER   69.3

KARPOV TO MOVE

queen to b6 leave Black helpless. The finish of the game is amusing for everyone except Unzicker. White has all the time in the world and simply exchanges the white-squared bishops and then infiltrates on the white squares. Black is powerless to prevent the execution of White's plans.

32 Bb1-c2

Heading for h5.

32 ...Be8-f7

33 Ne2-g3   Nd8-b7

34 Bc2-d1   h7-h6

35 Bd1-h5   Qe7-e8

36 Qd2-d1   Nb7-d8

37 Ra2-a3

The shuffling of the rooks is not strictly necessary, but is played as a safety measure to avoid any possible trouble.

37 ...Kg8-f8

Black cannot improve his position, and must just wait for the axe to fall.

38 Ra1-a2   Kf8-g8

39 Nh2-g4   Kg8-f8

40 Ng4-e3   Kf8-g8

41 Bh5xf7+   Nd8xf7

42 Qd1-h5   Nf7-d8

43 Qh5-g6   Kg8-f8

44 Ng3-h5   Black resigns

It is easy to see why!

Game 70

BLACK Kaválek   Sicilian Defence, Maroczy Bind
Nice Olympiad (A Final), 1974

Karpov increases his small spatial advantage in the ending until the positional and tactical threats overwhelm the black game. The final stages bring about strangulation of the black pieces, and Kaválek resigns as he is about to lose a second pawn. This game is a further example, although not such a good one, of Karpov's approach to rook-and-opposite-coloured-bishop endings. Here, as in Games 33 and 35, it is the tactical elements that decide the outcome.

1 c2-c4   c7-c5

2 Ng1-f3   g7-g6

3 d2-d4   c5xd4

4 Nf3xd4   Nb8-c6

5 e2-e4   Ng8-f6

6 Nb1-c3   d7-d6

7 Bf1-e2   Nc6xd4

The old variations with 7 ... Bg7 8 Be3 or 6 ... Bg7 7 Be3 Ng4 8 Qxg4 Nxd4 9 Qd1 are not popular in master chess, and the text move is the usual way in which this position is played.

8 Qd1xd4   Bf8-g7

9 Bc1-g5

Other possibilities here are

(a) 9 0-0 0-0   10 Qe3! Be6 (Gligorić recommends 10 ... Nd7 and 11 ... Nc5) 11 Bd2 Qb6?! (Better is 11 ... a6) 12 b3 Qxe3 13 Bxe3 with advantage to White (Petrosian-Browne, Nice Olympiad 1974).

(b) 9 Be3 0-0 10 Qd2 Be6 11 Rc1 Qa5 12 b3 a6! 13 f3 Rfc8! with counter-play for Black.

9 ... 0-0

It is strange that Kaválek chose this move here. A month or two earlier he had reached the same position as White against Visier at Lanzarote. Visier played 9 ... 0-0, Kaválek played 10 Qe3, and after 10 ... Qa5 11 0-0 Be6 12 Rac1 Rfc8 13 b3 a6 14 a4

Qb4 15 Bd1! Rab8 16 Qe1! White stood better, and won eleven moves later.

The major continuation here is 9 ... h6 10 Be3 0-0 11 Qd2 Kh7 12 0-0 Be6 when both the following are good for White:

(a) 12 Bd4 Rc8 14 b3 a6 15 Qe3! Nd7 16 Bxg7 Kxg7 17 f4 (Timman-Ribli, Amsterdam 1973).

(b) 13 f4 Rc8 14 b3 Qa5 15 a3 Bd7 16 f5 (Larsen-Fischer match 1971).

10 Qd4-d2   Bc8-e6

11 Ra1-c1   Qd8-a5

12 b2-b3   Rf8-c8

13 f2-f3   a7-a6

14 Nc3-a4   Qa5xd2+

15 Ke1xd2 *(see Diagram 70.1)*

Such endings as this are always favourable for White, who has a spatial advantage that Black will find difficult to combat. If for example Black were to engineer a freeing break by b7-b5 he would merely convert White's spatial advantage into a Q-side pawn majority. So Black can only wait for a chance to free his position by exchanges, or for a moment when a b7-b5 advance will be 'tactically and positionally playable'. White on the

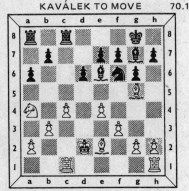

KAVÁLEK TO MOVE   70.1

KARPOV

other hand will first rearrange his
pieces into their most constructive
positions and then play for a pawn
attack on the K-side or in the centre
(i.e. e4-e5) in order to cramp the
black position still further. The threat
of 16 Nb6 can easily be met, but
when the white knight arrives on d5
it exerts its maximum pressure on the
black position.

15 ... Rc8-c6

16 Na4-c3   Ra8-c8

17 Nc3-d5   Kg8-f8

Black has a difficult choice here. He
is not afraid of doubling his pawns by
18 Bxf6 or 18 Nxf6, since the white
king would prevent exploitation of
the then-weak d6 pawn by the white
rooks. On the other hand the exchange 17 ... Bxd5 18 exd5 R6c7 has
a lot to be said for it. The two bishops
are conceded, but Black's position is
solid and difficult to exploit.

18 Bg5-e3   Nf6-d7

19 h2-h4!

The threat of 20 h5 cannot be met
by 19 ...h5 as 20 Nf4 Nc5 21 b4!?
or 21 Nxe6+ Nxe6 22 g4 are both
strong continuations for White. Thus
Black is after all forced to play the
exchange mentioned in the previous
note.

19 ... Be6xd5

20 e4xd5   Rc6-c7

21 h4-h5   Kf8-g8

Without the exchange on move 19
this move would leave the e7 pawn
en prise.

22 f3-f4

Both denying the black knight the
use of the e5 square and preparing to
force a further weakness on the black
pawn-structure by 23 Bg4. The two
white bishops together with the
general K-side pawn-storm now taking
place quickly force a deterioration in
Black's position

22 ... Nd7-c5

23 Be2-g4   Nc5-e4+

24 Kd2-d3   f7-f5

25 Bg4-f3   b7-b5

Black must act quickly to get any
counterplay at all. Both 25 ... Nc5+
26 Ke2 followed by 27 g4 and 25 ...
Nf6 26 h6 Bh8 27 Bb6 Rd7 28 Rce1
leave Black in a hopeless mess. After
the text move White must beware of
the possibility of infiltration on the
b- or c-files.

KAVÁLEK   70.2

KARPOV TO MOVE

26 g2-g4!   b5xc4+

27 Rc1xc4   Rc7xc4

28 b3xc4   Ne4-c5+

Black must move his knight, since the
immediate 28 ...Rb8 loses a pawn to

29 Bxe4 fxe4+ 30 Kxe4.

29 Be3xc5!

White gives up the two bishops, and at the same time allows bishops of opposite colours. At first sight this is a strange decision, but the impetus of the attack must be maintained, and in fact this impetus carries White through to win.

29 ... Rc8xc5

Black must be able to achieve counter-play quickly and so avoids 29 ... dxc5 30 h6 Bd4 31 gxf5 gxf5 32 Rh5 Rf8 33 Bg2, which wins comfortably for White. Also possible is the simple 31 Rb1 when Black will find it im-possible to answer the infiltration of the white rook.

30 h5-h6 Bg7-f8

After 30 ... Bh8 31 Rb1 is strong.

31 Kd3-c3?!

Karpov the materialist begins to take over. Geller in his notes to the game suggests 31 g5! here. After 31 ... Ra5 32 Rb1 Rxa2 (32 ... Ra3+ 33 Rb3) 33 c5! White is winning: e.g.

(a) 33 ... dxc5 34 d6! Ra3+ 35 Ke2 Rxf3 (if 35 ... exd6 36 Bd5+ Kh8 37 Rb8 mates in a few moves) 36 d7! and wins.

(b) 33 ... Ra3+ 34 Ke2 Rc3 (34 ... Rxf3 35 Kxf3 dxc5 36 Ra1 wins easily for White) 35 c6 Kf7 (what else is there?) 36 Ra1 and White wins.

It is a pity that Karpov did not crown his attack with such a brilliant finish.

31 ... f5xg4

32 Bf3xg4 Kg8-f7!

Although this move loses a pawn it represents Black's only drawing chance.

33 Bg4-e6+ Kf7-f6

34 Be6-g8 Rc5-c7

Threatening 35 ... Bxh6 36 Rxh6 Kg7 drawing.

35 Bg8xh7! e7-e6

36 Bh7-g8 e6xd5

37 h6-h7

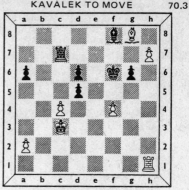

KAVÁLEK TO MOVE 70.3

KARPOV

37 ... Bf8-g7?

A blunder that allows White to win easily. Better was 37 ,.. Rxc4+ 38 Kd3 Bg7 when

(a) 39 h8=Q? Bxh8 40 Rxh8 Rc8! draws (but not 40 Kg7? when 41 Bxd5 Rc5 42 Rg8+ Kh7 43 Bb3 wins for White).

(b) 39 Bxd5! Rc5 40 Be4 and Black must lose at least one pawn. e.g.

(b1) 40 ... d5 41 Kd4 Ra5 42 Bxd5.

(b2) 40 ... Bh8 41 Rh6 Kg7 42 Rxg6+ Kxh7 43 Rxd6+ Kg8 44 Rxa6.

(b3) 40 ... Rc8 41 Rg1.

In all three cases the endings are lost for Black, but he can put up a much better fight than he is able to in the game.

38 Bg8xd5

Naturally 38 h8=Q is weak because of 38 ... Bxh8 39 Rxh8 Rc8! drawing (39 ... Kg7? loses to 40 Rh7+).

38 ... Bg7-h8

39 Kc3-d3 Kf6-f5

40 Kd3-e3 Rc7-e7+

41 Ke3-f3 a6-a5

42 a2-a4

Zugzwang. Black cannot move the bishop; so he must choose between:

(a) 42 ... g5 43 Rh5 Rg7 (43 ... Kg6

44 Rxg5+ Kxh7 45 Be4+ Kh6
46 Rg6+ Kh5 47 Rxd6 also wins for
White) 44 Be4+ Kf6 45 Rh6+ Ke7
46 f5! winning easily.

(b) 42 ...Kf6 43 Be4 with effects similar
to those in the game.

(c) 42 ...Re8 43 Rg1! Re7 44 Be4+!
Rxe4 45 Rg5+ winning comfortably.

Kavalek chooses the fourth possibility.

42 ...Re7-c7

43 Bd5-e4+ Kf5-f6

44 Rh1-h6 Rc7-g7
Also hopeless is 44 ...Kg7 45 Rxg6+
Kxh7 46 Rxd6+.

45 Kf3-g4 **Black resigns**
Again it is zugzwang. This time Black
must lost the valuable g6 pawn.
A beautiful ending by Karpov—ample
revenge for his loss to Kavalek at
Caracas in 1970.

Game 71

BLACK Korchnoi   Sicilian Defence, Dragon Variation
Candidates' Match (final, second game) Moscow 1974

It was interesting that Korchnoi chose the Dragon in his first game with
black. His defences to 1 e4 are all of the aggressive kind—the Dragon
Variation of the Sicilian and the Winawer Variation of the French are his
two favourites, although the Alekhine, the Pirc, and occasionally the López
also feature in his repertoire.

This first black was a disaster for Korchnoi. Karpov 'improved' on the
current theory of the opening and won quickly and convincingly. Korchnoi
did not try this opening again in the match, but switched instead to the
French Defence. The game itself must have been depressing for Korchnoi,
since many hours of opening analysis were immediately wasted.

1 e2-e4 c7-c5

2 Ng1-f3 d7-d6

3 d2-d4 c5xd4

4 Nf3xd4 Ng8-f6

5 Nb1-c3 g7-g6

6 Bc1-e3 Bf8-g7

7 f2-f3
Karpov embarks upon the sharpest of
all the variations against the Dragon—
the Rauzer attack.

7 ...Nb8-c6

8 Qd1-d2 0-0

9 Bf1-c4
After 9 0-0-0 Black has Konstantinov's
fine sacrifice 9 ...d5!

9 ...Bc8-d7

10 h2-h4 Ra8-c8
The alternative plan for Black is to
deploy his pieces by 10 ...Qa5 and
11 ...Rfc8 (see Game 4). The text
move and continuation were played
by Korchnoi in his match with Geller
in the previous candidates' series in
1971.

11 Bc4-b3 Nc6-e5

12 0-0-0 Ne5-c4
This exchange is a necessary part of
Black's plan. After 12 ...Qa5 Black
has reached a poor variation of the
alternative plan discussed in the
previous note since he would have
the 'wrong' rook on c8.

13 Bb3xc4 Rc8xc4

14 h4-h5!

A standard sacrifice in this position. A slow build-up would achieve nothing, since Black's counterplay by 14 ... Qa5 and 15 ... Rfc8 would be too dangerous. The opening of the h-file increases White's chances tremendously, and so is well worth the pawn. A similar idea occurred in Game 4.

14 ... Nf6xh5

To continue with Q-side operations immediately by 14 ... b5 14 ... Qa5 or 14 ... Qc7 would allow White to open the h-file by 15 hxg6 and thus exert great pressure on the black position. Black aims to sacrifice the exchange on c3 at a suitable moment and accepts this gambit pawn in the hope of gaining both material and positional compensation for his rook. After such a sacrifice not only would one of White's most dangerous pieces (his knight on c3) be removed but also Black would seize the initiative and force White to defend. All these variations have been analysed in great depth, and both players had so far played quickly.

15 g2-g4

The immediate 15 Bh6? loses to 15 ... Rxd4!

15 ... Nh5-f6

KORCHNOI   71.1

KARPOV TO MOVE

16 Nd4-e2!

A fine move, showing a true understanding of the position. Geller chose the sharp continuation 16 Bh6 in the fourth game of his Candidates' quarterfinal match with Korchnoi, Moscow 1971. The continuation 16 ... Nxe4! 17 Qe3 Rxc3 18 bxc3 Nf6 19 Bxg7 Kxg7 20 Rh2 Qa5 21 Nb3 Qxa2 22 Qxe7 Qa3+ 23 Kb1 Re8 24 Qxd6 Qxd6 25 Rxd6 left White with a slightly superior game, which he eventually won, but analysis of this line showed that 20 ... Rg8 or 20 ... Re8 (Zuckerman) would have been better for Black. After a spell in defence he can switch to counterattack and maintain the balance. Karpov's move has three ideas behind it. Firstly the K-side attack by 16 Bh6 is delayed by one move, but when it does come there will be a threat (after 17 Bh6) of 18 Bxg7 Kxg7 19 Qh6+ Kg8 20 g5 Nh5 21 Ng3 or 21 Nf4 with a mating attack. Secondly an exchange sacrifice by Black on c3 will now be useless, because White will be able to recapture with the e2 knight. (With the knight on d4 the weakening of the Q-side pawns, as in the Geller-Korchnoi game above, gives Black adequate counterplay against the white king.) Thirdly Black is threatened with 17 e5! dxe5 18 g5 which wins a piece for White. So a feasible defensive try of 16 ... Re8 would now lose a piece.

Korchnoi tries the theory recommendation but Karpov has an improvement ready for this line too.

16 ... Qd8-a5

17 Be3-h6   Bg7xh6

18 Qd2xh6   Rf8-c8

Now Black is prepared to meet 19 g5 Nh5 20 Ng3 (or 20 Nf4) by 20 ... Rxc3, when he has at least enough counterplay to draw.

19 Rd1-d3!

Another move in the class of Karpov's 16th. The threat to the Q-side pawns is now removed, so that 20 g5 Nh5 21 Ng3 Rxc3 22 bxc3 Rxc3 23 Nxh5

gxh5 24 Rxh5 wins for White.
Previous analysis had been concerned
with the tries 19 Rd5 and 19 g5 but
the quiet text move is sufficient to
bring about the downfall of the black
position.
Korchnoi's next move is his best try
but even this loses. There is no reasonable defence to the threat outlined
above, and so this position must be
considered lost for Black.

19 ... Rc4-c5

KORCHNOI   71.2

KARPOV TO MOVE

The finishing combination is pretty and
concludes a brilliant performance by
Karpov.

20 g4-g5!

By luring the black rook from the c-file
White prevents counterplay by Rxc2+
in answer to his Nd5.

20 ... Rc5xg5

To delay this capture by 20 ... Nh5
21 Nf4 Rxg5 would be even worse for
for Black: 22 Rd5 Rxd5 23 Ncxd5
Qxa2 24 Nxh5 gxh5 25 Nxe7+ Kh8
26 Qf6 is mate.

21 Rd3-d5! Rg5xd5

22 Nc3xd5 Rc8-e8

Were the black knight to capture on
d5 White would mate by Qxh7+ and
Qh8. With the text move Black is
hoping for 23 Nxf6+ exf6 24 Qxh7+
Kf8 when his king escapes to e7. But
again Karpov has the answer.

23 Ne2-f4!

Threatening 24 Nxf6+ and 25 Nd5
preventing the escape of the king to
e7. It is now clear that there can be
no defence.

23 ... Bd7-c6

KORCHNOI   71.3

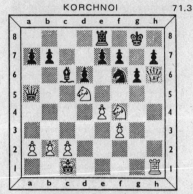

KARPOV TO MOVE

The alternative 23 ... Be6 loses to
24 Nxe6 fxe6 25 Nxf6+ exf6 26 Qxh7+
Kf8 27 Qxb7 Re7! 28 Qb8+ (28 Rh8+?
Kg7 29 Qxe7+ Kxh8 30 Qxf6+ Kh7
31 Qe7+ Kh6 32 Qxd6 Qxa2 gives
White some winning chances also)
28 ... Re8 29 Qxd6+ (29 Rh8+ Kg7!
and White must transpose into the line
above) 29 ... Kg8 (29 ... Re7 30 Rh8+
Kg7 31 Qxe7+ Kxh8 32 Qxf6+ this
time leaves White two pawns ahead;
29 ... Kf7 loses to 30 Qd7+ Re7
31 Rh7+ Kg8 32 Rxe7) 30 Qd7!
Then:

(a) 30 ... Qd8 31 Qh7+ Kf8 32 Qh8+
    Ke7 33 Qg7+ Kd6 34 Rd1+.

(b) 30 ... Rd8 31 Qh7+ Kf8 32 Qh8+
    Ke7 33 Qg7+ Kd6 34 Qxf6!

24 e4-e5!

The immediate 24 Nxf6+ exf6 25 Nh5
could be met by 25 ... Qg5+! 26 Qxg5
fxg5 27 Nf6+ Kf8! 28 Nxe8 Kxe8
29 Rxh7 g4! 30 fxg4 Bxe4 when
Black has good drawing chances. The
text move blocks the queen's route to
g5 and so 24 ... dxe5 now loses to
25 Nxf6+ exf6 26 Nh5.

Korchnoi tries the only other move.

24 ... Bc6xd5

25 e5xf6   e7xf6

26 Qh6xh7+   Kg8-f8

27 Qh7-h8+   Black resigns

After 27 ... Ke7 28 Nxd5+ Qxd5 (28 ... Kd8 29 Qxf6+ and 28 ... Kd7 29 Nxf6+ also win for White) 29 Re1+ White wins a rook, or queen for rook.

A beautifully balanced attack by Karpov, and a severe blow to Korchnoi's match preparations.

Game 72

BLACK Korchnoi   Petroff Defence
Candidates' Match, (final, sixth game) Moscow 1974

After his loss in the second game Korchnoi played the French Defence in the fourth game and succeeded in equalizing from the opening, and in gaining a slight endgame initiative. It was therefore a double surprise that Korchnoi should choose the Petroff Defence—firstly because he had achieved such a good position by playing the French and secondly because of the generally drawish nature of this particular opening. Korchnoi's style of play is not suited to this type of game and as we shall see his intentions were by no means passive. The key point in the game was between moves fourteen and sixteen when Korchnoi, unable to find a satisfactory continuation to his attack, used up almost all of his allotted time. When his flag fell on move 31 he was hopelessly lost.

1 e2-e4   e7-e5

2 Ng1-f3   Ng8-f6

3 Nf3xe5
Karpov prefers this move to the more aggressive line of 3 d4.

3 ... d7-d6

4 Ne5-f3   Nf6xe4

5 d2-d4   d6-d5
Smyslov played the passive 5 ... Be7 6 Bd3 Nf6 in Game 37.

6 Bf1-d3   Bf8-e7
The alternative is 6 ... Bd6 7 0-0 0-0 8 c4 when

(a) 8 ... c6 9 Qc2 Na6 10 Bxe4 dxe4 11 Qxe4 Re8 12 Qd3! Nb4 13 Qb3 Bf5 14 Bg5 with advantage to White (Keres).

(b) 8 ... Nf6 9 Nc3 dxc4 10 Bxc4 Bg4 11 h3 Bh5 12 Re1 gives White the edge.

7 0-0   Nb8-c6!
After 7 ... 0-0 8 c4 Nf6 9 Nc3 dxc4 (9 ... Nc6 is Keres's recommendation) 10 Bxc4 Bg4 11 Re1 Nbd7 12 h3 Bh5 13 g4 Bg6 White stands clearly better (Ree-Langeweg, Amsterdam 1968).

8 Rf1-e1
Karpov continues to play the theoretically best moves. 8 c4 Bg4 9 Nc3 allows Black to equalize by 9 ... Nxc3 10 bxc3 0-0 11 Rb1 dxc4 12 Bxc4 Na5 13 Bd3 c5 (Levenfish).

8 ... Bc8-g4

9 c2-c3
Keres analyses the line 9 c4!? Nf6 (9 ... Nxd4? loses to 10 Bxe4, whilst 9 ... f5 10 Nc3 Bxf3 11 gxf3 Nxc3 12 bxc3 0-0 13 cxd5 Qxd5 14 Qe2 and 9 ... Bxf3 10 Qxf3 Nxd4 11 Qe3 Nf5 12 Qh3 Nfd6 13 cxd5 Nf6 14 Bg5 [Chigorin-Schiffers, St. Peters-

burg 1879] are both strong for White)
10 cxd5 Nxd5 11 Nc3 0-0 12 Be4
Nf6 13 d5 (or simply 13 Bxc6 bxc6
14 h3) 13 ...Nb4 14 a3 Nxe4
15 Rxe4 Bxf3 16 Qxf3 Na6 17 b4
with advantage to White. Better for
Black in this line is simply 12 ... Be6.
An attempt to win a pawn by 9 Bxe4
dxe4 10 Rxe4 would lead to equality
after 10 ...Bxf3 11 Qxf3 (11 gxf3?
f5 12 Rf4 0-0 13 d5 Bg5 14 Ra4
Bxc1 15 Qxc1 Qxd5 gives advantage
to Black) 11 ...Nxd4 12 Qd3 Ne6.

9 ...f7-f5

10 Qd1-b3

After 10 c4!? best play for both sides
is 10 ...Bh4! 11 Bxe4! dxe4 12 d5
0-0 13 dxc6 exf3 14 Qxd8 Raxd8
15 cxb7 Rfe8 16 Rxe8 Rxe8 17 h3
with approximate equality (Tarrash-
Maroczy, Monte Carlo, 1902).

10 ...0-0

After 10 ...Bxf3 11 gxf3! Black
would have to lose a pawn.

11 Nb1-d2!

Lasker-Pillsbury, St. Petersburg 1895
went 11 Bf4? Bxf3 12 gxf3 Ng5
13 Kg2 Qd7 14 Qc2 Ne6 15 Bc1
Bd6 16 Nd2 Rae8 17 Nf1? Nexd4
18 Qd1 Rxe1 19 Qxe1 Nxf3! 20 Kxf3
f4 21 Qd1 Ne5+ 22 Ke2 Qg4+ 23 Kd2
Qxd1+ 24 Kxd1 Nxd3 with a winning
position for Black. Against 11 Nfd2
Schlechter gives 11 ...Nxf2! 12 Kxf2
Bh4+ 13 g3 f4! with a tremendous
attack, whilst 11 Qxb7 Rf6 12 Qb3
Rb8 13 Qc2 Rg6 leads to a position
similar to that in the game but with
Black having a tempo more. Karpov's
move is a significant improvement on
all this. The threat is to use the pin on
the a2-g8 diagonal to win a pawn at
e4 by 12 Bxe4 fxe4 13 Rxe4 or
12 Nxe4 Bxf3 13 Ng3!? Bg4 14 h3.

11 ...Kg8-h8 *(see Diagram 72.1)*

12 h2-h3!

Capablanca played 12 Nf1 in a match
game against Kostić in 1919, but after
12 ...Bxf3 13 gxf3 Nxf2! 14 Kxf2
Bh4+ 15 Ng3 f4 Black had a strong
attack.

KARPOV TO MOVE

As can be seen from the game referen-
ces given above this line is old and
has not been played much in the last
fifty years! One example however is
Stein-Anikaev, Kislovodsk 1972, which
continued here 12 Be2 Na5?! 13 Qa4
c5 14 Ne5 with slight advantage to
White. Gufeld gives 12 ...Rb8 as
advantageous for Black. Karpov's
accurate play brings him the best out
of the position.

12 ...Bg4-h5!?

The safe course of action was 12 ...
Bxf3 13 Nxf3 Rb8! when the
chances are about level—White's two
bishops are temporarily matched by
the well-posted black knight on e4.

13 Qb3xb7   Rf8-f6

14 Qb7-b3   Rf6-g6

15 Bd3-e2!

This move contains the black attack
by threatening simplification based on
16 Nxe4 fxe4 17 Ne5, or 16 Ne5
immediately. The point of Karpov's
12th move is now revealed—the bishop
on h5 is a liability in many cases, whereas on g4 it was secure, so that simplifying attempts such as those mentioned
above would be less effective.
(see Diagram 72.2)
The crucial position has now been
reached. How is Black to continue the
attack? He has two reasonable moves,

KORCHNOI TO MOVE   72.2

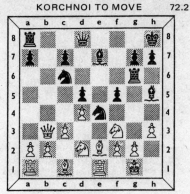

KARPOV

namely 15 ... Bd6 and 15 ... Bh4
(he could also try 15 ... Rb8 as a
prelude to either of these but the
white queen would be happier on d1
than on b3).

15 ... Be7-h4
After this move Black's attack runs
out of steam. The alternative leads to
fascinating complications: 15 ... Bd6
16 Ne5 (the only move to trouble
Black) and now:

(a) 16 ... Bxe5 17 Bxh5 Rxg2+ (17 ...
Qh4 18 Nxe4 Qxh5 19 Ng5! wins
for White) 18 Kxg2 Qg5+ when 19 Kf1
Qxh5 20 dxe5 Qxh3+ 21 Ke2 Qh5+
22 f3 d4! and 19 Bg4! fxg4 20 Nxe4
gxh3+ 21 Kxh3 Qh5+ 22 Kg2 dxe4
23 Be3 (23 dxe5 Qg4+ 24 Kf1 Qh3+
followed by 25 ... Nxe5 wins for
Black, and 23 Rxe4 Qh2+ 24 Kf1
Qh1+ wins a rook) 23 ... Rb8 with
chances for the sacrificed exchange
(Hartston and Keene).

(b) 16 ... Nxe5 17 Bxh5 Qh4! 18 Nxe4
(18 Rxe4 fxe4! 19 Bxg6 Rf8!!
20 Nxe4 [forced] 20 ... dxe4 21 Be3
Nxg6 and Black is a piece ahead)
18 ... Qxh5 (or 18 ... fxe4 19 Bxg6
[19 dxe5 transposes to the main line]
19 ... Nf3+! 20 gxf3 Qxh3 21 f4 Qg4+
with perpetual check) 19 dxe5
(19 Ng5 Nf3+! 20 gxf3 Qxh3 21 Re5
[21 f4 Rxg5+!] 21 ... Bxe5 22 dxe5
Qxf3! with advantage to Black) 19 ...

dxe4! 20 exd6 Qxh3 21 g3 Rxg3+
with perpetual check. The tempting
19 ... fxe4 loses to 20 Qxd5 Rf8
21 Qxe4 when Black has no compensation for his three-pawn deficit.

After such a string of exciting possibilities the game continuation is
something of an anti-climax. Korchnoi
had only ten minutes in which to make
his last 25 moves.

16 Re1-f1   Bh5xf3
There is no way in which Black can
maintain the pressure. For example

(a) 16 ... Ng5 17 Nxh4 Nxh3+ 18 Kh2
Qxh4 19 g3! Qg5 20 Ne4! when
White wins at least the exchange.

(b) 16 ... Bg5 17 Nxe4 Bxc1 18 Ng3
again winning the exchange.

(c) 16 ... Nxd2 17 Bxd2 Qe7 18 Qd1!
and Black has nothing left.

It appears that the whole attack is
worth only the draw illustrated in the
note above. Korchnoi plans to com-
plicate the position by sacrificing on
his next move, but Karpov's defence
is rock-solid and easily withstands the
black attack.

17 Nd2xf3   Bh4xf2+
18 Rf1xf2   Ne4xf2
19 Kg1xf2   Qd8-d6
20 Nf3-g5!
Removing all Black's tactical chances.
From here on it is all Karpov's way.

20 ... Ra8-f8
21 Qb3-a3!   Qd6-d8
22 Bc1-f4   h7-h6
23 Ng5-f3   Rf8-e8
24 Be2-d3   Re8-e4
25 g2-g3
Safety-first. No doubt 25 Bxe4 fxe4
26 Ne5 Rf6 27 Nxc6 would also win.

25 ... Rg6-f6
26 Qa3-c5   g7-g5
27 Nf3xg5! *(see Diagram 72.3)*
This sacrifice not only removes Black's
tactical chances but also leaves White
several pawns ahead.

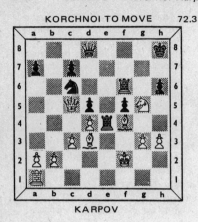

KORCHNOI TO MOVE   72.3

KARPOV

27 ... h6xg5

28 Bf4xg5   Re4-e6

29 Ra1-e1   Qd8-g8

30 h3-h4!
Again 30 Bxf6+ Rxf6 would leave Black some counterchances, owing to the bad position of the white queen.

30 ... Rf6-g6

31 Re1xe6
In this position Korchnoi lost on time. After 31 ... Rxe6 (31 ... Qxe6 loses to 32 Qf8+) 32 Bxf5 Qf7 33 g4 White has a crushing position. Another way is 32 Bb5 Nd8 33 Qxc7.

An interesting game, especially in the opening stages: what a pity Korchnoi did not play Petroff's Defence again later in the match.

Game 73

WHITE Korchnoi   Queen's Indian Defence
Candidates' Match (final, thirteenth game) Moscow 1974

In his press statement after the match Karpov commented that his best games were the second (Game 71) and the early part of this one. Certainly for the first thirty moves of this game Karpov is the master, but in a mutual time-scramble (most unusual for Karpov) both players make mistakes. Karpov's advantage becomes an equal game and then an inferior position, but by the resolute and determined defensive technique that he showed throughout the match, he is able to hold a most difficult endgame.

1 Ng1-f3   Ng8-f6

2 d2-d4   e7-e6

3 g2-g3   b7-b6

4 Bf1-g2   Bc8-b7

5 c2-c4   Bf8-e7

6 Nb1-c3   0-0
A safer continuation is 6 ...Ne4, which Karpov played in Game 75. The text move allows White to challenge for the e4 square immediately.

7 Qd1-d3

Korchnoi had previously played this in the eleventh game, whilst he chose 7 Qc2 in the fifth and nineteenth.

7 ...d7-d5
Black is unwilling to allow 8 e4, and so challenges White's central pawns.

8 c4xd5   Nf6xd5

9 Nc3xd5   e6xd5

10 0-0   Nb8-d7

11 Rf1-d1   *(see Diagram 73.1)*
White is in a quandary as to where to develop his queen's bishop. Against a

KARPOV TO MOVE   73.1

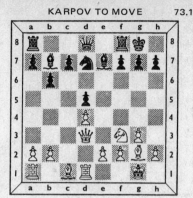

KORCHNOI

set-up with the black c-pawn on c7 or
c6 this piece would have an excellent
post at f4. On the other hand, if Black
were to advance his c-pawn to c5 then
the fianchetto of this bishop would
prove useful for attacking the black
central pawns. In the eleventh game
Korchnoi chose 11 Bf4 but after
11 ...c5! 12 dxc5 bxc5 13 Rfd1 Nf6
14 Qc2 Qb6 15 Nd2 Rfe8 he stood
no better. In this game Korchnoi
delays the development of his queen's
bishop, hoping that Black will choose
the premature 11 ...c5.

11 ...Rf8-e8!
So now Korchnoi must choose.

12 Bc1-e3
After 12 Bf4 c5 13 dxc5 bxc5 the
position would be similar to that given
above. Korchnoi strives to reach new
paths.

12 ...Be7-d6

13 Ra1-c1   a7-a5

14 Qd3-c2   c7-c6
Black is in no hurry to open up the
position to the power of the white
bishops. His position is perfectly
solid and so he waits for White to
produce a constructive plan.

15 Nf3-e1
The idea is to exchange the black-
squared bishops by 16 Nd3 and
17 Bf4.

15 ...Nd7-f6
Black could prevent the manœuvre
mentioned in the last note by 15 ...
Nf8 16 Nd3 Ne6 but he prefers
instead to lay a small trap.

16 Bg2-f3
After the natural 16 Nd3 Black has
the interesting try 16 ...Rxe3!?
17 fxe3 Ng4 18 Qd2 and now either
18 ...Nxh2 or 18 ...Qg5 19 Nf4
Bb4 20 Qd3 Ba6. In either case Black
has adequate compensation for the
material sacrificed.
The text move envisages the bishop-
exchange on f4 by bringing the knight
to g2. It also gives added protection
to the weak e2 pawn.

16 ...Ra8-c8

17 Ne1-g2   h7-h6

18 Be3-f4

KARPOV TO MOVE   73.2

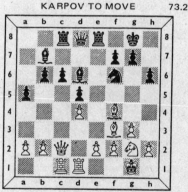

KORCHNOI

Korchnoi has at long last achieved his
objective. Whilst White's tortuous
manœuvres were going on Black has
been busy preparing for the central
pawn advance c6-c5.

18 ...c6-c5

19 Bf4xd6   Qd8xd6

20 d4xc5   Rc8xc5!
Generally speaking Black would try
to keep his pawn chain connected by
20 ...bxc5, but in this case White
cannot easily control the blockade

square d4 and is soon forced to re-
unite Black's central pawns.

21 Qc2-d2   Nf6-e4

22 Qd2-f4   Qd6-c6

23 Rc1xc5   b6xc5

24 Ng2-e3?!

This move leaves the white queen cut
off from the action on the Q-side and
is thus somewhat dubious. Better was
the simple 24 Qc1. Possibly Korchnoi
had underestimated the danger involved
in his play.

24 ...d5-d4

25 Ne3-c4   Qc6-a4

Threatening both the rook and the
knight. The white a-pawn is of little
significance at the moment but this
too is under fire from the black queen.

26 Rd1-c1

After 26 b3?! Qxa2 27 Bxe4 Bxe4
28 Nd6 Qxe2 29 Qxf7+ Kh7 30 Rc1
Bg6 Black has a clear plus.

26 ...Ne4-g5!

After 26 ...Qxa2? 27 Bxe4 Bxe4
28 Nd6 White wins at least the
exchange. But an interesting try was
26 ...d3!? 27 Bxe4 (27 exd3? loses
to 27 ...Ng5! 28 Bg2 Bxg2 29 Kxg2
Qc6+ 30 f3 Nxf3!) 27 ...Rxe4
(or 27 ...Bxe4 28 exd3 Bxd3
29 Ne5 with equality) 28 Qb8+ Re8
29 Qxb7 when 29 ...dxe2 30 Ne3!
Rxe3 31 fxe3 Qd1+ gives a drawn
queen-and-pawn ending. Black could
also try the highly adventurous
29 ...Qc2!? when 30 Ra1! dxe2
31 Ne3 Rxe3 leads to the same drawn
ending.

27 Qf4-f5

After 27 Bg2 Bxg2 28 Kxg2 Qc6+
White would be lost. *(see Diag. 73.3)*

27 ...Ng5xf3+?

Up to this point Karpov's play had
been accurate, and with one more
accurate move — 27 ...g6! — he
would have had Korchnoi in great
trouble: e.g.

(a) 28 Qg4? Bxf3 29 exf3 f5 wins the
queen

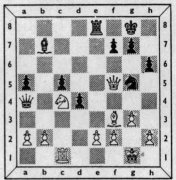

KARPOV TO MOVE   73.3

KORCHNOI

(b) 28 Qxc5 Bxf3 29 exf3 Nxf3+ 30 Kg2
(both 30 Kf1 and 30 Kh1 are strongly
answered by 30 ...Qd7!) 30 ...Ne1+
31 Kf1 Nd3 wins the exchange.

(c) 28 Qf6 Bxf3 29 exf3 Qd7! and
White's queen is in danger on account
of 30 ...Re6.

(d) 28 Qd3 Nxf3+ 29 exf3 Ba6 (also
29 ...Qc6 30 Nxa5 Qxf3 31 Qxf3
Bxf3 merits serious consideration)
30 Qb3 Qxb3 31 axb3 Bxc4
32 bxc4 Rb8, with a far superior
ending for Black.

28 e2xf3   Bb7-a6

29 Nc4-d6   Re8-e7

30 Qf5xc5   d4-d3

This strong passed pawn amply
compensates for the pawn deficiency.

31 Qc5-d5   Qa4-b4?!

Karpov could still have taken a draw
by 31 ...Qc2! 32 Rxc2 Re1+ 33 Kg2
dxc2, when White is forced to take
perpetual check by 34 Qxf7+ Kh7
35 Qf5+ etc.

32 Kg1-g2

Both players were short of time, but
Korchnoi is still trying to win! He had
a safe draw here by 32 Qa8+ Kh7
33 Qxa6 Re1+ 34 Rxe1 Qxe1+
35 Kg2 d2 36 Qd3+.

32 ...Qb4xb2

Probably better was 32 ... Rd7.
After the text move the advantage
swings in Korchnoi's favour.

33 Rc1-c6 Qb2-e5?

The safest way to draw was by 33 ...
Bb7! when 34 Nxb7 Qxb7 35 Qd8+
Kh7 36 Qxd3+ g6 gives White an
extra pawn but no real winning
chances.

34 Qd5xe5?

Korchnoi misses the winning 34 Nc8!
The options for Black are:

(a) 34 ... Bxc8 35 Rxc8+ Kh7 36 Qxd3+
g6 37 Qd8.

(b) 34 ... Qxd5 35 Nxe7+ Kh7
36 Nxd5 d2 37 Ne3.

(c) 34 ... Bb7 35 Nxe7+ Qxe7 36 Qd6
Qe2 37 Qb8+ Kh7 38 Qxb7 d2
39 Qb1+! followed by 40 Rd6.

(d) 34 ... Re8 35 Qxe5 Rxe5 36 Rxa6
Re8! 37 Na7 Ra8 38 Rxa5 d2
39 Rd5 Rxa7 40 Rxd2.

In all cases White has a winning advantage, although there is still a slight
hope for Black in line (d).

34 ... Re7xe5

35 Nd6-e4 Ba6-b5

Both players were forced to play
quickly to reach the time control at
move 40. It is creditable that throughout this period both players reject the
obvious drawing possibilities. Here
for example Black could draw simply
by 35 ... Bb7, since 36 Rc5 loses to
36 ... Rxe4 37 fxe4 d2.

36 Rc6-d6 f7-f5

37 Ne4-c3 Bb5-c4

38 f3-f4 Re5-c5

39 Kg2-f3 Kg8-f7

Here or at either of his next two
turns, Black could have equalized
completely by 39 ... Bxa2! 40 Nxa2
Rc2, trapping the white knight.
Whether Karpov missed this possibility or whether he thought he held
the advantage is not clear, but surely
he would have done better to take the
draw.

40 Kf3-e3 Kf7-e7

41 Rd6-b6 Rc5-c8

42 Rb6-b7+ Ke7-f8

43 Rb7-a7

At last White prevents the trick
pointed out at move 39.

43 ... Rc8-c5

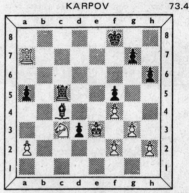

KARPOV   73.4

KORCHNOI TO MOVE

Korchnoi now spent 41 minutes in
sealing his move! The obvious 44 Kd4
gives White nothing after 44 ... Rc8
45 Rxa5 d2! when 46 Rxf5+ Bf7! or
46 Ke3 Rd8 47 Nd1 Rd3+. Korchnoi
opts for a quiet yet constructive move
which does not substantially change
the nature of the position. This allows
him to analyse the position at leisure.

44 h2-h4 h6-h5

45 a2-a3 Bc4-a6!

46 Ke3-d2

White's advantage is small but clear.
The black a- and d-pawns are both
weak and the knight is more manœuver-
able than the bishop. Black's last move
helps to guard the a-pawn from the
white rook. The point is that
46 Rxa6 Rxc3 47 Rxa5 g6 48 a4
Ra3 gives an ending that is drawn
despite White's extra pawn.

46 ... Rc5-c6

47 Ra7-d7 Ba6-c4

48 Nc3-d1   Bc4-b5

49 Nd1-e3   g7-g6

50 Rd7-d5   Rc6-b6

51 Ne3-d1   Kf8-f7

52 Nd1-b2
Although 52 Nc3 wins a pawn it leads to the same drawn ending as in the last note, by 52 ...Ba6 53 Rxa5 Rb2+ 54 Ke3 Rc2 55 Rxa6 Rxc3. The text move is a more direct attempt to win a pawn.

52 ...Bb5-a6

53 Nb2-a4
Naturally 53 Nxd3 Bxd3 54 Rxd3 would be a clear draw.

53 ...Rb6-c6

54 Rd5-c5
An exchange of rooks would enhance White's chances considerably. The black rook cannot be allowed to the seventh rank.

54 ...Rc6-e6

55 Rc5-e5   Re6-c6

56 Na4-c5   Ba6-c4

57 Nc5-a4   Bc4-a6

58 Re5-c5   Rc6-e6

59 Rc5-c7+   Kf7-e8

60 Na4-c3   Re6-b6

61 Nc3-d1   Rb6-e6

62 Nd1-e3   Re6-b6

63 Rc7-c5
At last Korchnoi takes the initiative by sacrificing his back f-pawn for the black a-pawn.

63 ...Rb6-b2+

64 Kd2-c3   Rb2xf2

65 Rc5xa5   Ba6-b7

66 Kc3xd3   Rf2-f3
The net result of White's combination is a general reduction in material. Black regains his lost pawn, but in the meantime White can advance his a-pawn and king to give himself a positional advantage.

67 Kd3-d4   Ke8-d7

68 Ne3-c4   Rf3xg3

69 a3-a4   Kd7-c7

70 Ra5-c5+   Kc7-b8

71 Nc4-e5
The threat is 72 Nd7+ Ka7 73 Ra5+ Ba6 74 Nc5 winning a piece.

71 ...Bb7-e4

72 Rc5-c3
The purpose of this move is to provide the white king with an entry square to the Q-side. The exchange of rooks would give White a winning ending.

72 ...Rg3-g1

73 Kd4-c5   Kb8-c7

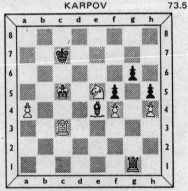

KARPOV   73.5

KORCHNOI TO MOVE

Black must prevent the further advance of the white king. For example 73 ...Rh1 74 Nxg6 Rg1 75 Ne5 Rh1 is met by 76 a5 Rxh4 77 Kb6, when mate is imminent.

74 a4-a5   Rg1-a1

75 Kc5-b5+   Kc7-d6

76 a5-a6
After 76 Rg3 Kd5 77 Nxg6 Kd4 Black's active king position, as in the game, compensates fully for his pawn minus.

76 ...Ra1-b1+

77 Kb5-a5   Rb1-a1+

78 Ka5-b6   Ra1-b1+

79 Kb6-a7   Kd6-d5!

Black's active king will ultimately be his saviour. Against passive play White would first capture the g6 pawn and then arrange his king on b8, his pawn on a7, and his rook on b6, when Rb6-b7, cutting the bishop's diagonal, would win.

80 Rc3-c6   Rb1-f1

81 Ka7-b6

After 81 Rb6 Rxf4 82 Nxg6 Rg4 83 Kb8 Kc5! 84 Rf6 Rg1 Black draws comfortably.

81 ... Kd5-d4

82 Rc6-c4+   Kd4-e3

83 Rc4-a4

Korchnoi is trying the traditional method of forcing the pawn home, and at the same time he sets a couple of devious traps. But Karpov is up to the task and defends brilliantly.

83 ... Be4-a8!

Both 83 ... Kxf4 84 a7 Kxe5 85 Rxe4+ and 83 ... Rxf4 84 Nc6! win for White. After the text move White must rethink his winning plans. The bishop on a8 must eventually be removed by the white king but in the meantime Black is able to construct a satisfactory defence.

84 Ne5xg6   Ke3-f3!

On g4 the black king will keep the white knight tied up for the rest of the game.

85 Kb6-c7   Rf1-d1

86 a6-a7   Kf3-g4

87 Ra4-a6   Kg4-g3

88 Ra6-a3+   Kg3-g4

89 Ra3-a5   Rd1-b1

90 Ra5-a6   Rb1-d1

91 Ra6-d6   Rd1-a1

92 Kc7-b8   Ba8-e4

93 Rd6-d7   Kg4-f3

94 Rd7-g7

After 94 Rb7 Bxb7 95 Kxb7 Rb1+ Black draws easily.

94 ... Ra1-a6

95 Kb8-c8   Kf3-g3

96 Kc8-d8   Draw agreed

White can make no further progress. With the exception of the period when he was in time-trouble Karpov played this game with great accuracy, both in the early stages when he held the initiative, and later when he was defending. Both players consistently avoided taking a draw, and this grim determination was typical of the whole match.

Game 74

WHITE Korchnoi   Catalan Opening
Candidates' Match (final, seventeenth game) Moscow 1974

The middle part of the match was fairly even: both players defended accurately the marginal swings from the openings. Every single game was fiercely contested, and no position given up as a draw until all possibilities of a win had been exhausted.

It was in this, the seventeenth game, that a further breakthrough, again in Karpov's favour, brought the tally of wins to 3-0.

1 d2-d4

Korchnoi opened most games with 1 c4. This time he tries new territory.

1 ... Ng8-f6

2 c2-c4   e7-e6

3 g2-g3

This order of moves deters Black from adopting a Queen's-Indian-type arrangement with 3 ...b6.

3 ...d7-d5

Both 3 ...c5 and 3 ...Bb4+ are playable, but the text move is more in tune with Karpov's general style.

4 Bf1-g2 d5xc4

5 Ng1-f3

White need not hurry to regain the pawn by 5 Qa4+, and simply completes his K-side development first.

5 ...c7-c5

This move and his previous one are typical of Karpov's approach to such a position. He prefers to play the freeing manœuvres at an early stage rather than to set up a solid but cramped position.

6 0-0 Nb8-c6

In Nikolaevsky-Bannik, Kiev 1955, Black tried 6 ...cxd4 7 Qxd4 Qxd4 8 Nxd4 a6 9 Nd2 Bc5 10 Nc2 c3 11 bxc3 Nbd7 but White's pressure on the black Q-side more than compensated for his slightly weakened pawn-structure. Also 6 ...a6 7 dxc5 Qxd1 8 Rxd1 Bxc5 9 Ne5 gives White the edge.

7 Qd1-a4

Taimanov analyses the interesting alternative 7 Ne5!? Korchnoi played this move gainst Ivkov in the USSR v. Yugoslavia match in 1964. The game continued 7 ...Bd7 8 Nxc6 Bxc6 9 Bxc6+ bxc6 10 Qa4 Qb6 11 dxc5 Bxc5 12 Qxc4 0-0 13 Nd2 Nd5 14 e4 Nf6 15 Nb3 Be7 16 Be3 Qb5 17 Rac1 Ng4 18 Bc5 with advantage to White.
The main line leads to an equal ending: 7 Ne5!? Nxe5 8 dxe5 Qxd1 9 Rxd1 Nd5! 10 Na3 (or 10 Nc3 Nxc3 11 bxc3 Be7 12 Rb1 0-0 13 Bxb7 Rb8 14 Be4 Rxb1 15 Bxb1 with equality) 10 ...c3 11 Bxd5 exd5 (11 ...cxb2 12 Bc6+! bxc6 13 Bxb2 and White stands a little better) 12 Nb5 cxb2 13 Bxb2 Kd7 14 Rxd5+

Kc6 15 Nc3 Be6 16 Rd2 Be7.

7 ...Bc8-d7

Black would have the inferior ending after 7 ...cxd4 8 Nxd4 Qxd4 9 Bxc6+ Bd7 10 Rd1 Bxc6 11 Qxc6+ bxc6 12 Rxd4. A similar idea occurs in the Grünfeld Defence. Another idea is the manœuvre 7 ...Nd7, when 8 dxc5 Bxc5 9 Qxc4 0-0 10 Nc3 a6 gives a position offering chances to both sides.

8 Qa4xc4

Theory recommends 8 dxc5! with the continuation 8 ...Na5 (8 ...Bxc5 9 Qxc4 Be7 10 Nc3 Rc8 11 Rd1 leaves White with an active position full of possibilities: Korchnoi-Antoshin, 1955) 9 Qc2 Bxc5 10 Ne5! Rc8 11 Nc3 Nc6 (11 ...b5 12 Bg5 Qb6 13 Rad1 is too dangerous for Black) 12 Nxc4 0-0 13 Rd1 with the better game for White.

8 ...c5xd4

More aggressive would have been 8 ...b5!? when 9 Qd3 c4 10 Qc2 Rc8 11 e4 Be7 12 Rd1 (Vukic-Pfleger, Ybbs 1968) and now 12 ...Nb4 gives an interesting position with equal chances. The move chosen by Karpov is in keeping with his general plan of exchange in the centre, but it allows Korchnoi some central pressure along the open c- and d-files.

9 Nf3xd4 Ra8-c8

KARPOV 74.1

KORCHNOI TO MOVE

So far the game has gone as both
players wanted. Korchnoi has some
central pressure and Karpov has
achieved relative freedom for his
position.

10 Nb1-c3 Qd8-a5?!
A strange move. Better was 10 ...
Nxd4 11 Qxd4 Bc5 12 Qd3! Bc6!
13 Qxd8+ Kxd8, or 12 Qh4 Bc6
13 Rd1 Qb6!?. In either case Black's
development is better than in the
game.

11 Rf1-d1 Bf8-e7
After 11 ... Nxd4 12 Qxd4 Bc5
13 Qh4 Bc6 14 Bxc6+ Rxc6 15 Bg5
Be7 16 Ne4 Nxe4 17 Bxe7 Black is
in trouble.

12 Nd4-b3 Qa5-c7
The alternative was 12 ... Qb4, when
13 Qd3 0-0 gives an unclear situation.

13 Nc3-b5
With this and his next two moves
Korchnoi gains the two bishops.

13 ... Qc7-b8

14 Nb3-c5 a7-a6
Both 14 ... Na5 and 14 ... Ne5 are
still met by 15 Nxd7.

15 Nc5xd7 Nf6xd7

16 Nb5-c3 Nd7-e5

17 Qc4-a4
The alternative was 17 Qe4 0-0
18 Bf4. Korchnoi intends to sacrifice
the two bishops to establish a rook
on the seventh rank.

17 ... 0-0

18 Bc1-f4 Qb8-a7

19 Bf4xe5 Nc6xe5

20 Qa4-e4 Ne5-c6

21 Rd1-d7 *(see Diagram 74.2)*

White has achieved his aim. The rook
cannot be undermined by 21 ... Rfd8
22 Rad1 Rxd7 23 Rxd7 Rd8? because
24 Qxc6! wins a piece for White. So
temporarily at least Karpov must leave
the rook alone and try to get counterplay against the white Q-side pawns.

KARPOV TO MOVE   74.2

KORCHNOI

21 ... Be7-f6

22 Ra1-d1 Qa7-b6
Now 22 ... Rfd8? would lose prettily
after 23 Qxc6!

23 Qe4-c2 Nc6-a5

24 Rd1-d3
With this and his next move White is
preparing the advance b2-b4.

24 ... h7-h6

25 a2-a3 Rc8-c7

26 b2-b4?
Stronger was 26 R3d6! After 26 ...
Nc6 27 Na4 Rxd7 28 Rxd7! Qb5
29 Bxc6 (the threat was 29 ... Nd4)
29 ... Qxc6 30 Qxc6 bxc6 Black is
in some difficulties, although he still
has plenty of drawing chances.
Sounder is 26 ... Qc5 27 b4! (so that
if 27 ... Qxc3? 28 Rxc7 wins the
exchange) 27 ... Qc4 28 bxa5 Rxd7
29 Rxd7 Qxc3 30 Qxc3 Bxc3 with
good drawing chances, for example:

(a) 31 Bxb7 Bxa5 32 Bxa6 Rd8!
33 Rb7 Rd1+ 34 Kg2 Ra1 35 Rb5
Rxa3 36 Be8, when White has some
mating chances but little else.

(b) 31 Rxb7 Rc8! 32 Ra7 Rc5!
33 Rxa6 Rxa5 34 Rxa5 Bxa5 with a
drawn ending.

Korchnoi spent half of his remaining
ten minutes in playing his 26th move,

and was now left in severe time-trouble.

26 ... Rc7xd7

27 Rd3xd7   Rf8-c8!
Now 28 bxa5 Qxa5 regains the piece
for Black and reaches a level ending.
In striving for more Korchnoi blunders.

28 Rd7-d3   Na5-c4

29 Nc3-e4   Qb6-c7

30 Ne4-c5?
Better was 30 Nxf6+ gxf6 31 Rc3 b5
when White has the smallest of advantages. After the text move however he
is lost.

KARPOV TO MOVE   74.3

KORCHNOI

30 ... Nc4-e5!
Threatening both the rook by Nxd3
and the knight by b6.

31 Rd3-d2
The alternative, and possibly the best
try, was 31 Rc3, when 31 ... b6
32 Bb7 (32 Ne4 loses to 32 ... Nf3+!)
32 ... Rd8! (Both 32 ... bxc5?
33 Rxc5, and 32 ... Re8 33 Ne4!
Nf3+ [33 ... Qxb7? 34 Nd6 Qd7
35 Nxe8 wins for White] 34 exf3

Bxc3 35 Qxc3 Qxb7 36 Nd6 are
insufficient) 33 Nxe6 Nf3+ 34 Bxf3
Qxc3 35 Qxc3 Rd1+ 36 Kg2 Bxc3
37 Nc7 a5 38 Nd5 Bxb4! 39 axb4
a4 wins for Black, since the a-pawn
costs White a whole piece. Nevertheless the ending of bishop and five
pawns against rook and four (if it is
possible for White to reach it) offers
some drawing chances for White.

31 ... b7-b6

32 f2-f4
There is simply no useful move for
White.

32 ... b6xc5

33 f4xe5   Qc7xe5

34 Bg2-b7   Rc8-c7

35 Qc2-e4
If 35 Bxa6, then 35 ... cxb4 is more
than adequate.

35 ... Qe5-a1+

36 Kg1-g2   Qa1xa3

37 b4xc5   Rc7xc5
Two pawns down, Korchnoi only
plays on because of 'impetus'—he is
still racing to reach the time control.

38 Rd2-d3   Qa3-a5

39 Qe4-f3   Qa5-b6

40 Rd3-d7   Rc5-f5
The time control is passed. The white
king is hopelessly exposed and is now
hunted down very quickly.

41 Qf3-g4   Qb6-f2+

42 Kg2-h3   g7-g6

White resigns

Karpov's victory in this game was by
no means as convincing as his other
two wins, but his excellent defence in
a difficult position deserved reward.

Game 75

WHITE Korchnoi   Queen's Indian Defence
Candidates' Match (final, twenty-third game) Moscow 1974

After his losses in the nineteenth and twenty-first games Karpov's lead was only three wins to two. It was on this game, Korchnoi's last white, that the fate of the match would depend. A nicely timed knight manœuvre brings Karpov a slight advantage, but as in the final game, where he was a clear pawn ahead, he is content to settle for a draw and thus clinch the match.

1 d2-d4	Ng8-f6
2 c2-c4	e7-e6
3 Ng1-f3	b7-b6
4 g2-g3	Bc8-b7
5 Bf1-g2	Bf8-e7
6 Nb1-c3	Nf6-e4

In all the previous Queen's Indian Defences Karpov played 6 ...0-0. In games 11 and 13 Korchnoi chose 7 Qd3 and in games 5 and 19, 7 Qc2. Karpov avoids this variation because of his nineteen-move loss in game 19. The text choice is the theoretical continuation, and a safer and more reliable move.

7 Bc1-d2

This move has become popular recently The older variations, 7 Qc2 or 7 Nxe4, have less bite.

7 ...Be7-f6

Karpov follows a safe and tested way to equality, as was to be expected.

8 0-0   0-0

9 Qd1-c2

Smyslov-Olafsson, Moscow 1971, continued 9 Rc1 c5 10 Nxe4 Bxe4 11 Bc3 d6 12 Qd2 Nc6 13 dxc5 Bxc3 14 Rxc3 bxc5 15 Rd1 Qe7 16 Ne1 Bxg2 17 Kxg2 Rad8 18 Nf3 Rd7 19 Qc2 Rfd8 with a slight advantage to White.

9 ...Ne4xd2

10 Qc2xd2   d7-d6

Karpov intends to play c7-c5 at an opportune moment, and thus contest the centre.

11 Ra1-d1

Here or on the next move White could have achieved the advantage by e2-e4, but the text move is by no means bad.

11 ...Nb8-d7

KARPOV   75.1

KORCHNOI TO MOVE

12 Nf3-e1?!

Not only does Korchnoi fail to occupy the centre by 12 e4, but worse he allows Black a comfortable road to equality. Better was 12 e4. The game Krogius-Liberzon 34th USSR Championship (semi-final), Irkutsk 1966, continued 12 e4 e5 13 Nd5 Re8 14 Rfe1 exd4 15 Nxd4 Nc5 16 b4 Bxd4 17 Qxd4 Ne6 18 Qb2 a5 19 a3 axb4 20 axb4 f6 21 f4 c5! 22 bxc5 Bxd5 23 Rxd5 bxc5 24 e5 fxe5 25 fxe5 Nd4 26 Rxd6 Qxd6! and Black won.

12 ...Bb7xg2

13 Ne1xg2
Again Korchnoi chooses an inferior
continuation. Better was 13 Kxg2 as
can be seen by his next two moves.

13 ... Qd8-e7

14 Ng2-e1   c7-c5!
Completing the equalization process.
Although 15 dxc5 Nxc5 16 Qxd6
Qxd6 17 Rxd6 wins a pawn, Black
can immediately regain it by 17 ...
Bxc3 18 bxc3 Ne4 19 Rd3 Rfd8 or
19 ... Rac8. The initiative is now in
Karpov's hands.

15 Ne1-c2   Ra8-c8

16 b2-b3   Rf8-d8

17 e2-e4
Many moves too late. Karpov now
brings his knight to a more active
square and by bombarding the d4
pawn brings about a favourable liquid-
ation of forces.

17 ... Nd7-b8!
Heading for c6, from where it can
bring pressure to bear on the white
centre. Black has no reason to fear
18 d5, for 18 ... Bxc3 19 Qxc3 exd5
20 exd5 leaves White with no advantage.

18 Rf1-e1
Since White cannot improve his position by a central pawn advance, he
simply triples his major pieces on the
d-file in anticipation of its opening.

18 ... c5xd4

19 Nc2xd4   Qe7-b7
Preparing Nc6, which could at the
moment be strongly met by 20 Nxc6
Rxc6 21 Nd5! with clear advantage
to White. Now 20 Ndb5 would be
premature not on account of 20 ... a6?
21 Nxd6 Rxd6 22 Qxd6 Bxc3
23 Qd8+ with mate next move, but
because of 20 ... Nc6 followed by
21 ... a6.

20 Re1-e3   a7-a6

21 Qd2-e2
After 21 Rd3 Nc6! is both playable
and strong, since the rook's position
on d3 may be exploitable: e.g.

(a) 22 Nxc6 Rxc6 with at least equality
   for Black.
(b) 22 N3e2?! Ne5 23 Re3 d5!∓
(c) 22 Nf3 b5 23 cxb5 axb5∓

21 ... Nb8-c6

22 Nd4xc6   Qb7xc6

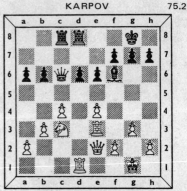

KARPOV   75.2

KORCHNOI TO MOVE

Black has seized the initiative. His
bishop is far more effective than
white's knight, and the threat of a
break by b5 more than compensates
for the slight weakness of the d6 pawn.
The fact that this initiative peters out
to a draw is due solely to the state of
the match.

23 Re3-d3   h7-h6!
The immediate 23 ... b5 allows
24 cxb5 axb5 25 e5! with advantage
to White.

24 a2-a4   Qc6-c5

25 Qe2-d2   b6-b5!
By his last two moves Karpov has
shown that he is willing to settle for
a draw. The end is inevitable: neither
side can afford to deviate from the
drawing line.

26 a4xb5   Bf6xc3   27 Qd2xc3   a6xb5

28 Rd3-d4   Qc5-c7   29 Qc3-b4   e6-e5

Draw agreed
After 30 Rxd6 Rxd6 31 Qxd6 Qxd6
32 Rxd6 bxc4 33 bxc4 Rxc4 the
ending is completely equal.

Tournament tables

Sixth International Youth Tournament
Groningen   December 1967—January 1968

		1	2	3	4	5	6	7	8	Total
1	Karpov (USSR)	–	½	1	½	1	1	1	½	5½
2	Jocha (Hungary)	½	–	½	1	1	½	1	½	5
3	Levi (Poland)	0	½	–	0	1	1	1	1	4½
4	Zara (Romania)	½	0	1	–	½	1	0	½	3½
5	Timman (Holland)	0	0	0	½	–	1	1	1	3½
6	Moles (Ireland)	0	½	0	0	0	–	1	½	2
7	Hostalet (Spain)	0	0	0	1	0	0	–	1	2
8	Ligterink (Holland)	½	½	0	½	0	½	0	–	2

World Junior Championship   Stockholm   August 1969
Preliminaries

		1	2	3	4	5	6	7	Total
1	Karpov (USSR)	–	½	1	½	½	1	1	4½
2	McKay (Scotland)	½	–	0	1	½	1	1	4
3	Payrhuber (Austria)	0	1	–	½	0	1	1	3½
4	Torre (Philippines)	½	0	½	–	½	1	1	3½
5	Hug (Switzerland)	½	½	1	½	–	0	½	3
6	Sznapik (Poland)	0	0	0	0	1	–	1	2
7	Fridjonsson (Iceland)	0	0	0	0	½	0	–	½

Final

		1	2	3	4	5	6	7	8	9	10	11	12	Tot
1	Karpov (USSR)	–	½	1	½	1	1	1	1	1	1	1	1	10
2	Adorjan (Hungary)	½	–	1	½	½	½	1	½	1	0	½	1	7
3	Urzica (Romania)	0	0	–	1	½	1	½	½	1	½	1	1	7
4	Kaplan (Puerto Rico)	½	½	0	–	½	1	1	½	1	0	½	1	6
5	Andersson (Sweden)	0	½	½	½	–	0	½	1	½	1	½	1	6
6	Neckar (C'slovakia)	0	½	0	0	1	–	1	1	½	½	1	0	5
7	Juhnke (W. Germany)	0	0	½	0	½	0	–	1	½	1	1	1	5
8	Vogt (East Germany)	0	½	½	½	0	0	0	–	½	1	½	1	4
9	Vujacic (Yugoslavia)	0	0	0	0	½	½	½	½	–	1	1	½	4
10	McKay (Scotland)	0	1	½	1	0	½	0	0	0	–	0	1	4
11	Diaz (Cuba)	0	½	0	½	½	0	0	½	0	1	–	1	4
12	Castro (Columbia)	0	0	0	0	0	1	0	0	½	0	0	–	1

Caracas International Tournament   June–July 1970

	1	2	3	4	5	6	7	8	9	10	11	12	13	14	15	16	17	18	Total
1 Kavalek	–	½	0	1	½	1	½	1	½	½	½	1	1	1	1	1	1	1	13
2 Panno	½	–	½	½	½	½	½	1	½	½	½	1	1	½	1	1	1	1	12
3 Stein	1	½	–	1	½	½	½	½	1	½	0	1	½	½	1	1	1	1	12
4 Benko	0	½	0	–	½	½	½	1	1	½	1	½	½	1	1	1	1	1	11½
5 Ivkov	½	½	½	½	–	1	½	½	½	½	½	½	1	1	1	1	½	1	11½
6 Karpov	0	½	½	½	0	–	1	½	1	½	½	1	½	1	1	1	1	1	11½
7 Parma	½	½	½	½	½	0	–	½	½	½	1	½	½	½	½	1	1	1	10
8 Sigurjonsson	0	0	½	0	½	½	½	–	1	½	1	½	1	½	½	1	1	1	10
9 Barcza	½	½	0	0	½	0	½	0	–	½	1	½	1	1	½	1	1	1	9½
10 Bisguier	½	½	½	½	½	½	½	½	½	–	½	½	½	0	½	1	1	1	9½
11 Addison	½	½	1	0	½	½	0	0	0	½	–	½	½	½	1	1	1	½	8½
12 O'Kelly	0	0	0	½	½	0	½	½	½	½	½	–	½	1	½	1	½	1	8
13 Ciocaltea	0	0	½	½	0	½	½	0	0	½	½	½	–	1	1	½	1	½	7½
14 Cuellar	0	½	½	0	0	0	½	½	0	1	½	0	0	–	½	½	½	1	6
15 Yepez	0	0	0	0	0	0	½	½	½	½	0	½	0	½	–	½	1	1	5½
16 Villaroel	0	0	0	0	0	0	0	0	0	0	0	0	½	½	½	–	½	1	3
17 Caro	0	0	0	0	½	0	0	0	0	0	0	½	0	½	0	½	–	1	3
18 Slussar	0	0	0	0	0	0	0	0	0	0	½	0	½	0	0	0	0	–	1

Student Olympiad   Mayaguez, Puerto Rico   June–July 1971

Preliminary Group 1

	1	2	3	4	5	Total
1 USSR	–	4	3	3	3	13
2 Austria	0	–	2½	2	3½	8
3 Puerto Rico	1	1½	–	3½	2	8
4 Peru	1	2	½	–	3½	7
5 Ecuador	1	½	2	½	–	4

Final

	1	2	3	4	5	6	7	8	9	Total
1 USSR	–	3½	4	2½	4	4	4	4	3½	29½
2 USA	½	–	1½	2½	2½	3½	4	3	4	21½
3 Canada	0	2½	–	2	3	3½	2	4	4	21
4 Israel	1½	1½	2	–	2½	3½	2½	3	4	20½
5 Iceland	0	1½	1	1½	–	2	2½	2½	3½	14½
6 Brazil	0	½	½	½	2	–	2	3	2½	11
7 Austria	0	0	2	1½	1½	2	–	2	2	11
8 Puerto Rico	0	1	0	1	1½	1	2	–	2½	9
9 Colombia	½	0	0	0	½	1½	2	1½	–	6

Karpov scored 7½/8 on board 3.

38th USSR Championship Riga November–December 1970

	1	*2*	*3*	*4*	*5*	*6*	*7*	*8*	*9*	*10*	*11*	*12*	*13*	*14*	*15*	*16*	*17*	*18*	*19*	*20*	*21*	*22*	*Total*
1 Korchnoi	–	0	½	1	1	1	1	½	1	½	½	1	1	½	½	1	1	1	½	1	½	1	16
2 Tukmakov	1	–	½	½	½	½	½	½	0	½	½	1	1	1	½	1	½	1	½	1	1	1	14½
3 Stein	½	½	–	½	½	½	½	1	½	1	½	1	1	½	½	½	1	1	1	0	½	1	14
4 Balashov	0	½	½	–	0	½	½	½	½	0	½	½	1	1	½	1	1	1	1	1	1	0	12½
5 Gipslis	0	½	½	1	–	½	½	½	½	½	½	½	1	½	½	1	½	½	0	1	½	1	12
6 Karpov	0	½	½	½	½	–	½	½	½	1	0	½	1	½	½	1	1	1	½	½	½	½	12
7 Savon	0	½	½	½	½	½	–	½	½	½	1	½	½	0	½	½	½	1	1	1	1	½	12
8 Averbach	½	½	0	½	½	½	½	–	½	½	0	½	1	0	½	½	1	½	½	1	1	½	11
9 Podgajec	0	1	½	½	½	½	½	½	–	½	½	0	1	1	½	½	½	½	½	½	0	1	11
10 Bagirov	½	½	0	1	½	0	½	½	½	–	1	½	0	1	½	1	0	0	0	1	1	½	10½
11 Dementiev	½	½	½	½	½	1	0	1	½	0	–	½	½	1	0	0	½	0	1	1	½	½	10½
12 Liberson	0	0	0	½	½	½	½	½	1	½	½	–	0	½	1	0	1	½	1	½	1	½	10½
13 Doroshkevich	0	0	0	0	0	0	½	0	0	1	½	1	–	½	1	1	½	0	1	1	1	1	10
14 Holmov	½	0	½	0	½	½	1	1	0	0	0	½	½	–	½	½	½	½	½	½	1	1	10
15 Antoshin	½	½	½	½	½	½	½	½	½	½	1	0	0	½	–	0	0	½	1	½	½	½	9½
16 I. Zaitzev	0	0	½	0	0	0	½	½	½	0	1	1	0	½	1	–	½	0	1	1	½	1	9½
17 Vaganian	0	½	0	0	½	0	½	0	½	1	½	0	½	½	1	½	–	1	0	½	½	1	9
18 Mikenas	0	0	0	0	½	0	0	½	½	1	1	½	1	½	½	1	0	–	1	0	0	1	9
19 Karasev	½	½	0	0	1	½	0	½	½	1	0	0	0	½	0	0	1	0	–	½	1	1	8½
20 Platonov	0	0	1	0	0	½	0	0	½	0	0	½	0	½	½	0	½	1	½	–	1	1	7½
21 Zeitlin	½	0	½	0	½	½	0	0	1	0	½	0	0	0	½	½	½	1	0	0	–	0	6
22 Moisejev	0	0	0	1	0	½	½	½	0	½	½	½	0	0	½	0	0	0	0	0	1	–	5½

39th USSR Championship Leningrad September–October 1971

	1	*2*	*3*	*4*	*5*	*6*	*7*	*8*	*9*	*10*	*11*	*12*	*13*	*14*	*15*	*16*	*17*	*18*	*19*	*20*	*21*	*22*	*Total*
1 Savon	–	½	½	½	1	1	½	1	½	½	1	1	1	½	½	1	½	½	½	½	1	1	15
2 Smyslov	½	–	½	1	½	½	½	½	½	½	½	½	½	½	1	½	½	1	1	1	½	1	13½
3 Tal	½	½	–	½	1	0	1	0	½	½	1	1	½	1	½	0	1	1	1	½	½	1	13½
4 Karpov	½	0	½	–	½	1	½	½	1	½	½	½	½	½	½	1	0	1	1	1	½	1	13
5 Balashov	0	½	0	½	–	1	1	½	½	0	0	0	½	½	1	½	1	1	½	1	1	1	12
6 Stein	0	½	1	0	0	–	½	1	1	0	1	½	½	½	½	1	½	1	½	0	1	1	12
7 Bronstein	½	½	0	½	0	½	–	1	½	1	½	1	½	1	0	1	1	½	0	0	½	1	11½
8 Polugaevsky	0	½	1	½	½	0	0	–	1	1	½	1	½	½	½	½	½	½	1	1	½	0	11½
9 Taimanov	½	½	½	0	½	0	½	0	–	1	1	0	½	1	½	½	1	0	½	1	½	1	11
10 Kapengut	½	½	½	½	1	1	0	0	0	–	½	0	½	0	½	½	½	0	1	1	1	1	10½
11 Krogius	0	½	0	½	1	0	½	½	0	½	–	½	0	1	1	½	1	1	½	½	½	½	10½
12 Lein	0	½	0	½	1	½	0	0	1	1	½	–	½	0	1	0	½	1	0	½	½	1	10
13 Platonov	0	½	½	½	½	½	½	½	½	½	1	½	–	½	0	0	0	½	1	1	1	0	10
14 Geller	½	½	0	½	½	½	0	½	0	1	0	1	½	–	1	0	½	½	0	½	½	1	9½
15 Karasev	½	0	½	½	0	½	1	½	½	½	0	0	1	0	–	1	½	½	½	0	1	0	9
16 Shamkovich	0	½	1	0	½	0	0	½	½	½	½	1	1	1	0	–	0	0	½	1	½	0	9
17 Vaganian	½	½	0	1	0	½	0	½	0	½	0	½	1	½	½	1	–	0	0	½	1	0	8½
18 Nikolaevsky	½	0	0	0	0	0	½	½	1	1	0	0	½	½	½	1	1	–	1	0	½	0	8½
19 Tukmakov	½	0	0	0	½	½	1	0	½	0	½	1	0	1	½	½	1	0	–	½	0	½	8½
20 Grigorian	½	0	½	0	0	1	1	0	0	0	½	½	0	½	1	0	½	1	½	–	0	½	8
21 Djindjinhashvili	0	½	½	½	0	0	½	½	½	0	½	½	0	½	0	½	0	½	1	1	–	½	8
22 Zeitlin	0	0	0	0	0	0	0	1	0	0	½	0	1	0	1	1	1	1	½	½	½	–	8

Alekhine Memorial Tournament Moscow November–December 1971

	1	*2*	*3*	*4*	*5*	*6*	*7*	*8*	*9*	*10*	*11*	*12*	*13*	*14*	*15*	*16*	*17*	*18*	*Total*
1 Karpov	–	½	½	½	½	½	½	½	1	1	1	½	½	1	½	½	½	1	11
2 Stein	½	–	½	½	½	½	½	½	1	½	½	1	½	½	½	1	1	1	11
3 Smyslov	½	½	–	1	½	½	½	½	½	½	½	½	1	½	½	1	1	½	10½
4 Petrosian	½	½	0	–	½	1	½	½	½	½	1	½	½	½	1	½	1	½	10
5 Tukmakov	½	½	½	½	–	½	½	½	½	½	1	½	½	½	1	½	1	½	10
6 Spassky	½	½	½	0	½	–	½	½	½	½	0	1	1	1	½	½	½	1	9½
7 Tal	½	½	½	½	½	½	–	1	½	½	0	½	0	½	½	1	1	1	9½
8 R. Byrne	½	½	½	½	½	½	0	–	½	1	0	½	½	1	1	½	½	½	9
9 Bronstein	0	0	½	½	½	½	½	½	–	½	0	½	½	½	1	1	1	1	9
10 Hort	0	½	½	½	½	½	½	0	½	–	1	½	1	½	½	½	½	1	9
11 Korchnoi	0	½	½	0	0	1	1	1	1	0	–	1	½	0	1	0	½	½	8½
12 Gheorghiu	½	0	½	½	½	0	½	½	½	½	0	–	1	½	½	½	½	½	7½
13 Ólafsson	½	½	0	½	½	0	1	½	½	0	½	0	–	1	0	½	½	1	7½
14 Savon	0	½	½	½	½	0	½	0	½	½	1	½	0	–	½	½	½	1	7½
15 Balashov	½	½	½	0	0	½	½	0	0	½	0	½	1	½	–	1	0	½	6½
16 Uhlmann	½	0	0	½	½	½	0	½	0	½	1	½	½	½	0	–	½	½	6½
17 Parma	½	0	0	0	0	0	½	½	0	½	½	½	½	½	1	½	–	½	6
18 Lengyel	0	0	½	½	½	0	0	½	0	0	½	½	0	0	½	½	½	–	4½

Hastings International Tournament December 1971–January 1972

	1	*2*	*3*	*4*	*5*	*6*	*7*	*8*	*9*	*10*	*11*	*12*	*13*	*14*	*15*	*16*	*Total*
1 Karpov	–	0	1	1	½	½	½	½	½	1	½	1	1	1	1	1	11
2 Korchnoi	1	–	½	½	½	½	0	1	1	1	½	1	1	½	1	1	11
3 R. Byrne	0	½	–	½	½	1	1	½	½	½	1	0	½	1	1	1	9½
4 Mecking	0	½	½	–	½	1	½	½	1	½	½	1	½	1	1	½	9½
5 Gligorić	½	½	½	½	–	½	½	½	½	½	½	½	½	½	1	1	8½
6 Najdorf	½	½	0	0	½	–	1	½	½	1	½	½	1	½	½	1	8½
7 Andersson	½	1	0	½	½	0	–	½	½	1	½	½	½	½	½	1	8
8 Unzicker	½	0	½	½	½	½	½	–	½	½	1	1	½	½	½	½	8
9 Pfleger	½	0	½	0	½	½	½	½	–	½	½	½	½	½	1	1	7½
10 Kurajica	0	0	½	½	½	0	0	½	½	–	½	½	1	½	1	1	7
11 Ciocaltea	½	½	0	½	½	½	½	0	½	½	–	½	½	½	½	½	6½
12 Botterill	0	0	1	0	½	½	½	0	½	½	½	–	½	½	0	1	6
13 Hartston	0	0	½	½	½	0	½	½	½	0	½	½	–	½	1	½	6
14 Keene	0	½	0	0	½	½	½	½	½	½	½	½	½	–	½	0	5½
15 Markland	0	0	0	0	0	½	½	½	0	0	½	1	0	½	–	1	4½
16 Franklin	0	0	0	½	0	0	0	½	0	0	½	0	½	1	0	–	3

Student Olympiad Final   Graz, Austria   July 1972

	1	2	3	4	5	6	7	8	9	10	Total
1 USSR	–	2	3½	2	3½	3½	3½	3½	3½	3½	28½
2 Hungary	2	–	1½	2	2½	2	2½	2½	2	2½	19½
3 West Germany	½	2½	–	1½	2	2½	1½	3	3½	2½	19½
4 USA	2	2	2½	–	2	1½	2	1½	2½	2	18
5 Bulgaria	½	1½	2	2	–	2½	2	2	3	2	17½
6 Israel	½	2	1½	2½	1½	–	1½	3	3	2	17½
7 Romania	½	1½	2½	2	2	2½	–	1½	2	2½	17
8 Cuba	½	1½	1	2½	2	1	2½	–	1	2½	14½
9 Denmark	½	2	½	1½	1	1	2	3	–	2½	14
10 England	½	1½	1½	2	2	2	1½	1½	1½	–	14

Karpov scored 4½/5 on board 1.

20th World Chess Olympiad   Skopje, Yugoslavia   Sep–Oct 1972

Preliminary Group 1

	1	2	3	4	5	6	7	Total
1 USSR	–	3½	4	2½	4	4	4	22
2 Denmark	½	–	3	2	2½	3	4	15
3 Belgium	0	1	–	3	3	3½	3½	14
4 Cuba	1½	2	1	–	2½	2½	3½	13
5 Finland	0	1½	1	1½	–	4	3½	11½
6 Dominican Republic	0	1	½	1½	0	–	3	6
7 Luxemburg	0	0	½	½	½	1	–	2½

20th World Chess Olympiad Skopje, Yugoslavia September–October 1972

Final

	1	2	3	4	5	6	7	8	9	10	11	12	13	14	15	16	Total
1 USSR	–	1½	2½	2	2½	2½	3	2½	3	3½	3½	3	3½	2	3	4	42
2 Hungary	2½	–	2½	2½	2	2½	2½	2½	2½	3½	3½	3	2	4	1½	3½	40½
3 Yugoslavia	1½	1½	–	1½	2	2	2	3	3	2½	3	3	3½	3	2½	4	38
4 Czechoslovakia	2	1½	2½	–	1½	2½	2½	2½	2	1½	1½	2½	3½	2½	4	3	35½
5 West Germany	1½	2	2	2½	–	2½	2½	2½	2½	2½	2½	2	2	3	2	3	35
6 Bulgaria	1½	1½	2	1½	1½	–	2½	3	2½	2½	2	2½	2½	2	2½	2	32
7 Romania	1	1½	2	1½	1½	1½	–	2	2	3	2½	2½	2½	3½	2	2½	31½
8 Holland	1½	1½	1	1½	1½	1	2	–	2½	3	3	2	2½	1½	2	2½	29
9 USA	1	1½	1	2	1½	1½	2	1½	–	2½	3	3	1½	2½	2½	2	29
10 East Germany	½	½	1½	2½	1½	1½	1	1	1½	–	2½	2	2	3	4	2½	27½
11 Spain	½	½	1	2½	1½	2	1½	1	1	1½	–	2	3½	3	1½	3	26
12 Poland	1	1	1	1½	2	1½	1½	2	1	2	2	–	2	2	2	2	24½
13 Denmark	½	2	½	½	2	1½	1½	1½	2½	2	½	2	–	2	2½	1½	23
14 Argentina	2	0	1	1½	1	2	½	2½	1½	1	1	2	2	–	2½	2	22½
15 Sweden	1	2½	1½	0	2	1½	2	2	1½	0	2½	2	1½	1½	–	1	22½
16 Switzerland	0	½	0	1	1	2	1½	1½	2	1½	1	2	2½	2	3	–	21½

Karpov scored 13/15 on board 1.

'Fried Chicken' Tournament San Antonio, USA November–December 1972

	1	*2*	*3*	*4*	*5*	*6*	*7*	*8*	*9*	*10*	*11*	*12*	*13*	*14*	*15*	*16*	*Total*
1 Karpov	–	½	0	1	½	½	1	½	½	1	1	½	½	1	1	1	10½
2 Petrosian	½	–	½	1	½	½	½	1	1	½	½	½	1	½	1	1	10½
3 Portisch	1	½	–	0	1	1	½	1	½	½	½	½	1	½	1	1	10½
4 Gligorić	0	0	1	–	½	½	1	½	½	1	1	½	½	1	1	1	10
5 Keres	½	½	0	½	–	1	½	1	1	1	½	0	½	1	1	½	9½
6 Hort	½	½	0	½	0	–	½	0	1	½	1	½	1	1	1	1	9
7 Suttles	0	½	½	0	½	½	–	½	½	½	½	1	1	1	1	1	9
8 Larsen	½	0	0	½	0	1	½	–	0	1	0	1	1	1	1	1	8½
9 Mecking	½	0	½	½	0	0	½	1	–	½	1	½	1	1	½	1	8½
10 D. Byrne	0	½	½	0	0	½	½	0	½	–	0	1	½	1	1	1	7
11 Browne	0	½	½	0	½	0	½	1	0	1	–	½	1	0	0	1	6½
12 Evans	½	½	½	½	1	½	0	0	½	0	½	–	0	½	½	1	6½
13 Kaplan	½	½	0	½	½	0	0	0	0	½	0	1	–	1	½	0	5
14 Campos	0	0	½	0	0	0	0	0	0	0	1	½	0	–	1	½	3½
15 Saidy	0	0	0	0	0	0	0	0	½	0	1	½	½	0	–	1	3½
16 Smith	0	0	0	0	½	0	0	0	0	0	0	0	1	½	0	–	2

Budapest International Tournament February–March 1973

	1	*2*	*3*	*4*	*5*	*6*	*7*	*8*	*9*	*10*	*11*	*12*	*13*	*14*	*15*	*16*	*Total*
1 Geller	–	½	1	½	½	1	½	½	1	½	½	½	1	1	1	½	10½
2 Karpov	½	–	1	1	1	½	½	½	½	½	½	½	1	½	½	½	9½
3 Adorjan	0	0	–	½	½	½	½	½	½	½	1	1	1	½	½	1	8½
4 Vaganian	½	0	½	–	½	½	1	½	½	½	1	½	½	½	1	½	8½
5 Hort	½	0	½	½	–	0	1	½	½	1	1	1	0	1	½	½	8½
6 Szabo	0	½	½	½	1	–	½	½	½	½	½	1	½	1	½	½	8½
7 Antoshin	½	½	½	0	0	½	–	½	1	½	½	1	0	½	1	1	8
8 Bilek	½	½	½	½	½	½	½	–	½	½	½	1	½	½	½	½	8
9 Csom	0	½	½	½	½	½	0	½	–	½		½	1	½	1	½	7½
10 Ribli	½	½	½	½	0	½	½	½	½	–		0	½	1	½	½	7
11 Ciocaltea	½	½	0	0	0	½	½	½	½	½		½	1	½	½	½	6½
12 Velimirović	½	½	0	½	0	0	0	0	½	1		–	1	0	1	½	6
13 Sax	0	0	0	½	1	½	1	½	0	½		0	–	½	½	1	6
14 Hecht	0	½	½	½	0	0	½	½	½	0		1	½	–	0	1	6
15 Lengyel	0	½	½	0	½	½	0	½	0	½		0	½	1	–	½	5½
16 Forintos	½	½	0	½	½	½	0	½	½	½		½	0	0	½	–	5½

Interzonal Tournament Leningrad June 1973

	1	2	3	4	5	6	7	8	9	10	11	12	13	14	15	16	17	18	Total
1 Karpov	–	½	½	1	½	½	1	1	½	½	1	½	1	1	1	1	1	1	13½
2 Korchnoi	½	–	1	½	1	1	½	½	1	1	1	1	1	½	0	1	1	1	13½
3 R. Byrne	½	0	–	½	1	½	½	½	1	½	1	1	1	½	1	1	1	1	12½
4 Smejkal	0	½	½	–	0	0	½	1	1	½	0	1	1	1	1	1	1	1	11
5 Larsen	½	0	0	1	–	1	1	0	½	0	0	1	½	1	1	½	1	1	10
6 Hübner	½	0	½	1	0	–	½	1	½	1	½	1	1	½	½	½	0	1	10
7 Kuzmin	0	½	½	½	0	½	–	0	½	1	½	½	½	1	1	1	1	½	9½
8 Gligorić	0	0	½	0	1	0	1	–	½	0	½	½	1	½	½	0	1	1	8½
9 Taimanov	½	0	0	0	½	½	½	½	–	½	½	1	½	½	1	½	1	½	8½
10 Tal	½	0	½	½	1	0	0	1	½	–	1	1	0	½	0	1	0	1	8½
11 Quinteros	0	0	0	1	1	½	½	½	½	0	–	0	½	0	½	1	½	1	7½
12 Radulov	½	0	0	0	0	0	½	½	0	0	1	–	1	1	½	½	1	1	7½
13 Torre	0	0	0	0	½	0	½	0	½	1	½	0	–	½	½	1	1	1	7
14 Uhlmann	0	½	½	0	0	½	0	½	½	½	1	0	½	–	½	½	½	1	7
15 Rukavina	0	0	0	0	0	½	0	½	0	1	½	½	½	½	–	0	1	½	6½
16 Tukmakov	0	0	0	0	½	½	0	1	½	0	0	½	0	½	1	–	½	1	6
17 Estévez	0	0	0	0	0	1	0	0	0	1	½	0	0	½	0	½	–	1	4½
18 Cuéllar	0	0	0	0	0	0	½	0	½	0	0	0	0	0	½	0	0	–	1½

European Team Championship Bath, England July 1973

	1	2	3	4	5	6	7	8	Total
1 USSR	–	5½	5	5½	5½	6½	5½	7	40½
2 Yugoslavia	2½	–	4½	6	6½	4½	4½	5½	34
3 Hungary	3	3½	–	6½	5½	5½	5½	3½	33
4 Poland	2½	2	1½	–	5	4	5½	4½	25

5 West Germany	2½	1½	2½	3	–	4½	4½	5½	24
6 England	1½	3½	2½	4	3½	–	4½	4½	24
7 Romania	2½	3½	2½	2½	3½	3½	–	5	23
8 Switzerland	1	2½	4½	3½	2½	3½	3	–	20½

Karpov scored 5/6 on board 4

40th USSR Championship Moscow October 1973

	1	*2*	*3*	*4*	*5*	*6*	*7*	*8*	*9*	*10*	*11*	*12*	*13*	*14*	*15*	*16*	*17*	*18*	*Total*
1 Spassky	–	½	½	½	½	½	½	½	½	0	1	½	1	1	1	1	1	1	11½
2 Karpov	½	–	1	1	0	½	½	½	½	1	½	½	1	½	½	½	½	1	10½
3 Korchnoi	½	0	–	½	½	½	½	½	½	1	½	½	1	1	½	1	1	½	10½
4 Kuzmin	½	0	½	–	½	½	½	½	½	½	1	½	½	1	1	1	1	½	10½
5 Petrosian	½	1	½	½	–	½	½	½	½	½	½	1	½	½	½	½	1	1	10½
6 Poługaevsky	½	½	½	½	½	–	½	1	½	½	½	1	1	½	½	½	½	1	10½
7 Geller	½	½	½	½	½	½	–	½	1	½	0	½	½	0	½	1	1	0	8½
8 K. Grigorian	½	½	½	½	½	0	½	–	½	+	½	1	½	1	½	0	0	½	8½
9 Keres	½	½	½	½	½	½	0	½	–	½	½	0	½	½	½	½	½	1	8
10 Savon	1	0	0	½	½	½	½	–	½	–	½	½	½	½	½	½	½	1	8
11 Taimanov	0	½	½	0	½	½	1	½	½	½	–	1	0	½	½	½	½	½	8
12 Tal	½	½	½	½	0	0	½	0	1	½	0	–	½	½	1	½	½	1	8
13 Rashkovsky	0	0	0	½	½	0	½	½	½	½	1	½	–	½	½	½	½	1	7½
14 Tukmakov	0	½	0	0	½	½	1	0	½	½	½	½	½	–	½	½	½	1	7½
15 Averkin	0	½	½	0	½	½	½	½	½	½	½	0	½	½	–	½	0	1	7
16 Smyslov	0	½	0	0	½	½	0	1	½	½	½	½	½	½	½	–	½	½	7
17 Sveshnikov	0	½	0	0	0	½	0	1	½	½	½	½	½	½	1	½	–	0	6½
18 Beliavsky	0	0	½	½	0	0	1	½	0	0	½	0	0	0	0	½	1	–	4½

Madrid International Tournament November–December 1973

	1	2	3	4	5	6	7	8	9	10	11	12	13	14	15	16	Total
1 Karpov	–	½	½	½	1	1	½	½	½	1	½	1	1	1	1	½	11
2 Tukmakov	½	–	½	½	½	½	1	0	1	1	1	½	1	1	½	1	10½
3 Furman	½	½	–	½	1	1	½	½	½	½	1	0	1	½	1	1	10
4 Hort	½	½	½	–	½	½	1	1	½	½	½	½	½	1	½	1	9½
5 Uhlmann	0	½	0	½	–	½	½	½	1	1	½	1	½	1	1	1	9½
6 Andersson	0	½	0	½	½	–	½	½	1	½	½	1	1	1	½	1	9
7 Portisch	½	0	½	0	½	½	–	½	½	1	1	1	½	½	1	1	9
8 Browne	½	1	½	0	½	½	½	–	½	½	½	1	1	½	1	0	8½
9 Ljubojević	½	0	½	½	0	0	½	½	–	½	1	1	½	1	1	1	8½
10 Planinc	0	0	½	½	0	½	0	½	½	–	1	0	1	0	1	1	6½
11 Panno	½	0	0	½	½	½	0	½	0	0	–	½	1	½	1	½	6
12 Calvo	0	½	1	½	0	0	0	0	0	1	½	–	½	½	0	½	5
13 Kaplan	0	0	0	½	½	0	½	0	½	0	0	½	–	1	½	1	5
14 Pomar	0	0	½	0	0	0	½	½	0	1	½	½	0	–	½	1	5
15 Garcia	0	½	0	½	0	½	0	0	0	0	0	1	½	½	–	½	4
16 Bellon	½	0	0	0	0	0	0	1	0	0	½	½	0	0	½	–	3

Candidates' Match (quarter-final) Moscow January–February 1974

	1	*2*	*3*	*4*	*5*	*6*	*7*	*8*	*Total*
Karpov	½	½	½	1	½	1	½	1	5½
Polugaevsky	½	½	½	0	½	0	½	0	2½

Candidates' Match (semi-final) Leningrad April–May 1974

	1	*2*	*3*	*4*	*5*	*6*	*7*	*8*	*9*	*10*	*11*	*Total*
Karpov	0	½	1	½	½	1	½	½	1	½	1	7
Spassky	1	½	0	½	½	0	½	½	0	½	0	4

21st World Chess Olympiad Nice, France June 1974

Preliminary Group 1

	1	*2*	*3*	*4*	*5*	*6*	*7*	*8*	*9*	*Total*
1 USSR	–	4	3½	3	3	3½	4	4	4	29
2 Wales	0	–	2½	2½	1½	3	4	3½	4	21
3 Scotland	½	1½	–	2	2½	3	3½	4	4	21
4 Poland	1	1½	2	–	2½	2½	2½	4	4	20
5 Brazil	1	2½	1½	1½	—	2½	2½	2½	4	19
6 Mongolia	½	1	1	1½	1½	–	3	3	3½	15
7 Puerto Rico	0	0	½	1½	1½	1	–	3	3½	11
8 Jordan	0	½	0	0	½	1	1	–	2	5
9 Dutch Antilles	0	0	0	0	0	½	½	2	–	3

21st World Chess Olympiad Nice, France June 1974

A Final

	1	2	3	4	5	6	7	8	9	10	11	12	13	14	15	16	Total
1 USSR	–	2½	3	2	3	2	3½	3½	3	3	4	3½	2½	2½	4	4	46
2 Yugoslavia	1½	–	1½	2	2½	1	2½	2	3½	2	3½	3	3	3½	2	4	37½
3 USA	1	2½	–	1½	2½	2	1½	3	2½	3	3	2	3½	2½	3½	2½	36½
4 Bulgaria	2	2	2½	–	2	1½	2	2	2	3	3	3	3	2	2½	4	36½
5 Holland	1	1½	1½	2	–	2	2	2	2½	2½	2½	3½	2½	3	3	4	35½
6 Hungary	2	3	2	2½	2	–	2½	1	1½	2½	2½	1	2½	3½	3	3½	35
7 West Germany	½	1½	2½	2	2	1½	–	2	2	2½	2½	2½	2	2½	3	3	32
8 Romania	½	2	1	2	2	3	2	–	2	2	2	2	3	1	2½	2½	29½
9 Czechoslavakia	1	½	1½	2	1½	2½	2	2	–	3	1½	1	2	3	3½	2½	29½
10 England	1	2	1	1	1½	1½	1½	2	1	–	2	2	2	2	2	3½	26
11 Spain	0	½	1	1	1½	1½	1½	2	2½	2	–	3	2	2½	1½	3	25½
12 Philippines	½	1	2	1	½	3	1½	2	3	2	1	–	1	2	2½	2½	25½
13 Sweden	1½	1	½	1	1½	1½	2	1	2	2	2	3	–	2	1½	2½	25
14 Argentina	1½	½	1½	2	1	½	1½	3	1	2	1½	2	2	–	2	1½	23½
15 Finland	0	2	½	1½	1	1	1	1½	½	2	2½	1½	2½	2	–	2½	22
16 Wales	0	0	1½	0	0	½	1	1½	1½	½	1	1½	1½	2½	1½	–	14½

Karpov scored 12/14 on board 1.

Candidates' Match (final) Moscow September–November 1974

	1	2	3	4	5	6	7	8	9	10	11	12	13	14	15	16	17	18	19	20	21	22	23	24	Total
Karpov	½	1	½	½	½	1	½	½	½	½	½	½	½	½	½	½	1	½	0	½	0	½	½	½	12½
Korchnoi	½	0	½	½	½	0	½	½	½	½	½	½	½	½	½	½	0	½	1	½	1	½	½	½	11½